Books are to be returned on or before
the last date b

D0279933

Play It Again, Sam

Retakes on Remakes

EDITED BY

Andrew Horton and Stuart Y. McDougal

with an Afterword by Leo Braudy

UNIVERSITY OF CALIFORNIA PRESS
Berkeley   Los Angeles   London

University of California Press
Berkeley and Los Angeles, California

University of California Press, Ltd.
London, England

© 1998 by
The Regents of the University of California

Library of Congress Cataloging-in-Publication Data

Play it again, Sam : retakes on remakes / edited by Andrew Horton and Stuart Y. McDougal ; with an afterword by Leo Braudy.
   p. cm.
Includes bibliographic references and index.
ISBN 0-520-20592-8 (cloth : alk. paper). — ISBN 0-520-20593-6 (pbk. : alk. paper)
   1. Motion picture remakes.   I. Horton, Andrew.   II. McDougal, Stuart Y.
PN1995.9.R45P58   1998
791.43′75—dc21
                                         97–175
                                          CIP

Printed in the United States of America
9 8 7 6 5 4 3 2 1

The paper used in this publication meets the minimum requirements of American National Standards for Information Sciences—Permanence of Paper for Printed Library Materials, ANSI Z39.48–1984.

CONTENTS

PART TWO · DISTANT RELATIVES:
CROSS-CULTURAL REMAKES

PART THREE · ALTERED STATES:
TRANSFORMING MEDIA

ILLUSTRATIONS AND TABLE

FIGURES

TABLE

Introduction

Andrew Horton and Stuart Y. McDougal

I don't invent: I steal.
JEAN-LUC GODARD

I.

This collection of original essays is dedicated to exploring the scope and nature of remakes in film and in related media, in Hollywood as well as in the cinemas of other nations. We are concerned with remakes as aesthetic or cinematic texts and as ideological expressions of cultural discourse set in particular times, contexts, and societies. Although there has been considerable recent work in film as an intertextual medium,[1] the remake has received relatively little critical attention to date.[2]

Remakes themselves, however, continue to proliferate. Case in point: the 1994 summer blockbuster *Maverick*. This film suggests some other genre and cultural boundaries we wish to explore beyond the obvious level of new films made from old. In what sense is the film *Maverick* a "remake" or "makeover" of the old James Garner television show that began in 1957, the year Mel Gibson, who plays Maverick in the movie, was born? What exactly are the boundaries of a remake? At what point does similarity become simply a question of influence? And what is the difference between a remake and the current television label "spin-off"? Darren Star, creator of *Beverly Hills 90210*, agrees that his more recent show, *Melrose Place*, is a twenty-something spin-off of his earlier high school series, which, in turn, he claims, is a spin-off of the film *The Breakfast Club*. How do we define the complex relations between these texts?

Our collection of essays responds to these questions in a variety of ways and suggests some of the directions that others may follow, either with a more theoretical interest in defining "remakes" or with a more focused interest in cultural studies and the meanings of repetition in whatever shades of difference such texts may suggest.

II.

We begin with the nature of narrative itself. Edward Branigan has recently reexpressed a definition of narrative this way: "[N]arrative is a perceptual activity that organizes data into a special pattern which represents and explains experience" (3). Narratives, therefore, wherever they are found, both represent and explain or comment on by their structure or content, tone or characterization, experiences from "real" life. A remake is, of course, a particular form of narrative that adheres to Branigan's definition but with an additional dimension. We could paraphrase Branigan to say the remake is a "special pattern which re-represents and explains at a different time and through varying perceptions, previous narratives and experiences." And how do we read such a pattern?

"I don't know whether to look at him or to read him," says Robert Mitchum playing a tough detective in Martin Scorsese's 1991 *Cape Fear*, as he watches a strip search of the heavily tattooed Robert De Niro, who plays Max Cady, Mitchum's original part in the 1962 version of the film. As we consider cinematic remakes, our dilemma is Mitchum's: do we simply watch or read these texts?

Like Mitchum, of course, we do both. As viewers, we can't help both viewing and reading—that is, teasing out narrative inferences, pleasures, contradictions, and implications of any film. But a film like *Cape Fear*, advertised as a reworking of an earlier film, forces us to read in a different way, by considering its relationship to the earlier film. Are remakes then merely another instance of a state of affairs as old as recorded literature? The Greek dramatists retold classical myths and Homer borrowed almost everything in his epics while transforming the materials to his own ends. Chaucer and Shakespeare also borrowed liberally from their precursors. As the centuries passed, the relationship between such texts often became much more self-conscious. John Dryden's *All for Love* (1678) was a reworking of Shakespeare's *Anthony and Cleopatra*, and audiences were expected to respond to it as such. Ruby Cohn has chronicled the many transformations of Shakespeare on the twentieth-century stage in *Modern Shakespeare Offshoots*. Such intertextual relationships have proliferated in modern times. In a universe of ever-expanding textuality, the relationships in a text such as James Joyce's *Ulysses* (1922) between Joyce and Homer (to say nothing of Joyce's reworkings of Dante and Shakespeare) are complex indeed. How do cinematic remakes differ from any modern work that is itself a tissue of other works? In Jorge Borges's story "Pierre Menard, Author of the Quixote," the title character is quite literally rewriting part of the novel *Don Quixote*. Borges's story questions notions of textuality, intertextuality, and originality, issues that have become central in modern literary debates. Through her work on Bakhtin, Julia Kristeva introduced the notion of *in-*

tertextuality, a term to designate the ways in which any text is a skein of other texts. Earlier texts are always present and may be read in the newer text. "The literary word," Bakhtin suggested, "is aware of the presence of another literary word alongside it." Thus texts form what Kristeva calls a "mosaic of citations," each modifying the other, and many modern authors, like Borges or T. S. Eliot in *The Waste Land,* have foregrounded this issue in their own work. In terms of intertextuality, then, remakes—films that to one degree or another *announce* to us that they embrace one or more previous movies—are clearly something of a special case, or at least a more intense one.

In *Palimpsestes* (1982), Gerard Genette expanded on Kristeva's notion of intertextuality through the elaboration of a number of separate categories. These categories form a useful way of situating cinematic remakes. Genette's first category is *intertextuality,* which he defines more restrictively than Kristeva as the "co-presence of two or more texts" in the form of citation, plagiarism, and allusion. The title of this collection of essays, for example, alludes to a famous line in *Casablanca,* a line that was remade (and made famous) as the title of a film by Woody Allen. Films emulate literature in this respect, as John Biguenet demonstrates in this volume, and this relationship has a clear bearing on the issue of remakes. Genette's second category, *paratextuality,* describes the relationships between the text proper and its title, intertitles, prefaces, postfaces, notes, epigraphs, illustrations, and so on. While these relations also apply to film, they are less central to the issue of remakes. Genette's third category is *metatextuality,* a "critical relationship *par excellence*" between texts in which one text speaks of another, without necessarily quoting from it directly. The example he cites is Hegel's use of Diderot's *Le Neveu de Rameau* in his *Phenomenology of Mind.* Although this relationship does sometimes occur in films, it is quite different from the relationship of texts within a remake. Metatextuality, as Genette notes, is closely related to his fifth category, *architextuality.* This category, the "most abstract" and the "most implicit," refers to the taxonomic categories of a work as indicated by the titles or, more often, by the subtitles of a text. This too is less applicable to remakes, although like the other categories it provides a context for a discussion of remakes. But the category that occupies Genette most centrally in *Palimpsestes,* and the one that has the most direct bearing on cinematic remakes, is the fourth type, *hypertextuality.* Genette defines hypertextuality as the relationship between a given text (the "hypertext") and an anterior text (the hypotext) that it transforms. In the literary example cited above, the hypotexts of James Joyce's *Ulysses* would include *The Odyssey, The Divine Comedy,* and *Hamlet.* This category provides an apt way of discussing cinematic remakes and connects them to other intertextual relationships. In the strictest use of the term *remake,* a new text (the hypertext) transforms a hypotext. But although Genette's distinctions provide a useful way of discussing the remake, his terminology does not take us far enough. For our concern here is not only with the remake as a category in Hollywood, where a given film is based on an earlier film, but with an extension of the boundaries of the term *remake* to include as well works resulting from the contact between diverse cultures and different media. Bill Nichols has recently written of the "blurred boundaries" between fiction and nonfiction today, but his remarks apply to the blurred boundaries between remakes and the texts they draw from or refer to as well. Nichols observes, "Deliberate border violations serve to announce a contestation of forms and purposes. What truths, drawing from what ethics, politics, or ideology, legitimizing what actions, do different forms convey?" (x). We can substitute "narratives" for "forms" and suggest that the remake both pays tribute to a preexisting text and, on another level, calls it into question, as Nichols suggests. And although cinematic remakes—from Anthony Quinn's 1958 remake of his father-in-law Cecil B. DeMille's swashbuckling New Orleans saga, *The Buccaneer* (1938), in which Quinn was himself a minor star, to Philip Kaufman's 1978 chilling remake of Don Siegel's 1956 *Body Snatchers* to Kevin Costner's 1991 *Robin Hood: Prince of Thieves*—can stand alone as entertainment and as independent narratives, independence is not what attracted us as editors and/or contributors to this project. This is quite purely a collection dedicated to the pleasure of the pirated text, where remakes constitute a particular territory existing somewhere between unabashed larceny and subtle originality. Remakes, in fact, problematize the very notion of originality. More so than many other kinds of films, the remake and, as we shall see, the makeover—a film that quite substantially alters the original for whatever purpose—invite and at times demand that the viewer participate in both looking at and reading between multiple texts.

Beyond simple remakes of one film to another with the same title and story, we are also interested in extending the definition of remake to include a variety of other intertextual types. What dynamics and dimensions are involved in cross-cultural remakes in which language, cultural traditions, psychology, and even narrative sense may differ greatly. Kurosawa's *Seven Samurai* (1954) was influenced by John Ford's westerns, and it in turn became the basis for the Hollywood remake *The Magnificent Seven* (1960). How do we begin to discuss such a complicated transposition? The titles may or may not be the same and the films may or may not stick to the original narratives, but their relation to those narratives is secure. This, we shall see, especially seems to occur in cross-cultural examples, such as Emir Kusturica's *Time of the Gypsies* (1989), which is perhaps better called a makeover of Coppola's *Godfather* done in terms of Yugoslav gypsy culture. And then there are those films that simply allude to or quote from previous films. What does it mean in *Honey, I Blew up the Kid* to have Japanese tourists look up at a fifty-foot-high kid and shout "Godzilla!" Or when the first word we see posted on the side of the tourists' bus in *The Man Who Knew Too Much* is "CASABLANCA"? Such questions have a bearing on notions of intertextuality. As films proliferate, so do the relations between them.

In the days when the Hollywood studios held sway, remakes provided a fertile source of material for the theaters' voracious appetites. The bottom line then, as now, was money, and since the studio owned these properties it could cannibalize them at will. John Huston's 1941 film *The Maltese Falcon* was the third time Warner Brothers had filmed Dashiell Hammett's novel. In recent years, high profits have been garnered by adapting French films for the American screen. The French film *Three Men and a Cradle* (1985), for instance, grossed slightly over $2 million in the United States, but the Hollywood remake, *Three Men and a Baby* (1987), has, to date, pulled in over $168 million.

But the issues cannot be explained in terms of finances alone. Sometimes, as with *The Maltese Falcon,* the remake is a return to an earlier noncinematic source. Is the filmmaker trying to correct the earlier adaptation, to render a more accurate version of the original text? Here textuality provides but a limited explanation for the remake. In addition, films remake other media—comic books, for example, in *Superman, Dick Tracy,* and countless other recent films. And films themselves are source texts for other media, among them television and radio. To what extent do these media remake their sources? And finally, what motivates a filmmaker to remake his own work, as Alfred Hitchcock does in *The Man Who Knew Too Much?* The term *remake,* then, comprises a broad range of possibilities.

The specific focus of this volume is the phenomenon of movie remakes, especially as practiced in Hollywood. As we approach the end of the century, Hollywood possesses a considerable history it can remake and recycle. One issue seems abundantly simple: there is a film and, for one reason or another, it is remade and re-released at a later date. The differences between the two versions may be significant: in *Cape Fear,* Scorsese paid complicated attention to why and how Max Cady was framed (the withholding of evidence that the rape victim was a nymphomaniac); or they may be trivial: what does it suggest about Max Cady in the contemporary version that he drinks Evian water from a plastic bottle, while Robert Mitchum drank an endless supply of Bud from cans in the original? The more recent film is defined, in part, by these very differences. After all, at this writing *Casablanca* and *Gone with the Wind* are in production or preproduction as updated remakes, and the only thing we can be sure of is that they will differ significantly from their originals. They will tell us as much about our own concerns in the nineties as they will about the films upon which they are based.

The more we think about the issue of remakes, the more we can see how

many significant strands of narrative, cinema, culture, psychology, and textuality come together. Taking the largest possible view—that of human psychology and development—we can, for instance, make the following observation. Experience and development themselves depend upon recognizable
patterns of repetition, novelty, and resolution. John Belton has recently
written that part of the point of the classical Hollywood film system of narration and style is not only that these films share many narrative and production elements but that, given their similarities, "each strives to be different as well" (*American Culture/American Film*). The remake, especially the
Hollywood remake, intensifies this process: by announcing by title and/or
narrative its indebtedness to a previous film, the remake invites the viewer
to enjoy the *differences* that have been worked, consciously and sometimes
unconsciously, between the texts. That is, every moment of every day, we
experience what is familiar, what seems "new," and we learn somehow to
resolve the difference so we can continue to focus. It was Victor Shklovsky
who argued in the early decades of this century that the function of art was
to defamiliarize the familiar—to make us experience the commonplace in
new ways. One way of achieving this, he noted, was repetition with a difference. In one sense, remakes exemplify this process. They provoke a double
pleasure in that they offer what we have known previously, but with novel
or at least different interpretations, representations, twists, developments,
resolutions.

But there are also, as John Belton makes clear, strong *cultural* and *historical* levels to our experience of cinema. To watch Robert Mitchum in the
original 1962 *Cape Fear* and Robert De Niro in Martin Scorsese's 1991 version is not just to watch widely differing acting and directorial styles but to
experience the historical and cultural changes that have occurred within
the twenty-nine years separating these films. The dark elements in the original are definitely threatening, but they appear threatening in black and
white at a seemingly less complicated period in American history and culture. One year later, John F. Kennedy was dead and America had entered
a true "cape fear" and also a "cape hope" as the sixties began in full force
on all fronts—civil rights, Vietnam, the coming of age of the baby boomers,
and so on. Scorsese's *Cape Fear,* however, echoes many of the fears and preoccupations of today, caught in stylishly controlled color. Today, after the
Los Angeles riots of 1992; rising crime of all sorts, including serial killings
and drug abuse; and the decline of many of our institutions from education
to government itself, Americans share a different kind of "cape fear." De
Niro's edgy performance and Scorsese's restless camera capture much of
this contemporary tension in what is still a "classical" Hollywood narrative,
but with certain distinct flourishes.

Our investigation of remakes, therefore, takes us into several distinct
areas: the personal (psychological), the sociocultural (political-cultural-

anthropological), and the artistic (cinematic narrative: style-substance-presentation). We will be concerned with all of these "voices" as they speak to us in each film, although the individual essays in this collection may focus upon one or more of them. This collection of essays, then, attempts to map out the field and begin clarifying the nature of these relations.

III.

The tripartite division of our collection suggests our major concerns. Part 1 (framed by the essays of Robert Eberwein and Biguenet) focuses on both the nature of remakes and on some of the ways Hollywood has handled this never-ending source of material. Eberwein's essay provides a useful context for understanding remakes within a "framework emphasizing contextualization" and an "analysis of conditions of spectatorship." Biguenet hones in on a particular aspect of the remake, the cinematic allusion. Taken together, the essays argue for a broader understanding of intertextuality in cinema than has commonly been explored.

The whole collection, in fact, celebrates a variety of critical perspectives regarding the remake. Beyond the general divisions established, we encouraged these invited essayists to employ various strategies for considering repeated and recreated texts.

The first pair of essays considers the films of Alfred Hitchcock, a filmmaker whose work has had an incalculable influence on later filmmakers. Robert Kolker offers a refreshingly original examination of *Cape Fear* and *Basic Instinct* as efforts to rework Hitchcock but which, for the most part, fail "to get the figures and the figuration right." Stuart McDougal considers Hitchcock as a director who "continuously re-explored themes and techniques from his earlier work." McDougal's study of *The Man Who Knew Too Much* sheds light on the workings of a director who always felt there was another chance to revise his past work and "get it right" in terms of new demands and interests.

Turning to a popular work that has been remade many times, *Cineaste* editor Dan Georgakas takes a decidedly political and ideological approach to the various versions of *Robin Hood*. He concludes that "the entertainment genre romance of Flynn is closer to historical truth and the myth than Costner's politically correct version so many decades later."

A pair of essays consider the different ways musicals remake earlier sources. Jerry Delamater works with *A Star Is Born* to map out four specific forms of remakes building on principles posited by Altman, Feuer, Delamater, Collins, and others. Krin Gabbard makes use of a variety of versions of *The Jazz Singer* to detail the oedipal narrative "that may have attracted each of the stars to the story in the first place."

Another examination of the relationship between the oedipal narrative and cinematic remakes is provided by Harvey R. Greenberg, a practicing New York psychiatrist. Dr. Greenberg takes a psychoanalytic look at Stephen Spielberg's remake of *A Guy Named Joe* (1943) in his *Always* (1990), relating it to possible unresolved conflicts between the filmmaker and his father. Beyond his "case study" of Spielberg, however, Greenberg clarifies the oedipal condition of the remake as he views it, concluding that "the remaker, simultaneously worshipful and envious of the maker, enters into an ambiguous, anxiety-ridden struggle with a film he both wishes to honor and eclipse."

Part 2 of our collection pays attention to the transformation of narratives across national and cultural boundaries. Realizing that for Hollywood to redo foreign films or for other countries to reshape Hollywood narrative much more is at play than simply translating from English to French or German or Japanese, each of these essays also explores the cultural and aesthetic dynamics of such makeovers.

Hollywood's raid on foreign narratives is given sharp attention by David Wills in his examination of Jim McBride's version of Jean-Luc Godard's *Breathless* and by Michael Brashinsky in his study *The Last House on the Left*, Wes Craven's makeover of Ingmar Bergman's *The Virgin Spring*. Drawing on his studies of Jacques Derrida, Wills sees film itself as "a web of quotations" and the remake, in this case McBride's *Breathless*, as only a more blatant form of the whole process of representation. Brashinsky deftly chronicles the transformation of a European high art film into a Hollywood B film.

Andrew Horton and Patricia Aufderheide explore the reverse tradition as Hollywood narratives become the basis for foreign films. Using the Yugoslav makeover of the Coppola *Godfather* films in Emir Kusturica's *Time of the Gypsies,* Horton concludes that cinematic makeovers are in part an attempt by foreign filmmakers to feel connected to a world film community and in part a nostalgic impulse at a moment in media history when cinema itself appears in danger of being replaced by other entertainment media. Aufderheide turns to the Far East and details how Hong Kong imitates Hollywood "unabashedly" but, in the process, winds up reflecting much that is prevalent in contemporary Hong Kong culture.

The effect of gender on very different postmodern remakes is the subject of essays by Lucy Fischer and Chris Holmlund. Fisher maps the indebtedness of Pedro Almodovar's *High Heels* (1991) to Douglas Sirk's *Imitation of Life* (1959) and analyzes it as a postmodern remake through its "highly parodic" intertextuality, its many citations to mass culture, its intermingling of fact and fiction, its crossing of genres, and its presentation of gender. Holmlund stretches the boundaries of a remake even further through her detailed examination of the ways two experimental filmmakers, Su Friedrich and Valie Export, reshape Hollywood products. How, she asks, does celluloid surgery resemble plastic surgery? Using the analogy of the ways in which transsexuals and transvestites disturb gender categories, Holmlund demonstrates how experimental filmmakers transform earlier mainstream movies in their own works. In the process she raises a number of important questions about gender, genre, and the relationships between experimental and commercial films.

The final three essays in the collection explore the connections between Hollywood films and three other media: the comics, radio, and television. Luca Somigli examines the differences between "visual narratives on film and paper," clarifying the narrative possibilities of each form, before turning his attention to the ways in which film has drawn upon comic books for material and techniques. Peter Lehman directs our attention to the differences between radio and film. What happens, Lehman asks, when a film is retold as an episode in a radio series? Lehman underscores the important relations between radio and film in the thirties and forties, when directors, writers, actors, and technicians were working in both media. And Elisabeth Weis shows what happens when a film becomes a series on television, where the narrative can be expanded almost limitlessly. Her essay tells us a great deal about the cultural, technical, and narratological differences between a Hollywood film and a popular television series, at the same time that it extends our definition of the remake.

Part 2 concludes with the deathless appeal of vampire narratives. Lloyd Michaels broadens his dialogue on *Nosferatu* beyond vampires while noting that cinema itself is a specific signifying system that is haunting, since the referent is not an object or place that can be said to have an actual, even recoverable existence. Ira Konigsberg takes on Francis Ford Coppola's recent *Dracula* and all previous retellings of this story and suggests a popular cultural view of these films that reflects "changing fears and fascinations toward sex, seduction, and mortality."

IV.

Let us return for a moment to *Maverick*. At what point should we begin a discussion of this film made "from" the television series? The answer, we suggest, depends on one's particular interests. *Maverick* as a remake or spin-off is a complicated case, for it was written by William Goldman, who also wrote *Butch Cassidy and the Sundance Kid* (among many other films) and who worked closely with director George Roy Hill. Hill not only directed *Butch Cassidy* but *The Sting* as well, a film many critics have suggested *Maverick*, the movie, followed rather too closely.

To begin a discussion of *Maverick*'s borrowings thus takes in a number of films the audience may or may not recognize: who can watch Mel Gibson, as he nearly falls into the Grand Canyon, without thinking of two women who purposely drove into the canyon in the film *Thelma and Louise,* clearly "remade" from *Butch Cassidy and the Sundance Kid*—but twenty years later from a woman's point of view! Allusions, spin-offs, makeovers, and remakes—all of these terms are needed to characterize the complex nature of a work like *Maverick.*

The spirit that shapes a work like *Maverick* has been picked up by filmmakers from Hollywood to Hong Kong as they have sought to enrich the possibilities of their medium by transforming novels, comic books, symphonies, television series and, more recently, video games into films and vice versa. If Maverick can return to the big screen, what cinematic-comic-novelistic figure will be next? And in what form?

V.

We celebrated the first century of cinema in 1995. One recognition of this centennial was an imaginative film project entitled *Lumière and Company* (*Lumière et Compagnie*). A French-Spanish-Swedish co-production, this compilation documentary is an omnibus film made up of fifty-two-second pieces shot by thirty-nine directors from around the world using a camera originally used by the Lumière brothers to shoot the first film, fifty-two seconds in length (*Variety,* 51).

Each director, including Peter Greenway, Costa-Gavras, James Ivory, David Lynch, Liv Ullmann, John Boorman, Spike Lee, Theo Angelopoulos and many more, was asked to shoot whatever he or she pleased but under the same circumstances as the Lumière brothers one hundred years ago: "homemade" film, with natural lighting and nonsync sound.

As the second century of cinema begins, surely this creative collage is tribute to the power of cinema to remake its magic but, as always, with both familiar and new styles, images, and messages.

NOTES

1. See, for example, James Goodwin, *Akira Kurosawa and Intertextual Cinema* (Baltimore: Johns Hopkins University Press, 1994), and T. Jefferson Kline, *Screening the Text: Intertextuality in New Wave Cinema* (Baltimore: Johns Hopkins University Press, 1992).

2. See, for example, Michael B. Druxman, who provides a sketchy survey of the field in *Make It Again, Sam: A Survey of Movie Remakes* (New York: A. S. Barnes and Company, 1975); and Doris Milberg, *Repeat Performances* (New York: Broadway Press, 1990); and Robert A. Nowlan and Gwendolyn Wright Nowlan, *Cinema Sequels*

and Remakes, 1903–1987 (Jefferson, North Carolina: McFarland, 1989), two volumes that provide listings and synopses.

WORKS CITED

Bahktin, Mikhail. *The Dialogic Imagination.* Austin: University of Texas Press, 1981.
———. *Rabelais and His World.* Cambridge: MIT Press, 1968.
Belton, John. *American Culture/American Film.* New York: McGraw-Hill, 1994.
Branigan, Edward. *Narrative Comprehension and Film.* New York: Routledge, 1992.
Cohn, Ruby. *Modern Shakespeare Offshoots.* Princeton: Princeton University Press, 1978.
Genette, Gerard. *Palimpsestes: La Littérature au second degré.* Paris: Editions du Seuil, 1984.
Kristeva, Julia. *Sēmeiōtikē: recherches pour une sémanalyse.* Paris: Editions du Seuil, 1969.
"Lumiere and Company." *Variety* (December 4–10, 1995).
Nichols, Bill. *Blurred Boundaries: Questions of Meaning in Contemporary Culture.* Bloomington: Indiana University Press, 1994.
Shklovsky, Victor. "Art as Technique," *The Film Factory: Russian and Soviet Cinema in Documents, 1896–1939,* edited by Richard Taylor and Ian Christie, Cambridge: Harvard University Press, 1988.

PART ONE

Next of Kin:
Remakes and Hollywood

ONE

Remakes and Cultural Studies

Robert Eberwein

In this essay I propose a suggestion, based on an application of aspects of cultural studies, that is designed to provide a methodologically coherent approach to thinking about various kinds of remakes.[1] I urge a *re*-contextualization of the original and its remake, achieved by an analysis of conditions of spectatorship.[2]

It is difficult to know where to begin in theorizing remakes. It seems that many of the studies of remakes do not go much beyond a superficial point-by-point, pluses-and-minuses kind of analysis.[3] Often this kind of discussion employs a common strategy: the critic treats the original and its meaning for its contemporary audience as a fixity, against which the remake is measured and evaluated. And, in one sense, the original *is* a fixed entity.

But in another sense it is not. Viewed from the fuller perspective of cultural analysis over time, the original can—I am arguing that it must—be seen as still in process in regard to the impact it had or may have had for its contemporary audience and, even more, that it has for its current audience. A remake is a kind of reading or rereading of the original. To follow this reading or rereading, we have to interrogate not only our own conditions of reception but also to return to the original and reopen the question of its reception. Please understand that I am *not* arguing that a return to the original will necessarily yield a "new" meaning in the film that has hitherto been missed by shortsighted critics. Rather, I am arguing that a fresh return to the period may help us understand more about the conditions of reception at the time and, hence, offer us a fuller range of information for comparing the original and its audience with the remake and its audience. To demonstrate the point, I will use as my particular focus the original and remake of *Invasion of the Body Snatchers* (Don Siegel, 1956; Phil Kaufman, 1978). I have chosen this film largely because it has been remade again by Abel Ferrara. I am sure that the most recent remake will evoke stimulating commentaries on the relation between itself and its predecessors, but I doubt that anyone writing about the new film will be able to position it fully in terms of its contemporary reception. And that is because a contemporary audience is fixed by its spatiotemporal restrictions. We are inside a particular historical and cultural moment that may in fact account for certain aspects of the film Ferrara made recently. It will remain for later critics to look back and speculate on the conditions of reception for the film in a way that I am convinced we really can't since we are inside the historical and cultural moment.

In a recent essay in *Framework* on Caribbean cinema, Stuart Hall makes some telling points that can serve to introduce the argument I want to make about our investigations of remakes as these both posit and depend on certain assumptions about audience reception. Specifically he addresses the concept of cultural identity as a construct emerging from the Caribbean cinema. But the applicability of his comments to assumptions about a shared cultural identity is pertinent to consideration of any cinema assumed to "reflect" the culture in which it is produced. According to Hall: "The practices of representation always implicate the positions from which we speak or write—the positions of *enunciation*. What recent theories of enunciation suggest is that, though we speak, so to say 'in our own name,' of ourselves and from our own experience, nevertheless who speaks, and the subject who is spoken of, are never exactly in the same place. Identity is not as transparent or unproblematic as we think. Perhaps . . . we should think . . . of identity as a 'production,' which is never complete, always in process, and always constituted within, not outside, representation" (68). Cultural identity "is not a fixed essence at all, lying unchanged outside history and culture" (71).

I am appropriating Hall's view of cultural identity and considering it in relation to the way we posit culturally inflected unity in originals and remakes. As you can tell, one of my basic concerns here is whether we can talk about remakes as if they and their audience were "lying unchanged, outside history and culture"—as if, in other words, interpretation can assume a fixed timeless cultural identity.

Some comments on the original and remakes of *Invasion of the Body Snatchers* will illustrate the point. Nora Sayre, for example, writes: "(In the Fifties, many believed that Communist governments turned their citizens into robots.) So the political forebodings of the period spilled over into science fiction, where subservience to alien powers and the loss of free will were so often depicted, and the terror of being turned into 'something evil' became a ruling passion. The amusing 1978 remake of *Invasion of the Body Snatchers* did not perpetuate the social overtones—instead it concentrated on conformity and surrendering the capacity to feel, and few of the scenes

Figure 1. Beware of huge pods found at night! A pod conceals its startling secret in Don Siegel's original *Invasion of the Body Snatchers* (1956).

had the impact of Kevin McCarthy's climax in the original, when he stood
on a highway, screaming at passing trucks and cars, 'You fools, you're in
danger . . . ! They're after us! You're next! You're next!' " (184).

Richard Schickel's comment on the remake of *Invasion of the Body Snatchers* (1978) is equally relevant: "In its day, *Invasion* made a moving and ex-
citing film. Among other things, it was a metaphorical assault on the times
when, under the impress of McCarthyism and two barbecues in every back-
yard, the entire Lonely Crowd seemed to be turning into pod people. (See
figure 1.) The remakers have missed that point, failing to update the metaphor so that it effectively attacks the noisier, more self-absorbed conformity
of the '70s" (82).

Both Sayre and Schickel make what seem for a variety of reasons to be
unwarrantable assumptions about audiences and reception that then become the basis of interpretive judgments. Each treats the original as having
completed the acts of reflecting its culture and conveying its meanings once
and for all. But this is a problematic position to maintain, particularly as a
ground of critical judgment, because the position elides two questions: what

do we know of the specific audience for the first film? and what do we know of its multiple audiences over time? The position supposes that within a homogeneous audience locked in its own time and space—the time and space of the film's release—there had been cultural agreement and unanimity about interpretive questions when the film appeared.

Any film that survives will have audiences over time. A film that is remade encounters new audiences, individuals who might not have encountered the original if someone hadn't decided to remake the older film. The question of why later filmmakers appropriate earlier films is an issue deserving at least a brief digression at this point. Various suggestions have been made to account for the existence of remakes. These explanations range from the purely economic to the highly personal. For example, it is a critical commonplace that Hollywood studios have recycled films as a way of saving money by using properties to which they already hold the rights—hence remakes of older films. On one level, this explanation could be applied universally to account for all remakes, since no film is made in order to *lose* money.

But there are at least a couple of reasons why this explanation is too simple or at least incomplete. First, we have evidence that some directors with sufficient clout and economic support may remake a film for personal reasons. For example, Frank Capra explains why he remade *Lady for a Day:* "I wanted to experiment with retelling Damon Runyon's fairy tale with rock-hard non-hero-gangsters"—hence *A Pocketful of Miracles* (Silverman, 26). In addition, Franco Zeffirelli claims he remade *The Champ* (King Vidor, 1931; 1979) because he identified strongly with the family problems figured in the older film. He had seen it as a child and been moved. Having seen it more recently, he says: " '[T]he whole trauma came back, the whole syndrome of anguish.' He remembered that Richard Shepherd, an MGM executive, had invited him to make a movie in this country. 'I called him and said I wanted to do a remake to *The Champ*' " (Chase, 28).

Second, Harvey Greenberg has suggested even more complex reasons possible for wishing to remake a film, various forms of "Oedipal inflections" evident in different kinds of relationships between older and newer filmmakers: first, "unwavering idealization" in the faithful remake; second, "the remaker, analogous to a creative resolution of childhood and adolescent Oedipal conflict, eschews destructive competition with the maker, taking the original as a point of useful, unconflicted departure"; third, "the original, as signet of paternal potency and maternal unavailability/refusal, incites the remaker's unalloyed negativity"; and, fourth, "the remaker, simultaneously worshipful and envious of the maker, enters into an ambiguous, anxiety-ridden struggle with a film he both wishes to honor and eclipse." The latter is the "contested homage" Greenberg sees at work in Steven Spielberg's *Always* (115ff.).

In addition, we can think of one remake that is the product of neither economics nor psychoanalytic conflict. As Lea Jacobs has explained, Universal had hoped to *re-release Back Street* (John Stahl, 1932) in 1938, but, because it ran afoul of the Production Code Administration, headed by Joe Breen, the studio ended up having to *remake* the film (Robert Stevenson, 1941): "[T]he film had been . . . criticised by the reform forces at the time of its original release; in particular, it had been attacked by Catholics connected with the Legion of Decency. The story . . . was said to generate sympathy for adulterers and to undermine the normative ideal of marriage as monogamous. When Breen argued against a re-release of the 1932 version, Universal agreed to do a remake" (107).

It is useful to consider Phil Kaufman's stated reasons for wanting to remake *Invasion of the Body Snatchers* in light of this information:

> In 1956, the science-fiction consciousness of the public was limited, and now it's greatly expanded, so you could deal with certain things in different ways. . . . There were a lot of articles coming to my attention about how we were being bombarded from outer space, saying that diseases are coming from outer space. . . . There were political overtones to the original film, and there are two sides on this. What was the original saying? Was it anti-Communist? Was it anti-anti-Communist? I don't know the answer to that. It's interesting to examine the original film both ways, because both theories seem to make sense. Obviously those political overtones don't apply to our film. . . . I also feel that paranoia or fear is a very important thing. I don't think this film would have been worthy of a remake during the period of the Vietnam war, because at that time there was a high consciousness about where we were. The fears hanging over everyone's heads—particularly young people's—gave them a sense of mortality. . . . I think that in the last couple of years, we've been losing that sense of mortality. Fear is very valuable in a time of complacency (Farber, 27).

In addition, Kaufman says, "It seems to me . . . that this is a perfect time to restate the message of *Body Snatchers*. . . . We were all asleep in a lot of ways in the Fifties, living conforming, other-directed types of lives. Maybe we woke up a little in the Sixties, but now we've gone back to sleep again. We've taken some of the things that were expressed *about* the original film—that modern life is turning people into unfeeling, conforming pods who resist getting involved with each other on any level—and we're putting them directly into the script" (Freund, 23). (See figure 2.)

Interestingly, in none of Kaufman's comments, or in the reviews cited above, do we get anything that addresses the historical-cultural moment when the original film actually appeared. It was released without any acknowledgment in the *New York Times* (advertising or reviews) at the end of February 1956. There are very few reviews that Albert LaValley has been able to assemble in his invaluable edition of the script and commentary. In

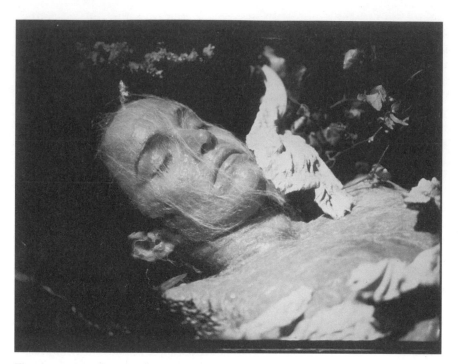

Figure 2. A pod person slumbers in Phil Kaufman's *Invasion of the Body Snatchers,* the 1978 remake.

subsequent years, as far as I have been able to determine, no one has fully come to terms with the moment of the film's release in regard to the audience and the country receiving it. But, as George Lipsitz, one of the major American proponents of cultural studies, reminds us in a discussion of other works, any film "responds to tensions exposed by the social moment of its creation, but each also enters a dialogue already in progress, repositioning the audience in regard to dominant myths" (169). Equally pertinent is Michael Ryan's observation: "The 'meaning' of popular film, its political and ideological significance, does not reside in the screen-to-subject phenomenology of viewing alone. That dimension is merely one moment in a circuit, one effect of larger chains of determination. Film representations are one subset of wider systems of social representation (images, narratives, beliefs, etc.) that determine how people live and that are closely bound up with the systems of social valorization or differentiation along class, race and sex lines" (480).

I want to talk about the dialogue already in progress when the original emerged, with the hope of putting us in closer contact with the audience that experienced the film. First, I want to clarify somewhat more fully the question of the communist menace. By the time the film appeared, Senator Joseph McCarthy, whose attack on communists is consistently used to interpret the film's meaning (anti-communist? anti-anti-communist?), had already started to lose power. Joseph Welch's stinging condemnation of him had occurred in 1954. In 1955, the year that *Invasion of the Body Snatchers* was being made, while there continued to be investigations of communists, some of them proceeding from McCarthy, news accounts reveal a partial unraveling of the charges and sentences that had resulted from the activities of McCarthy and Roy Cohn. As a matter of fact, in the very months that the film was being made (March 23 to April 18, 1955), the convictions of two men were reversed on the grounds that one Harvey M. Matusow had admitted to lying when he said they were communists. Matusow claimed he had been coached by Roy Cohn. The latter was exonerated of that charge. Still, in the context of a year when other convicted communists were being released (some to be retried) and when, according to *Facts on File,* "the Eisenhower administration, reacting to criticism of its employee security program, revised its procedure to insure that accused Govt. workers received 'fair & impartial treatment' at the hands of Govt.," it is clear that the overwhelming period of paranoia and the domination of McCarthy and Cohn had started to ease significantly (*Facts on File,* March 3–9, 1955: 75. Also February 24–March 2; March 10–16; April 21–27). Thus, we need to be careful about the extent to which we: 1) attribute a particular mind-set to a contemporary audience confronting a film supposedly illustrating the communist menace (whether from the left or the right); 2) use this mind-set to fix the film's meaning; and 3) criticize a remake for failing to reproduce it.

There are two historically relevant matters that can be advanced as having more than a casual relevance to the contemporary audience. The first involves what for want of a better term I will call the discourse of medicine. Peter Biskind talks about the treatment of doctors generally in right-wing films but hasn't fully explored the following with reference to *Invasion* (60–61). In 1954, Dr. Jonas Salk had discovered a vaccine that would apparently stop polio. The vaccine was tested in 1955 and put to use that year. On February 6, 1956 (a few weeks before the release of *Invasion*), Salk and his predecessors who worked to develop the vaccine were honored by the Department of Health, Education, and Welfare. The citation is worth quoting, particularly in light of cold-war rhetoric: "A community needed a bell tower to warn its people against attack. Everyone helped to build it, and the whole was greater than the sum of its parts. When it was finished, the feeling of gratitude of each man for his neighbor, for what each had contributed, was showered upon but one—and he was among the last to contribute. But all knew that the end could not have come without the beginning and without all that had transpired in between" ("Salk Award," 74). Jonas

Salk was one of two doctors whose status approached that of the venerated. The other was Paul Dudley White, President's Dwight Eisenhower's personal physician and the person honored not only for helping Eisenhower pull through his heart attack but also for having started to change the health habits of Americans. Dr. White's status as personal physician and as national spokesperson for health was of particular significance at the moment the film was being released, because the nation was poised to hear whether Eisenhower would run again for election. There had already been considerable campaign activity among Democratic candidates, particularly between Estes Kefauver and Adlai Stevenson, who were seeking the nomination. It was assumed that Eisenhower's decision, when it came, would be predicated on Dr. White's estimate of his health and fitness to run. The week before the film opened, White and the medical advisers had said he was "able"; the title of an article in *Life* for February 27, 1956, on the matter was: "Doctors Say He's Able—Is He Willing?" (38–39).

Thus at the point of the film's appearance, one can see a valorization almost approaching the hagiographic of two doctors: Salk, who had saved the children from attack; and White, who had saved the president and was helping to change physical behavior in the nation's citizens. The latter's work had an inescapably political dimension, given his association with administrative and hence political stability.

In addition, there was evidently strong support for the medical profession in general. *Time* reported on a survey done by the American Medical Association: "To no one's surprise, the A.M.A. concluded that doctors stand comfortingly high in public esteem. Only 82% of the 3,000 people polled have a regular family physician, but of those who do, 96% think well of him" ("Patients Diagnose Doctors," 46). That same week, the magazine reported on a training program developed at the Menninger Psychiatric Clinic in Topeka, Kansas, in which the Menninger brothers counseled various business leaders and managers in ways of using "psychology and psychiatry . . . to help them with their problems" in the workplace ("Psychiatry for Industry," 45).

In such a historical and cultural context, it is worthwhile to consider the possible impact of *Invasion of the Body Snatchers,* specifically the impotency of those associated with the medical discourse in the film. The psychiatrist Danny Kaufman (Larry Gates), the family doctor Ed Pursey (Everett Glass) who delivered Becky, and the nurse Sally (Jean Willes) are all taken over by the pods. It is Sally who is conducting the transformation of her own baby when Dr. Miles Bennell (Kevin McCarthy) spies on her home. Only in the narrative frame added after previews of the film is Miles restored to viability within the medical community; this occurs when Dr. Bassett (Richard Deacon) and Dr. Hill (Whit Bissell), another psychiatrist, begin to believe his story after hearing of the truck accident and the cargo of pods. My point is that such a unilateral and comprehensive presentation of medicine as succumbing to an alien force (involving nursing, general practice, and psychiatry) can be imagined to have had some resonance with the audience, but in a way that doesn't involve conformity or conspiracy.

An even more significant historical-cultural consideration I want to point out has to do with the events of February 1956 as they pertained to civil rights. *Brown v. Board of Education* in 1954, and a subsequent ruling in 1955 in which the phrase "with all due deliberate speed" was used in reference to public education, were very much on the collective minds of the citizens in 1956. Early in February, Miss Autherine Lucy had entered the University of Alabama in Montgomery under court order. After two calm nights (she was not permitted to stay in the dormitory), various demonstrations erupted, including cross burnings. She was dismissed from the institution by the trustees in order to insure harmony. This action occasioned different kinds of agitated reactions. Some students protested the trustees' action. Democrats campaigning for the presidential nomination were asked what they would do to enforce the court decree if they were president. At the same time, on February 21, "115 persons were indicted by a county grand jury . . . in Montgomery, Ala. . . . on charges of instigating a Negro mass boycott of City Line buses. . . . The boycott began Dec. 5, 1955, after Mrs. Rosa Parks, a Negro, was fined $14 for refusing to give up her seat" (*Facts on File*, February 15–21: 61). The following week, a Gallup poll reported that "Southern whites disapproved the Supreme Court's school desegregation ruling by a 80%–16% majority" (*Facts on File*, February 22–28, 1956: 68). In the first week of the film's release, *Life* carried an essay by Nobel Prize winner William Faulkner, "A Letter to the North," in which he defends the position of going slowly in the integration process. Although he says segregation is an "evil," "I must go on record as opposing the forces outside the South which would use legal or police compulsion to eradicate that evil overnight" (51). He concludes by asserting "that 1) Nobody is going to force integration on [the Southerner] from the outside; 2) [t]hat he himself faces an obsolescence in his own land which only he can cure: a moral condition which not only must be cured but a physical condition which has got to be cured if he, the white Southerner, is to have any peace, is not to be faced with another legal process or maneuver, every year, year after year, for the rest of his life" (52).

The use of language couched in reference to cures and illness is significant. A month earlier, in an article entitled "South Rises Again in Campaign to Delay Integration," *Life* had run a picture of a Pontiac automobile carrying a Confederate flag and a banner taped to the side: "Save Our Children from the Black Plague" (22–23). And the previous year, according to William J. Harvie, in testimony before the Supreme Court, a Virginia attorney working for delay in integration said: "Negroes constitute 22 percent of the population of Virginia . . . but 78 percent of all cases of syphilis and 83 percent of all cases of gonorrhea occur among the Negroes. . . . Of course the incidence of disease and illegitimacy is just a drop in the bucket compared to the promiscuity[;] . . . the white parents at this time will not appropriate the money to put their children among other children with that sort of background" (63).

In addition, according to the *New York Times,* during that month there were renewed instances of states such as Georgia and Mississippi introducing "nullifying" bills and "interposition" bills. The former type of bill simply denies the application of federal rulings to an individual state; the latter involves states enacting laws to defend their own jurisdictions by countering federal legislation ("Miss Lucy *v.* Alabama," 1; "Georgia Adopts 'Nullifying' Bill," 16). In addition, there was movement to "abolish public schools, create gerrymandered school districts and set up special entrance requirements" ("School Integration Report," 7).

All this is offered not to say that *Invasion of the Body Snatchers* contains a previously undiscovered allegory about racism but, rather, to suggest that we ought to remember that the film entered a dialogue, to use Lipsitz's phrase, of considerable tension. In this regard, it is interesting to consider several scenes from the original in which the action and language seem pertinent.

In the first of these scenes, Miles, suspecting that a gas station attendant who had earlier serviced his car may be one of the invaders, stops his car and discovers two pods hidden in the trunk. He pulls them out and sets them on fire. The camera lingers on the flames as they envelop the pods. Burning of alien forces at night in a way that emphasizes the flames against the darkness might well have reminded contemporary audiences of the cross burnings that had recently occurred.

Second, as Miles and Becky (Dana Wynter) watch unobserved from his office, townspeople gather in the square while the pods are being distributed to trucks that will carry them to various communities beyond Santa Mira. As he sees the full implication of the spread of the pods and the infiltration of the aliens into neighboring communities, Miles describes the situation to Becky in terms of a "malignant disease spreading throughout the country."

Third, during the frenzied sequence on the highway, Miles tries to stop motorists and warn them. Specifically (in a shot in which he virtually addresses the camera) he warns: "Those people are coming after us. They're not human. You fools, you're in danger. They're after you, they're after all of us. Your wives. Your children." It is hard not to see a connection between the film's depiction of a threatening, destabilizing force from within the society, characterized in terms of disease, taking over lives, and threatening wives and children, and the current discourse going on in the country in which individual states tried to avoid what was perceived as a similarly de-stabilizing force, one characterized as a disease.

I make no claim that this information about the context of reception for the 1956 *Invasion* will help us understand the 1978 film any better. But it may help to define the differences between the two films somewhat more finely and in a way that goes beyond what I submit has not been sufficiently complete. What's at issue is a cultural version of Michel Foucault's *episteme* or what in another context Ann Kaplan has called the "semiotic field" of a work (41). As scholars and critics making comparative evaluations, we en-rich our work to the extent that our positioning of the original in relation to the remake comes to terms with the forces and dialogues that shaped the works as well as those into which it entered. In fact, with this kind of comparative approach, we may find ourselves better positioned to comment on the relation between original and remake.[4]

The remake of *Invasion of the Body Snatchers* was released December 22, 1978. Within the month, events occurred that could not have been antici-pated in any way by the filmmakers but that provide a grim background for its reception. First was the discovery of the mass suicides led by Jim Jones at the People's Temple of Jonestown, Guyana. Pictures of the more than nine hundred suicides appeared in newspapers and, in color, in maga-zines like *Time* and *Newsweek*. Reports of the suicide made it clear that some of the victims were forced to participate. According to *Facts on File*, "As for the dissenters, some appeared to have been browbeaten into drinking the poison and others appeared to have been murdered by zealous cult mem-bers. Guyanese sources told the *New York Times* Dec. 11 that at least 70 of the bodies found at Jonestown bore fresh injection marks on their upper arms. The marks presumably showed that the poison had been injected into these victims by others, since it was very difficult for a person to inject himself in that part of the body" (*Facts on File*, December 15, 1978: 955).

Such information and pictures must have resonated in those members of the audience aware of it who were watching the weirdly charismatic psychiatrist Dr. David Kibner (Leonard Nimoy) inject Matthew Bennell (Donald Sutherland) and Elizabeth Driscoll (Brooke Adams) with a "light sedative" that would cause them to sleep and, subsequently, to die as they were taken over by the aliens. The international reaction to the horribly disturbing mass suicide had its counterpart in the national response to the news that, within a few weeks, two teenagers committed suicide in a suburb in New Jersey; they were "the third and fourth Ridgewood, N.J., youngsters to die by their own hands in the past 18 months." One explanation offered was that attention paid to the Jonestown disaster may have triggered the recent suicides, but others, according to *Time*, "[saw] a deeper malaise," including school pressures and family difficulties ("Trouble in Affluent Sub-urb," 60).

Ironically, the December 4 story about Jonestown included a quotation from San Francisco Mayor George Moscone, who, according to *Time*, "received important help from Jones in his close 1975 election [and had] appointed him to the city's housing authority in 1976. (Said the mayor about last week's horror: 'I proceeded to vomit and cry.')" ("Messiah from the Midwest," 27). Within the week, Moscone was dead, having been shot along with Harvey Milk by Dan White. In a creepy coincidence, the film is set in San Francisco and includes a scene in which Matthew seeks Kibner's help in reaching the mayor by phone. As far as I have been able to determine, the association of the suicides and murders, of Jones, Moscone, and Milk, and San Francisco, and the turbulent atmosphere of death in the month of December seem not to have entered into contemporary reviews of the film. Indeed, the opposite seems to be the case if Pauline Kael's laudatory review is examined. She notes: "The story is set in San Francisco, which is the ideally right setting because of the city's traditional hospitality to artists and eccentrics. . . . San Franciscans often look shell-shocked. . . . The hip-idyllic city, with its ginger-bread houses and its jagged geometric profile of hills covered with little triangles and rectangles, is such a pretty plaything that it's the central character" (48).

Our own period has recently seen a revival of interest in conspiracy theories in regard to the assassination of John F. Kennedy because of the interest generated in conjunction with Oliver Stone's film (*JFK*, 1991). The audience for *Invasion of the Body Snatchers* during the last week of 1978 and the beginning of 1979 was learning that the House of Representatives Select Committee on Assassinations "concluded Dec. 30 that President John F. Kennedy 'was probably assassinated as a result of conspiracy' in 1963. . . . The committee also said that on the basis of circumstantial evidence 'there is a likelihood' that Dr. Martin Luther King Jr. was slain as a result of conspiracy. . . . The findings came at the end of the committee's $5.8 million, two-year inquiry into the assassinations of the two leaders. . . . The committee flatly stated that none of the U.S. intelligence agencies—the Central Intelligence Agency, the Federal Bureau of Investigation, and the Secret Service—were involved in the Kennedy murder. The three agencies cleared were, however, criticized for their failings during the assassination and in the investigations after. The Justice Department was also attacked for its direction of the FBI probe" (*Facts on File*, December 31, 1978: 1002). Such information could well have hit a collective nerve in the audiences watching the futile attempts of Matthew Bennell and his friends. It's not that Kaufman gives any evidence of wanting to build in considerations of assassination conspiracy theories; rather, the film, with its frightening depiction of a conspiracy involving the police, the municipal government, and the secret service appears at a time when a major committee is raising the possibility of conspiracies and denying that the highest government agencies are involved. The threat of conspiracy in the remake seems, from our perspective, to have even more potential relevance to its audience in 1978 than the already fading threat of a communist conspiracy had for the audience of 1956.

Another dimension of the semiotic field worth noting concerns the pods themselves. Certainly one of the most disturbing scenes in the films occurs when we watch the creatures reproducing while Matthew sleeps. Kaufman examines the creatures with uncompromising (and unnerving) scrutiny as they emerge struggling from their pods, swathed in weblike mucus and uttering little cries. After being awakened by Nancy Bellicec (Veronica Cartwright), Miles uses a spade to attack the pods and, in one particularly gruesome shot, is seen splitting open the head of the one that resembles him.

In this scene the film enters a dialogue about abortion that was raging then and is even more violent now. Nothing that Kaufman has said even hints at any self-conscious imposing of a thesis on abortion into the film. Just as I linked the earlier film to civil rights, I here try to contextualize the images in terms of the audience's historical and cultural position in relation to the controversy. What is clear to me is that such images entered a semiotic field in which the legal and medical status of the fetus had already been hotly debated. In 1978, there had been several cases nationally in which "consent" agreements had included provisos that women seeking abortions had to view photographs of fetuses or be given descriptions of them by doctors. According to *Facts on File*, the law in Louisiana "required the doctor to describe 'in detail' the characteristics of the fetus, including 'mobility, tactile sensitivity, including pain, perception or response, brain and heart function, the presence of internal organs and the presence of external members' " (September 29, 1978: 743).

There was also legal consideration of the fetus's ability to withstand a saline abortion, most immediately in connection with the trial of Dr. William Waddill, a California physician accused of having strangled a twenty-eight- to thirty-one-week-old infant after it survived an abortion (Lindsay, 18). Audiences watching the film and Bennell's "murder" of his double might well have been affected by the abortion controversy, particularly since they had watched the character kill something that, recently emerged from its pod, was more "alive" than "dead."[5]

I am grateful to Lucy Fischer for suggesting that another dialogue in which the film can be seen engaging concerns in vitro fertilization, a medical phenomenon that had occurred for the first time earlier in 1978. In July of that year in England, Drs. Patrick Steptoe and Robert Edwards succeeded in effecting the conception of a child for Lesley and Gilbert John Brown ("British Awaiting Birth," 1). That same month, a much less happy case of in vitro fertilization was reported. The John Del Zio family was suing the Columbia-Presbyterian Medical Center, charging that Dr. Raymond L.

Vande Wiele "deliberately destroyed" the embryo produced in 1973 at the hospital ("Childless Couple Is Suing Doctor," 26). One concern raised during the trial by lawyers defending Columbia University was that the experiment's outcome was uncertain: "[The Del Zio's] physicians, the lawyer said, had no way of knowing whether their efforts would produce a 'monster birth' or a normal child" ("2 Charge 'Jealous' Doctor," 9). Shortly after this scene, Kaufman's film does in fact reveal a monster effected by this process. As a result of a partial aborting of the pod birth process, a dog acquires the head of the Union Square singer seen earlier in the film. Again, an audience in 1978 could reasonably be expected to have a certain amount of exposure to this medical information about a different kind of birth process, one in which there is a fear of something going wrong.

I want to conclude by quoting George Lipsitz again. He speaks of "sedimented historical currents" and of "sedimented networks and associations" that are more than merely intertextual references. His comment seems pertinent to our consideration of remakes and their originals: "The presence of sedimented historical currents within popular culture illumines the paradoxical relationship between history and commercialized leisure. Time, history, and memory become qualitatively different concepts in a world where electronic mass communication is possible. Instead of relating to the past through a shared sense of place or ancestry, consumers of electronic mass media can experience a common heritage with people they have never seen; they can acquire memories of a past to which they have no geographic or biological connection. The capacity of electronic mass communication to transcend time and space creates instability by disconnecting people from past traditions, but it also liberates people by making the past less determinate of experiences in the present" (5). This is true, but I would add that we have to work at this by reconstructing as much as possible the historical contexts, just as someone years hence will try to recover ours.

KINDS OF REMAKES: A PRELIMINARY TAXONOMY

1. a) A silent film remade as a sound film: *Ben Hur* (Fred Niblo, 1926, and William Wyler, 1959); b) a silent film remade by the same director as a sound film: Ernst Lubitsch's *Kiss Me Again* (1925) and *That Uncertain Feeling* (1941) or Cecil B. DeMille's *The Ten Commandments* (1923 and 1956); c) a major director's silent film remade as a sound film by a different major director: F. W. Murnau's *Nosferatu* (1922) and Werner Herzog's *Nosferatu, the Vampire* (1979).
2. a) A sound film remade by the same director in the same country: Frank Capra's *Lady for a Day* (1936) and *A Pocketful of Miracles* (1961); b) a sound film remade by the same director in a different country

in which the same language is spoken: Alfred Hitchcock's *The Man Who Knew Too Much* (1934, England, and 1954, United States); c) a sound film remade by the same director in a different country with a different language: Roger Vadim's *And God Created Woman . . .* (1957, France, and 1987, United States).

3. A film made by a director consciously drawing on elements and movies of another director: Howard Hawks's and Brian DePalma's *Scarface* (1932 and 1983); Alfred Hitchcock's *Vertigo* (1959) (and *Rear Window* [1955] and *Psycho* [1960]), and DePalma's *Obsession* (1976), *Body Double* (1984), and *Raising Cain* (1992).

4. a) A film made in the United States remade as a forcign film: *Diary of a Chambermaid* by Jean Renoir (1946, France) and Luis Buñuel (1964, France); b) a film made in a foreign country remade in another foreign country: *Yojimbo* (Akira Kurosawa, 1961) and *A Fistful of Dollars* (Sergio Leone, 1964); c) a foreign film remade in another foreign country and remade a second time in the United States: *La Femme Nikita* (Luc Besson, 1990, France), *Black Cat* (1992, Hong Kong) (thanks to Scott Higgins), and *Point of No Return* (John Badham, 1993); d) a foreign film remade in the United States: *La Chienne* (Jean Renoir, 1931) and *Scarlet Street* (Fritz Lang, 1945) and *Breathless* (Jean-Luc Godard, 1960, and Jim McBride, 1983).

5. a) Films with multiple remakes spanning the silent and sound eras: *Sadie Thompson* (Raoul Walsh, 1928), *Rain* (Lewis Milestone, 1932) and *Miss Sadie Thompson* (Curtis Bernhardt, 1953); b) films remade within the silent and sound eras as well as for television: *Madame X* (Lionel Barrymore, 1929 [the third silent remake of the silent film]; Sam Wood, 1937; David Lowell-Rich, 1966 [the Lana Turner version]; and, for television, Robert Ellis Miller, 1981 [with Tuesday Weld]).

6. a) A film remade as television film: *Sweet Bird of Youth* (Richard Brooks, 1962, and Nicholas Roeg, 1989); b) a film remade as a television miniseries: *East of Eden* (Elia Kazan, 1955, and Harvey Hart, 1981); c) a television series remade as a film: *Maverick* (Richard Donner, 1994) and *The Flintstones* (Brian Levant, 1994).

7. a) A remake that changes the cultural setting of a film: *The Big Sleep* (Howard Hawks, 1946, United States, and Michael Winner, 1978, Great Britain); b) a remake that updates the temporal setting of a film: *Murder, My Sweet* (Edward Dmytryk, 1944) and *Farewell My Lovely* (Dick Richards, 1975); *A Star Is Born* (William Wellman, 1937, George Cukor, 1954, and Frank Pierson, 1976); *Out of the Past* (Jacques Tourneur, 1948) and *Against All Odds* (Taylor Hackford, 1984); c) a remake that changes the genre and cultural setting of the film: *The Lives of a Bengal Lancer* (Henry Hathaway, 1935) re-

made as a western, *Geronimo* (Paul H. Sloane, 1939); the western *High Noon* (Fred Zinnemann, 1954) remade as the science fiction film *Outland* (Peter Hyams, 1981).

8. a) A remake that switches the gender of the main characters: *The Front Page* (Lewis Milestone, 1931); *His Gal Friday* (Howard Hawks, 1941); b) a remake that reworks more explicitly the sexual relations in a film: William Wyler's *These Three* (1936) and *The Children's Hour* (1961); *The Blue Lagoon* (Frank Launder, 1949, and Randal Kleiser, 1980).

9. A remake that changes the race of the main characters: *Anna Lucasta* (Irving Rapper, 1949, with Paulette Goddard; Arnold Laven, 1958, with Eartha Kitt).

10. A remake in which the same star plays the same part: Ingrid Bergman in the Swedish and American versions of *Intermezzo* (Gustav Molander, 1936, and Gregory Ratoff, 1939); Bing Crosby in *Holiday Inn* (Mark Sandrich, 1942) and *Holiday Inn* (Michael Curtiz, 1954).

11. A remake of a sequel to a film that is itself the subject of multiple remakes: *The Bride of Frankenstein* (James Whale, 1975) and *The Bride* (Frank Roddam, 1985).

12. Comic and parodic remakes: *Frankenstein* (James Whale, 1931) and *Young Frankenstein* (Mel Brooks, 1954); *Strangers on a Train* (Alfred Hitchcock, 1951) and *Throw Mamma from the Train* (Danny DeVito, 1987).

13. Pornographic remakes: *Ghostbusters* (Ivan Reitman, 1984) and *Ghostlusters* (1991); *Truth or Dare* (Alex Kashishian, 1991) and *Truth or Bare* (1992) (thanks to Peter Lehman).

14. A remake that changes the color and/or aspect ratio of the original: *The Thing* (Christian Nyby, 1951, black-and-white; John Carpenter, 1982, color and Panavision); *Invasion of the Body Snatchers* (Don Siegel, 1956, black-and-white and Superscope; Phil Kaufman, 1978, color and 1.85 to 1 aspect ratio).

15. An apparent remake whose status as a remake is denied by the director; Michelangelo Antonioni's *Blow-Up* (1966) and Francis Ford Coppola's *The Conversation* (1974).

This taxonomy doesn't cross-reference films. Clearly, some could be put in more than one category. *The Big Sleep,* for example, updates the temporal *and* cultural settings. In addition, the list doesn't address any number of relevant production and economic aspects: the role of the star as an element in developing the remake (Barbra Streisand and the 1976 *A Star Is Born*); variations in advertising, marketing, and distribution practices from period to period, genre to genre, country to country; historical data about the studios' decisions on remaking; comparative financial data on the original and remake; issues of acquiring rights; distinguishing among the major and minor studios (e.g., an MGM remake of an MGM picture? a United Artists remake of an Allied Artists picture?); and epochal analyses of remaking practices—for example, comparative data regarding the number of remakes in the period of "classical Hollywood cinema" as opposed to during the sixties and later periods.[6]

Even more problematic, the taxonomy itself doesn't address the issue of adaptation: are there any films in the various categories that can claim a common noncinematic source? If so, is it correct to call a film a remake or a new adaptation (e.g., *Madame Bovary*, Vincente Minnelli, 1949; Claude Chabrol, 1991)? Are there stages left out between the original and remake, as occurs for example when a play intervenes between the original and the remake (e.g., *The Wiz*)?

NOTES

1. See the end of this chapter for a tentative taxonomy of remakes.

2. Druxman, Milberg, and Nowlan offer commentary on remakes.

3. Essays by Thomas Doherty and Douglas Kellner provide welcome exceptions to the typical comparative studies of remakes.

4. Stuart Samuels concludes that the 1956 film "[d]irectly or indirectly . . . deals with the fear of annihilation brought on by the existence of the A-bomb, the pervasive feeling of paranoia engendered by an increasing sense that something was wrong, an increasing fear of dehumanization focused around an increased massification of American life, a deep-seated expression of social, sexual, and political frustration resulting from an ever-widening gap between personal expectation and social reality, and a widespread push for conformity as an acceptable strategy to deal with the confusion and growing insecurity of the period" (216).

5. For commentary on the abortion controversies, see Rubin and Milbauer.

6. See Simonet for comparative data on the number of remakes made by studios before and after conglomerate takeovers.

WORKS CITED

Biskind, Peter. *Seeing Is Believing: How Hollywood Taught Us to Stop Worrying and Love the Fifties.* New York: Pantheon Books, 1983.

"British Awaiting Birth of Baby Conceived in Laboratory Process." *New York Times*, 12 July 1978, sec. 1, pp. 1, 13

Chase, Donald. "The Champ: Round Two." *American Film* 3, no. 9 (July–August 1978): 28.

"Childless Couple Is Suing Doctor." *New York Times*, 16 July 1978, sec. 1, p. 26.

"Doctors Say He's Able—Is He Willing?" *Life*, 27 February 1956, 38–39.

Doherty, Thomas. "The Fly." *Film Quarterly* 40, no. 3 (spring 1987): 38–41; "The Blob." *Cine-Fantastique* 19, no. 1–2 (January 1989): 98–99.

Druxman, Michael B. *Make It Again, Sam: A Survey of Movie Remakes.* Cranbury, N.J.: A. S. Barnes, 1975.

Facts on File Yearbook 1955. Vol. 15. New York: Facts on File, 1956.

Facts on File Yearbook 1956. Vol. 16. New York: Facts on File, 1957.

Farber, Stephen. "Hollywood Maverick." *Film Comment* 15, no. 1 (January–February 1979): 26–31.

Faulkner, William. "A Letter to the North." *Life,* 5 March 1956, 51–52.

Freund, Charles. "Pods over San Francisco." *Film Comment* 15, no. 1 (January–February 1979): 22–25.

"Georgia Adopts 'Nullifying' Bill." *New York Times,* 14 February 1956, sec. 1, p. 16.

Greenberg, Harvey Roy. "Raiders of the Lost Text: Remaking as Contested Homage in *Always,*" this volume, 115–130.

Hall, Stuart. "Cultural Identity and Cinematic Representation." *Framework* 36 (1989): 68–81.

Harvie, William J. III. *From Brown to Bakke: The Supreme Court and School Integration, 1954–1978.* New York: Oxford University Press, 1979.

Jacobs, Lea. "Censorship and the Fallen Woman Cycle." In *Home Is Where the Heart Is: Studies in Melodrama and the Woman's Film,* edited by Christine Gledhill, 100–112. London: BFI Books, 1987.

Kael, Pauline. "Pods." *The New Yorker,* 25 December 1978, 48, 50–51.

Kaplan, E. Ann. "Dialogue." *Cinema Journal* 24, no. 2 (winter 1985): 40–41.

Kellner, Douglas. "David Cronenberg: Panic Horror and the Postmodern Body." *Canadian Journal of Political and Social Theory* 13, no. 3 (1989): 89–101.

LaValley, Albert J., ed. *Invasion of the Body Snatchers.* New Brunswick: Rutgers University Press, 1989.

Lindsay, Robert. "Coast Doctor's Murder Trial Draws Abortion Foes' Interest." *New York Times,* 10 April 1978, sec. 1, p. 18.

Lipsitz, George. *Time Passages: Collective Memory and American Popular Culture.* Minneapolis: University of Minnesota Press, 1990.

"Messiah from the Midwest." *Time,* 4 December 1978, 22, 27.

Milbauer, Barbara. *The Law Giveth: Legal Aspects of the Abortion Controversy.* New York: Atheneum, 1983.

Milberg, Doris. *Repeat Performances: A Guide to Hollywood Movie Remakes.* Shelter Island, N.Y.: Broadway Press, 1990.

"Miss Lucy v. Alabama." *New York Times,* 12 February 1956, sec. 4, pp. 1–2.

Nowlan, Robert A., and Gwendolyn Wright Nowlan. *Cinema Sequels and Remakes, 1903–1987.* Jefferson, N.C.: McFarland and Co., 1989.

"Patients Diagnose Doctors." *Time,* 13 February 1956, 46.

"Psychiatry for Industry." *Time,* 13 February 1956, 45.

Rubin, Eva R. *Abortion, Politics and the Courts: Roe v. Wade and Its Aftermath.* Westport, Conn.: Greenwood Press, 1982.

Ryan, Michael. "The Politics of Film: Discourse, Psychoanalysis, Ideology." In *Marxism and the Interpretation of Culture,* edited by Cary Nelson and Lawrence Grossberg, 477–486. Urbana: University of Illinois Press, 1988.

"Salk Award." *Time,* 6 February 1956, 74.

Samuels, Stuart. "The Age of Conspiracy and Conformity: *Invasion of the Body Snatch-*

ers." In *American History/American Film: Interpreting the Hollywood Image,* edited by John E. O'Connor and Martin A. Jackson, 203–217. New York: Frederick Ungar Publishing Co., 1979.

Sayre, Nora. "Watch the Skies." In LaValley, 184.

Schickel, Richard. "Twice-Told Tales." *Time,* 25 December 1978, 82.

"School Integration Report: The Situation in 17 States." *New York Times,* 19 February 1956, sec. 4, p. 7.

Silverman, Stephen M. "Hollywood Cloning: Sequels, Prequels, Remakes, and Spin-Offs." *American Film* 3, no. 9 (July–August 1978): 24–27, 29.

Simonet, Thomas. "Conglomerates and Content: Remakes, Sequels, and Series in the New Hollywood." *Current Research in Film* 3 (1987): 154–162.

"South Rises Again in Campaign to Delay Integration." *Life* 6 February 1956, 22–23.

"2 Charge 'Jealous' Doctor Killed 'Test-Tube Baby.' " *New York Times,* 18 July 1978, sec. 2, p. 9.

"Trouble in Affluent Suburb." *Time,* 25 December 1978, 60.

TWO

Algebraic Figures:
Recalculating the Hitchcock Formula

Robert P. Kolker

Alfred Hitchcock was a director of elegant solutions. His best films are well-tuned cinematic mechanisms that drive the elements of character, story, and audience response with a calculated construction that creates, anticipates, yet never quite resolves the viewer's desire to see and own the narrative. Hitchcock's films make us believe that we understand everything even while they leave us unsettled about what we have seen and unsure about our complicity in the event of seeing itself. Even his less-than-perfect films, in which too much is spoken and too much resolved, there are sequences or shots of formal inquisitiveness that concentrate the attention and reveal a filmmaker who, although his interest is less than thoroughly engaged, can formulate a cinematic idea and calculate it to a small perfection. Hitchcock is one of the few commercially successful filmmakers who give the viewer pleasure by means of his formal deliberations. For popular cinema—a form of expression dedicated to hiding its formal structures—this is a major achievement.

But there is an unsettling anomaly at work here. The elegance of Hitchcock's formal structures and the pleasure we take in watching them in operation belie the content they generate: images and narratives of violence and disruption; attacks on complacency and routine; sexual cruelty and a disturbing misogyny are created in visual and narrative fields whose eloquence and intelligence seem to transcend their content. Something of a sadomasochistic pattern is put into operation. We reverberate to the shocks endured by Hitchcock's characters and take a peculiar pleasure in the way they are perceived and the way in which we perceive them. We delight in the cunning with which the director represents this violence and respond favorably to the eloquence of the moral ambiguities that result in our pleasurable assent to violence and madness. When we see culpability and evil

portrayed as the twins of innocence and rectitude, we accept this contradiction with an almost smug knowingness. The pain of the revelation of
moral complexity and uncertainty (which repels us in, for example, the
political sphere) is accepted in the aesthetic as the insight of a clever interpreter of modernity. The calculation of it all, the almost obsessive construction of narrative, the composition and cutting of shots that force us to respond in predetermined ways to seemingly uncontrolled or uncontrollable
acts, Hitchcock's complete command of our perceptions, turns upon reception into delight. We find pleasure in his authority and enlightenment in
his calculations. Hitchcock and his audience are able to have it all ways:
plot, character, suspense, fear, pleasure; a formal structure never invisible,
yet intrusive only when one desires it to be; a structure of moral ambiguity
lurking below the level of immediate cognition, all firmly buttressing the
pleasure of narration.

Hitchcock calculated himself as part of the overall structure of his work.
He foregrounded his presence by appearing in his films; he developed an
instantly recognizable persona on television; and he entered the popular
imagination with a distinctiveness unrivaled by any other filmmaker in fifties and early sixties American culture. This success on all levels created
the event of the director as celebrity. His films were known; and he (or
rather the public persona he created) was known through the work of film
reviewers, who referred to almost any film that used suspense, shock, or a
"surprise ending," as "Hitchcockian." His work was conflated into an adjective and misappropriated as a genre. It's not surprising that, with all this,
Hitchcock became a very special example to the generation of film students
turned filmmakers in the late sixties and early seventies.[1]

This is a special group of writers and directors, which now dominates
American filmmaking. While not all were students in the literal sense (a
few of them, like Martin Scorsese, did take degrees in film school, while
others may have attended briefly or not at all), they were a generation who
learned about film by watching movies on television and in repertory movie
houses. Unlike their Hollywood predecessors, who learned filmmaking as
a trade, coming up the studio ranks, many of the young filmmakers of the
late sixties and early seventies saw film as a form of expression: subjective
and malleable. One manifestation of that expression, one way of impress-
ing subjective response and a love of the cinematic medium was by alluding to and quoting from other films. Hitchcock and John Ford were the
touchstones for these new directors, and the films—*The Searchers* (1956)
and *Psycho* (1960) in particular—the foundation for much of their work.[2]

The phenomenon of allusion, quotation, and imitation in film is complex. We need to divide some of the strands of these activities to understand what the new filmmakers were about and how Hitchcock plays a role
in their work. The business of filmmaking has always thrived on the fact

that viewers remember films, stories, stars, and genres. The repetitions and sequels and cycles that Hollywood needs in order to reproduce narratives in large numbers depended—and depends still—on the viewer's ability to recall, respond to, and favor particular films. There is a discrete contradiction operating here. The classic American style of moviemaking and reception depends upon transparency and a kind of virgin birth. Every film emerges whole and new, actively suppressing its technical, stylistic, or historical origins. Yet audiences are depended upon to recognize similarities and repetitions from film to film, and indeed they *must* do this. If they did not, they would have no desire to see stars, plots, generic elements, narrative patterns repeated; and without that desire to fulfill, Hollywood filmmaking could not exist.

The post-fifties, post–French New Wave generation of American filmmakers exploited the contradictions. They too looked to repetition and depended upon audience recognition, yet did not care to make their work completely transparent. They did not want to hide the genesis of their films or suppress the fact that films come not from life or from an abstract convention of "reality" but from other films. Their films recalled not only broad generic paradigms or the sexual attractions of certain players but specific images, the narrative structure of individual films, the visual and storytelling stratagems of particular filmmakers. They interrogated that aspect of filmmaking that combines commercial necessity (repetition and imitation) with the work of the imagination (allusion and quotation) in order to provoke the audience into recognizing film history, and in doing so pleased the viewer by asking for her response and her knowledge. The cinema of allusion is made out of a desire to link filmmaker and viewer with cinema's past and inscribe the markings of an individual style by recalling the style of an admired predecessor. At its worst, it is an act of showing off; at its best, a subtle means of giving depth to a film, broadening its base, adding resonance to its narrative and a sense of play, and, through all of this, increasing narrative pleasure.

Various filmmakers refer to and incorporate other films in various ways, as John Biguenet demonstrates in his essay elsewhere in this book. Among the most interesting are the subtle allusive acts that operate on the level of pure form. In these instances, allusion is not quite the appropriate term, for here filmmakers are working with and advancing basic visual experiments tried out by their predecessors. Hitchcock is a particularly apt example, because he was constantly playing with formal devices, looking for ways in which elements of composition, cutting, and camera movement could be employed to express a state of mind or clarify perception, to bring the viewer into the progression of the narrative or hold her at arms length.

When Spielberg uses a formal Hitchcockian device in *Jaws* (1975), combining a tracking shot with a zoom, each moving in opposite directions, to communicate a tense moment of perception and recognition, the result is powerful and terrifying. Hitchcock had experimented with the technique in *Vertigo* (1958) to indicate Scottie's fear and loss of control as he hangs from a roof or races up the steps of the mission steeple. He used it as a point-of-view shot, expressing his character's terrified perception of his situation. Spielberg expands its use to express not only the character's but the audience's response: it becomes the viewer's point of view as the sheriff, Brody, thinks he sees the shark in the water, while character and background simultaneously shrink from and expand into each other. Toward the end of *Goodfellas* (1991: a film of great, imaginative "tryings out" and experiments), Martin Scorsese refines the device even further. In a diner, Jimmy and Henry sit by a window, talking. The camera tracks very slowly toward them, while the scene outside the window zooms in at a faster speed in the opposite direction. The sequence impresses the characters' dislocation and prepares for the major turn in the narrative, when Henry betrays his gangster friends.

Such examples carry allusion beyond the point of play, inside joke, or plot device into the very system of visual narrative structure. They demonstrate that filmmakers work like artists in any other media: they learn from, copy from, and expand upon the work of their predecessors, exploring and exploiting their own tradition. The degree of success that each attains, however, is not equal. Brian De Palma, for example, has done the simplest arithmetic exercises based upon the Hitchcock equations. He alludes to Hitchcock's plot structures and plays with visual and editorial devices. Unquestionably, the majority of American filmmakers who attempt to recalculate the Hitchcock formula wind up diminishing the work of their subject. Rather than recreate or rethink the moral structures of the Hitchcock mise-en-scène, they simply exploit it, sometimes very quietly, as if out of desperation. Paul Verhoeven's and Joe Eszterhas's *Basic Instinct* (1992) is an example of an exploitation film in which sexual violence is made a metaphor for moral bankruptcy. But the metaphor is rendered useless because the film depends on its ability to sexually arouse its audience to assure its commercial success. The film enacts what it seems to condemn, leaving no space for introspection or comprehension of the viewer's own complicity in the film's narrative affairs. Despite the fact that Eszterhas keeps reaching into two of Hitchcock's most disturbing and questioning films about sexuality, *Vertigo* and *Marnie* (1964), he allows no space for speculation, only manipulation. A central premise of *Vertigo*, that male sexual obsession can be carried to the point of destroying both the subject and object of the obsession, is reduced in *Basic Instinct* to various sets of exclusive sexual provocations, in which a man and two women maneuver one another into sexual thralldom (a mainstay of popular romantic literature and middle-brow, commercial soft-core pornographic film), with the threat of death hanging over every encounter. From *Marnie* comes the figure of the sexually tormented woman, psychologically broken into multiple characters, yielding, destructive, finally psychotic, and, in a ploy Hitchcock would never indulge, murderous.

Hitchcock's misogyny is well documented. But despite the suspicion and distrust of women manifested in much of his work, there is almost always an understanding that women, when they are figures pursued and possessed by men, are fantasies made up by men. They are (as Tania Modleski points out in *The Women Who Knew Too Much*) fictions that belie innate personality and female desire, fictions that subordinate the female to the neurotic, often psychotic, male gaze. *Notorious* (1946) and *Vertigo* play upon this transformation, the latter film elevating it to a semblance of tragedy. *Marnie* examines the phenomenon in almost clinical fashion, as a woman, honest about her neurotic dysfunction, is reduced and finally raped by a man who believes he can transform her.

Eszterhas and Verhoeven do not care for abstractions or meditations on transformation. The central figures of *Basic Instinct* are present only to exploit and use one another, and the audience most of all. Hitchcock's troubled and abused woman is here turned into a sexual destroyer, and none of the shots of the Michael Douglas character driving along the California coast carry the weight of existential fear and sexual anxiety borne by Jimmy Stewart's Scottie as he pursues his phantom of desire through the streets of San Francisco. *Basic Instinct* is an example of the exhaustion of allusion and the employment of Hitchcockian technique as an act of exploitation and despair. To *do* Hitchcock may convince a filmmaker or his producer that he may be *like* Hitchcock, and with such similarity may come respect and admiration and ticket sales. But in the end, very few directors—perhaps only Martin Scorsese in America and Claude Chabrol in France—understand that recalculating Hitchcock means understanding the mathematics of the original formula, thinking the way Hitchcock thought, and reformulating the original so that the results not only allude to but reinterpret it. Again, it is a matter of comprehending Hitchcock's mise-en-scène: the spatial articulation of his films, which includes the way his characters are situated and the way they look at each other and are looked at by the camera. It is the mise-en-scène itself that gives voice to ambiguities of sexuality and the violence of the everyday, the subjects that most engaged Hitchcock in his best work.

Scorsese has made two films that actively engage Hitchcock. *Taxi Driver* (1976) reformulates *Psycho* (while it simultaneously situates its narrative pattern in *The Searchers*). Within the figures, gestures, and ideological and cultural practice of the late seventies, Scorsese finds analogues for the return of the repressed, which Hitchcock represented in the late fifties. *Taxi Driver* incorporates dread, angst, and threat in the figure of Travis Bickle, whose world is as tentative and malperceived as was Norman Bates's in *Psycho*. *Cape Fear* (1991), certainly a less complex and resonant film than *Taxi Driver*, uses Hitchcock in more devious ways than its predecessor. Rather than elide and reconstruct the methods of one film within another (as *Taxi Driver* does with *Psycho*, embracing as much as remaking it), *Cape Fear* uses Hitchcockian technique to solve some problems. Just as Hitchcock used the perceptual structures of film to solve thematic puzzles and simultaneously engage and distance his audience, Scorsese turns to Hitchcock to solve other kinds of problems and provide a kind of secret narrative structure for a film that even its director admits is a minor, unashamedly commercial work. Within this "secret narrative" lie some of the most interesting reformulations of Hitchcock, unobtrusively, and with a great deal of humor and play.

When *Cape Fear* was being edited late in the spring of 1991, Scorsese gave a talk about the filmmaker Michael Powell at the Library of Congress as part of a program celebrating British cinema. He made a number of interesting revelations. One concerned the extent to which his own imagination was nurtured by cinema, and the fact that the choices he made and the problems he solved in creating his films depended in excruciating detail upon other films. He said, for example, that the close-up of De Niro's eyes during *Taxi Driver*'s credit sequence was suggested to him by a similar shot of the eyes of a gondola oarsman in Michael Powell's little-known film, *Tales of Hoffman* (1951). This is more than allusion or the simple celebration of cinematic community. It is, rather, the activity of a profound, subjective intertextual imagination that links Scorsese with the modernist writers of the teens and twenties and with the cinemodernists like Godard in the sixties, who looked to the writers and filmmakers who proceeded them as the usable past that must inform their own work. For the modernist, a "new" text is built from the appropriation and accretion of other texts. In a basic, material way, modernism demands that the works of imagination remain viable and usable, that they exist as the seeds of other works. Through such incremental nurturing a history of the imagination is written.

At its very best, the modernist act of allusion reveals form and structure through dialectical play. A new work, coherent in its own structure, gains that coherence by absorbing and restructuring other works. A kind of imaginative space is marked out that is open to other spaces and in that openness is made secure. "These fragments I have shored against my ruins," T. S. Eliot writes—or rather quotes—in *The Waste Land*. This is intertextuality as imaginative redemption; and that is precisely what is going on in *Cape Fear*, a secret remake, knowledge of which reveals the film as joke and intricate reformulation, a way of knowing Hitchcock and absolving Scorsese.

At his Library of Congress talk, Scorsese made an admission of sorts. In return for the financial and moral support given *The Last Temptation of Christ*

(1988), he owed Universal Pictures six films. *Cape Fear* was the first of these, and it was consciously and eagerly made quickly, cheaply, and with an eye on the box office. As an indulgence in the thriller-horror genre, and drawing upon a multitude of sources, it was aimed to please its audience and its creator. Part of that pleasure was in the remaking of an earlier film of the same title and basic plot structure, J. Lee Thompson's 1962 *Cape Fear* (a Universal property). Were it only a remake of this earlier film, it would be a somewhat interesting aside in Scorsese's career, a successful attempt at a commercial film (as big a moneymaker as Scorsese has had and an even better film than an earlier commercial attempt, *The Color of Money,* 1986, which was itself not a remake, but an extension of yet another film, *The Hustler,* 1961). But it is apparent that Scorsese calculated to produce something more than a quickie remake. He would, in effect, create a number of remakes in one: within the remake of the 1962 *Cape Fear* would be embedded a kind of remake of three minor Hitchcock films from the early fifties: *Stage Fright* (1950), *I Confess* (1953), and *Strangers on a Train* (1951). In other words, having decided to do a minor film within his own canon, he turned to films in Hitchcock's canon in order to discover how a minor film could best be done: to try, in effect, to recreate a minor Hitchcock film. The result is still not anything more than a minor film; yet it is one that plays a game of intertextual counterpoint, a modernist exercise in popular form in which one film adopts the plot of its predecessor while gaining a deeper structure through an allusive tag game with three Hitchcock films. The result is enormous pleasure for the maker of the film and the viewer who perceives the games being played.

All this becomes even more interesting when we realize that Thompson's 1962 *Cape Fear* is itself a Hitchcockian exercise, a film that plays upon *Psycho,* or, more accurately, the atmosphere of *Psycho* and its reception. The production of Thompson's film is explicitly connected to Hitchcock. Bernard Herrmann, who wrote the score for *Psycho* (as he did for most of Hitchcock's fifties films), wrote the music for Thompson's *Cape Fear.* (Scorsese had Elmer Bernstein—an old hand at film music—reorchestrate a souped-up version of the same score for his film. He furthered the *Psycho* connection by having Saul Bass design credits somewhat similar to those he designed for *Psycho.*) George Tomasini, Hitchcock's regular editor, who cut *Psycho,* edited Thompson's film. Martin Balsam, who plays the detective Arbogast in *Psycho,* plays a police detective in *Cape Fear.* Gregory Peck, who had starred in Hitchcock's *Spellbound* (1945) and *The Paradine Case* (1948), plays Sam Bowden (Scorsese gives both Balsam and Peck small roles in his version of *Cape Fear,* as he does Robert Mitchum, the original Max Cady. (See figure 3.) There are visual references to *Psycho* in the 1962 *Cape Fear,* well before the time that allusions were to become prominent in American cinema: in the sequence where two detectives mount the steps in a boarding house

Figure 3. Evoking Hitchcock through casting: Martin Balsam, Robert Mitchum, and Gregory Peck in the original *Cape Fear* (1962) directed by J. Lee Thompson.

where Max Cady has brutalized a young woman, the camera tracks them up the stairs as it does Arbogast when he visits Norman's mother.

Thompson's film explores issues of violent sexuality, just becoming explicit in film as a result of *Psycho*. He examines "normal" middle-class people intruded upon by a psychotic, uncontrollable, and ultimately unknowable individual, and he observes an ordinary and plain middle-class landscape turned suddenly threatening by an amoral and dangerous presence. In short, Thompson attempts to recreate the mise-en-scène of *Psycho:* a gray, ugly world charged with violence and sadomasochistic sexuality, a world of ordinary people put in danger, a world of psychotic presences teasing and seducing middle-class morality and straining its oppressive limits. *Psycho* had come as a challenging and changing force onto the site of fifties American cinema, which, superficially, was as quiescent and predictable as the culture in which it was made. Few films outside of low-budget crime movies spoke to the political and moral despair of the period. To be sure, some of the decade's melodramas—notably those of Douglas Sirk and Nicholas Ray—suggested the fears and threats of domesticity on a social level above that represented in the gangster film. But these works almost always indulged in an obligatory, if ironic, recuperation of at least one of the main characters in an attempt to negate the terrors of dissolution within the narrative. Hitchcock, in *The Wrong Man* (1956) and *Vertigo*, began a concerted effort to represent a world that was not recuperable, a world hostile to ordinary emotional life in which individuals were shown as helpless in face of uncontrollable events, incapable of normal responses, and destructive of themselves and others. Together, these films spoke the unspeakable in a decade devoted to amnesia and evasion. In *Psycho*, finally, the articulation of despair was stated with such violence that there was no longer a possibility of recuperation.

Psycho placed the grimness of *The Wrong Man* within the emotional abyss of *Vertigo* and out of the two created a physical and emotional landscape unrelievedly barren and violent. It did this with such force and self-consciousness, and such self-awareness, that it startled viewers not only with the blackness of its vision, but its humor, the unrelenting notion that some kind of joke was being played. *Psycho*, as its creator never tired of saying, was in fact a joke, a story that kept giving itself away in the process of its telling. But its playfulness made its seriousness all the more disturbing, and the force of its darkness penetrated American film and slowly changed it. Thompson's *Cape Fear*, coming less than two years after *Psycho*, was among the first to reproduce its fearsome insistence that the disruption of madness is a given in a world that counts on an illusory continuum of the ordinary.

But let's be clear. The 1962 *Cape Fear* has none of the complex resonance of *Psycho*. It does, in the character Max Cady, have its own version of Norman Bates, the madman who, from moment to moment, appears normal and self-contained (it is interesting to note that Scorsese, in his version of *Cape Fear*, is uninterested in this bit of Hitchcockian drollery: his Max Cady is a fearsome crazy man, a parody of recent unkillable movie monsters, a self-proclaimed "big bad wolf," a sadistic creep from beginning to end). It also has its middle-class family, a much more respectable family than Hitchcock's unpleasant petite bourgeoisie in *Psycho*, whose grim world is turned over by the madman's appearance. The origins of Thompson's family are the ordinary fifties domestic melodramas, not the grim hotel rooms and storefront offices of the inhabitants of *Psycho*. What the original *Cape Fear* takes from *Psycho* and exaggerates are its elements of sexual perversity and the inescapable attractions to evil, its bland black, white, and gray landscape that absorbs and gives back threat from the madman's indwelling. Here—though not as subtly as in *Psycho*—smugness and seduction, propriety and corruption work smoothly, implicitly together.

By 1991, few representations of sexuality and violence were still considered transgressive in cinema. The host of *Psycho* imitations during the intervening years had raised the ante of violence simulated and depicted to appalling levels. In 1962, Thompson's Cady does the literally unspeakable and unseeable to the young woman he picks in a bar. The act goes on behind closed doors. Afterward, the woman will not even tell the police what Cady did, and she leaves town. In Scorsese's film, the young woman is sexually active and insecure, she was Bowden's lover, and Cady picks her up and brutalizes her not as a general threat to Bowden, but as a specific act of revenge. The act does not go on behind closed doors. We are privy to Cady's sadism: he breaks the woman's arm, bites a chunk out of her face, and spits it across the room. Scorsese, as is often his wont, throws representations of violence in our face because he likes to; because he knows a large part of the audience likes it; because (in his better films, at least) such images are among the articulate essentials of the world he is mediating and a vital component of the character is he is creating within this world. But something else is happening in his *Cape Fear.* Scorsese is attempting to refashion the moral landscape of the original film. His Sam Bowden is something of a pompous fraud who concealed evidence at Max Cady's trial (a morally correct but legally culpable act). Therefore, Cady's vicious actions come not from madness simply but from an insane sense of righteousness and revenge. Unlike his predecessor, he acts as Bowden's bad conscience; he is— and here Scorsese begins to get closer to Hitchcock—Bowden's double, his own corruption made flesh, the bleakest image of his own desires and destructiveness. Seduction and pain are not merely the ways Cady uses to get back at Bowden; they are ways of exposing the worst of Bowden to himself.

For Hitchcock, the creation of the double was a means of structuring moral ambiguity, which I noted earlier is so basic to his work. More than most filmmakers, he builds his mise-en-scène out of a counterpoint of gazes, of characters looking at each other and the viewer looking at the characters within spaces that contextualize those gazes as intrusive, threatening, and violent. The possibility of visualizing one character as a reflection of the other, or one act or gesture as a mirroring of the desire of the other, grows easily out of such structures. With looks and gestures, Hitchcock rhymes his doubles: Charlie and young Charlie are introduced with similar shots in *Shadow of a Doubt* (1943). Sam stands by his reflected image in the mirror as he attempts to face down Norman Bates in the motel office in *Psycho.* Judy-Madeleine in *Vertigo* is a double doubled: she is the fault line of Scottie's psychosis, his desire made impossible flesh. And in turn she is two women to him: one the person someone else created, who Scottie turned into the image of his beloved, the other the "real" woman he thinks is someone else and proceeds to recreate again into the image of his love. Often the doubling structure takes place in the exchange between image and viewer, the latter given an image of sadomasochistic desire through his or her assent to the characters' actions on screen and thereby becoming a kind of fantastic double of the character on the screen.

Each of the three fifties Hitchcock films that Scorsese draws on for his *Cape Fear*—*Stage Fright, I Confess,* and *Strangers on a Train*—is built on the concept of the double. *Stage Fright* is the most subdued of them. Were it not for the fact that it is so flat and arrhythmic, its performances so without energy, it could well be the most interesting, for it doubles and quadruples its doubles, setting up what should be an intricate structure in which many of the major characters play roles, making believe they are other than what they appear to be, and lie to themselves and the audience (the body of the narrative is told in a flashback that communicates false information), each reflecting the other's bad faith. Jane Wyman's Eve attempts to protect her boyfriend from the accusation of murder, one presumably committed by Marlene Dietrich's Charlotte Inwood (an aloof and potentially powerful character, who the film manages to humiliate and almost destroy in its rush to recuperate Eve). (Cf. Modleski, 115–17.) That the murder was committed by Jonathan, Eve's boyfriend, becomes fairly clear late in the film but is not fully revealed until a powerful sequence in which a clearly psychotic Jonathan admits his crime and his madness in the prop area of a theater. Scorsese draws this sequence, like a thread through the eye of a needle, into the high school episode of *Cape Fear.* In the 1962 version, Sam Bowden's daughter is pursued—or rather thinks she is pursued—by Cady in her school. Scorsese is uninterested in such simple images of pursuit and more concerned with the inexplicable sexual seductiveness of Cady and the effect of that seductiveness on Bowden's daughter. Echoing the penultimate sequence in *Stage Fright,* he places the man and woman in a stage set (here an expressionist image of a cottage on the stage of a high school auditorium) where Cady awakens the sexuality of Danielle Bowden and puts her under his control.

In the source sequence from *Stage Fright,* Eve retains a great deal of control in the face of the madman: both sit in the darkness with a slit of light over their eyes. One-shots—shots in which only one character is seen—of each predominate and the suggestion of mirroring images is strong. But Hitchcock is not quite able to press the doubling structure and its sense of the uncanny because his Eve is, finally, too good and too protected. *Stage Fright* fails because its central character is recessive and continually under patriarchal control. Her father and her police detective lover are never far away. She soothes the madman and leads him out of hiding, only to have him escape and be killed by a falling stage curtain. Scorsese puts his Eve— Sam Bowden's daughter Danielle—at greater risk. The unprotected child, marginalized by her bickering parents, is at the mercy of the mad seducer and seemingly all too ready to become his accomplice. Both characters play roles in this scene: Danielle the innocent child; Cady the wise, almost scholarly teacher. But unlike Hitchcock's Eve, Scorsese's has no control and becomes very receptive to Cady's sexual advances. The misogyny here is off-putting. Scorsese's suggestion that the innocent girl is the willing agent for seduction, and through seduction a weak link between Cady and her father, diverts the intensity of the moral conflict between Cady and Bowden, suggesting finally that Cady—monster though he is—finds ready access for his brutality in the willingness of the women he meets. At least Hitchcock's Eve can control her psychotic friend, though this control is mediated by the male protection that surrounds her.[3]

As I noted, the source sequence in *Stage Fright* gives the female character an extraordinary amount of control over the madman. In Scorsese's version, the young woman melts in sexual passivity in the face of Cady's seductive menace, for Cady *is* seduction and brutality; he is the vengeful, destructive father. It is just this destructive impulse that seems to emanate from the ordinary that attracts Scorsese to the two other Hitchcock source films, *I Confess* and *Strangers on a Train*. Both films deal with loss of control, with a character who takes over and begins mediating another's life. The primary figures—Father Logan in *I Confess* and Guy in *Strangers on a Train*—attempt to live the straightest and most orderly of lives. Their relationship with figures of madness and violence plays out Hitchcock's most obsessive concern: the disruption of the mundane by the unexpected appearance of the uncontrollable destroyer, and the manifestation of that destroyer as a double of the straight and orderly hero.

In *I Confess,* Hitchcock creates one of his most passive characters (matched only by Manny Balestraro in *The Wrong Man*, made a few years later in 1957). The narrative is structured upon the unwillingness of Montgomery Clift's Father Logan to identify the handyman Otto Keller, who confesses to him the murder of a man who, coincidentally, has been blackmailing Logan over a love affair he had before becoming a priest. The film fails precisely because of Logan's enforced passivity within a mise en-scène of unrelenting heaviness. The spaces surrounding Logan are too foreboding, too oppressive for what is essentially a narrative of a man who traps himself within his own theology. Hitchcock permits no breathing space and no alternative for the pitiable oppression of all the characters. Like Bowden in Scorsese's *Cape Fear,* Father Logan cannot act against his oppressor, who becomes, in effect, his active principle, a figure of otherness, violence, and retribution, who manages not merely to keep the main character under his control but to manifest his impotence at every turn. The difference is that Logan's passivity is based upon religious commitment— a priest cannot expose the man who has confessed to him—whereas Bowden's passivity is based partly upon the seeming indestructibility of Cady but mostly on the fact that it is Cady who carries and exposes the moral imperative. Bowden is paralyzed by the brute and emotional force of his own corruptibility; it is as if there were a pact between him and his double that forces each into the other's embrace. This notion of mutuality is missing from *I Confess,* which is why the film only lurks in the background of *Cape Fear.* But it is central to *Strangers on a Train.* The notion of an unwitting pact, of characters mirroring one another because of a corrupt and not quite unconscious bond between them, connects the films so strongly that Scorsese reenacts at least three sequences.

Strangers on a Train is the most notable bad film from Hitchcock's early fifties period. Unable to create a usable script with Raymond Chandler, he had it completed by a relatively unknown writer. Unwilling and unable to do anything more than suggest the homosexual implications of the relationship between the two main characters or to follow through on the inherent corruption of the film's putative hero, Guy, Hitchcock palliates his actions by giving Guy a girlfriend—a senator's daughter—whose presence dilutes the narrative and defocuses the mise-en-scène. The best sequences in the film are those between Guy and Bruno, where the former's breathless mock innocence and the latter's chattering and infectious lunacy play off each other in a way that gives neither character the upper hand, but Bruno the lead in a kind of lighthearted maliciousness. The film thrives on their interchanges and on the strange and often amusing appearances of Bruno as Guy's dark watcher, his alter ego calling him into account to execute his part of their contract, that Guy kill Bruno's father in return for his having killed Guy's unpleasant wife. The film breaks apart when it centers upon Guy's relationship with the conventional "good woman" (the "bad" woman, Guy's sexually active wife, is so obnoxious that her death becomes a pleasure, a mere function of Bruno's mischief making, a devaluation of the woman by turning her into a function of her husband's dissatisfaction and his friend's psychosis) and then collapses in the theatrics of the fairground with its out-of-control carousel that kills Bruno. It ends in bathos with the cute interplay between Guy, his intended, and a priest on a train.

The complexity of the film—the little there is of it—lies in its insistence that Guy and Bruno are so intertwined as to be each other's double. Bruno is Guy's secret-sharer who does his murderous deed, emerging from his unconscious to do its bidding. Hitchcock signals this in a series of episodes in which Bruno imposes himself within Guy's and the viewer's visual field, an object of threat that calls one into account, an image of the unconscious made flesh (cf. Barton). Three of Bruno's appearances have this effect. The first occurs after Bruno has killed Guy's wife. Guy returns to his Washington home, and as he goes up the front stairs in the dark (the camera severely canted in a Dutch tilt), Bruno's spectral voice calls to him. A reverse shot reveals nothing but the darkened gate in front of the house. The second reverse shows Bruno emerging from the dark, as if dissolving into presence, beckoning Guy to him with a purposive, exaggerated gesture. The second appearance is in broad daylight. Guy drives by the Jefferson Memorial with a policeman, who is with him to observe his movements (the police think he has murdered his wife). In a long shot, from Guy's point of view, Bruno is seen, a stark, still, menacing, dark figure against the white columns of the monument, a corruption of the public space, a projection of Guy's bad conscience. The third appearance is at a tennis match, another public space in which Bruno appears, again in a dark suit, completely still amid the spectators, all of whom turn their heads following the play on the field. Bruno stares straight ahead at his alter ego.[4]

For Hitchcock, the dark double dominates the hero's perceptual space and devalues and obliterates the protective aura of the public spaces he inhabits, becoming the sole object of the fearful gaze. For Scorsese, the figure of menace is mostly private, a part of fantasy, a projection of a bad dream. To be sure, Cady appears to Bowden in public. He stares down Bowden during a Fourth of July parade sequence, which has its direct parallel for Scorsese in the tennis match in *Strangers on a Train*. Like Bruno in the viewing stands, Cady stares out of the crowd straight ahead at Bowden, dominating him and the surroundings. In the Hitchcock film, Guy pursues Bruno after the match, only to find him talking genially with members of Guy's entourage at tea. The parade sequence in *Cape Fear* occurs early in the film, when Bowden is unclear about Cady's plans and furious at the intrusion into his life. He runs through the parade and attacks his evil twin, only to be pulled back by bystanders who are unaware of Cady's threat. Guy in *Strangers* is a fairly passive character throughout; he acts as if aware that Bruno is more spectral than real, more him than not. Bowden begins by taking a manly stance before his alter ego, only to find that Cady, like Bruno, is too persistent, clever, and righteous (and, unlike Bruno, too physically powerful) to be easily undone. Bowden too becomes passive, depending, like Bruno, on others in his attempts to outwit Cady. Only at the end of the narrative, when the detectives fall away or are killed, and when the women have failed to subdue the monster during the furious storm, does Bowden do successful physical battle with his alter ego.

The other appearances of Cady that echo *Strangers on a Train* are of different effect and intent. Here Scorsese specifically presents the villain as fantastic emanation of the main characters, as nightmare. The first occurs after Sam and his wife make love, a sequence rendered unharmonious and troubling as the image turns to negative and Leigh gets out of bed in slow motion, goes to the mirror and applies lipstick, an act interrupted by fades to red. She goes to the window and looks out at the Fourth of July fireworks (suggested, perhaps, by a sequence from Hitchcock's *To Catch a Thief*, and which is part of the hallucinatory apparatus of the film—Sam and Leigh comment earlier that it is strange to see the fireworks the day before the Fourth). She goes to the window and her gaze is locked by the image of Cady sitting on the garden wall. Three times she sees him, and each time Scorsese returns to her look of amazement and terror, just as

Hitchcock returns to Guy's amazed look when he sees Bruno at the Jefferson Memorial.[5]

Unlike Bruno, Cady is not an emanation solely of the male character. His maliciousness crosses gender and in many ways reflects the film's questions about gender. Scorsese's characters in *Cape Fear* are filled with sexual anxiety, troubled by domestic discord, and unable to deal with their child, who is just coming into her sexuality. Cady is the very spirit of discord, the insinuation of meanness and sexual panic; he is the trickster, the shape changer who comes in the night to scare people and mess with their lives. He does this when he appears to Leigh on the wall and again in the third appearance that parallels *Strangers on a Train*. Bowden and a private detective have booby-trapped the house to catch Cady, and Bowden is trying to sleep. He awakes, looks, and Cady appears inside by the window, first in negative, then positive, as Bowden returns the gaze, rubbing his eyes. The sequence parallels Bruno's appearance in the dark in front of Guy's house, beckoning Guy to tell him that he has carried out his part of the "bargain" and killed Guy's wife. Cady's appearance is a reminder too that his violence has been done. He has killed the housekeeper (and, like Norman Bates, put on a wig to look like her) and then killed the private detective. This is the final insinuation. From here the film, sticking close to its source, externalizes the psychological into the physical, climaxing with the bravura pyro-and aquatechnics of the fight on the houseboat in the storm.

Where Bruno acted as a kind of exclamation point for Guy, a sharp reminder that his hoped-for life of calm and fame as the tennis-playing husband of a senator's daughter might not work, Cady is a dash—on the other side of which are obscene phrases and threatening remarks, the violence of a corrupted heterosexuality and the meanness of religious hysteria. Bruno was a clear marker of Guy's potential murderousness and his attraction to the sexual other. In the early fifties, Hitchcock was still able and willing to circumscribe his doubles, to localize and finally recuperate the good twin back into a life that might not be normal (after all, he or she was contaminated by the experience with the other, and from the early forties on, the "happy endings" that Hitchcock was compelled to attach to his narratives were deeply compromised by the narrative events that came before). By the time he made *Vertigo* and *Psycho*, there was no need for a polite recuperation. In the latter film particularly, the claustrophobic world that surrounded the characters who were each others' shadow encapsulated the culture at large and signaled the end of the possibility of redemption. Scorsese adopts this grim view. The characters of *Cape Fear* do not triumph with the hard death of Cady, just as Guy is never completely freed of Bruno or the audience itself completely freed of Norman Bates.

Throughout the fifties, Hitchcock was thinking about domesticity. Along with Sirk and Nicholas Ray, though more darkly and with a greater sense of terror, he represented in film the culture's own fears of eruptions from the inside and threats from the outside. He spoke of the domestic as the place of vulnerability and danger. Hitchcock went further than most in his perception of domestic arrangements as dead places where madness dwells. No longer a barrier against the unknown and unwanted, the domestic was the shell that only barely kept evil and corruption from spilling out. *Psycho* proposes the necessary eruption of evil out of the protective barrier of the domestic fantasy of corruption or, more accurately, and according to its own imagery, a swirling down into the swamp of despair of all illusions of safety and control, all rational fantasies of the domestic. Thompson's *Cape Fear* domesticates this vision. While it reproduces the figure of madness imposing itself upon the middle-class family and threatens it with sexual release, it manages to return some measure of control to the good man and to allow the family a measure of recuperation.

Scorsese's *Cape Fear* directly extends the Hitchcockian proposal of *Psycho* while speaking to the nineties' belief that corruption is the norm and will appear to spoil any pleasure that might be fantasized. Eliding the fifties domestic melodrama into *Psycho*'s response to these films, referring to Hitchcock's doubles films of the early part of the fifties, and then adding to the mix *Nightmare on Elm Street* and its sequels and such items as *Fatal Attraction, Pacific Heights, Sleeping with the Enemy,* and their ilk, Scorsese makes a film that speaks of an ongoing danger to a never stable and always illusory harmoniousness. (He speaks as well, with an almost ideal cynicism, to his audience's *desire* to be frightened by the ineluctable presence of destructive corruption.) In his *Cape Fear* and its predecessors, the domestic scene is always already troubled and discordant. Max Cady appears only as the final agent of this discordance, as bad conscience, evil twin, and lord of misrule—the innate violence of the family given flesh, its sexual repressions unleashed (see figure 4).

Cape Fear is a film of accretions; it builds upon its predecessors and then exaggerates their various parts. The specific Hitchcock allusions help keep it grounded, somewhat. They help introduce a measure of moral ambiguity within a film that otherwise throws all moral concerns to the winds in its quest for the bloodiest and most sexually violent effects. As if Scorsese were aware that, in this film made for the purest commercial reasons, there would have to be an anchor for a filmmaker who was able to seed commercial conventions with unconventional perception, he calls upon Hitchcock as an aesthetic and narrative source. Hitchcock becomes *Cape Fear*'s point of good faith, part of the calculation of an equation that maintains connections, factors in film history, and yields a few interesting returns. Were *Cape Fear* a better film, it would have further interrogated the possibilities of restating certain Hitchcockian perceptions and premises. As it is, it confirms Scorsese's own best modernist impulses and the ongoing usefulness

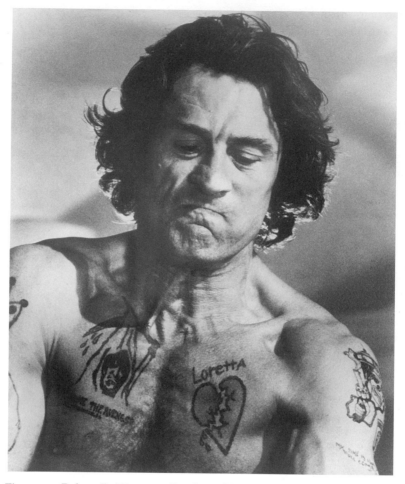

Figure 4. Robert DeNiro as evil twin and lord of misrule in Martin Scorsese's *Cape Fear* (1991), the remake. Photograph by Phil Caruso.

of Hitchcock to filmmakers who know the importance of maintaining links, of borrowing and alluding as a means of maintaining ground and balance. A calculated risk.

NOTES

1. A good study of Hitchcock's reputation can be found in Robert E. Kapsis, *Hitchcock: The Making of a Reputation* (Chicago: University of Chicago Press, 1992).

2. It was the French who first indulged in the allusive act in the late fifties; it was also the French who first gave serious critical attention to Hitchcock. André

Bazin published an essay in 1950, and he visited Hitchcock on the set of *To Catch a Thief* in 1955. *Cahiers du Cinéma* devoted an issue to Hitchcock in 1954; Claude Chabrol and Eric Rohmer published a book on Hitchcock in 1957; François Truffaut published his famous interview in the mid-sixties. Chabrol and Truffaut both exercised some Hitchcockian options in their filmmaking.

3. Another weakness lies in the construction of the sequence. After the initial pleasure at the design of the set—the strange-looking cottage on the high school stage—in which the characters play out their game, one's attention lapses. The sequence is too long; there are too many repetitious one-shots of each of the characters. The intensity of their interaction would have been better expressed by composing them both in the frame and refraining from cutting. When Scorsese uses a lot of one-shots or over-the-shoulder shots in expository sequences, it can indicate his lack of full commitment to the film. There was much of this in *Cape Fear* and *The Color of Money*.

4. Another unexpected appearance of Bruno occurs when Guy and his fiancée visit the National Gallery in Washington. There is no real menace here: just an interruption of strained domesticity.

5. In the original *Cape Fear*, Sam's wife also has bad dreams and when she awakes thinks she sees Cady: it's only a clothes rack. Similarly, the man who the Bowdens' daughter thinks is pursuing her in the high school is only the janitor. Scorsese abjures these peekaboo conventions of the horror-thriller.

Another take (or remake) of this essay, with full-motion images, is available in the September 1994 issue of the online, subscription journal, *Postmodern Culture*. The URL is http://muse.jhu.edu/journals/postmodern_culture/

WORKS CITED

Anobile, Richard J. *Alfred Hitchcock's Psycho*. New York: Avon Books, 1974.

Barton, Sabrina. " 'Criss-Cross': Paranoia and Projection in *Strangers on a Train*," *Camera Obscura*, no. 25–26 (1991).

Carroll, Noël. "The Future of Allusion: Hollywood in the Seventies (and Beyond)." *October*, no. 20 (spring 1982).

Kapsis, Robert E. *Hitchcock: The Making of a Reputation*. Chicago: Univ. of Chicago Press, 1992.

Modleski, Tania. *The Women Who Knew Too Much: Hitchcock and Feminist Theory*. New York and London: Methuen, 1991.

Truffaut, François. *Hitchcock*. New York: Simon and Schuster, 1984.

Wood, Robin. "The American Nightmare: Horror in the Seventies." *Hollywood from Vietnam to Reagan*. New York: Columbia Univ. Press, 1986.

THREE

The Director Who Knew Too Much: Hitchcock Remakes Himself

Stuart Y. McDougal

L. B. Jeffries [James Stewart]: Why would Thorwald want to kill a little dog?
Lisa [Grace Kelly]: Because it knew too much.
REAR WINDOW

Scottie [James Stewart]: One doesn't often get a second chance.
VERTIGO

The notion of a remake becomes complex with a filmmaker like Alfred Hitchcock, who was continuously and obsessively remaking his own work. Such a practice is well documented among modern writers: Yeats, Auden, and Marianne Moore, for example, frequently rewrote their earlier poetry. Prose writers have this luxury less often, because of the greater costs of publishing fiction. The exceptions usually involve collected editions, such as the New York Edition of Henry James's work, a publishing event that gave him the opportunity to revise his work and write extensive introductions. Similarly, Graham Greene revised his short fiction when publishing his *Collected Short Stories*. For literary scholars as well as publishers, these revisions raise problematic issues about whether one text should be privileged over another. Does a publisher print the long version of Marianne Moore's "Poetry / I, too, dislike it" or the final short version? Or both?

Because of the economics involved, the situation with film is much more complicated. With the advent of video, some films have been reissued in multiple versions, from a choice of wide-screen or pan-and-scan to, more recently, the director's cut. But very few directors have been able to remake an earlier work of their own; Hitchcock is one of them.[1] Before considering *The Man Who Knew Too Much,* which Hitchcock first made in 1934 and filmed a second time twenty years later, I would like to comment on the centrality of remaking as a process in all of Hitchcock's work. Throughout his career, Hitchcock remade his early work in a variety of ways, combining his exploration of the expressive potential of film with a desire for technical perfection.

Hitchcock often remade a single shot or a transition between shots. One of the most innovative transitions in his early sound films occurs in *The Thirty-Nine Steps* when Hannay's landlady enters his flat, finds the recumbent body of Annabella Smith with a knife in her back, and screams. Hitchcock cuts directly from a close-up of her screaming face to the express train carrying Hannay to Scotland. Her scream blends with the harsh, piercing whistle of the train and seems to be propelling Hannay northward. Try as he will, Hannay cannot escape her scream or the accusations that will accompany it. Hitchcock had experimented with a similar transition as early as *The Lodger* (1927). Here the close-up of a screaming woman is followed by a black screen (as in the opening of the film) or by exposition (as in the flashback concerning the lodger's sister). In *Blackmail* (1929), Hitchcock's first sound film, a shot of Alice, the heroine, screaming at the sight of an outstretched hand on the London street is followed immediately by a shot of the screaming landlady as she discovers the body of the murdered artist. Hitchcock refines this idea through a series of films until he is satisfied with the effect. In *The Thirty-Nine Steps,* he succeeds in combining the shock of the abrupt transition with continuity on several levels.

One could cite many other such examples like this from Hitchcock's work. But his remaking extends beyond the single shot or juxtaposition of shots. Entire sequences are remade, as well. In addition, Hitchcock takes extended themes and remakes them in different contexts, often culminating in an entire film devoted to that theme. Thus, Hitchcock introduces the theme of "the wrong man" in *The Lodger,* a theme that he will develop (in *The Thirty-Nine Steps* and elsewhere) before making *The Wrong Man* in 1957. Two years later, in *North by Northwest,* Hitchcock obsessively returns to this theme. Similarly, Hitchcock introduces the fear of heights in *The Lodger* and returns to it throughout his career before exploring this fear systematically in *Vertigo* (1958).

Hitchcock's continuous remaking of shots, sequences, and themes contributes to a sense of cohesion in his oeuvre. But there is yet another way in which remaking is central in his work—and that results from the fact that over 75 percent of his films are adaptations of novels, stories, or plays. Of his remaining films not based on literary sources, many are loose remakes of his earlier work. Thus, two of his "original" works, *Saboteur* (1942) and *North by Northwest* (1959), are in some sense American remakes of *The Thirty-Nine Steps;* the action in *Saboteur* traverses America from west to east at the outbreak of the Second World War; *North by Northwest* reverses that trajectory during the Eisenhower years of the cold war.

These different forms of remaking reflect Hitchcock's desire to get things right—they are a part of his obsession with the details of moviemaking as he developed as an artist. But in remaking an entire film, much more is involved. Deeply seated personal concerns shape his selection of a project as well as the ways in which he transforms an earlier project while remaking

LIVERPOOL JOHN MOORES UNIVERSITY
LEARNING SERVICES

it. A comparison of the two versions of *The Man Who Knew Too Much*, then, will clarify Hitchcock's development as an artist as well as illuminate some of the psychological dynamics of his filmmaking.

The Man Who Knew Too Much (1934) was an enormous success in Britain and reestablished Hitchcock's reputation after several relative flops. It marked a return to the suspense genre and the development of an idea the Hitchcocks first discussed on their honeymoon at the Palace Hotel in St. Moritz in 1926 (Spoto, 94–95). The 1934 film chronicles the adventures of an English family whose vacation in St. Moritz is interrupted by the murder of a close friend and the kidnapping of their own daughter. As they struggle to get their daughter back, the couple have to rethink their relationship and assume new roles. The film is a study of the dynamics of a marriage as well as the conditions of spectatorship and passivity (related to both marriage and film viewing).

The Man Who Knew Too Much opens with a series of three performances, at each of which Bob, the husband (Leslie Banks), is a spectator and in two of which his wife, Jill (Edna Best), "performs" with a potential rival: a ski competition involving the potential rival, Louis Bernard (Pierre Fresnay), a dashing and mysterious Frenchman and a friend of Bob and Jill; a skeet-shooting competition between Jill and Ramon (Frank Vosper), another mysterious "foreigner"; and a ball where Jill and Louis Bernard dance together amid other couples in the hotel ballroom. The first two performances are disrupted by Betty (Nova Pilbeam), the Lawrence's precocious daughter, so that both Louis Bernard and Jill lose their respective competitions. The dance, observed by Bob and Betty, is fraught with sexual banter and an underlying sexual tension. It is the culmination of a series of flirtations between Jill and Louis Bernard. Bob picks up Jill's knitting project (a symbol of domesticity, if ever there were one) and hooks the end of one strand of wool on the button of Bernard's tuxedo. As the sweater comes unraveled, the couples on the dance floor become caught up in a web created by the strand of wool. Just as the film audience relaxes at the humor of the situation, Louis Bernard is shot and dies in Jill's arms. Jill, the skilled markswoman, is unable to provide any sort of protection for her dance partner and, like many sexually aggressive women in Hitchcock's films, she is punished for her behavior. The rapid movement from humor to horror is typical of Hitchcock, as is the sudden intrusion of death into a public and apparently secure situation. The metaphorical use of knitting suggests both the unraveling of Bob and Jill's relationship (as well as the unraveling of Bernard's life) and the simultaneous entanglement of Bob in the lives of others.

As Bob acts on the entreaties of the dying Bernard to seek out a note hidden in the handle of Bernard's shaving brush, he becomes implicated in a plot he is unable to comprehend. Before he can show the note to the police, he receives a message that his daughter has been kidnapped and will be harmed if he speaks out. He shares this note with his wife and she faints—a decisive moment in the development of her character. For the next third of the film, she is either absent or seen in a more passively feminine role, as when she clutches Betty's doll in the nursery. She won't assume an active role again until after her near-fainting in Albert Hall.

With the killing of Louis Bernard and the kidnapping of Betty, the villains are responsible for separating the two pairs clearly established as couples in the opening exposition: Jill and Louis Bernard and Bob and his daughter, Betty. Both of these losses represent wish fulfillments for the married couple: Bob is relieved of his rival and Jill is relieved of the daughter who was both a sexual threat and an impediment to her relationship with Louis Bernard. (Remember that Betty caused both her mother and Louis Bernard to fail in their respective competitions.)

As the Lawrences return to England from Switzerland, Hitchcock creates a "decisive . . . contrast between the snowy Alps and the congested streets of London" (Truffaut, 91–92). The disparity between the expansive spaces of the resort and the civilized interiors of the upper-middle-class hotel and the grimy, crowded cityscape is also a difference predicated on class. St. Moritz was a place known well by the Hitchcocks: they honeymooned there and returned often for holidays with their young daughter, Patricia, in tow. The Hitchcocks always stayed in a first-class hotel. In London, however, because of his Cockney accent, Hitchcock could not enter a first-class hotel without experiencing class discrimination. The settings in London—with the exception of Albert Hall—are all the lower-middle-class environment of Hitchcock's youth. The sense of authenticity in this version is strong because Hitchcock is using locales with which he is intimately familiar. Bob must enter the dark maze of lower-class London to rescue Betty. Only Jill remains outside and, in some ways, untouched by it.

In Hitchcock's original conception of the film, Jill was to have played a more central role in the London sequences, rather than be relegated to the sidelines until the Albert Hall scene. As Hitchcock explained to Truffaut, he planned to have Jill accompany Bob to the Tabernacle of the Sun, there to be hypnotized by Nurse Agnes. Then Jill would be taken to Albert Hall, where she would shoot the statesman herself. "On thinking it over," Hitchcock added, "I felt that even a crack shot might not aim accurately while in a hypnotic trance. So I dropped it" (Truffaut, 92). In eliminating Jill from this sequence, Hitchcock is forced to create a new accomplice for Bob in the person of Clive (Hugh Wakefield), the infantilized bachelor uncle. Clive is introduced in the nursery playing with the electric train he had given Betty. He represents the immature childishness that Bob must overcome. At the same time, Jill is at her most maternal in London after the loss of Betty. She clutches a doll in the nursery and faints on two occasions—something she would have seemed incapable of doing as a markswoman. She must succeed in bringing the feminine and masculine aspects of her character into alignment, just as Bob must become more assertive and responsible in order for the family to survive.

The London sequences concentrate on the activities of Bob and Clive, who behave like two adolescents. Clive accompanies Bob to the dentist and then to the chapel, where he is hypnotized and doesn't come to until Bob breaks a chair over his head during a fight with the villains. Clive escapes through the chapel window and telephones Jill. He urges her to go to Albert Hall. He then calls the police, who meet him in front of the chapel. In a scene that Hitchcock will remake in *North by Northwest,* the villains persuade the police that Clive is intoxicated and should be booked on drunk and disorderly conduct, leaving Bob locked inside. And that's the last we see of Clive. Without Clive, Bob can now begin to act more like an adult.

Although Hitchcock was correct in recognizing a problem with having Jill do the shooting in Albert Hall, there is an equal problem in eliminating her from this part of the action. When she goes to Albert Hall, she does so with the knowledge that an assassination is about to occur. (See figure 5.) She meets the killer (Ramon, her former antagonist in the shooting competition) and he hands her the brooch that she had given to Betty just prior to her last competition. It was the brooch which precipitated her loss in the competition with Ramon; now it represents Betty metonymically. The close-up of her left hand, juxtaposing the brooch with her wedding band, underscores her responsibility for her family, now in conflict with her public responsibility as a citizen. Jill enters the theater and sits alone in the back, her eyes searching the balcony for the killer and his target. She knows what is about to happen and as she considers the consequences, she becomes a surrogate for the film spectator who wants to intervene but is unable to. She begins to faint and the screen goes white. Suddenly a gun enters the blank screen from the right and turns toward the viewer—as though the gun had come from the depths of Jill's unconscious. Although she is no longer the one to pull the trigger in this scene, the connection between her and the rifle remains strong. When Jill comes to, she screams, thereby violating the decorum of the performance hall but succeeding in averting the assassination.

The Albert Hall sequence feels like it should be the climax of the film, and the shoot-out that follows has struck critics as something of an afterthought. When it becomes apparent that the assassin and his gang are going to be defeated, Abbott (Peter Lorre) declares that they will have to use the girl as a shield to escape from their headquarters. Here Bob plays an integral role and is wounded helping Betty to escape. He pushes her out the third-story window onto the roof, like a mother bird pushing a baby from the nest. Betty's separation from the family must be sanctioned by her

Figure 5. Preparing for the assassination attempt, as Ramon (Frank Vosper), Bob (Leslie Banks), Betty (Nova Pilbeam), and Abbott (Peter Lorre) listen to the recording in *The Man Who Knew Too Much* (1934).

father if she is to enter adulthood—and if Bob and Jill are to survive as a couple. As Betty makes her way across the roof, she resembles an actress making her debut by stepping gingerly across a stage, the footlights glaring in her eyes. If her father has facilitated this moment, her mother must sustain it. On the street below, Jill takes a rifle from the policeman, draws a bead on Ramon, and drops him in his tracks, as though he were a duck in a shooting gallery. Thus she vanquishes her earlier opponent, gets revenge for the murder of Louis Bernard, *and* saves her child. Bob, through her participation, has moved from being an apathetic childlike spectator to an active adult—first by overcoming the sinister dentist in his chair and discovering the hideout of the assassins, and then by freeing his daughter and helping her escape. Neither he nor Jill alone could have saved Betty; only by working together are they able to succeed. Betty, too, must take some initiative. The final shot of the film—with Bob and Jill embracing Betty, and with Jill reaching affectionately over to Bob—reaffirms their unity as a family. For the first time in the film, Bob and Jill appear as equals.

Hitchcock's dissatisfaction with the two climaxes in *The Man Who Knew*

Too Much can be seen in his structuring of the climax in his next film, *The Thirty-Nine Steps.* In some ways this can be viewed as a remake of the Albert Hall sequence. *The Thirty-Nine Steps* concludes with a sequence in the London Palladium that is not in the novel from which Hitchcock adapted the film. Like the Albert Hall sequence, the climactic scene takes place within a theater where innocent spectators wait to be entertained. The hero or heroine is a surrogate for the film viewer, as he or she looks from the performance on the stage to the audience and attempts to understand what is happening. In both cases the hero or heroine's life is at stake, although no one in the theater, except for the killer and the hero or heroine, knows this. The policeman comments to Hannay, as he attempts to lead him out of the theater, "You don't want to disturb these people. They're here to be entertained." For Hitchcock, spectators enter theaters to be entertained at their own risk: to remain passive is to incur self-destruction. In *The Thirty-Nine Steps,* Hitchcock uses this scene to solve the puzzle ("What are the thirty-nine steps?"), expose the villains, and unite the man and woman. It is the simultaneous resolution of all parts of the drama that makes this climax so satisfying.

Hitchcock began thinking about remaking *The Man Who Knew Too Much* as early as 1938, when David O. Selznick was negotiating with him to come to America to make *Rebecca* (Spoto, 248). At one point in their correspondence, Selznick suggested a remake of *The Man Who Knew Too Much*, noting that he was sure he could get Ronald Colman for the lead. In 1941, Selznick (who, like Hitchcock, had a fondness for adaptations and remakes) bought the rights to *The Lodger* and *The Man Who Knew Too Much.* He assigned John Houseman to help Hitchcock with a remake of the latter. By the end of 1941, Houseman wrote to Selznick that they had been working on a version that would begin in Sun Valley, Idaho, and move to Rio de Janeiro during Mardi Gras. Spies would plot to kill the president of Brazil during a concert at the Metropolitan Opera in New York, with the final encounter taking place at their hideout in Fort Lee, New Jersey. Hitchcock was apparently dissatisfied with the political aspects of the story and the characterizations of the American family (Spoto, 359), and he shelved the project for nearly a decade. By December of 1954, when Hitchcock spent the Christmas holidays in St. Moritz with his wife, he had decided to remake the film.

Apart from Selznick's interest in the project, why would Hitchcock choose this of all his earlier films to remake? Although he refused to state in interviews that he preferred the second version, he did go as far as to acknowledge in his self-deprecating way that "the first version is the work of a talented amateur and the second was made by a professional" (Truffaut, 94). Part of Hitchcock's dissatisfaction no doubt refers to his unhappiness with the climax in his first version. This problem is not addressed by Houseman's description of the new project (above), although it is treated somewhat in the 1955 remake. But there were other, more compelling personal reasons as well.

In the 1955 remake, Hitchcock works with different social, political, and geographical dynamics. Although this is usually referred to as the "American version," none of the movie takes place on American soil. Instead, Hitchcock presents the well-off American innocents abroad—first in North Africa and then, for most of the film, in London. Here the contrast is between the teeming marketplace of Marrakesh and the surprisingly deserted streets of London. Or, to contrast the two versions, between the cold, snowy alpine slopes and the hot, arid North African deserts, and between the lower-class London that Bob Lawrence and Clive explore and the middle- and upper-class London the McKennas pass through. In both versions the vacation locale aptly characterizes the protagonists: Bob Lawrence is cold and passionless while Ben McKenna is fiery tempered. Hitchcock has altered the dynamics of the family rather significantly. In place of the Lawrences about whom we know too little, we have an American family, about whom we know too much: Dr. Ben McKenna (James Stewart), Jo Conway McKenna (Doris Day) and their son, Hank (Christopher Olsen). The change of the child's sex is not accidental. With the marriage of Hitchcock's only daughter, Patricia, in 1952 and the birth of her first child in 1954, coupled with the reluctance of her husband to seek work in Hollywood, it had become apparent to Hitchcock that Patricia would not continue the acting career she had once pursued on the stage and more recently in *Stage Fright* (1959) and *Strangers on a Train* (1951).[2] There would be no one to carry on the Hitchcock name. Hitchcock's own wife, Alma Reville, had given up a very promising career (as writer, editor, and potential director) to submerge her identity in her husband's—although she continued for some time to have her name in the credits (as Alma Reville). Preoccupied with surnames and the patriarchal power they carry, Hitchcock plots a film in which the oedipal struggle (between father and son) reflects the dynamics of succession within his own family as well as his own struggle as a mature filmmaker with the earlier product of his youthful energy.

Hitchcock has transformed the externally motivated drama of the 1934 film into an internal quest for identity. This is clear in the altered nature of the MacGuffin (the device that propels the plot of his films forward). In the first version, the man from the Foreign Office appeals to the Lawrences' patriotism by comparing the possibility of this assassination to another Sarajevo. In the remake, by contrast, the conflict remains within the family, as the ambassador of an unidentified country attempts to have his own prime minister assassinated.

The opening sequence of the second version, which takes place on a bus from Casablanca to Marrakesh, sets up a crucial encounter that clearly indicates the oedipal dynamics of the conflicts. Hank is bored by doing nothing but watching the scenery, which reminds him of an earlier vacation with his family in Las Vegas, so he gets out of his seat in the back of the bus and makes his way forward. Suddenly the bus lurches forward, and Hank loses his balance. As he reaches out for support, he grabs the veil of an Arab woman seated on the aisle, thereby exposing her face. She remains mute (a characteristic of women in the film) but her outraged husband speaks for her and screams at Hank, while pursuing him back to his seat. Hank's father is puzzled and unable to protect him; an ugly confrontation is averted only by the intervention of a polished European who understands the customs and language (Arabic) of Morocco. The European then joins the McKennas, introduces himself as Louis Bernard, and explains what has happened. As we learn later, this is the first of several cases of mistaken identity, since Bernard assumes at first that the McKennas are the English-speaking assassins (i.e., the Draytons) he is seeking. Before they have reached Marrakesh, Bernard has adroitly questioned Ben so that he has elicited considerable information about the McKennas. The detailed exposition sets up the film's dynamics—one of them being, as Jo comments, that Louis Bernard knows a great deal about Ben and his family and but that they know very little about Louis Bernard.

Jo's suspicions here are related to her ambivalence about being the object of the gaze of others. As subsequent incidents demonstrate—her passing an English couple (the Draytons) while entering the hotel and her later encounter with them at a restaurant—Jo is suspicious by nature. It is only after she and Ben have spoken with the Draytons in the restaurant that we learn why people might stare at her—she is a well-known singer who has performed in Europe as well as America, something Louis Bernard had failed to recognize. Names tend to shield identities. Indeed, the relation between that patriarchal signifier, the surname, and identity is crucial in this film. The doctor's own name, McKenna, is a play on knowledge ("ken") and hence the title of the film, as well as on Hitchcock's "MacGuffin." When Ben introduces Louis Bernard to his family, he begins with "Mrs. McKenna" and then introduces Hank. A moment later he refers to his wife as Jo. "But I thought his name was Hank," Bernard declares. Ben corrects him and then adds, "Nobody knows her by any other name." "I do," his son says: "Mommy." His son's correction underlines the significance of names in this film. For Mrs. McKenna is also Jo Conway, the well-known singer. And Jo is a woman, not a boy, just as the Ambrose Chapel sought by Jo and Ben will turn out to be a place and not a person.[3] The instability of identity in this version is emphasized by the fact that the McKennas remain on foreign soil throughout the film (either in North Africa or London), where differences in language and customs confound them.[4]

A related issue is introduced when Hank pulls the veil from face of the

Moslem woman. Of Hitchcock's critics, only Robin Wood has underscored its significance (Wood, 367). The veil obscures the woman's identity from everyone but her husband. Similarly, Ben McKenna has insisted that his wife give up her identity (as Jo Conway, the singer) to become Jo McKenna, the doctor's wife. In addition, he has required his wife to put aside her voice (like the Moroccan woman, who immediately covers her mouth), her singing, except, apparently, in moments of relaxation with her son. As we learn in the scenes that follow, Jo has paid a great price for this—with her reliance on tranquilizers and her monthly fights with her husband. Although she and her son, Hank, are very close, her relationship with her husband is somewhat strained.

The veil has an additional significance. In removing it, Hank violates a woman's privacy. It is as close to undressing a mother figure as he comes in this film and a surrogate father must intervene to protect him. The dynamics of the family have been altered by this act for which the boy must ultimately pay.

In *Rear Window* and *Vertigo*, Hitchcock's two films with James Stewart that bracket *The Man Who Knew Too Much*, the characters played by Stewart have been viewed as—among other things—surrogates for the director. In *The Man Who Knew Too Much* Ben McKenna has assumed the prerogative of the director to rename his wife—from Jo Conway to Mrs. McKenna—and to remake her as a domestic figure. (He also controls her behavior, as in the scene when he drugs her.) To underscore this point, Hitchcock has cast a woman known primarily as singer in a dramatic role. By focusing on Jo's voice—as that which saves the prime minister in Albert Hall and helps save Hank in the embassy—Hitchcock has created a work with a greater thematic consistency than the original. Her voice is precisely that link between her personal and professional identities (as well as a link with her son), a link that her husband has attempted to suppress by concealing her identity and insisting that she remain off the stage. Unlike the first version, however, the heroine has put aside this skill before the beginning of the film, and it is the source of much friction between them. Ben insists that motherhood cannot coexist with a career, and he has forced Jo to stop singing. It will be necessary to reforge this link to save Hank, and this will require adjustments in Ben as well as Jo.

In remaking *The Man Who Knew Too Much*, Hitchcock retained the structure of the original but changed the characterizations and many of the incidents. As we have seen, the opening exposition is much more thorough. Louis Bernard becomes a surrogate father for Hank (on the bus) and a mysteriously foreign and attractive presence for Jo. The film has two bedroom scenes (always an important location in a Hitchcock film), and the first involves Louis Bernard. He has been invited for drinks in the McKenna's hotel room in Marrakesh and apparently arrives while they are still dressing. When the scene opens Ben is standing before the mirror fixing his necktie and Jo is adjusting her dress and singing for Hank—and for Louis Bernard, who listens with a drink in his hand in the next room. Her husband in very much on the sidelines here, as was the husband at the dance sequence in the first version. But here the scene furthers the oedipal drama, as mother dances with son. Indeed, as Jo sings and dances with Hank, she displays a greater intimacy with him than she ever does with her husband. Finally, Jo moves to Barnard's side on the balcony, and he mixes a drink for her as she interrogates him intensely. The scene is disturbed by a knock on the door. A bilingual stranger glances across the room and recognizes Louis Bernard before apologizing by saying he was looking for someone else. The moment of recognition that occurred on the public ski slope in the first version has here been shifted to the private spaces of the parents' bedroom. This act of recognition will have dire consequences for Louis Bernard.[5]

The relationship between the McKennas and the kidnappers (the Draytons) is also strikingly different in the remake. Clearly, Hitchcock intends for the Draytons to double for the McKennas, quite unlike the psychopathic couple in the first version.[6] In the opening exposition, the McKennas are mistaken for the Draytons by Louis Bernard. The couples pass each other in a moment of odd recognition before their hotel and the Draytons introduce themselves later that evening to the McKennas at a restaurant in Marrakesh—a scene that comes to include all the principals in the action, except for Hank. (By this time, the Draytons know of the relationship between Louis Bernard and the McKennas). The Draytons join the McKennas, sitting like mirror images across the table. Ben's physical awkwardness, lack of manual dexterity, and boorishness about foreign customs point to deeper flaws in his character. His repressed anger erupts twice, when Louis Bernard enters with a woman and Ben threatens to go over and make a scene, and when he is unable to eat chicken with his fingers. It is the Draytons who mollify him, and they conclude by making plans to visit the marketplace together the next morning. The viewer, like the McKennas, accepts the Draytons without suspicion. In the marketplace, Mrs. Drayton forms a bond with Hank, as the two wander around. Ben and Jo are left on their own. They begin friendly banter about the exchange of operations and body parts for their vacation ("A gall stone for my dress.") which connects them with Louis Bernard (he "buys" and "sells") and prepares us for the exchange about to take place. The conversation gradually leads to their greatest moment of intimacy: "I'd like to know when we're going to have another baby," Jo declares. Before Ben can respond, Hank interrupts their intimacy, and almost immediately a police chase disrupts the marketplace. Hitchcock follows the chase through the streets until we see one of the two Arabs being pursued stab the other in the back with a knife. The dying

Arab struggles through the marketplace with a knife in his back, while the police continue to follow his assailant. He spots the McKennas and stumbles forward. Ben moves cautiously toward him and then catches him as he falls. The dark greasepaint on his face stains Ben's hands and Louis Bernard is unmasked. Ben, the doctor who practices at the Good Samaritan Hospital, is unable to offer the slightest assistance. With his recognition of Louis Bernard, Ben is now fully implicated in the plot that began with Hank's careless gesture. "Why should he pick me out to tell?" Ben asks Jo as they move away from the dead man. For the same reason that Hannay is picked out in the Music Hall at the beginning of *The Thirty-Nine Steps:* because he is an innocent foreigner, totally unconnected with the plot. But, of course, this is only a partial answer. Louis Bernard has been killed for his knowledge, and this knowledge becomes a burden Ben must now carry. An exchange has taken place and this new knowledge separates Ben from his son and imperils his son's existence. He must first reluctantly share the burden with his wife (but only after drugging her) and then work with her to help bring Hank back. Jo's role in this activity depends on her shifting identity, from Mrs. McKenna to Jo Conway and to some combination of the two at the end of the film. Ben will be required to rethink his own identity as well.

Jo's domestic identity has depended very much on her relationship with her son. Louis Bernard's comment about their names is the first suggestion of their intimacy, and the scene in their hotel bedroom with Bernard confirms this. Jo and Hank sing "Que Sera, Sera" and dance together as well. The lyrics of the song ("When I was just a little boy, I asked my mother, what would I be") develop the mother-son relationship further. When Hank is gone, then, Jo's own identity is threatened.

In England, the conflict between Jo's two selves—Mrs. McKenna and Jo Conway—becomes exacerbated. At the airport Jo is greeted like a celebrity by her British fans. When she and Ben arrive at the hotel, a group of old friends come by, one of whom addresses Ben as Mr. Conway.[7] For them, Ben is an appendage of Jo; a pleasant American, but someone who has stood in the way of her return to the London stage. Ironically, he is responsible for this unscheduled stop and it is he who will insist that she perform again in England.

In both versions, the search in London for the child is marred by serious conceptual problems. As noted earlier, the British version leaves Jill on the sidelines while Bob and Clive seek the child. In the remake, Ben goes off on a wild-goose chase when he mistakes the name of a place for the name of a person—another example of the problematic nature of naming and the complexity of identity. On the way to the taxidermist's shop, the son (Ambrose Chapel Jr.) had overtaken the father (Ben McKenna) and at the shop chaos results from the confusion of the father (Ambrose Chapel Sr.) with his son. Versions of the oedipal struggle are everywhere in the

film. So is the confusion that confronts an American in a foreign culture—
even when the cultures share a common language. Although the scene is
both threatening and mysterious, Hitchcock later acknowledged it to be a
failure.[8]

The scene demonstrates that Ben's intellect is no match for Jo's intuition.
It was Jo, after all, who was first suspicious of Louis Bernard and later the
Draytons; Ben succeeded in convincing her through logical argumenta-
tion that her suspicions were ill founded, only to discover that she had
been right all along. It is Ben who looks up "Chapel, Ambrose" and races
off to confront the villains who turn out to be innocent taxidermists. During Ben's absence Jo realizes—in response to a comment by her friend,
Val—that Ambrose Chapel, like Albert Hall, is a place, not a person. She
finds the church and is later joined there by Ben. She then leaves Ben in
the church with the service still in progress to telephone the Scotland
Yard inspector who had earlier offered them assistance. When the police
fail to help her, Jo seizes the initiative and goes alone to find the inspector at Albert Hall, leaving Ben behind in the chapel. This reverses the trajectory that had taken her from being Jo Conway (the theater) to Mrs.
McKenna (the chapel). The chapel is the first of two locations—the other
being the embassy—that are off limits to the police and where, as a
result, the McKennas are on their own. In both of these locations, Ben
must overcome earlier handicaps, both physical (by climbing the rope to
the bell tower) and emotional (by reasserting his patrimony in the embassy).

The Albert Hall sequence of the remake is one of the great set pieces in
Hitchcock's work. In an attempt to make the sequence the logical climax
of the remake, Hitchcock expands it considerably and stresses the element
of performance. But unlike the first version, where Jill arrives at Albert Hall
with a clear idea of why she is there and what will happen, here Jo is motivated solely by her desire to seek the help of Inspector Buchanan. Instead,
Jo encounters the assassin, whom she recognizes as the mysterious intruder
who had knocked on their door in Marrakesh, when they were entertaining
Louis Bernard. She watches him disappear upstairs as Buchanan enters with
the prime minister and his entourage and mounts the opposite staircase.
Alone, Jo looks from one staircase to the other, trying to figure things out.
She enters the theater, studies one box and then another, and finally realizes
what is about to happen. Hitchcock builds suspense as he cuts from the
orchestra to the singers to Jo and to the boxes containing the gunman and
the prime minister, choreographing this action to the music. The audience
keeps waiting for the crescendo that seems to be continually receding.[9]
Finally Jo is joined by Ben, but he is not at her side when the climax comes.
As Ben attempts unsuccessfully to thwart the gunman, the music reaches
its climax and Jo, the professional singer, cries out, giving voice to her re-

Figure 6. Doris Day performs "a tranquil coda" in *The Man Who Knew Too Much* (1955).

pressed desire. Only too late does Ben succeed in finding the assassin, who jumps from his box and falls to his death.

The final sequence takes place at the embassy of the prime minister, where a reception in his honor is taking place. By building continuity between this scene and the preceding sequence in Albert Hall, it becomes much less of an anticlimax. The McKennas contrive to be invited, and on the way there Ben tells his wife that she must sing so that he can have an opportunity to search the embassy for Hank, whom Buchanan has told them is being hidden there. At the embassy, the prime minister introduces Jo to the other guests as "the American singer, Jo Conway." The veil has been removed, and it is as Jo Conway—and not Jo McKenna—that she will be able to help save her son. To emphasize the relationship between this scene and the Albert Hall sequence, Hitchcock has the injured prime minister say to Jo, "I beg you, madame, a tranquil coda to conclude a dramatic evening." And it is a coda, in which the dramatic moments of the Albert Hall sequence are replayed and resolved. (See figure 6.)

Once again Hitchcock uses a musical number as a ticking clock. Before the arrival of the McKennas at the embassy, Hitchcock has shown us the ambassador upbraiding Drayton for his failed attempt. "I want that child removed from this embassy . . . and removed in such a way that he won't be able to say any more where he has been tonight." This time it is Jo, and not the Hitchcock surrogate Bernard Herrmann, who calls the tune. The song, "Que Sera, Sera" is "remade" to focus on her: "When I was just a little girl," she sings, changing the sex from the first time we had heard this song. It is now her song, and we know that Ben must find Hank before she finishes singing. Hitchcock takes his camera through the vast corridors and empty staircases of the embassy as Jo's song fills the halls, finally reaching the room where Hank is hidden. Hank hears the song and thinks he must be dreaming; Mrs. Drayton hears it as well and, fearing for the boy's life, asks if he can whistle the tune—as we have heard him do in the hotel room in Marrakesh. Mother and son begin a duet, and father pursues the sounds to the upper levels of the embassy. But the song is over before Ben reaches the room. Hitchcock cuts to the interior of the room and we see the door-knob being turned from the outside. Mrs. Drayton, fearing that it is her husband, screams and Ben breaks down the door and enters. The confusion between Mr. Drayton and Dr. McKenna is significant. By screaming, Mrs. Drayton has just assumed Jo's role in the Albert Hall sequence and has gained sympathy from the audience as a result.[10] Ben must show that he is capable of protecting his son, as he was unable to do at the beginning of the film, and he must rescue Hank from his "mother." He must also defeat Drayton, his parental rival. Drayton appears, gun in hand, and reasserts his control just as Ben is about to flee with Hank. Deserting his wife, Drayton attempts to leave the Embassy with Hank and Ben as his cover. The three descend the vast staircase, in a remake of the staircase scene at the end of *Notorious*.[11] As Drayton holds the gun in his pocket, its resemblance to a phallus is unmistakable. Halfway down the staircase, Ben turns suddenly and lurches toward Drayton—duplicating the action of his son on the bus at the beginning of the film. Drayton falls and the gun goes off in his pocket, killing him.

By having the assassins try "to liquidate one of their own big shots" (Buchanan), Hitchcock has internalized the action upon which the film pivots. The political intrigue provides a perfect parallel for the struggle within the McKenna family, between the domineering and manipulative father who knows too little, rather than too much, about the needs of his family, and his wife. When Jo and Hank sing in the hotel room in Marrakesh, "When I was just a little boy, I asked my mother . . . " Ben interrupts them for the benefit of Louis Bernard and says, "He'll make a fine doctor." There is a strong tension in this film between the rigid, rational, head-strong power of the patriarchy—embodied in Dr. McKenna—and the in-tuitive, "musical" intelligence of his wife, Jo, as well as a concern with pa-triarchal succession and oedipal struggle that is lacking in the first version.

Knowledge, for Dr. McKenna, begins with the death of Louis Bernard, Hank's surrogate father and Jo's potential suitor. This death precipitates the loss of McKenna's son, Hank, who is kidnapped by another surrogate father and a surrogate mother (the Draytons). The McKennas' success in finding Hank in London is possible only through a reconceptualization of their roles as husband and wife. Similarly, Hank's maturation depends upon a separation from his parents. When they are reunited as a family, they are vastly different from the trio we saw vacationing in Marrakesh. They have earned the right to be together.

Earlier I noted that this film shared characteristics with *Rear Window* and *Vertigo* insofar as it could be read as an allegory of some of film's properties. After hearing Louis Bernard's words in the marketplace, Ben asks, "Why should he pick me out to tell?" Similarly, near the end of *Vertigo*, Scottie (Jimmy Stewart) asks Judy, "Why did you pick on me? Why me?" Scottie has spent considerable time and energy remaking Judy in the image of a woman he once loved, a woman who herself was the remake of her former lover's dead wife. In addition, she was the remake of an historical antecedent, the "mad Carlotta." *Vertigo* is in part a meditation on the process and consequences of remaking by a director for whom this had been a lifelong concern. So too is *The Man Who Knew Too Much*. As we have seen, both versions revolve around an exchange: a child for a secret. The remake itself is a form of exchange, as Hitchcock rethinks the relations between texts, between characters (real and fictional), and between the work of a younger, more exuberant director and a mature craftsman.[12] In demonstrating that a director can shape those relations at will, Hitchcock affirms the power of art to renew itself continually.

NOTES

1. An interesting recent example is *The Vanishing*, first made in 1989 by the Dutch filmmaker George Sluizer and remade by him in Hollywood in 1992–93.

2. In her final appearance in one of her father's films, *Psycho* (1960), Patricia played a recently married woman who complains about headaches on her honeymoon.

3. In the first version, Clive comments over the phone to Betty that Albert Hall is a place and not a person. The confusion of places in the second version begins with Hank's remark about how North Africa looks exactly like Las Vegas, the city they had visited the previous summer. The confusion between personal and professional identities is underscored by casting Doris Day as Jo and Bernard Herrmann as the conductor.

4. This is in contrast to the Lawrences, who act out much of the drama within a taxi-ride's distance of their own apartment.

5. This glance of recognition recalls Thorwald's equally penetrating and chilling gaze across the courtyard at L. B. Jeffries in *Rear Window*.

6. See, for example, Robin Wood (368 ff.) for discussion of these parallels.

7. This mistake is shared by critics as well. Robin Wood speaks of the Conways (368).

8. However, Hitchcock reuses the taxidermy theme to good effect in *Psycho*.

9. Wendy Lesser argues that the musical piece itself is a "remaking" of the earlier piece and demonstrates how any musical performance continually remakes a musical score. She also stresses the way Bernard Herrmann is a surrogate for Alfred Hitchcock throughout this scene.

10. This is the culmination of a positive characterization of Mrs. Drayton that Hitchcock has been developing throughout the film. The turning point comes shortly before this, when—in the ambassador's study—the order is given to kill the boy and Mrs. Drayton cries out in horror. It is another element in the conscious creation of the Draytons as doubles for the McKennas.

11. In *Notorious,* Devlin (Cary Grant) had rescued Alicia (Ingrid Bergman) from her father figure, Sebastian (Claude Rains), while Sebastian's mother looked on. Note that *Notorious* begins with doors opening to reveal Alicia's real father—whom she must renounce—and closing on her husband-father figure, whom she must also renounce.

12. See Wendy Lesser for a more detailed discussion of the relationship between *Vertigo* and *The Man Who Knew Too Much* (141–144).

WORKS CITED

Bogdanovich, Peter. *The Cinema of Alfred Hitchcock.* New York: Museum of Modern Art Film Library, 1963.

Bonitzer, Pascal. "The Skin and the Straw." In *Everything You Always Wanted to Know about Lacan (But Were Afraid to Ask Hitchcock)*, edited by Slavoj Zizek. New York: Verso, 1992.

Cameron, Ian. "The Mechanics of Suspense." In *Movie Reader,* edited by Ian Cameron. New York: Praeger, 1972.

———. "Suspense and Meaning." In *Movie Reader,* edited by Ian Cameron. New York: Praeger, 1972.

Durgnat, Raymond. *The Strange Case of Alfred Hitchcock or, the Plain Man's Hitchcock.* Cambridge: MIT Press, 1974.

Finler, Joel W. *Hitchcock in Hollywood.* New York: Continuum, 1992.

Hark, Ina Rae. "Revalidating Patriarchy: Why Hitchcock Remade *The Man Who Knew Too Much*." In *Hitchcock's Rereleased Films: From Rope to Vertigo,* edited by Walter Raubicheck and Walter Srebnick. Detroit: Wayne State University Press, 1991.

Kapsis, Robert E. *Hitchcock: The Making of a Reputation.* Chicago: University of Chicago Press, 1992.

Leff, Leonard J. *Hitchcock & Selznick.* New York: Weidenfeld and Nicholson, 1987.

Leitch, Thomas M. *Find the Director and Other Hitchcock Games.* Athens: University of Georgia Press, 1991.

Lesser, Wendy. *His Other Half: Men Looking at Women through Art.* Cambridge: Harvard University Press, 1991.

Rohmer, Eric, and Claude Chabrol. *Hitchcock: The First Forty-Four Films.* Trans. by Stanley Hochman. New York: Frederick Ungar, 1979.

Rothman, William. *Hitchcock: The Murderous Gaze.* Cambridge, Harvard University Press, 1982.

Ryall, Tom. *Alfred Hitchcock & the British Cinema.* Urbana, Ill.: University of Illinois Press, 1986.

Sloan, Jane E. *Alfred Hitchcock: A Guide to References and Resources.* New York: G. K. Hall, 1993.

Spoto, Donald. *The Art of Alfred Hitchcock: Fifty Years of His Motion Pictures.* New York: Hopkinson and Blake, 1976.

———. *The Dark Side of Genius: The Life of Alfred Hitchcock.* Boston: Little, Brown, 1982.

Sterritt, David. *The Films of Alfred Hitchcock.* New York: Cambridge University Press, 1993.

Truffaut, François. *Hitchcock.* New York: Simon and Schuster, 1983.

Weis, Elisabeth. *The Silent Scream: Alfred Hitchcock's Sound Track.* Rutherford, N.J.: Fairleigh Dickinson University Press, 1982.

Wood, Robin. *Hitchcock's Films Revisited,* New York: Columbia University Press, 1989.

Yacowar, Maurice. *Hitchcock's British Films.* Hamden, Conn.: Archon Books, 1977.

FOUR

Robin Hood: From Roosevelt to Reagan

Dan Georgakas

A half century separates *The Adventures of Robin Hood* (1938) from *Robin Hood: Prince of Thieves* (1991). Although each film was conceived as a popular entertainment and star vehicle with the profit motive paramount, they faithfully reflect the political and cinematic ethos of their eras. More specifically, *Adventures* embodies the political confidence and creativity of the late 1930s and *Thieves* the cultural confusion and aberrant individualism of the late 1980s. The former also reflects the dominant characteristics of the studio system and the latter those of the poststudio system.

Rather than original and remake, the films are better considered as quasi-independent adaptations, for their time and place, of a beloved popular myth constantly reprised in various media. The 1991 *Thieves* was certainly aware of its illustrious 1938 predecessor and a number of other *Robin Hood*s in between, including a well-received television series.[1] The 1938 version, in turn, was aware of the highly successful Douglas Fairbanks 1922 silent *Robin.* Nevertheless, the cinematic strategies of the films are far more reflective of their social settings than of the usual problematics of cinematic remakes. Despite vastly different aesthetic merits as genre films, each proves to be an example of film as an extremely valuable cultural artifact.

Adventures, made during a time when the travails of the Great Depression were beginning to ease, was produced by Warner Brothers, the studio most closely linked to President Franklin Roosevelt. The New Deal had recently passed labor legislation that was making possible the unionization of millions of industrial workers, while the government itself was employing millions more to work on repairing the nation's infrastructure. In Hollywood, a Jewish-dominated studio system had been consolidated and was in the early phase of its most creative period. Despite the studios' vigorous opposition to the unsuccessful California gubernatorial campaign of socialist Upton Sinclair in 1934, the industry was left-of-center on most issues. Swelled by refugees from Nazi persecution and moved by the valor of Loyalist Spain, Hollywood was ardently antifascist. Hollywood was also at this time informed by Washington that the president would welcome motion pictures that extolled democratic values and presented England in as positive a light as possible. While not a direct or conscious response to these political currents, *Adventures* faithfully reflected them in its energetic espousal of democratic values rooted in the culture of the common people of England.

Costume action films had done well for Warner Brothers in the past, and after seeing Erroll Flynn in *Captain Blood* (1935) Jack Warner thought he would be ideal in the title role for what would be the studio's highest-budgeted film to date. The script that came from Norman Reilly Raine and Seton I. Miller was faithful to Robin Hood folklore. The major thrust, spiced with a low-key romance and feudal weaponry, is restoration of legitimate government.[2]

When King Richard the Lion-Hearted is delayed returning from the Crusades, his brother, Prince John (Claude Rains), aided by Sir Guy of Gisbourne (Basil Rathbone), conspires to usurp the throne. They lead a group of Norman lords in an economic and sometimes literal destruction of the Saxon countryside in what amounts to a replay of the original Norman Conquest some hundred years earlier. Robin of Locksley Hall, a Saxon, stands as the only noble in the realm who will take up arms in defense of Richard's throne. He spits out his challenge to Prince John at a lavish banquet and then proceeds to Sherwood Forest to rally the Saxon masses of Nottinghamshire.

As played by Flynn, Locksley has no ambiguities. When Locksley laughs, he puts his hands on hips and tosses back his head. To make his speeches more dramatic, he leaps to a tabletop or a tree stump to stand slightly above his audience. He dons the garments and cap of the masses. He is cheeky yet charming. Never for an instant do we doubt his cause will prevail. Never for an instant do we mistake him for a real person. He is a myth. He is— Robin Hood. (See figure 7.)

Robin's political agenda is spelled out for the masses in several speeches. He ends his initial Sherwood rally by having his followers swear an oath not only to Richard but to "our people." The so-called outlaws vow that they will help the poor, the aged, the widowed, and victims of injustice. Rather than bandits, they are Loyalists, a kind of popular militia. Almost a guerrilla band. Later, the sheriff of Nottingham (Melville Cooper) will complain that he cannot capture them because the people of Nottingham inform the outlaws of his every move.

In contrast to their depiction fifty years later, the common people are extremely competent. They are so skilled in warfare that they never lose a

Figure 7. Olivia de Havilland as Marion and Errol Flynn as Robin
Hood bring solid star power to the old legend, in Michael Curtiz's *The
Adventures of Robin Hood* (1938).

battle with either the sheriff's men or the prince's knights. They make their
forest sanctuary impregnable and set up a roadhouse for liaisons with outside supporters. Their counterattacks soon put an end to the most brutal
of the Norman expropriations and tax collections.

Among the band's aristocratic supporters is Lady Marian (Olivia De
Havilland), King Richard's niece. Originally she is not at all taken with
Robin, whom she finds an offensive braggart and probable traitor. Once

shown what is really going on in Sherwood Forest, however, her attitudes change and in the course of her conversion, she falls in love with Robin. Although garbed from head to toe in clinging garments that leave only the skin of her face exposed, she manages to be sensual while preserving an air of modesty. The gallant Robin makes one foray to her castle room, and a single chaste kiss is sufficient to seal their commitment. When Prince John and Sir Guy realize where Marian stands, they plot to murder her as soon as John gains the throne.

From the vast Robin Hood folklore available to further the plot, the screenwriters selected two elements: the recruitment of Friar Tuck and the archery contest. Each is given a political twist antithetical to the values of the 1991 adaptation. Friar Tuck (Eugene Pallette), who wears a tin helmet at all times, is introduced to Robin as one of the most dangerous swordsmen in England. Portly though he may be and much as he loves his ale, Tuck has sworn a vow of poverty and is militantly pro-Richard. After some mandatory macho swordplay, Tuck joins the Sherwood band. Throughout the film, he will be counterpoised to High Church officials who cooperate with John. The echoes of Spain are again obvious.

Robin's renown as an archer serves as the basis for a sequence that illustrates how the best leader can be guilty of hubris. Prince John sponsors an archery contest to lure his adversary from the forest. Against all counsel, Robin participates. The other archers, all commoners, are the best marksmen from each region of the kingdom. They are so skilled, in fact, that Robin can only win by piercing his opponent's arrow with a double bull's eye. The legendary shot reveals the man disguised as a tinker to be Robin Hood, and he is immediately arrested.

Once more the common people demonstrate their organizational and military skills. Marian's lady-in-waiting, who has become romantically linked with one of Robin's stalwarts, arranges for Marian to meet with the Sherwood leaders at the roadhouse. They plan what becomes a successful rescue of Robin. This reversal of the standard formula—a female and commoners rescuing the male leader—is emblematic of an era in which artistic works frequently featured strong women and militant workers. A disguised King Richard (Ian Hunter) now appears on the scene and quickly discovers who is loyal to his cause. The balance of the film's action deals with Richard's restoration to power by military force and the reforging of the Norman-Saxon peace symbolized by the marriage of Marian and Robin.

Many of the strengths of *Adventures* are the strengths of the studio system. The film's swift and bold sequences reflect the confidence of the filmmakers in their craft and purpose. Michael Curtiz directs with his usual verve and has Robin go through a series of strides, leaps, and swings, often with weapons in hand. All the stunts were done by Flynn himself and his Australian accent gives his speech a distinctive quality that is not quite English but definitely not American. The action is punctuated throughout with a rousing score that won Erich Wolfgang Korngold an Academy Award and set a genre standard.

Each of the major and supporting roles is played to stereotype, but played brilliantly. Among the outstanding performances are Rathbone's insidious Guy, Pallete's garrulous Tuck, Rains's epicene John, and Hunter's regal Richard. Even so able a scene stealer as Alan Hale is hard pressed to hold his own as the jovial Little John. The fluidity of the performances is aided by the fact that these contract players worked regularly with one another and a limited number of technicians. Their efforts are further enhanced by gorgeous costumes and lavish sets designed to fully exploit a new color process the studio introduced with *Adventures*. The sets are brightly lit to highlight the colors and reinforce the general sense of camaraderie and optimism.

Adventures proved to be Warner Brothers' biggest moneymaker of the year and one of the industry's top ten hits. From a genre perspective, it has been judged one of the best films of its kind in the Hollywood canon. Content to work with mythic elements never taken beyond two dimensions, *Adventures* boldly asserts a profound democratic ethos and faith in justice. Fifty years later, this fanfare to the common people remains as fresh and vivid as the now classic comic books of the same era.

The national ethos evident when *Thieves* was being made was decidedly different from that of the New Deal. Although the cold war had been "won," there was a sense of national decline. Domestic and international financial scandals were endemic, the United States had become a debtor nation for the first time since World War I, and parents feared their children would not have as good a life as they had enjoyed. Trust was often placed in invisible market forces to handle intractable cultural problems. In Hollywood, the old studio system was gone. Rather than a steady stream of modest moneymakers, the industry was now dependent upon blockbuster hits. The studios were less manufacturing complexes than financial fulcrums that mounted projects whose success increasingly depended on bankable stars.

The new Robin Hood venture had the backing of Warner Brothers, the producer of the Flynn epic. The linchpin of the new star vehicle was Kevin Costner, already a bankable star in the United States and about to become internationally bankable as the star of *Dances with Wolves*. Costner, in fact, arrived on the Robin Hood set only three days after completing work on *Dances*. His involvement with the new film was mainly due to his personal friendship with director Kevin Reynolds. (See figure 8.)

The script of *Thieves,* mostly developed by Pat Denshaw, made no effort to remain faithful to the myth of Robin Hood. The basic strategy was to update the story with politically correct ideology and a stab at deconstruc-

Figure 8. Kevin Costner stars as Robin Hood and Morgan Freeman as Azeem in *Robin Hood: Prince of Thieves* (1991), a politically correct revamping of *Robin Hood*.

tion. To those ends, Denshaw grafted racial and sexual liberation themes to the myth and opted for medieval muck and grit rather than medieval tapestry and pomp. Perhaps fearing comparison with Flynn, Robin was written as a clumsy everyman, more often confused than in command. Further complicating the script's design were elements intended to mock the genre itself. Any of these strategies might have produced an interesting film, but the amalgam resulted in a clumsy bag of tricks often in conflict with one another. If *Adventures* may be thought of as successful high baroque, then *Thieves* is failed rococo.

Characteristic of the film's mood is the dark lighting that renders even Sherwood Forest as a dismal place. Most drab is Robin himself, in costume, speech, character, and manner. Costner remains the country bumpkin baseball fan of *Field of Dreams*. His occasional attempt at an English accent is quarterhearted at best. He is awkward and witless, lacking charm as a military leader or lover. Scenes that try to give the character some mythic qualities are undone by realistic but unnecessary details that often lapse into the worst nationalistic excesses.

The film limps to a false start by placing Robin in the Holy Land as a Crusader. We first see him as a prisoner about to be beheaded in a Jerusalem dungeon. Through a not very convincing trick, he foils his executioners even as the fatal blade descends. The purpose of this contrived gambit is to introduce fellow captive and escapee Azeem the Moor (Morgan Freeman). Thus, the conditions are set for a possible medieval version of the white guy/black guy buddy films such as the *Lethal Weapon* series, so successful in the 1980s.

In order to justify Azeem remaining with Robin, the film offers the notion that Azeem feels morally obliged to stay with Robin, who has just saved his life, until Azeem can return the favor. This white man's notion of Near East morality is even more bizarre as Azeem is otherwise shown as intellectually and technologically superior to all the European characters. Azeem proves to be too old to be Robin's buddy and too young to be his surrogate father. There is no chemistry between them and Azeem becomes a burden to the film's plot. Much like the huge ceremonial sword Azeem carries about as if it were a fighting weapon, the character of the Moor is just a gimmick that fails.

The two men return to England in a process mercifully left vague. Robin soon discovers that his father has been murdered by the sheriff of Nottingham (Alan Rickman) on the false charge of devil worship. The sheriff emerges as the major villain of the film as he plunders the countryside for personal profit while also lusting after Lady Marian. The Norman-Saxon plot line is totally ignored and Prince John's machinations are a side issue. Unlike the somewhat goofy sheriff of 1938, the 1991 sheriff is a psychopath who seems to have wandered into the film from a performance of the Theater of the Ridiculous. His confidant is the witch Mortianna (Geraldine McEwan), who may also be his mother. Mortianna comes with unsightly warts, black pots, snakes, and other Halloween-like paraphernalia. The two characters are so overplayed that the term *camp* would be generous. Against such silly and unworthy foes, even Flynn or Fairbanks would have had a hard time appearing heroic.

The Nottingham commoners are an equally uninspiring lot. They are presented as ignorant farmers, unaware of their economic rights under feudalism and totally unskilled in weapons. Robin has to cajole them to rebel, and he and Azeem must work very hard to make them even minimally competent as fighters. The filmmakers have no sense of the English yeoman tradition or the role of the English longbow in military history. Several scenes have Robin using a crossbow as if it were a pistol, a slighting of the longbow that works as poorly as Mortianna's concoctions.

Robin's followers arrive with wives and children who set up a tenement house din in the green. The individuals are a depressing lot often lacking in common sense and speaking in a variety of accents. Friar Tuck (Michael McShane) is the worst of the lot. Void of any political or religious dimension, he is loyal to whoever provides him free ale. His conception is too sophomoric to offer comic relief, much less add a note of cynicism. Not surprisingly, the Sherwood camp is not very neat or ably defended. The sheriff locates it through a simple ruse, destroys it, and takes numerous captives.

In direct contrast to 1938, it is Robin who rides to the rescue of the masses. The key element in this action is a high-tech weapon of its day, gunpowder, which is miraculously provided by Azeem. Miraculous it must be, as gunpowder was not actually used in war for another fifty years. Azeem also comes up with a telescope four hundred years ahead of its time. The problem is not just feel-good black history, as the sheriff uses printed wanted posters more than two hundred years before the invention of the printing press. These elements are not offered as technological comedy as in *A Connecticut Yankee in King Arthur's Court,* but as realism. This indicates either an inexcusable sloppiness in research or utter contempt for the viewing audiences' sense of history.

The ethnic sensitivity of the film is as threadbare as its historical accuracy. Having gone out of its way to honor non-European culture, the film has the Sherwood camp overrun by a horde of Celts imported by the sheriff. These men and women are as wild as the creatures that forced Hadrian to build his wall in pre-Christian times. One wonders how the Celts got to Nottingham undetected and what is to happen to them once the battle is over. Never for an instant do we think Celtic culture is anything but utterly barbaric.

The character of Lady Marian (Mary Elizabeth Mastrantonio) is also bungled. Her first encounter with Robin is contrived so that she can pass off her muscular maid as herself in order to get behind Robin and place a blade to his back while garbed in an outfit that appears to be left over from *The Mark of Zorro.* Her original suspicion of Robin is never clarified, and one wonders how long Robin has been away if he cannot differentiate between the curvaceous Marian and her hefty maid. Nevertheless, the two quickly fall in love. While more verbally and sexually liberated (on the surface at least) than previous Marians, the 1991 Marian proves helpless before the sheriff's intrigues. Robin must literally catapult himself over a castle wall to rush to her rescue as she is being raped by the sheriff. Azeem gets the job of dispatching Mortianna.[9] Yet another odd twist to the tale involves the return of Richard the Lion-Hearted. The king plays no role in the plot, and when he shows himself in the last scenes, he is not Richard at all, but Sean Connery. That is, we are expected to respond to him as Connery, not as a character. We are to remember that he has played an aged Robin in *Robin and Marian* and that he is the quintessential Agent 007. Connery is not listed in the credits or any of the film's advertising. The manner of his presentation is cinematic self-reference at its most juvenile.

The film's subtitle is also meaningless. Robin is neither prince, nor thief. Never once do we see him rob the rich, much less give to the poor, the

essence of his modern myth. With religious, class, ethnic, and political issues absent, character motivation is largely individualistic. Rather than a
bottom-up mass rebellion, the film shows trickle-down elite leadership.
Without their clumsy former Crusader, the people of Nottingham would be
hapless victims of the nutty sheriff, with nary a thought of Prince John or
King Richard.

Critical reaction to *Thieves* was savage. The film was considered far too
violent and sexually explicit for children and too artless for adults. But the
studio's faith in the bankable star was vindicated. *Robin Hood: Prince of
Thieves* had the good fortune to be released after the fabulously successful
Dances with Wolves. Enough Costner fans were generated by *Dances* to make
Thieves a financial success. For all its aesthetic shortcomings, *Thieves* was
also in tune with many of the cinematic trends of its day. As the American century entered its last decade, novelty increasingly passed as originality, incoherence as style, plagiarism as homage, and cynicism as candor.
Challenging gender and ethnic themes were toyed with but never seriously engaged. Literary and historical names were appropriated for their
recognition value without much concern for their original context. Having
lost faith in the future, American cinema also seemed to have lost faith in
the past.

NOTES

1. The Hollywood producer Rob Wood, a longtime fan of the television series,
has recently repackaged these episodes, colorizing them, reediting them to include
slow motion for action scenes, and updating the music for today's audiences, with
pleasing results.

2. The plot line of *Adventures* is heavily influenced by the themes introduced
by Sir Walter Scott's *Ivanhoe* (1819). J. C. Holt, *Robin Hood* (London: Thames and
Hudson, 1982), 183–186, discusses how this differs from previous Robin Hood
themes.

3. The filmmakers apparently had no discomfort in having a black man kill an
older white woman as the means of repaying his debt to a white male. Nor do the
filmmakers have much sensitivity to the kind of feminist view of witches found in
the often-reprinted essay "Witches, Midwives, and Nurses" by Barbara Ehrenreich
and Deirdre English; much less do they take into consideration mainstream schol-
arship such as Alan C. Kors and Edward Peters, *Witchcraft in Europe, 1100–1700*
(Philadelphia: University of Pennsylvania Press, 1972).

WORKS CITED

Bartlett, Neil. "The Voyeur's Revenge," *Sight and Sound* 2, no. 5 (September 1992).
A light-hearted homosexual response to Flynn's Robin Hood.
Buehrer, Beverly Bare. "Robin Hood: Prince of Thieves." In *Magill's Cinema Annual,*

1992. Pasadena: Salem Press, 1992. Strong on historical errors in the film. Bibliography provides references to eighteen popular reviews of the film.

Hirschhorn, Clive. *The Warner Brothers Story.* New York: Crown Publishers, 1979. Heavily illustrated studio history.

Holt, J. C. *Robin Hood.* London: Thames and Hudson, 1982. Traces the origins and evolution of the Robin Hood legend from before its first written expression in 1450. Cinema, however, is not discussed.

Pyle, Howard. *The Merry Adventures of Robin Hood.* New York: Charles Scribners, 1883. A rendering that had a huge mass audience in the United States for decades.

FIVE

"Once More, from the Top": Musicals the Second Time Around

Jerome Delamater

Working on *My Sister Eileen* (1955), the musical remake of the 1942 comedy, actress Betty Garrett noted how often choreographer Bob Fosse made them repeat dance routines during rehearsals. "I never worked as hard in my life as I did with Bob. He never stopped. He had one phrase: 'Once more.' About five o'clock at night he'd give a little criticism and then say, 'Once more,' and at 7:30 you'd still be doing it once more" (Delamater, 205). With the musical perhaps more than with other genres the phrase "once more," often coupled with "from the top," so important in rehearsals of musical groups, seems the apt metaphor for remakes. Whether it is an attempt to strive for perfection, an opportunity to reinterpret familiar material, or a chance to modify a particular performance to suit different times, repeating the dance, the song, the musical routine, or—in this case—the entire film "once more" suggests that Hollywood periodically recapitulates its own artifice. Since the musical, above all, is a genre of artifice, that artifice reinforces the genre's basic purpose: to conceal conservative ideology with a formal innovation that often gives the illusion of progressive ideology.

The formulaic nature of all genres makes it possible to consider at least three different kinds of musical remakes.[1] The first is simply another version of the original (like the 1951 *Show Boat* and the 1962 *State Fair*), using essentially the same material but with a different cast and possibly different formal approaches. A second type takes a nonmusical entity and explores its material by introducing the genre's primary semantic elements—song and dance. (*High Society* [1956] and *Silk Stockings* [1957], for example are musical remakes of *The Philadelphia Story* [1940] and *Ninotchka* [1939] respectively.)[2] A third type, the reinterpretations—what some choose to call makeovers—use the essential narrative material of an earlier musical but give it a new gloss with, as in the case of *The Wiz* (1978), more contemporary music and an urban, ethnic identity.[3] All three types continue the "once more" metaphor as they explore the nature of entertainment and the interaction of song and dance with narrative.

One trilogy of films, in particular, embodies many of the issues raised by the show-musical subgenre[4] *and* by remakes. The 1937 melodrama *A Star Is Born* (itself influenced by the 1932 *What Price Hollywood?*)[5] was remade twice. Its second incarnation in 1954 is an illustration of a musical version of a nonmusical, while its third in 1976, also a musical, is probably best considered as a reinterpretation or makeover of the second version.[6] (There was also a major, nonmusical, radio adaptation, starring Judy Garland and Walter Pidgeon, in 1942.) These three films demonstrate changes in how Hollywood has viewed itself (or perhaps more accurately how Hollywood has wanted itself to be viewed), the nature of changes in American popular music, and the role of remakes as vehicles for stars and as embodiments of the ideology of entertainment.

The turmoil striking Hollywood in the early fifties—turmoil brought on by the Paramount decrees in 1948 (causing studios to divest themselves of their theater chains) and by television's ascendancy as the primary form of American entertainment—resulted in a number of remakes as producers and studios attempted to cash in on the successes of the past. Warner Brothers' musical remake of *A Star Is Born*,[7] directed by George Cukor, fulfilled two functions at that time. First, it gave Warner Brothers a chance to exploit an established star long associated with MGM, a studio renowned for musicals. Second, it gave them a chance to explore one of the new technologies—it was Warner's first CinemaScope film[8]—then being used to compete with television. Reviewing the film several decades later provides an instructive lesson about the turmoil-ridden studios of 1954 as compared with the self-confident ones seen in the 1937 film. Warner Brothers' *A Star Is Born* suggests a last-gasp, nostalgic view, belied by the film's own production history. Earlier, in 1950 and 1951, the studio had radically restructured its operating system, terminating or renegotiating contracts, dismissing personnel, and generally reducing overhead (Schatz, *Genius of the System,* 437–38), and one of the ironies of this film is that it presents a picture of a system that the studio was then in the process of dismantling.

Although in the late forties and early fifties the studios introduced an occasional star within the system established years before, as was illustrated by Janet Gaynor's Esther Blodgett-Vicki Lester in the 1937 film, that route to stardom was becoming increasingly rare. Compared to what was really occurring in Hollywood, therefore, the path by which Judy Garland's Blodgett becomes Vicki Lester seems anachronistic. In both films the studio attempts to alter her appearance (although the movie star Norman Maine, her newfound friend, helps her resist and maintain her "natural" look) and changes her name without any consultation with her. Gaynor's Blodgett at

Figure 9. At the end of the 1937 *A Star Is Born,* Vicki Lester (Janet Gaynor), accompanied by her grandmother (May Robson), her pal Danny (Andy Devine), and the studio patriarch, Oliver Niles (Adolphe Menjou), attends a studio premiere where she will declare herself to be "Mrs. Norman Maine."

least listens to the process by which a choice of a new name is made, but the Garland Blodgett discovers the change when she goes to the pay window and is told her check is under L. Similarly in both films the studio sees Esther's marriage to Norman purely in terms of its economic value to the studio. Matt Libby, Niles Studio's public relations officer, says that they have no right to get married quietly; they are stars and have a responsibility to the studio and to the public. Although ostensibly criticizing the studio-controlled, star-making process, both films nevertheless emphasize the "special magic" of stardom (Dyer, 10), a myth that Hollywood long fostered as part of its perceived economic well-being. (See figure 9.)

Certain adjustments to a new, poststudio era are evident, however, in the 1954 version. Perhaps the most obvious concession to the problems affecting Hollywood occurs during Oliver Niles's discussion with Norman about his contract. Having been instructed by the "New York boys" to buy out Norman's contract, Niles says, "They can't afford you anymore, Norman. You're too big a risk. Those big, fat, blush days when a star could get drunk and disappear and hold up production for two weeks are over." He continues, "No one can afford it anymore. Things are too tough." The 1954 film also de-emphasizes luck as the essential factor in the rise to stardom. Gaynor's Blodgett in 1937, very much the girl next door, pines for Hollywood from afar, struggles to break into films when she does get there (through the generosity of her grandmother), and finally gets her chance: she is waitressing at a party where she catches Norman Maine's fancy. By contrast, Garland's Blodgett is already in show business: she is singing at the benefit performance for which Norman Maine arrives drunk and unable to perform. According to the film, it isn't just luck that creates stars. Obvious talent and hard work provide Esther with the opportunity to meet Norman Maine, and, a point that the "Born in a Trunk" number reinforces, people like her "can't quite be called an overnight sensation, for it began many years ago." In a limited way the 1954 *A Star Is Born* acknowledges that an era is ending, but it simultaneously camouflages the industry's difficulties in order to reassure its audience of the rewards of entertainment.

If Garland's Esther Blodgett inconsistently suggests someone rising to stardom in a milieu that was in disarray, Barbra Streisand's Esther Hoffman rises to stardom in a totally different milieu altogether. Movies no longer provide the means for stardom; indeed, by 1976 *Hollywood* has become less a metonymy for the movies than a metaphor for all of show business, with a special emphasis here on music and the recording business. Popular entertainment, once embodied in the movies almost exclusively, has become spread across a variety of media. The first two films reveal something of the workings of the film industry at two different periods whereas the last one depicts "the disorienting surge and psychic voltage of the concert world, its race and disarray" (Stewart, 180). The self-reflexivity implicit in the first two films' inquiries into the exploitation of film stars has become an affirmation, albeit illusory, of one individual's resistance to that kind of control. "Why should I want to change my name?" Esther Hoffman insists at one point, noting all the practical problems—like changing one's driver's license—that would ensue. Similarly, during a rehearsal for a show, she resists a planned walk down a flight of stairs and at another point comments, "They hire me—then they want to change everything about me." Despite her claims of independence, however, Esther Hoffman must yield to the financial exigencies of the music business when she agrees to cancel her long-desired tour with her husband. Streisand's Esther functions in a more inclusive world of show business and in a more socially conscious era than either Gaynor's or Garland's character, but the results are the same: stardom has its price, but entertainment provides redemption.

The motivation for remaking *A Star Is Born* in 1954 lay with Sid Luft, the film's producer (then Judy Garland's husband), and with Garland herself (Haver, 24), and the 1976 remake, although originally John Gregory Dunne's idea, became exclusively Streisand's project (Pierson, 49–50). Both remakes accentuate the role of the star and the use of a given film to show-case a star. Each version of *A Star Is Born* may detail the rise of an unknown, but does so through extremely well-known performers, albeit ones at different stages of their careers. Janet Gaynor "was considered to have out-grown [her earlier] woman-child persona" by the time she made *A Star Is Born,* but Selznick thought her still capable of playing Esther; a similar return to former type was evident in Fredric March's Norman Maine, as well (Schatz, *Genius of the System,* 182). Ultimately the melodrama of 1937 has two leading roles of equal strength, but changing the film to a vehicle for Judy Garland in 1954 completely changed the film's emphasis.[9] The melodramatic qualities of the story, evident in all three versions, nevertheless yield to musical ones because of the stars in the two remakes. Cukor's film was the means for Judy Garland's comeback as a movie star. Indeed, her first appearance, singing "Gotta Have Me Go with You," seems an allusion to her MGM films: "The song and performance would have nicely fit into almost all of the earlier Garland musicals" (Jennings, 329). Having been fired by MGM in 1950, however, Garland was beset by personal problems that had become part of her myth and even part of the singing persona that predominates in this remake. In "The Man That Got Away," the second song of the film, "singing becomes a means of expressing tragedy, heart-break, alienation" (Feuer, *The Hollywood Musical,* 119), the underlying thrust of the film. (See figure 10.) Barbra Streisand, on the other hand, was at the height of her career in 1976. Her domination of *A Star Is Born* (she contributed to the writing and even, as Kris Kristofferson, her co-star, saw it, the directing [Burke, 208–9]) was another manifestation of a desire to play out aspects of her own life. The credited director has recounted at length how, during preproduction, Streisand debated the degree to which her autobiography should be reflected in Esther Hoffman (Pierson, 50). If James Mason's character in the 1954 film becomes through role reversal the "fictional counterpart of the neurotic, self-destructive person that Garland [had] become" (Jennings 333), then Streisand's Esther Hoffman directly fulfills everything that Streisand herself has become by 1976. Richard Dyer even suggests that among the "number of cases on which the totality of a film can be laid at the door of the star" the case can be made "most persuasively" for Streisand's *A Star Is Born* (Dyer, 175).

The resemblances among the three films lie almost exclusively on the narrative level and emphasize the melodrama of the films; what makes the two remakes most interesting, however, is their commitment to the principles of the musical. Certain scenes from Wellman's film are almost duplicated in Cukor's film, for example, and fragments of dialogue similarly recur, but the two musical remakes operate on a different level of intertextuality, one that stresses the semantics of the genre. The Garland and Streisand films use music as a way of exploring the main character's rise to

Figure 10. Demonstrating to the film's audience as well as to Norman Maine that she has "that little something extra" that is star quality, Esther Blodgett (Judy Garland) sings "The Man That Got Away" in the 1954 remake.

stardom, as the means to define the relationship with the man who discovers her, and as an illustration of the star's innate ability. Janet Gaynor's Esther is first seen in the Blodgett farmhouse defending her fascination with Hollywood, whereas Garland's Esther and Streisand's Esther, already residents of Hollywood, are both introduced singing. Prophetic of her subsequent role in the film, Garland's Esther, lead singer of a group, replaces Maine at the Actor's Relief Fund Benefit; she then has to battle him into submission when he tries to interrupt their performance. Streisand also has to battle her Norman—Kris Kristofferson's rock star is named John *Norman* Howard—when they first meet; after his behavior has interrupted her performance of the song "The Queen Bee," she confronts him: "You're blowin' my act!" In both cases the first song each sings—even though spoiled by their soon-to-be leading man—functions to define who they are. Garland's "Gotta Have Me Go with You" truly replaces Norman when considering the lyrics, which sound like his later appeals to her; in other words, Garland's Esther even sings Norman's song for him:

Hey there, shy one, come be my one.
You want a love that's truly true,
You gotta have me
Go with you.
You want to live high on the wire.
You want to have bells that'll ring
You want to have songs that'll sing
You gotta have me go with you.

Streisand actually sings *two* first songs—both disturbed by John Norman—
that clearly identify her in terms of her future relationship with him and
in terms of her ambitions. (See figure 11.) In "The Queen Bee" she yearns
for a man in an overtly sexual way:

It is so frustratin'
When you're really into matin'
And there ain't no lovin' man around.

Her second song becomes a statement of her goals:

I want to learn what life is for.
I don't want much,
I just want more.
Ask what I want, and I will sing.
I want everything, everything.

Whatever the melodramatic implications of the narratives, both remakes
subordinate those implications to other concerns at the outset and demonstrate that the female lead is a singer and performer and a star soon to be
reckoned with.

Similarly the Garland and Streisand characters get their big breaks
through singing, and this moment helps further to move the remakes away
from their roots in melodrama and to define them as musicals. In the 1937
film, Norman, in a discussion with Esther in the studio cafeteria, describes
the need for an actress who clearly fits Esther perfectly, and then the two
together—with little persuasion—convince Oliver Niles that she should
play opposite Norman in his next film; by contrast, the 1954 and 1976
films use totally different but strongly persuasive *musical* constructs. In both
cases the male is the catalyst for the big break, but the situation demonstrates that the character is a latent star—and the performance demonstrates that the performer is a real star.[10] In the 1954 film, knowing that
the studio is desperately seeking a replacement singer for a leading role,
Mason's Norman sets up a situation for Niles to overhear Garland-Esther
singing. Garland-Esther has previously demonstrated to Norman and to
the film's audience that she has "that little something extra" that makes
star quality; now she needs to do so to the studio head, which she does by

Figure 11. Barbra Streisand (as Esther Hoffman) belts out a song in the montage sequence from her tour without her husband in *A Star Is Born* (1976) and foregrounds the reasons that she is a star.

reprising "The Man That Got Away," the song by which she had earlier proved herself to Norman. Streisand's Esther has also previously proved herself to both John Norman and to the film audience, but, whereas the two earlier Esthers also needed the imprimatur of a studio head, this Esther needs the acclaim of a concert audience, an audience within the film.[11] John Norman provides her with that opportunity by, in a singular moment of selflessness, setting up the situation for her to sing at his concert. This is clearly not a spontaneous whim; he has even recruited the other members of her former singing group, the Oreos, to back her up at her stage debut. Everything about the performance—within the film and through the film—suggests that the rising star Esther Hoffman *is* the fully established star Barbra Streisand. As she prepares to begin her song, the camera shoots her from behind, glamorously silhouetted against the lights aimed at the concert stage, her hair highlighted with the aura of a halo. As she sings (one important line is "They can hold back the tide, but they can't hold back the woman in the moon"), she captivates her audience while simultaneously demonstrating that nothing will hold back this Esther from fulfilling her goal of attaining "everything, everything." While fulfilling the function of the character she plays, Streisand foregrounds herself and the demonstrable reasons that she is, in fact, a star.

In certain respects only the 1976 *A Star Is Born* provides the opportunity for the male lead also to participate in the film as a musical. Throughout all three films the nature of the love relationship of the two main characters and Norman's systematic physical and psychological deterioration are akin to those melodramas in which "the well-meaning patriarch [is reduced] to a confused helpless victim of his own good intentions" (Schatz, *Hollywood Genres*, 239). In the 1954 film the musical rituals of courtship and romance remain solely Garland's province, thereby confining James Mason's character to the melodrama of the film. Although Norman Maine proposes to her within a musical background (Esther in a rehearsal has just made it clear through the lyrics of a song that she is open to his proposal: "To share a journey that leads to Heaven's door / You'll find is what I'm here for"), he is far more the observer of, than the participant in, their relationship. In the 1937 film Norman and Esther (by now Vicki Lester) do appear together in a film, but in 1954 they don't even do that. Norman's observer role is especially noticeable during her performance for him at home when she sings "Someone at Last." This all-stops-out performance, characterized by hopeful lyrics ("Somewhere there's a someone for me" and "With my someone I'll be someone at last"), is belied by what is actually occurring in the characters' lives. She has become someone because of him, but as he sits there observing her *being* someone, he realizes that he has become a no one; at the end of her show for him, having just been called Mr. Lester by a delivery boy, he gets himself a drink—the first since their marriage. In contrast, Kris Kristofferson's John Norman does participate in their musical rituals of love and courtship. Although he too is the observer during Esther's first concert performance (and her second song, "I Believe in Love," is one of her strong solo statements of their relationship), previously, following the conventions of the genre, they performed love duets. The first occurs when she plays her own composition on his piano and he improvises lyrics ("Then you came inside my life / Now I'm lost inside of you") to her music, leading directly to their first physical contact and love making; the second occurs during her first recording session when he joins her—albeit hesitantly—in singing "Evergreen," a real declaration of their commitment. Photographed in a single take with both of them together, sharing the frame equally, "Evergreen" shows one side of their relationship. In the subsequent scene, when he has subordinated his performance to give her the big break, they are presented separately through crosscutting as he watches her; the unity of "Evergreen" has given way to what will be the divisions of their separate careers.

One of the most revealing comparisons of the three films concerns the externally imposed "house husband" role that the three Normans assume after their careers have ended. In the first two films the scenes are narratively and formally very similar, even beginning with the close-ups of golf balls that Norman is hitting somewhat indolently. By contrast, John Norman persists in his business: he is playing the guitar and then, with ominous resonances from the earlier movies, begins composing a song, "One More Look at You," the line with which the first two Norman Maines exited as they left to commit suicide. Significantly it is a love song, more appropriate for Esther to sing; just as John Norman throughout the film has given Esther her opportunities, likewise Esther has influenced John Norman's song-writing style, which will—in the end—become his chance for musical immortality. Nevertheless, for all of its contemporary references (John Norman has a problem with alcohol *and* cocaine), its ostensibly updated modifications of the male-female interaction, and its adherence to the semantics of the musical genre, the 1976 film still implies, as did the earlier films, that being reduced to "house husband" is the prelude to suicide. Women can succeed in these films only at the expense of a man, and the films always present this as an innate tragedy.

In their endings all three demonstrate commitment to the genre, but the third also demonstrates this commitment throughout. After Norman Maine has committed suicide, Esther Blodgett receives a lecture in the show-must-go-on philosophy. Her grandmother delivers it to her in the 1937 film, her friend and former band partner Danny McGuire in the 1954 film. In both films, however, the dictates of melodrama supersede those of the musical. As Esther steps up to the microphone to say a few words to her public, the film ends with her proudly asserting her subordination to a man, to domesticity, and to a way of life that she has never really known in Hollywood: "Hello, everybody, this is Mrs. Norman Maine." The 1937 film underscores that irony when, reminiscent of the film's opening, it cuts to a shot of the last page of the shooting script, allowing the audience to read what it has just witnessed and simultaneously to hear the swelling music that the script says should accompany the ending. The 1954 film is less reflexive but no less melodramatic. After the audience at the Actor's Relief Fund Benefit (the cyclical nature of the experience suggested by returning to the scene of the film's opening) gives Mrs. Norman Maine a standing ovation, the camera frames her center stage then pulls back into extreme high-angle long shot; on the sound track a choir sings "It's a New World," Vicki's hit song, which she sang for Norman on their honeymoon and which she was singing as he prepared to die for her, a song that in its initial use reinforced the "new-found promise" of her marriage *and* her career. Its use here is ambiguous, however, and reinforces her obsession with the past, with Norman. Had Vicki-Garland herself sung, as in fact the announcer had said she would when introducing her, the strengths of the genre would have carried other implications, that Vicki has overcome the past and can now move on—the show really can go on. Having no final song for the star, however, reinforces the sense that the film may not be a musical at all; it ends as melodrama. Having originally subordinated her identify to the studio's patriarch by accepting a new name, she further suppresses her identity as a star by reveling in being Norman Maine's widow.[12]

The 1976 film, therefore, is the only one to deliver a fulfilled musical destiny to the lead character at the end. Esther Hoffman doesn't need a lecture to recognize her obligations as a star (the equivalent inspiration to carry on is her discovery of the tape John Norman made of "One More Look at You"), nor does she subordinate herself to another person. As she steps out onto the stage for a memorial concert, an announcer intones, "Ladies and Gentlemen, Esther Hoffman Howard"; she has combined her identity with his, as it were. Moreover, this is to be a performance, one that recapitulates their relationship through song. Debuting "One More Look at You," the song he had written because of her influence, she allows his memory to continue through her performance; subsequently she segues into "Watch Closely Now," one of his signature pieces, which she delivers in his hard-rock style. Rather than giving in to the victimization of the melodrama heroine, Esther Hoffman is redeemed through performance, for the genre has always suggested that "the achievement of personal fulfillment goes hand-in-hand with the enjoyment of entertainment" (Feuer, "The Self-Reflective Musical," 171). Garland's Esther says, "I somehow feel most alive when I sing," but it is Streisand's Esther who demonstrates the necessity of that for the musical star. "This movie does not merely come alive in song; it is about lives lived, linked and ended in a lyric" (Stewart, 178).

Surely one of Streisand's motivations for wanting to do *A Star Is Born* was her view of herself as an heir to Judy Garland's musical legacy. The intertextual resonances of prior films that exist in all remakes would have been strong between the 1954 and 1976 versions of the film, particularly as embodied in the two female stars. (Although the general populace may have had strong memories of the 1937 film,[13] Janet Gaynor, who in 1954 had made no films since 1938 and who was not a singer, certainly had no following comparable to Garland's and Streisand's). Streisand's Esther had to give the illusion of an updated, popularly feminist character, however. Her Esther, for example, proposes to John Norman, but it is still only an illusion since one implication is that her redemption through stardom resides in John Norman. Moreover, Streisand's Esther must sing in a currently popular, rock-music idiom (by comparison one is reminded that Garland's film was being made just at the outset of the rock era), even though Streisand herself has always kept alive loyalties to older forms of popular music. At the end of the film, as Streisand sings Esther's tribute to John Norman, the ultimate conflation of character and performer breaks "down the barriers between art and life" (Feuer, "The Self-Reflective Musical," 171): The audience within the film does not applaud after Esther sings (indeed, the audience is never shown again once she starts singing). Instead by implication the audience *of* the film is invited to applaud *Streisand* at the end. Unlike Gaynor's Esther-Vicki, who is relegated to a scripted character at the end of the 1937 film, and also unlike Garland's Esther-Vicki, whom the diegetic audience does applaud (but for being Mrs. Norman Maine, not for her singing), Streisand's Esther (seen in freeze-frame close-up as the credits roll) affirms the power of popular entertainment by making the audience watching the film feel part of the process of entertainment. The musical's self-reflexivity and self-conscious heightening of emotion through song and dance become reinterrogated the second—and third—time around, but even when the films seem contemporary and fashionable, they still result only in the conclusions that have long sustained the genre: in this case, life is fulfilled through the illusions and myths of entertainment and popular culture.

NOTES

1. No less important in terms of the way the genre functions are the sequels-series, a possible fourth type. Sequels (e.g., *Grease II* [1982] and *Staying Alive* [1983]) are generally self-explanatory. Certain films function similarly to sequels but are properly called series since they follow the same patterns of other films but without necessarily addressing the activities of the same characters. (The most obvious examples are the *Golddiggers* and *Broadway Melody* films of the thirties.) Series films use an established formula and occasionally repeated material to take advan-

tage of earlier films' successes. However, unlike true remakes, which derive more or less from specific earlier films, series films use a broad array of antecedents.

2. *Silk Stockings* and *The Wiz* (and a few other films, *Sweet Charity* among them) are complicated by an intermediary step: a Broadway musical version of which these films are screen adaptations.

3. An alternate form of reinterpretation reverses the process and uses established songs but with newly developed narratives (e.g., *Singin' in the Rain* [1952] and *Pennies from Heaven* [1981]).

4. In *The American Film Musical* Rick Altman proposes three subgenres—the fairy tale musical, the show musical, and the folk musical—each with its own semantic and syntactic elements. All three have had their share of remakes, but partially because it has been the site of considerable critical attention the show musical seems especially profitable to explore in the context of remakes.

5. *What Price Hollywood?* produced by David O. Selznick, who also produced the 1937 *A Star Is Born* (directed by George Cukor, who also directed the 1954 remake), was clearly an inspiration for various scenes and moments in both the 1937 and 1954 films. The complicated romantic relationships of this film, however, as well as its attack on the press for invading a star's personal life, are so different from any version of *A Star Is Born* that it seems inaccurate to consider them specific remakes of *What Price Hollywood?* Patrick McGilligan suggests that "[i]ts tough storyline about the pressures of Hollywood stardom has been stolen from and remade many times" (80).

6. The screenplay credits for the 1976 *A Star Is Born* cite only a story by William Wellman and Robert Carson as its basis. According to the credits of the 1937 film, the Wellman-Carson story was itself the basis of the original screenplay. (David O. Selznick's uncredited contribution has been much recognized; see Haver and McGilligan.) The tale of the writing of the 1976 film reveals a great deal about the preproduction process of remakes. John Gregory Dunne and Joan Didion wrote the first two drafts while quite proudly having seen neither earlier version; they were interested only in the title recognition as a way of getting studio support for a film about the rock and roll business (Dunne, 30). After a third draft, the pair left the project, and numerous other writers (fourteen, according to Dunne) contributed versions. Subsequently the director, Frank Pierson, showing some allegiance to the two prior films, "past[ed] bits and pieces of every draft starting from 1936 into the third draft by Joan Didion and John Dunne" (Pierson, 52).

7. Any analysis of Cukor's *A Star Is Born* is complicated by textual questions. The film initially released was radically altered without the participation of the director or other principal creators. Although much footage was irretrievably lost, a restored version was released in 1983, which used master sound tapes, alternate takes not included in the director's cut, and still photographs to simulate narrative action. The full story has been documented by Ron Haver in *A Star Is Born: The Making of the 1954 Movie and Its 1983 Restoration.* I have used the restored version as my source.

8. The decision to use CinemaScope, a patented system controlled by Twentieth Century-Fox, was made only after Warner Brothers had failed in numerous attempts to exploit its own kinds of wide-screen processes. In fact, the decision to

use CinemaScope occurred only after several days—and three hundred thousand dollars worth—of production on the film (Haver, 126–32).

9. It is significant in this regard that Garland sings all the songs in the 1954 version; emphasis away from the male lead seems also the result of James Mason's being one of Cukor's alternate choices to play Norman Maine. Cary Grant—Cukor's first choice—adamantly refused, and Stewart Granger walked out after finding Cukor's methods incompatible with his own (McGilligan, 219–20).

10. Other than the conflation of Gaynor-Blodgett in the 1937 film, there is no demonstration that this Esther-Vicki has the ability to play a leading role. Indeed, the only two "performances" in the film thus far would argue otherwise: First, at the party where Gaynor's Esther meets March's Norman Maine, she adopts various guises as she offers hors d'oeuvres to the guests; second, just prior to the discussion with him in the cafeteria, she practices different voices for her first speaking part. Both instances suggest that she has no individual persona. Except for the short scene shown at the preview, throughout the film there is only hearsay evidence that this character is worthy of the designation *star.*

11. A further affirmation of Barbra Streisand's own acclaim by a concert audience—and perhaps an even greater blurring of the function of *audience* in this version of *A Star Is Born*—lies in the fact that the outdoor concert scenes of the film were filmed as part of a real concert for a crowd of fifty thousand who paid admission for an all-day performance. On the morning of the concert, Streisand, initially apprehensive about her reception by the audience ("These are rock and roll kids. They'll *hate* me. They'll boo me off the stage. What do they know about what I do?"), walked onstage, "looked at the crowd and said, '*Holy shit!*' They went crazy. *Crazy.* She *owned* them from that point on" (Graham and Greenfield, 374–75).

12. Robert Lang's *American Film Melodrama* provides a full discussion of the relationship between women's identity and patriarchy as fundamental to melodrama (3–13).

13. Wade Jennings asserts that the film itself had been re-released several times between 1937 and 1954 and that the film had also been adapted for radio on more than one occasion—not just in 1942 with Judy Garland (327).

WORKS CITED

Altman, Rick. *The American Film Musical.* Bloomington: Indiana University Press, 1987.

Burke, Tom. "Kris Kristofferson Sings the Good-Life Blues." *Esquire* 86 (December 1976): 126–28ff.

Delamater, Jerome. *Dance in the Hollywood Musical.* Ann Arbor: UMI Research Press, 1981.

Dunne, John Gregory. "The Coast: Gone Hollywood." *Esquire* 86 (September 1976): 30 ff.

Dyer, Richard. *Stars.* London: BFI, 1979.

Feuer, Jane. *The Hollywood Musical.* Bloomington: Indiana University Press, 1982.

———. "The Self-Reflective Musical and the Myth of Entertainment." In *Genre: The Musical,* edited by Rick Altman, 159–74. London: Routledge, 1981.

Graham, Bill, and Robert Greenfield. *Bill Graham Presents: My Life inside Rock and Out.* New York: Doubleday, 1992.

Haver, Ronald. *A Star Is Born: The Making of the 1954 Movie and Its 1983 Restoration.* New York: Knopf, 1988.

Jennings, Wade. "Nova: Garland in 'A Star Is Born.' " *Quarterly Review of Film Studies* 4, no. 3 (summer 1979): 321–37.

Lang, Robert. *American Film Melodrama: Griffith, Vidor, Minnelli.* Princeton: Princeton University Press, 1989.

McGilligan, Patrick. *George Cukor: A Double Life.* New York: St. Martin's, 1991.

Pierson, Frank. "My Battles with Barbra and Jon." *New York* 9 (November 15, 1976): 49–60.

Schatz, Thomas. *The Genius of the System: Hollywood Film-Making in the Studio Era.* New York: Pantheon, 1988.

———. *Hollywood Genres: Formulas, Filmmaking and the Studio System.* New York: Random House, 1981.

Stewart, Garrett. "The Woman in the Moon." *Sight and Sound* 46, no. 3 (summer 1977): 177–81f.

SIX

The Ethnic Oedipus:
The Jazz Singer and Its Remakes

Krin Gabbard

Apart from its initial popularity, *The Jazz Singer* (1927) ought to have held little appeal for remakers: the novelty of introducing talking and singing to a mass audience must have worn off rather quickly; changing racial attitudes ought to have made a narrative involving blackface obsolete if not off-limits; the title's reference to jazz should have discouraged studio bosses once jazz ceased to be a popular music in the 1950s; the emergence of the state of Israel in 1948 drastically altered the issues of Jewish assimilation that are crucial to the film's plot, as J. Hoberman (1991a) has argued; and the personality of Al Jolson weighs so heavily upon the 1927 film that any re-creation would seem to be impossible without him. Finally, in an article that was the inspiration for this paper, Michael Rogin (1992) has shown that the original film dramatized several subjects that Hollywood abandoned after the 1920s, most notably the rags-to-riches ascent of American Jews who broke out of the ghetto, some of whom "invented Hollywood" (Gabler, 1988).

Yet filmmakers repeatedly return to *The Jazz Singer.* Warner Brothers celebrated the twenty-fifth anniversary of the film's release with a 1952 remake directed by Michael Curtiz and starring Danny Thomas; playing a dramatic role for the first time in his career, Jerry Lewis appeared in a Ford "Startime" production directed by Ralph Nelson for NBC television in 1959; and Neil Diamond played the title role in a 1980 film directed by Richard Fleischer. There are also several films that seem to have much in common with the first *Jazz Singer* even if they do not bear the same title. Films such as *The Jolson Story* (1946), *The Benny Goodman Story* (1955), *St. Louis Blues* (1958), and even *La Bamba* (1987) raise questions about biopics and remakes in general and about the pivotal role of *The Jazz Singer* in particular. Almost by accident, the 1927 *Jazz Singer* provided filmmakers with a uniquely American template for dealing with oedipal and ethnic issues.

In arguing that a number of films are unconscious or unacknowledged remakes of *The Jazz Singer,* I am cautioned by the exchange between Seymour Chatman and Barbara Herrnstein Smith (Mitchell, 1981) that was first carried out in the pages of *Critical Inquiry.* Chatman posits a binary model of story and discourse, arguing that a "deep structure" or "basic story" can be transposed from one "discourse" to another, regardless of form, mode, or media. As an example of a basic story he cites *Cinderella,* which has existed "as verbal tale, as ballet, as opera, as film, as comic strip, as pantomime, and so on" (Chatman, 1981, 18). Smith seizes on this example to charge Chatman with subscribing to a "versionless version" of *Cinderella* that resembles a Platonic ideal: "unembodied and unexpressed, unpictured, unwritten and untold, this altogether unsullied *Cinderella* appears to be a story that occupies a highly privileged ontological realm of pure Being within which it unfolds immutably and eternally. If this is what is meant by the basic story of *Cinderella,* it is clearly unknowable—and, indeed, literally unimaginable—by any mortal being" (Smith, 1981, 212).

After quoting several folklorists who have assembled international catalogues of *Cinderella* stories, Smith finds that no rules exist to distinguish versions with most elements of the "basic story" from versions with only a few. As folklorists pile up more and more *Cinderella* stories from around the globe, Smith begins to suspect that if one of the folklorists had continued long enough, "all stories would have turned out to be versions of *Cinderella,*" and that *Cinderella* would turn out to be basically all stories (216). Like Raymond Bellour (1979), I occasionally suspect that all films are versions of the Oedipus story, and after recently immersing myself in musical biopics, I sometimes believe that all Oedipus stories are versions of *The Jazz Singer.*

Smith is right that the term "basic story" is so highly contingent as to be of questionable value, especially if narratologists do not rigorously examine the "hierarchies of relevance and centrality" (217) that they construct in order to arrive at basic-ness. Smith ends her essay by asking for a more thorough theory of narration that is more attentive to the cultural contexts in which narratives take place: "[I]ndividual narratives would be described not as sets of surface-discourse-signifiers that represent (actualize, manifest, map, or express) sets of underlying-story-signifieds but as the verbal acts of particular narrators performed in response to—and thus shaped and constrained by—sets of multiple interacting conditions" (222). On the one hand, my attempts to establish common threads running through the first *Jazz Singer* and its various remakes is not a search for basic-ness among texts composed centuries and continents apart. I will be looking rather at films produced in one country by a single industry over the relatively short span of fifty-three years. Furthermore, identifying the kernel of the 1927 film is somewhat different from positing a basic *Cinderella* since there is already a fully realized version of *The Jazz Singer* in contrast to some stripped-down, unembodied, Platonic version of *Cinderella*. On the other hand, a psychoanalytic reading of the *Jazz Singer* texts suggests that the strongly marked oedipal elements in the films constitute something like a universal core. But the oedipal tensions in the film and its remakes are inseparable from obsessions with popular music, ethnicity, assimilation, and reconciliation that are quite specific to America in general and to Hollywood in particular. Furthermore, the oedipal and racial dynamics of the films are deeply entwined not only with optimistic narratives of assimilation through music but also with the specifics of each era in which filmmakers (and critics) operate. As Smith might argue, it is impossible to separate out a "deep structure" of oedipal themes from the "surface-discourse-signifiers" unique to each text. Smith might also argue that any paraphrase of *The Jazz Singer* says as much about the paraphraser as it does about the film. So, I lay a few cards on the table at this point and declare my commitment to a flexible model of psychoanalysis that acknowledges the impact of cultural change on American obsessions as they are repeatedly played out in popular narratives. I also assert that the first *Jazz Singer* occupies a special role in American cinema, in effect establishing a set of conventions for narratives about race and oedipal conflict in which the hero transcends his ethnic background through success as a popular entertainer imitating African Americans. An especially large number of subsequent films have been based closely enough on these conventions to be called remakes.

For my purposes then, the defining plot elements of *The Jazz Singer* (1927) are as follows: 1) in 1920s America, a boy from 2) a working-class 3) Jewish family with 4) strong feelings toward his mother wants to 5) sing popular songs or "jazz," much to the chagrin of 6) a father who is a cantor and who insists that his son follow in his footsteps. The father disowns the boy only to 7) forgive him on his deathbed. Helping the son in his singing career is 8) a young and attractive gentile woman who is more advanced in show business and who soon becomes the love interest for the son. A not incidental element in the story is the polysemous moment when the son 9) masquerades as an African American male just as he must simultaneously confront his romantic ties to the shiksa and the oedipal crises in his own family. As Rogin (1992) has argued, the blacking up of Jack Robin (Al Jolson) endows him with a more overt sexuality at the same time that it eases his path to assimilation by concealing his Jewishness. At the optimistic, multiculturalist conclusion, the son is able 10) to combine his commitment to "jazz" with his love for his family and their heritage by singing Kol Nidre with vaudeville body English. (Compare Jack's gesturing at the synagogue with the comportment of the eminent cantor Josef Rosenblatt who stands motionless when he sings in *The Jazz Singer,* unwilling to make any concessions to show business beyond appearing in the film.)[1]

Obviously my scheme of ten elements can be expanded and numerous subcategories can be teased out of each element.[2] I have not, for example, mentioned any secondary characters, any details of the son's progress toward stardom, or any effects of the film's racism and sexism. I have tried rather to identify the crucial constitutive elements of *The Jazz Singer* that are most likely to be restated in subsequent films and most relevant to my theses about the role of music in fables of Oedipus and assimilation. My scheme has the further advantage of lending itself to the following table, in which I have marked with an *x* each element that a remake shares with the original.

I have deliberately omitted the reference to America in the 1920s, the first element on my list above, because all of the films take place at different times in America: like most remakes, the first three take place in the same present as when they were made, and the four biopics are anchored in the life history of a famous individual. There also appear to be no films resembling *The Jazz Singer* that center on women, unless we include films like *Coal Miner's Daughter* and *Sweet Dreams,* in which a lower-class, rural milieu might supply the heroines' ethnicity. Given Hollywood's insistence on gender hierarchies, any female variant of *The Jazz Singer* would almost certainly have to focus on the moment in which the heroine upsets the apple cart by surpassing her male lover. The various versions of *A Star Is Born,* in which the success of a female star results in the suicide of her husband, may provide a better example of what happens to *The Jazz Singer* when its gender roles are reversed.[3]

I have also omitted the reconciliatory conclusion, the last element on my list, because I consider this to be the sine qua non for any remake of *The Jazz Singer:* virtually all of the films on the table exhibit some version of it. If, to use Rick Altman's terminology, the table summarizes the semantics of the film and its remakes, *The Jazz Singer*'s conclusion is essential to the film's syntax (Altman, 1986). To distinguish it from the "fairy-tale musical" and the "folk musical," Altman describes the "show musical" as a narrative about a show business couple whose onstage romance and backstage love affair culminate in a final production number (Altman, 1989). For Altman, the semantics of the show musical involve the production of a play, a revue, a film, or some kind of show while the syntax involves the dovetailing of a love plot with the success of the show. As a film from the early stages of the show subgenre—Altman (1989) places the film first in his chronological listing of show musicals—*The Jazz Singer* splits the finale into two small production numbers instead of one large one: after Jack receives his father's blessing at the old cantor's deathbed, he sings his jazzy Kol Nidre in the

TABLE 1   *The Jazz Singer* and Its Remakes

	Class	Jews?	Does mother indulge son?	Does son sing jazz?	Does father oppose son at first?	Does father forgive son later?	Does son love a shiksa?	Does son wear blackface?
Jazz Singer (1927)	Lower	Yes	Yes	Yes	Yes	Yes	Yes	Yes
Jazz Singer (1952)	Middle	X Yes	X Yes	No	X Yes	X Yes	Lover is Jewish	No
Jazz Singer (1959)	X Lower	X Yes	X Yes	No	X Yes	No?	X Yes	No, a clown face
Jazz Singer (1980)	X Lower	X Yes	No mother	No	X Yes	X Yes	X Yes	X Yes
The Jolson Story (1946)	X Lower	X Yes	X Yes	X Yes	X Yes	X Yes	X Yes	X Yes
Benny Goodman Story (1955)	X Lower	X Yes	X Yes, but opposes shiksa at first	X Plays jazz	X Yes, then dies early	X Yes	X Yes	No, but plays with blacks
St. Louis Blues (1958)	X Lower	No	Close to Aunt Hagar	X Yes	X Yes	X Yes	X Eartha Kitt	No, but sings with orchestra
La Bamba (1987)	X Lower	No	X Yes	No	X Competition with brother	X Reconciled with brother	X Yes	No, but changes name

synagogue; a title card then explains that "the season passes—and time heals—the show goes on" just before Jack is seen on the stage of the Winter Garden theater singing "Mammy" under cork while his mother and Mary Dale, his gentile lover, look on adoringly. As David Desser (1991) has argued, "[A]n overdetermined form of mother love represses the intermarriage component" (399), one of several elements in the conclusion that could easily disrupt the film's utopian view of assimilation. "Success in the American mainstream, a breakthrough into stardom, a breakout of the ghetto, 'naturally' brings with it the WASP woman. Intermarriage becomes secondary to assimilation" (Desser, 1991, 399).

Significantly, Jack Robin's final return to the stage, along with the reaction shots of doting Jewish mother and shiksa lover, is not in Alfred A. Cohn's original shooting script for *The Jazz Singer.* Nor can these scenes be found in the principal sources for the film—Samson Raphaelson's 1922 short story, "Day of Atonement," and his play, *The Jazz Singer* (Carringer, 1979). The shooting script ends with Jack in the synagogue where he may have ended his show business career by walking out on the opening night of a Broadway show. Although Raphaelson wrote "Day of Atonement" with Al Jolson's own story in mind (Carringer, 1979, 11), the story ends with the hero actually choosing to remain a cantor. The triumphant but slightly incoherent "Mammy" finale was added to the film by Warners, if only for the sake of a more upbeat ending. Like most show musicals, nearly all of *The Jazz Singer* remakes are more economical, placing the weight of the reconciliation primarily in a concluding stage act: the protagonist may in fact return to the synagogue or its equivalent, but the final stage performance is more clearly motivated, with the father usually surviving to enjoy the show along with the rest of his son's adoring fans. What the father eventually comes to understand is what the hero and the story (in most of the remakes) have been saying all along, "that Jack's jazz singing is fundamentally an ancient religious impulse seeking expression in a modern, popular form" (Carringer, 1979, 23). Or as the film itself states in its first title card, "[P]erhaps this plaintive, wailing song of jazz is, after all, the misunderstood utterance of a prayer."

This kind of oedipal reconciliation may be unique to American popular culture. In contrast to the reassuring ending of America's *The Jazz Singer,* Hoberman (1991a) has found a turn-of-the-century Yiddish tragedy from Poland that foreshadows the plot of the film even though Raphaelson probably had no knowledge of it when he wrote "Day of Atonement." In *Der Vilner Balebesl,* later filmed in Yiddish as *Overture to Glory* (1940), a talented cantor's desire to see the world leads him to a successful career as an opera singer and eventually into the arms of a Polish countess. When he returns home to his village, however, he finds that his wife has gone mad and his child has died.[4] "In Europe, the fruits of assimilation were seen as madness, ruin, and death. In America, of course, it was a different story" (Hoberman 1991a, 64).

Robert B. Ray (1985) has placed Hollywood's paradigm of reconciliation alongside "American myths of inclusiveness," part of the fundamental belief that options are eternally available in the New World: "Often, the movies' reconciliatory pattern concentrated on a single character magically embodying diametrically opposite traits. A sensitive violinist was also a tough boxer (*Golden Boy*); a boxer was a gentle man who cared for pigeons (*On the Waterfront*). A gangster became a coward because he was brave (*Angels with Dirty Faces*); a soldier became brave because he was a coward (*Lives of a*

Figure 12. The Jewish jazz singer and his shiksa: Al Jolson and May McAvoy star in Alan Crosland's *The Jazz Singer* (1927).

Bengal Lancer)" (58). Similarly, a jazz singer who abandons his family for the stage can also lead the congregation in prayer on the most solemn of holy days, then return to the stage as a great success and still have the love of his mother and a beautiful shiksa. (See figures 12, 13, and 14.) (Although the myth implies that limitless possibilities are open to all Americans, the vast majority of American films suggests that Hollywood is willing to extend such wide-ranging freedom only to white males, even if they are Jewish.)

Even after the upbeat ending was added to the 1927 *Jazz Singer*, there was still the tragic possibility that Jack Robin could lose the stage career he so desperately sought: both his manager and Mary Dale follow him to his parents' apartment to caution him firmly about walking out on an opening night. In the remakes, however, the jazz singers face no such crises; rather, the heroes of the 1952 and 1980 versions arrive at their respective synagogues with little anxiety about career-ending absences on Broadway. In the 1952 version, when the summons to sing Kol Nidre comes on the same afternoon as the hero's important opening night, a quick call for the understudy is issued, and the heroine expresses only sympathy when the Danny Thomas character departs for home; no title card or expository dialogue is necessary to explain the jump from Danny singing in the syna-

Figure 13. The Jewish jazz singer and his shiksa: Danny Thomas and Peggy Lee star in Michael Curtiz's slick but professionally crafted remake of *The Jazz Singer* (1953).

gogue to Danny singing in the theater. In the 1980 version, Jakie Rabino-witz (Neil Diamond) has just ended a rehearsal by telling his musicians to take the day off for Yom Kippur when his father's friend arrives with the plea that Jakie replace his ailing father back home: singing Kol Nidre has no effect whatsoever on the progress of the singer's career. Whereas the cantor in the 1927 film declares his love for his son but never articulates his acceptance of Jack's vocation as a singer, the father in almost all of the remakes comes to accept and actually appreciate his son's music.

As many critics pointed out, the path to reconciliation in the 1952 re-make is so smooth that little tension remains to drive the narrative. Edward Franz, who plays Danny Thomas's father in the 1952 version, is not a poor cantor in a Lower East Side ghetto, but the well-heeled leader of a congre-gation in an affluent section of Philadelphia. Not only is the cantor thor-oughly assimilated into urban society; he also appears to be quite comfort-able with popular culture, at one point singing every word of a rapid-fire soap commercial that his son recorded for radio. The father's demand that

Figure. 14. The Jewish jazz singer and his shiksa: Neil Diamond is featured in his motion picture debut, along with Lucie Arnaz, in Richard
Fleischer's cliché-packed re-remake of *The Jazz Singer* (1980).

his son follow in a family tradition of several generations of cantors takes
on the marks of a neurotic symptom, a familiar convention during Hollywood's romance with psychoanalysis in the 1950s (Gabbard and Gabbard,
1987). Coming to his senses on his sickbed just before his son sings Kol
Nidre, the cantor himself delivers the film's message that the popular entertainer can express a divine spirit. After giving his blessing to Jerry's show
business career, the cantor adds, "Only I want you to remember that wherever you sing, always lift your head high and raise your voice to god, the

way you did in the temple." Even the problem of intermarriage is solved by having Peggy Lee, Danny Thomas's love interest, drop a line about attending a seder to hint that she too may be Jewish.

Although Laurence Olivier's cantor in the 1980 *Jazz Singer* leads a less affluent congregation on Eldridge Street on the Lower East Side of Manhattan, and although he is never overheard equating popular music with religion, he is entirely won over when Jakie shows the old man a photograph of his grandson, "Charlie Parker Rabinowitz." The reference to the canonical jazz saxophonist and composer seems motivated primarily by the anachronism of the film's title and by the vestiges of white appropriation of black culture that seem obligatory in a *Jazz Singer* remake. The largely perfunctory citation of Charlie Parker may also have stemmed from Diamond's desire to shore up his dubious claim to hipness. In the decidedly unhip conclusion of the film, Olivier is caught up in the crowd's semi-Dionysian abandon while Diamond sings "Coming to America," a hymn to assimilationism so unproblematic that the Democratic Party adopted the song for its national convention in 1988. Diamond's American melting-pot jingoism is expressed symbolically in the finale by his red, white, and blue outfit set off by a scarf worn like a prayer shawl.[5]

If the 1952 and 1980 films tilt toward easy reconciliation, Jerry Lewis's 1959 television production retains a sense of the tragic possibilities in the story of the ethnic Oedipus. Lewis plays a clown, rather than a singer, who is about to appear in his first national TV program when he is called back to the synagogue. With no time to wipe off his makeup, the son arrives at the last minute to sing Kol Nidre in *clown* face as his father expires and the film ends. Scott Bukatman (1991) has attributed the bizarre, nonresolution of the program's ending to Lewis's own "unresolved conflicts of identity" (192).[6] Whatever his reasons, Lewis remained true to the original spirit of Raphaelson's story and play, both of which emphasized the assimilating Jew's dilemmas rather than his successful negotiation of career and oedipal conflicts. Like the authors of the 1952 remake, Lewis appeared to be uninterested in the original film's appropriation of black culture.

Even accounting for the inevitable changes that characterize the vast majority of remakes, the 1952 and 1980 *Jazz Singers* respond powerfully to agendas unknown to filmmakers in 1927: as Smith (1981) would argue, each new *Jazz Singer* was radically refashioned as its "narrators" formulated new stories to accommodate the profound changes in American culture. Danny Thomas appears in uniform at the opening of the 1952 remake, a GI faced with the problems of adjustment reminiscent of those in successful predecessor films like *The Pride of the Marines* (1945), *The Best Years of Our Lives* (1946), and *The Men* (1950). Although the film was also made in the shadow of several problem films that dealt with anti-Semitism, such as *Gentlemen's Agreement* (1947) and *Crossfire* (1947), hatred of the Jews is hardly an issue in Curtiz's film. In fact, the film is so careful to avoid Jewish stereotypes that the principals might as well be Episcopalians.

The 1952 film also omits any reference to African Americans, either real or mimicked through blackface. My research has turned up nothing to indicate that Warner Brothers made a conscious decision to eliminate any reference to blackface, and almost without exception the reviews of the film make no mention of the omission. By 1952, the civil rights movement may have been sufficiently successful with its consciousness-raising to have made the practice forbidden, even in a film that must have quickly brought to mind Al Jolson, the best-known of all blackface performers, whose long and highly visible career had ended with his death just two years earlier.[7]

Richard Fleischer's 1980 version was motivated primarily by the personal fixations of Neil Diamond, who insisted on script changes throughout production in order to bring the story more in line with his own life story (Wiseman, 1987, 256). The most significant omission is the protagonist's mother, so essential to the oedipal hysteria of the original and most of the remakes. Blackface, on the other hand, returns. Diamond and Fleischer may have intended a tongue-in-cheek homage to the 1927 film when they inserted an early scene in which Jakie Rabinowitz reluctantly puts shoe polish on his face in order to replace the missing member of an African American singing group that is performing his songs in a black nightclub. At least initially, the scene is played for laughs as Jakie tries to conceal his misgivings with the black makeup. At the dawn of the era of Reagan and Bush, however, the sequence is especially disturbing in its invocation of racial stereotypes that were soon to become more pervasive than they had been during previous decades. If in 1927 blackface authorized sexuality and emotional vulnerability, in the 1980 *Jazz Singer* blackface appears to authorize violence against obstreperous blacks and the fantasy of loyal retainers fighting alongside the white hero: after an angry black man in the audience notices that Jakie has neglected to put color on his hands ("That ain't no brother; that's a white boy!"), he rushes the stage and sets himself up for a sucker punch from the hero. As members of the soul group come to his aid and the entire club breaks into pandemonium, the film activates clichés from bar fights in westerns as well as from myths about the natural inclination of black people to violence. The film also upholds Hollywood's old racial hierarchies by suggesting that a group of black singers is dependent on a white man for their music. Although there is no question that whites in general and Jews in particular have made substantial contributions to the evolution of jazz and black popular music, the film acknowledges the crucial role of African Americans in jazz history only in the name of Jakie's son.

If each of the three titled remakes departs substantially from the semantics and syntax of the original, the four biopics in table 1 line up more agreeably with my characterizations of the 1927 film. On the one hand, this

phenomenon may be related to the need for self-identified remakes to update their plots in order to separate themselves from the original. The frequently hagiographical biopics, on the other hand, tend to be more conservative and consequently fall back on well-established conventions. *The
Jolson Story* (1946), for example, represents a self-announced biography of
Jolson after a progression of *Jazz Singer* texts—story, play, screenplay, and
final film—each moved closer to Jolson's own story. Almost all of the semantic elements of the 1927 film reappear in *The Jolson Story*, although the
syntax begins to break down in the film's final third, which chronicles the
star's temporary retirement, his separation from his wife, and the beginnings of his comeback. The reconciliation with father comes quickly and
easily even before the young Asa Yoelson changes his name to Al Jolson:
after the child runs away from home, he is taken to a Catholic boys' home
where his parents arrive to see him singing "Ave Maria." When the elder
Yoelson complains, "[S]inging without his cap on," an Irish priest strikes
the principal ecumenical note of all *The Jazz Singer* films when he says, "It's
not so much what's on the head as what's in the heart, is it, Cantor?" The
father's smile indicates his agreement and concession to his son's wishes;
with the film less than fifteen minutes old, the man becomes the ardent
follower of his son's career, thus setting an example for the 1952 and 1980
titled remakes. On one of the boy's visits home, the father even tells his
son that he need no longer wear a yarmulke. Jolson's real father passed
away when Jolson was quite young (Goldman, 1988). The oedipal aggres-
siveness of the first *Jazz Singer* surely became less appealing after so many
Jewish fathers had died in the Holocaust, perhaps motivating the makers
of almost all the post-1945 *Jazz Singer*s to allow the fathers to live on and
achieve satisfying reconciliations with their sons.

In addition to anticipating the much greater attention to career progress
that characterizes the subsequent remakes of *The Jazz Singer, The Jolson Story*
goes farther than any of the films in exploring the significance of blackface. For reasons that are never really explained, Jolson first blacks up while
appearing in a variety show that features a blackface performer. When
the white minstrel man is too drunk to perform one night, Jolson sponta-
neously replaces him; coincidentally, Lou Dockstader, the leader of a well-
established minstrel troupe, is in the audience. Jolson's desire to work in
blackface appears to grow out of his interest in African American music,
but the film offers no evidence that the young Jolson has previously heard
blacks in performance even though he begins improvising and syncopating
his vocal solos early in his career. Only after he has joined Dockstader's
minstrel show does Jolson arrive in New Orleans and wander into a gathering of blacks to hear a fairly slick version of Dixieland jazz. Jolson has a
revelation, that the staid repertoire of the minstrel troupe can be transformed by actually playing black music in blackface. He tells Dockstader

that he wants to sing what he has just experienced: "I heard some music tonight, something they call jazz. Some fellows just make it up as they go along. They pick it up out of the air." After Dockstader refuses to accommodate Jolson's revolutionary concept, the narrative chronicles his climb to stardom as he allegedly injects jazz into his blackface performances. This of course allows the audience to appreciate Jolson's foresight in predicting the popularity of jazz, but it also suggests that this ethereal music—picked out of the air by simple black folk—needs the genius of someone like Jolson to give it solidity and validity. After the brief scene in New Orleans, African Americans are never seen again, nor is there any subsequent reference to jazz and Jolson's appropriation of black music. In the scenes that follow, however, the blacked-up Jolson is granted license to play the trickster, impishly but endearingly rewriting stage shows as they unfold in front of audiences. Whereas blacking up allowed a certain freedom of sexual expression for Jolson in the first *Jazz Singer,* in the *Jolson Story* it becomes associated with harmless mischief.

Once we accept a semantic change from singing to playing the clarinet, *The Benny Goodman Story* becomes an almost transparent reworking of *The Jazz Singer.* The hero never puts on blackface, but he does have critical encounters with black musicians in which their proximity seems to act upon his sexuality and emotional expressivity. The mythological characteristics of African Americans that Jack Robin puts on along with burnt cork are acquired by Goodman when blacks are simply nearby. When the young Benny plays his first job with a white dance band on a riverboat in Chicago, he is introduced to a young woman who is about to become his first date until she ridicules him for wearing short pants. Almost immediately he wanders into a performance by the black intermission band led by New Orleans trombonist Kid Ory (played by Ory himself) and notices that the musicians have no music. "We just play what we feel," explains Ory. "Playing the way you feel," muses Goodman. "Say, could I sit in?" Immediately, the young clarinetist becomes an accomplished improviser, presumably finding in African American music the perfect means for overcoming his wounded feelings.

Donna Reed is later introduced into *The Benny Goodman Story* as Alice Hammond, the gentile woman from New York society whom the mature Goodman (Steve Allen) eventually marries. Their romance is off to a slow start until Benny has returned to Chicago at the pinnacle of his first great success. Standing next to Fletcher Henderson, the black bandleader whose arrangements contributed mightily to Goodman's success, Goodman is reintroduced to Kid Ory, who offers the praise, "You have the best band I ever heard anyplace." At this moment, Alice walks in, and Benny is about to approach her in earnest. Reversing the situation of his first sexual humiliation, Benny quickly thanks Ory for his compliment and then hands his clarinet to Henderson, adding, "Fletch, could you hold this, please?" Now a more fully sexualized individual, Goodman no longer needs black musicians to tutor him about feelings, although the film does seem to relate their proximity (and easy dismissal) to his romantic energies.[8]

For all the patronizing and marginalizing of black jazz artists in *The Benny Goodman Story,* the film does in fact acknowledge the contribution of Henderson as well as Teddy Wilson and Lionel Hampton (both played on-screen by themselves) to Goodman's career. The appearance of Wilson, Hampton, and Buck Clayton with Goodman at the re-creation of the triumphant 1938 Carnegie Hall concert that ends the film is a dramatic change from the mimicking of black performers that concludes the 1927 *Jazz Singer.* The end of *The Benny Goodman Story,* with its several black performers, is one of the most inclusive of the many reconciliatory finales in the cycle of show musicals. As in *The Jazz Singer,* this unorthodox performance by a jazz musician is presented as a gamble that might endanger his career. Appropriately, the romance plot culminates at this concert when we are told that Goodman is asking Alice to marry him by means of a clarinet solo, a proposal she accepts by nodding her head. This wedding proposal doubles the marriage of jazz and classical music symbolized by a Carnegie Hall concert attended entirely by socially prominent New Yorkers, who depart from their usual behavior at concerts by tapping their feet in rhythm. Goodman's adoring mother is seated next to the clarinetist's fiancée at the concert, recalling the reaction shots of Jack Robin's mother and lover at the end of *The Jazz Singer.*

The Benny Goodman Story is of course another film about successful assimilation by a Jewish musician. Its perhaps unconscious debt to *The Jazz Singer* suggests that the 1927 film had definitively established the rules by which such a story should be told, even one alleged to be true. Although there is no Kol Nidre at the conclusion of the film, *The Benny Goodman Story* also follows *The Jazz Singer* in forging a rapprochement between Jewish culture and the mainstreams of American culture. The word "Jew" is never uttered in the film, though the accents of Benny's parents provide one of several obvious references to the family's Jewishness. At another point, Mrs. Goodman has a brief moment of hesitancy about Benny's courtship of the upper-class, gentile Alice, in which she tells the younger woman, "You don't mix caviar and bagels." Generally, the film displaces anxieties about social class and ethnicity into a conflict over musical tastes—a conflict that is of course much more easily resolved both here and in the many *Jazz Singer* narratives in which music is the preferred path to assimilation. Since Alice prefers classical music to jazz, her admiration for Benny grows substantially when she discovers that he is capable of what the film identifies as an expert reading of Mozart's Clarinet Concerto.

But there are a number of subtle signs that Benny has also retained his

Jewish heritage in his "hot music." At several transitional moments in *The Benny Goodman Story*, Benny plays a melancholy tune alone at night on the rooftop of his building. Anyone with a passing knowledge of Goodman's music would be able recognize the tune as "Goodbye," a song written in fact by Gordon Jenkins that became the closing theme for the Goodman band. When played solo by Goodman (who dubbed in all clarinet solos for Steve Allen), the minor melody of the song also bears the signifiers of Jewish folk music. Even more strikingly, the final Carnegie Hall concert features a performance of "And the Angels Sing" with the famous trumpet solo by Ziggy Elman that quotes from the Jewish klezmer tune, "Der Shtiler Bulgar," part of an earlier version of the song entitled "Frahlich in Swing" (Sapoznik, 1987). With the *echt* WASP Martha Tilton taking the vocal chorus on "And the Angels Sing," Jewish is married to American even if klezmer does not quite accomplish the mixture of the sacred and the profane that ends *The Jazz Singer.*

A case can be made that remakes of *The Jazz Singer* can involve non-Jewish groups so long as they are sufficiently marginal. With slight semantic changes, *St. Louis Blues* (1958) and *La Bamba* (1987) address many of the same questions as the original 1927 film. In the former, Nat King Cole plays W. C. Handy, the African American man who was the first great popularizer of the blues. Handy's father is a minister who strongly disapproves of secular music and insists that his son pursue a respectable career as a school teacher. Although the hero's mother is dead, he is frequently indulged by his Aunt Hagar (Pearl Bailey). Like all the mothers in the *Jazz Singer* texts, surrogate mother Aunt Hagar inevitably sides with the boy in his oedipal struggles with father.

In *St. Louis Blues,* the young W. C. Handy is fascinated by the work songs he hears from black laborers and begins writing songs that show the influence of these songs: even when the protagonist is black, American cinema is able to find an otherness in black music. Handy is soon playing and singing his songs in a cabaret whose featured performer is the sensually purring Eartha Kitt. Her otherness from Handy's strict Christian background puts her in much the same relationship to the hero as Mary Dale bears to Jack Robin. Kitt is certainly more outside the protagonist's tribe than was Peggy Lee in the 1952 *Jazz Singer.* In the final moments of *St. Louis Blues,* Handy appears in a tuxedo—in some sense, a cultural disguise—and sings the title tune before a symphony orchestra while his father stands backstage, accepting at last his son's vocation. Although the film's religious crisis is displaced into issues of social class and the sacralization of the concert hall, the ending resembles that of other *Jazz Singer* remakes in its suggestion that the son can be true to his artistic convictions *and* to the demands of his father.

In *La Bamba,* Ricardo Valenzuela (Lou Diamond Phillips) grows up playing rock and roll in Southern California in the 1950s, and his highly supportive mother takes an active role in his career. Although the boy's father is dead, the protagonist has a relationship with an older brother that adumbrates the conflict between father and son found in earlier *Jazz Singer* films: in fact, the film creates additional oedipal tension by indicating that Ricardo feels affection and later sympathy for the woman who is married to his brother, a former convict given to violent outbursts. Before he crosses over to success under the name Ritchie Valens, the Mexican American hero has already established a relationship with Donna, a blonde girl whose father strongly disapproves of the young man's ethnic and lower-class origins. Significantly, Ritchie has grown up in America listening to rock, specifically to black artists such as Little Richard, and never learned to speak Spanish. When his older brother takes him on a trip to Tijuana he hears a *norteña* band playing the old folk tune "La Bamba." The trip was arranged by the brother to take Ritchie to a brothel for his first sexual experience, part of the brother's attempts to acquaint Ritchie with the cultural heritage that Ritchie regards ambivalently (like the jazz singer's bar mitzvah?). In the film's multicultural solution, Valens sings the Spanish words to "La Bamba" while transforming the song with a rock beat and stage mannerisms borrowed from black rhythm-and-blues performers. As an assimilated Hispano-American, Valens draws his sexual power from blacks and his ethnic legitimacy from the Mexican band that he first heard in a bordello. The film ends when Ritchie dies in a plane crash at the height of his popularity, still adored by his mother and his blonde girlfriend and recently reconciled with his brother. Like the various jazz singers before him, Ritchie has successfully negotiated his ethnic and oedipal crises before the end of his short life.

By adding the "Mammy" finale to the originally scripted ending for *The Jazz Singer,* Warner Brothers helped cement a tradition that we now call the classical Hollywood cinema. Hoberman (1991a, 65) quotes one reviewer who attributed the revised ending to the persona of Jolson: "No audience would really expect to see Al Jolson give up show business—even in a film." A more general explanation of the change has been offered by Carringer (1979): "The story is transformed from a fable of adjustment (how the new generation finds its place in a cultural tradition) to a more characteristically American fable of success—open revolt against tradition, westward movement, the expenditure of energy, triumph, and the replacement of the values of the old by the values of the new." (27) I would qualify this characterization by adding that the resolution of oedipal tension must accompany the revolt against tradition if the fable is to be sufficiently appealing. Furthermore, the hero's appropriation of black American music may also be an essential part of the original *Jazz Singer*'s lasting influence: as Rogin (1992) has argued, Jack Robin does not sing the jazz of "The New Negro" and urban sophistication: instead he sings of a nostalgic return to the mythological plantation with its infantilized black slaves.[9] Jack Robin puts on a mournful demeanor with the burnt cork that is highly inconsistent with the cheerful opportunist we first meet at Coffee Dan's, where Jack practically dances as he eats his breakfast. Along with everything else it offers, blackface gives Jack a dimension of solemnity and filial piety that are otherwise absent in his single-minded pursuit of assimilation. The hero's return to the stage at the end is substantially less abrupt because of Jack's impersonation of a mournful and loyal momma's boy: the crime of Oedipus becomes less abhorrent. And by simultaneously hiding his Jewishness and putting on the satyr's mask, Jack can move closer to his gentile love object. If the upbeat finale of *The Jazz Singer* is crucial to the film's syntax, so is the borrowing of emotional and sexual capital from African Americans. This exchange of sexuality is especially significant in a culture that stereotypes blacks as hypersexual at the same time that it characterizes Jewish men as undersexed.

In this sense, the 1952 and 1980 remakes are not as close to the original as are *The Benny Goodman Story* and, to a large extent, *St. Louis Blues.* In the W. C. Handy film, the hero's final success resolves the oedipal crisis with his father; although Benny Goodman's father is absent at the end, the culture of the father is never abandoned as the son moves into gentile society. The regular proximity of Goodman to black musicians like Wilson and Hampton allows him to make this move without losing his soul, just as in *St. Louis Blues,* the devotion of W. C. Handy to the folk art of "simple" African American working men preserves his authenticity even as he stands in his tuxedo before a symphony orchestra. And as in *The Jazz Singer,* black vernacular music provides both protagonists with an acceptable context for their sexualization. By contrast, Danny Thomas and Neil Diamond have only the most tenuous connection to black culture both inside and outside their respective narratives. (Both Steve Allen and Nat Cole had substantial ties to jazz artists.) It has not been my intention in this essay to valorize films that exploit the "surplus symbolic value of blacks" (Rogin, 1992, 417) or for that matter the surplus symbolic value of gentile women. I am interested rather in how a seemingly unique film like the 1927 *Jazz Singer* can become a paradigm for American success stories, regardless of what they are called.

I thank Lewis Porter, Christine Holmlund, Ilsa Bick, Scott Bukatman, Robert Eberwein, and Louise O. Vasvari for their many helpful comments on earlier drafts of this essay.

NOTES

1. The part of Jack Robin's father was first offered to Rosenblatt with the promise of a salary as high as one hundred thousand dollars. According to Rosen-

blatt's biographer, the cantor refused because of his religious convictions but eventually agreed to appear in one scene as himself only after laying down strict conditions, including a ban on makeup (Rosenblatt, 1954, 289). I thank Lewis Porter for calling my attention to this text, as well as for many other helpful suggestions.

2. For a more rigorous approach to the semantics of films such as *The Jazz Singer*, I recommend the much more detailed "coding sheet" with no less than twenty-seven categories that George Custen (1992, 237–39) developed for his work on biopics.

3. In a curious way, the documentary of a tour by the pop singer Madonna, *Truth or Dare* (1991), vaguely recalls many of the conventions of the *Jazz Singer*, including a conflict with working-class ethnic parents, a (mildly blasphemous) recuperation of the family's religious heritage into the star's performance, and the wary reconciliation with the father. The sexual capital of African Americans is also a crucial factor in this narrative—Madonna tours with a troupe of black male dancers and with two female singer-dancers, one of whom is black. And like 90 percent of white pop singers today, Madonna relies heavily on vocal styles and body language steeped in African American traditions.

4. In his book on Yiddish cinema (1991b), Hoberman discusses *Der Vilner Balebesl* and several related films in greater detail. For studies that contextualize *The Jazz Singer* with other American films about Jews, see Erens (1984) and Friedman (1982).

5. In 1982, the SCTV (Second City TV) troupe did a parody of the Diamond film on their NBC series, in which the father—played by "Sid Dithers" (Eugene Levy) with dread locks—is a Jewish recording executive who wants his son to make hit records. The son, played by Al Jarreau (who is African American), wants to be a cantor. In still another *Jazz Singer* parody, Krusty the Klown told the story of his estrangement from his orthodox Jewish father on a 1992 episode of *The Simpsons:* as in so many of the remakes, the program culminates with the father accepting his son's profession and enjoying his performance, even to the point of throwing a pie at the "camera" as the episode ends.

6. Lewis, who owns exclusive rights to his 1959 *Jazz Singer*, has expressed dissatisfaction with the program and has made it unavailable for public viewing. I have obtained most of my information on Jerry Lewis's *Jazz Singer* in conversation with Scott Bukatman, an ardent student of Lewis's work, who was given access to the program by Lewis himself.

7. I can only speculate that Warner Brothers decided early on to omit blackface performance scenes from the 1952 *Jazz Singer* after receiving complaints about Doris Day's blackface imitation of Al Jolson in *I'll See You in My Dreams,* released one year earlier in 1951. *I'll See You in My Dreams,* like the 1952 *Jazz Singer*, was directed for Warners by Michael Curtiz and starred Danny Thomas. This was not the end of blackface in the cinema, however. In 1953, Joan Crawford performed under cork in *Torch Song.* As far as I can tell, the tradition does not reappear until it reaches a socially conscious stage with *Black Like Me* (1964). Elliott Gould does a brief parody of blackface and Jolson in *The Long Goodbye* (1973), and there is a sentimental but vaguely sinister revision of the practice in *Soul Man* (1986).

8. As the author of an article that employs psychoanalytic methodologies in order to insist upon the phallic nature of the jazz trumpet (Gabbard, 1992), I feel

compelled to comment on the scene in which Goodman, at a crucial moment in his sexual development, hands his clarinet to the black musician Fletcher Henderson. Although there may be moments when a clarinet is only a clarinet, the long black instrument can perhaps be conceptualized here as a prosthesis for Goodman's sexuality, first charged with phallic qualities when Goodman learns to play jazz from black artists. Even though the mature Goodman never abandons the clarinet in his public life, he eventually becomes sufficiently confident as a sexual being to put the prosthesis aside. Handing the phallic instrument to Fletcher Henderson while Kid Ory is present brings to completion a process that began when Ory taught Goodman the full potential of the clarinet while twice mentioning Fletcher Henderson's name in conversation. Hollywood's racial codes may have demanded that a woman like Donna Reed-Alice Hammond should require a suitor more sophisticated than one tutored by blacks, who simply "play what they feel." According to his logic, Goodman can successfully approach her only after he has put his large black prosthesis aside.

9. Rogin (1992) tends to overstate the racism inherent in the original *Jazz Singer*'s imitation of black music. Rogin implies that African American jazz artists of the twenties—he specifically names Louis Armstrong, Jelly Roll Morton, Fletcher Henderson, and King Oliver—played an urban, revolutionary music quite separate from Al Jolson-Jack Robin's songs of nostalgia for the old plantation (448). In fact, many of Rogin's canonical black jazz musicians performed exactly the kind of music that he lays at the door of Jolson and *The Jazz Singer*. During the 1920s and early 1930s, Louis Armstrong essentially built his popularity upon "coon" songs like "Sleepy Time Down South," "Shine," "Snowball," and "Shoe Shine Boy," while Fletcher Henderson recorded "Old Black Joe Blues," "Darktown Has a Gay White Way," and "Cotton Picker's Ball." In 1927 King Oliver recorded a song called "Aunt Jemima." While it is true that this repertoire was probably forced upon black entertainers by white impresarios, it is also true that this was the only system through which we can come to know these black entertainers. Rogin seems to suggest that a pure, uncorrupted, uncommercialized black music is somehow knowable without the apparatus of the culture industry.

WORKS CITED

Altman, Rick. *The American Film Musical.* Bloomington: Indiana University Press, 1989.

———. "A Semantic/Syntactic Approach to Film Genre." In *Film Genre Reader,* edited by Barry Keith Grant, 26–40. Austin: University of Texas Press, 1986.

Bellour, Raymond. "Alternation, Segmentation, Hypnosis: Interview with Janet Bergstrom." *Camera Obscura* 3–4 (1979): 93.

Bukatman, Scott. "Paralysis in Motion: Jerry Lewis's Life as a Man." In *Comedy/Cinema/Theory,* edited by Andrew S. Horton, 188–205. Berkeley and Los Angeles: University of California Press, 1991.

Carringer, Robert L., ed. *The Jazz Singer.* Wisconsin/Warner Bros. Screenplay Series. Madison: University of Wisconsin Press, 1979.

Chatman, Seymour. *Story and Discourse: Narrative Structure in Fiction and Film.* Ithaca: Cornell University Press, 1978.

——. "What Novels Can Do That Films Can't (and Vice Versa)." In Mitchell, 117–36.

Custen, George F. *Bio/Pics: How Hollywood Constructed Public History.* New Brunswick, N.J.: Rutgers University Press, 1992.

Desser, David. "The Cinematic Melting Pot: Ethnicity, Jews, and Psychoanalysis." In *Unspeakable Images: Ethnicity and the American Cinema,* edited by Lester D. Friedman, 379–403. Urbana: University of Illinois Press, 1991.

Erens, Patricia. *The Jew in American Cinema.* Bloomington: Indiana University Press, 1984.

Friedman, Lester. *Hollywood's Image of the Jew.* New York: Ungar, 1982.

Gabbard, Krin. "Signifyin(g) the Phallus: *Mo' Better Blues* and Representations of the Jazz Trumpet." *Cinema Journal* 32, no. 1 (1992): 43–62.

Gabbard, Krin, and Glen O. Gabbard. *Psychiatry and the Cinema.* Chicago: University of Chicago Press, 1987.

Gabler, Neal. 1988. *An Empire of Their Own: How the Jews Invented Hollywood.* New York: Crown, 1988.

Goldman, Herbert G. *Jolson: The Legend Comes to Life.* New York: Oxford University Press, 1988.

Hoberman, J. *Bridge of Light: Yiddish Film between Two Worlds.* New York: Museum of Modern Art, 1991.

——. "The Show Biz Messiah." In *Vulgar Modernism: Writing on Movies and Other Media,* 64–68. Philadelphia: Temple University Press, 1991.

McClelland, Doug. *Blackface to Blacklist: Al Jolson, Larry Parks, and "The Jolson Story."* Metuchen, N.J.: Scarecrow, 1987.

Mitchell, W. J. T., ed. *On Narrative.* Chicago: University of Chicago Press, 1981.

Ray, Robert B. *A Certain Tendency of the Hollywood Cinema, 1930–1980.* Princeton: Princeton University Press, 1985.

Rogin, Michael. "Blackface, White Noise: The Jewish Jazz Singer Finds His Voice." *Critical Inquiry* 18(1992): 417–53.

Rosenblatt, Samuel. *Yoselle Rosenblatt: The Story of His Life as Told by His Son.* New York: Farrar, Straus and Young, 1954.

Sapoznik, Henry, with Pete Sokolow. *The Compleat Klezmer.* Cedarhurst, N.Y.: Tara Publications, 1987.

Smith, Barbara Herrnstein. "Narrative Versions, Narrative Theories." In Mitchell, 209–32.

Wiseman, Rich. *Neil Diamond, Solitary Star.* New York: Dodd, Mead, 1987.

SEVEN

Raiders of the Lost Text: Remaking as Contested Homage in *Always*

Harvey R. Greenberg, M.D.

You cannot speak "on" such a text, you can only speak "in" it,
in its fashion, enter into a desperate plagiarism.
ROLAND BARTHES, *THE PLEASURE OF THE TEXT*

In poker, when cards are poorly shuffled and redealt the result is often a "ghost hand." If the last hand was good, its ghost is likely to be a poor, watered-down thing better left unplayed. In their long Hollywood history, most remakes of earlier films have been ghost hands, shallow attempts to trade on an original's smash success by using new stars, new technology, sometimes a new setting—but the remake is rarely as profitable as the first movie and artistically is best left unmade.[1]

By no means is remaking necessarily dictated by pursuit of gain alone. The new version may be sincerely or ironically intended as homage or satire; it may be intended to open up psychological-political possibilities latent in the original movie that its makers were unaware of, or that could not be pursued because of censorship (e.g., Blake Edwards's *Victor, Victoria* [1982]—a remake of a now forgotten German film of the thirties with a much more suppressed homoerotic subtext).[2]

Steven Spielberg's purposes in rehashing the World War II chestnut *A Guy Named Joe* (1943) into *Always* (1990) would appear to be located well beyond the profit principle. That war has been the director's preferred locale in many of his pictures: *1941* (1979), two of the *Indiana Jones* cycle (*Raiders of the Lost Ark* [1981] and *Indiana Jones and the Last Crusade* [1989]), and the underrated *Empire of the Sun* (1987).

Spielberg's father served as a radio operator with a B-25 bomber squadron in Burma as a young man (Tallmer, 1). Spielberg is proud of his parent's military career but has not spoken about any impact it might have had upon specific filmmaking choices. He clearly admires the hometown and frontline virtues commended by the media of the time—all that boyish spunk and good-humored doing without. He's been particularly enchanted by *A Guy Named Joe* since adolescence, has seen the film numerous times,

"What are you trying to do — win this war single-handed?"

Figure 15. An oedipal confrontation occurs, as teacher (Spencer Tracy), backed by his sidekick (Ward Bond), faces student (Van Johnson) in *A Guy Named Joe* (1943).

and greatly admires its director, Victor Fleming. He says he's always wanted to make an old-fashioned love story like the one in *Joe,* instead of the action spectaculars that have been his hallmark (Steranho, 46).

A Guy Named Joe was actually a slight piece of business scripted rather lumpishly by Dalton Trumbo and redeemed by Victor Fleming's crisp direction. Daredevil pilot Spencer Tracy, madly in love with free-spirited airperson Irene Dunne, loses his life diving on a Nazi ship, then joins a spectral squadron of dead heroes with a mission to instruct a new generation of live ones. Tracy's prize student, Van Johnson, falls for Dunne. By the conclusion, Tracy has renounced his jealousy, recapitulating the renunciation theme privileged in *Casablanca* and other World War II movies. He proudly lets Dunne go "out of my heart" into a star-spangled future with Johnson.

Tracy's sidekick in *A Guy Named Joe* is the sturdy Ward Bond. (See figure 15.) John Goodman, as an oafish replicant of the sidekick character, Al Yackey, that Bond played, asserts at the beginning of *Always* that there's no good war to be found in contemporary America:

Figure 16. Oedipal triangulation figures in *Always* (1989), as Richard Dreyfuss observes Holly Hunter in the arms of Brad Johnson. Photograph by John Shannon.

AL: What this place reminds me of is the war in Europe . . . which I personally was never at, but think about it. . . . [T]he beer is warm, the dance hall's a quonset, there's B26's outside, hotshot pilots inside, an airstrip in the woods. . . . It's *England,* man, everything but Glenn Miller! Except you go to burning places and bomb 'em until they stop burning. You see, Pete, there is no war here. This is why they don't make movies called *Night Raid in Boise, Idaho,* or *Firemen Strike at Dawn.* And this is why you're not exactly a hero for taking the chances you take. You're more of what I would call—a dickhead.

As implied in Al's speech, Spielberg's enterprise is to have the war refought, but by brave pilots who put out raging forest fires with chemicals dropped from ancient planes, like the ones his father flew. There are such outfits, and they do run enormous risks. But the director reduces his relocated narrative to negligible sound and fury—roaring piffle unable to carry the weight of the original's perilous combat context.[3]

As leads, Richard Dreyfuss and Holly Hunter own all the sexual spark of *Peanuts* kids. (See figure 16.) They bed tastefully, without a jot of sensuality. Both are literally dwarfed by their earlier counterparts. Spielberg nods to feminism by using Hunter in a role that clearly means to reprise her feisty producer in *Broadcast News* (1987), much as he used Karen Allen in *Raiders of the Lost Ark* as a tough-minded foil for Harrison Ford. By the end of *Raiders,* Allen had been reduced to an impotent screaming meemie. In *Always,* whether due to direction or scripting, Hunter's Dorinda has become a querulous tomboy. Dunne's read of the character is vastly more adult, competent, and sensuous on or off the ground. Intriguingly, her (and Tracy's) eroticism gains a keener edge from the implicit lack of consummation to their passion.

In *Always,* the couple's dialogue aims for the lucid sassiness of thirties and forties movies that conspicuously foregrounded equal footing between the sexes. But all too often lines reprise *The Goonies* (1985) rather than *Adam's Rib* (1949). Lacking the poignant edge of universal wartime insecurity, Dreyfuss and Hunter indulge inane New Age chatter about commitment, your thing, my thing, and so forth.[4] The oddly juvenile—and asexual—quality of their relationship infects Spielberg's work more definitively than ever, thoroughly subverting the unabashed romanticism of his project away from the bedroom as well.

In *A Guy Named Joe,* Tracy slow dances with Dunne at the officers' club, while a single flyer eyes her speculatively. In *Always,* at a dance in the firefighters' canteen, Hunter is besieged by a horde of grimy smoke jumpers who ogle and paw at her like moonstruck Boy Scouts. The sequence could have been filmed at sleep-away camp.

In the main, *Always* rates as an unfortunate ghost hand (about ghosts). The screenplay unwittingly telegraphs its own obituary via Yackey's admonition to Pete. *Always* is instructive about Spielberg's increasing blind spots: his childlike predilection for wretched excess, visually and aurally; his simple-minded admiration for male-bonded professionalism celebrated in the movies of Howard Hawks and John Ford; and, above all, his unreflective hankering—similar to Pete's—after what he evidently valorizes as an ideologically simpler era he never lived through (Spielberg was born in 1947) but chiefly experienced via its pop culture artifacts.

Essentially, *Always* interprets as a postmodern fantasy based on an agit-prop version of the war—one cracked mirror held up to another, Baudrillardian simulacra both. Whatever its shortcomings, *A Guy Named Joe* did possess a substantive ideological agenda. The film sought to console audiences that their loved ones weren't *really* dead—merely translated to a newer realm of struggle (Kael, 92–93). It aimed at alleviating the guilt of women who found new men after their husbands or boyfriends had been killed. It virtually elided any notion of fear or panic in combat, purveying the message that no matter how rough the fighting got, an American soldier would still acquit himself with grace and good humor even as he died.[5] Finally, *A Guy Named Joe* strongly promoted the value of teamwork over rugged individualism. In a sense, Pete had to die to learn from his ghostly new compatriots that the war could not be won by a seat-of-the-pants soloist.[6]

Compared to its source, *Always* is radically drained of ideological freight.

Yackey's "dickhead" speech reads as a Barthesian "inoculation" against the recognition that practically *nothing* except tepid romance is at stake in this juvenile text with its infantilized characters.[7] Spielberg centrally privileges nostalgia and pastiche, that mimesis of dead styles from the "imaginary museum" addressed by Jameson and other cultural critics.[8]

The film is resolutely ignorant of or uncaring about actual history;[9] for all its feminist pretensions, its sexual politics are deeply, if unpolemically, conservative. It is profoundly informed by the "aesthetic *frisson* in emptiness"[10] so often encountered in recent remakes and sequels. I have elsewhere addressed the articulating psychosocial factors and film industry practices implicated in this monumental vacuity, which emerged during Hollywood's virulent pursuit of blockbuster profits in the late seventies and eighties (Greenberg, 1993).

My specific psychoanalytic interest in *Always* is the intensely rivalrous spirit inhabiting Spielberg's "homage." Harold Bloom (1973) has theorized that many of the strongest poets were compelled by their anxiety about a predecessor's power to deviate sharply from his praxis. Instead of employing Bloom's "swerve," Spielberg plunges unabashedly into *A Guy Named Joe.* The metaphor is literally fleshed out in the establishing sequence of *Always,* a peaceful scene of two men fishing on a lake. Behind them, a hug PBX seaplane descends. Its foreshortened image slowly fills the screen, wavering ominously in the lambent air, until the anglers, alerted by the sudden, terrifying roar of its engines, dive out of their canoe, barely escaping destruction as the plane swoops down upon them.

This arresting sequence is extremely difficult to place within the film's narrative schema. It can only be linked diegetically with an anecdote Dorinda-Hunter relates to her new lover more than halfway through the film, about a flying vacation she took with Pete-Dreyfuss in a PBX seaplane rigged as a "scoop" craft. From the air, Pete saw a fire in a small town courthouse. He scooped up water from a nearby lake, dove upon the conflagration, completely missed the courthouse and disastrously flooded the town. Dorinda bubbles with laughter as she relates the episode. Her humor rings curiously callous for a character presented as so empathic, especially when one considers the misery that must have resulted from Pete's blunder.

The introduction may have been intended as a "raid" on audience sensibility reminiscent of the thunderclap establishing sequence of *Close Encounters of the Third Kind* (1977); perhaps the opening was also meant to anticipate Dorinda's tale about Pete's scooping water from the town lake. The connection in the conscious narrative between the two cinematic events is at best obscure. I suggest that this very tenuousness, along with Dorinda's unsympathetic humor, may be understood analytically as symptoms of an intriguing textual uneasiness, that it exemplifies strategies of isolation and crude denial, defenses against the occulted awareness within the film's text of its own bristling competitiveness with the original narrative. Under this rubric, the men in the boat, the town, and its people can be taken as one entire symbol of the source film, which Spielberg has raided and swamped in transgressive adulation.

Throughout *Always,* Spielberg and his writers tamper egregiously with scenes from *A Guy Named Joe* that worked adequately, adding a punched-up sound track and overwrought visuals. To cite but one example: in the original film's climax, Dunne steals the plane Van Johnson was supposed to pilot in a solo suicide mission, and bombs a Japanese ammunition dump, aided by the ghostly Tracy. The special effects in the sequence are modestly spectacular, thoroughly in style for a war film of the time. As Dunne returns to home base, Tracy speaks eloquently of the wonderful life waiting for her. She lands, and Tracy bids her good-bye.

Spielberg has Hunter steal the plane to extinguish a blaze that has trapped a platoon of smoke jumpers in a hard-to-reach mountain site. The pyrotechnics and acoustics of Hunter's overflight rival Luke Skywalker's run at the Deathstar. Afterward, Dreyfuss gives the Tracy farewell speech, virtually unchanged. The plane then stalls, crashes into the water and sinks like a stone. Hunter, in extremis and goggle-eyed, momentarily *sees* Dreyfuss. He pulls her to the surface, a few feet from the runway where her new lover is waiting. She walks toward him, Dreyfuss bids her good-bye, end of story.

Spielberg obviously must have believed these hyperbolic, clumsy changes (of which making Dreyfuss *visible* is the most risible, the latent rendered absurdly blatant) were artistically justifiable, satisfying elaborations. But inflicting them upon the yeoman work of the original appears as questionable as the enterprise of the Yiddish theater entrepreneur who earlier in the century advertised his company's production of *Hamlet* as a "*shoyshpil fun Vilyam Shekspir—farendert un farbesert*"—drama by Shakespeare, changed and improved.[11] One cannot know if the impresario was only repeating a hoary theatrical precedent: convincing himself he was after all only doing for Shakespeare what he believed Shakespeare had accomplished for Hollingshead.

The central issue for the purposes of this discussion is not the merits of *Always* relative to *A Guy Named Joe;* rather, it is the extraordinary merit the latter has "always" held for Steven Spielberg, along with the attendant possibility that an unconscious, oedipally driven competitiveness comprises the dark side of Spielberg's intense admiration for the original and its director. Some evidence can be adduced on this score from several anecdotes in Spielberg's biography.

The senior Spielberg has a background in electrical engineering, and he helped design early computer technology. He comes across as a pragmatic, hard-driving individual intensely passionate about scientific progress, equally passionate about conveying the wonders of the universe to an impressionable and admiring youngster: "With Dad everything was precision, accuracy. . . . He had the fastest slide rule in Arizona and spoke two languages: English and Computer. When I was a five-year-old kid in New Jersey . . . my dad woke me up in the middle of the night and rushed me into our car in my night clothes. . . . He had a thermos of coffee and had brought blankets, and we drove for about half an hour. We finally pulled over to the side of the road, and there were a couple hundred people, lying on their backs in the middle of the night, looking up at the sky. My dad found a place, spread the blanket out, and we both lay down. . . . He pointed to the sky, and there was a magnificent meteor shower . . . " (Margolis and Modderno, 102). This potent memory would later form the organizing stimulus for *Close Encounters of the Third Kind.*

Spielberg's first filmmaking experience involved emulation of, and competition with, his father: "A long, long time ago, I became interested in movie-making simply because my father had an eight-millimeter movie camera, which he used to log the family history. I would sit and watch the home movies and criticize the shaky camera movements and bad exposures until my father finally got fed up and told me to take over. I became the family photographer and logged all our trips" (Margolis and Modderno, 142, 144).

It would not be untoward to suggest that Spielberg's father thus inadvertently launched his son's career. Another episode speaks more pointedly to youthful rivalrous feelings. When Spielberg was eleven, his father came home and gathered the family in the kitchen: "He held up a tiny little transistor he had brought home and said: 'This is the future.' I took the transistor from his hand. . . . And I swallowed it. Dad laughed, then he didn't laugh; it got very tense. It was like the confrontation scene between Raymond Massey and James Dean in *East of Eden.* One of those moments when two worlds from diametrically opposite positions in the universe collide. It was as if I was saying, 'That's your future, but it doesn't have to be mine' " (Spielberg 62).

Spielberg's quotation from *East of Eden* is illuminating. In the movie, James Dean gives a classic performance as Cal Trask, a rebellious late adolescent desperately struggling to overcome his father's perennial displeasure, while wrestling with his own formidable ambivalence. The father is a stern, religious farmer who, like Spielberg's parent, worships scientific progress. He sustains massive losses in an ill-advised effort to send iced-down vegetables cross-country by rail. The scene Spielberg alludes to occurs after the father refuses to accept the gift of "dirty" money Cal made in crop-futures speculation during World War I. One notes that Cal's "tainted" agricultural enterprise was a spectacular success, whereas the father's failed abysmally, albeit "honorably," from the latter's censorious viewpoint.

Steinbeck's novel and the film derived from it are elsewhere singularly rich in oedipal resonances. Cal competes keenly with his brother Aaron for the father's love, as well as for Adam's fiancée. He seeks out his mother, a promiscuous hellion disowned by the father, now turned brothel owner, borrows money for his agricultural ventures from her, and later exposes her to Aaron after his father's rejection. Aaron's "good" persona obviously prefigures the preternaturally upright, idolized envied/resented paternal imago for Cal.

One may wonder if Spielberg discovered an analogous idealized father-rival in Victor Fleming. The leitmotif of *A Guy Named Joe* is the struggle in its hero's heart with another aviator over the same love object. Did a similar competition exist in Spielberg's psyche with Fleming, "possession" of the original film its aim, anxiety upon the prospect of fulfilling that aim inevitable?

From this perspective, Pete's "accidental" flooding of the town in Dorinda's tale takes on the ambiguous valence of a Freudian slip, where conflicted motive lies concealed beneath a gratuitous facade. Pete's surprising incompetence may be construed as a mask for Spielberg's ambivalent designs on *A Guy Named Joe* and its creator. It may be speculated that the director aimed consciously to "hit the target," that is, exhibit appropriate obeisance toward Fleming and his work, but could not resist indulging in a species of cinematic overkill and went considerably wide of the mark.

No proof should be drawn from the above that Spielberg is particularly "neurotic." One speaks here only to the presence—and possible influence—of unconscious conflictual residues in the director's films. On the evidence of biographical material as well as his own brief autobiography, he seems an engaging, assertive individual, who has labored exceptionally well under the stresses of his idiosyncratic craft, devoted to family and friends off the job.[12]

Setting aside the incidents previously described, there seems to have been little overt serious conflict between Spielberg and his father. He speaks of him consistently with affection and evidently remained close to him following his parents' divorce in his mid-teens. Spielberg has spoken of his mother with equal approval and not a little awe: "She had more energy than a hundred mothers her age. The image I have of her is of this tiny woman climbing to the top of a mountain, standing there with her arms out and spinning around. My mom was always like a little girl, who never grew out of her pinafore. . . . [S]he left a large wake" (Spielberg, 62).

While somewhat estranged from peers during late childhood and adolescence—accounts of the nature, degree, and hurtfulness of his alienation vary considerably from one report to the next—Spielberg indicates that life at home was generally happy. The temperamental differences between his parents did cause him distress, related by the director with characteristic boyish diffidence: "My mom and dad were so different. That's probably why they were attracted to each other. They both love classical music . . . [but] aside from that, they had nothing in common. . . . My mother was a classical pianist. She would have chamber concerts with her musician friends, in the living room, while in another room my father would be conferring with nine or ten other men in the business about how to build a computerized mousetrap. These opposite lifestyles would give me circuit overload. My tweeters would burn out and my only insulation would be my bedroom door[,] which remained closed for most of my life. I had to put towels under the jamb so I couldn't hear the classical music and the computer logic. . . . " (Spielberg, 62).

Spielberg's account could have been drawn from the pages of a Thomas Mann novel. He depicts himself as a suburban Tonio Kroger, his identifications riven between an artistically inclined, emotive mother and a burgher-like father firmly anchored in scientific and business reality.

It can be reasonably argued on the basis of available sources that the director emerged from the oedipal vicissitudes of early childhood with balanced, loving perceptions of his father—indeed of both parents. Against this favorable background, with further unstinting parental affection he was able to weather the internal turmoil and external stresses of his adolescence. Drawing upon his native creative endowment, he eventually forged a primary identification with his mother's artistic inclinations, but also internalized his father's scientific interests and business acumen. The result is the adult of today: an auteur-producer-entrepreneur extraordinaire, exceptionally skillful at Hollywood's intricate business and passionate in advancing the technical parameters of filmmaking, whose eyes are fixed literally and figuratively upon the stars.

However even an immensely successful, stable son who enjoys a harmonious relationship with his parents may still harbor considerable unconscious fantasy referable to childhood traumata, including the oedipal struggle. When that son is an artist, such fantasies may fuel his art, successfully or quite otherwise. For instance, Spielberg has little to say about the impact of his parents' separation, but its signature is written poignantly across the characters of Elliot in *E.T.* and Carry Guffey's wonderful toddler in *Close Encounters.*

Both are children of divorce, each the apple of his mother's eye (like Spielberg), uncontested victor on the oedipal field—a contest no little boy really wants to win. Each bears the stigmata of paternal loss—loneliness and longing openly articulated by Elliot and wordlessly by the younger child in his delighted tropism toward the blinding presence on the other side of the door. Recuperation of the father's absence is accomplished for both in a relationship with alien voyagers, themselves condensations of omnipotent father and achingly vulnerable child.

Human paternal surrogates in these and other Spielberg films are frequently portrayed as impersonal authoritarian oppressors or benevolent facilitators. Alternately, positive and negative paternal images are condensed in a single character. In *Close Encounters*, the polarization is manifested on the one hand by the officers who attempt to thwart Roy Neary and his fellow visionaries from realizing their quest, and on the other by Lacombe, the luminously intelligent director of the secret mountain project whose intervention sends Neary across the galaxy.

In *E.T.*, Keys, the leader of the team dispatched by the government to apprehend Elliot's "visitor," initially is presented as a cold, impersonal bureaucrat (Spielberg deliberately keeps him and his minions faceless in their early appearances). As the tale unfolds, Keys evolves into an increasingly sympathetic character. He can empathize with Elliot's neediness because of his own childhood yearning for an "E.T."

These divided representatives may be taken as embodiments of the child Spielberg's ambivalent perceptions of paternity—oedipally shaded, as-yet-unintegrated imagos of the powerful, beloved father who unveils the heavens to his adoring son, or the no less powerful, harsh authority figure who seeks to impose his iron will upon his resentful offspring. The negative side of the equation is further darkened by the specter of paternal abandonment, which appears to persistently haunt the director's imagination: abandonment through divorce in *E.T.* and *Close Encounters* (Spielberg's adolescent experience, projected backward upon those films' youngsters?), or through rank indifference in the case of Indiana Jones's work-obsessed father[13] and of the neglectful, fast-lane yuppie lawyer that a middle-aged Peter Pan has become in *Hook* (1992).[14]

I have noted in an earlier essay on Fellini that "the connection between the artist's triumphs or disasters in his creative life or his mundane affairs is incompletely understood at this stage of psychoanalytic theory" (Greenberg, 1975, 67). Pathobiography is an especially risky venture, often vitiated by dubious reportage, bias (including the myths artists spin around themselves), and scant clinical information. Freud himself acknowledged the limitations of interrogating Leonardo's oeuvre on the basis of a few historical details and a single, if trenchant, dream.

Acknowledging the fragmentary and inferential nature of supporting evidence, I submit that an oedipal gloss does offer modestly plausible grounds (internally plausible, that is, in terms of depth psychology) upon which to explicate the overreaching and excessive contrivance of *Always*. The only Spielberg film to treat heterosexual romance at length imbricates sexuality in a triangulation between two heroes and the woman they both love. The theme is common and ancient—and one that would seem to have proven particularly thorny for the director.

Other causes within and external to Spielberg's psyche life that may have contributed to the film's aesthetic deficiencies must also be properly recognized: these include other directorial psychodynamics[15] and the dynamics of collaborators; financial and other "realistic" exigencies; and the creative limitations of other major or minor players in the production.

Setting aside Spielberg's specific difficulties in remaking *A Guy Named Joe,* it does not seem untoward to suggest that an intrinsic oedipal configuration lies deeply embedded in the remaking process, waiting to be evoked in the triangle between remaker, maker, and the original movie—the more troublesome to the degree that the source is perceived by its remaker as a mysterious, ultimately unavailable plenitude.[16] Barthes's remarks on the text as maternal object, and the oedipal thrust of narrativity seem apposite here:

> The writer is someone who plays with his mother's body . . . in order to glorify [and] embellish it. (Barthes, 37)

> Doesn't every narrative lead back to Oedipus? Isn't storytelling always a way of searching for one's original, speaking one's conflict with the Law, entering into the dialectic of tenderness and hatred? (Barthes, 47)

Pace other contributing factors, one speculates on the extent to which the shape (perhaps the quality as well) of remaking depends upon the project's oedipal significance for the remaker—notably, on how competitive strivings evoked by the maker and source are processed intrapsychically and artistically.[17] (An oedipal dynamic would clearly have greatest impact when a director or another personality under its sway exerts central influence over the remaking project.)[18]

Depth exploration of this issue lies beyond the scope of this inquiry, but several possible outcomes can be tentatively advanced for those cinematic "cases" where the original may have a significant oedipal meaning for the remaker:

1. The text exists under the sign of unwavering idealization; the remaker forswears competitive designs and remains unreflectively, even stultifyingly "faithful," to it.

2. The remaker, analogous to a creative resolution of childhood and adolescent oedipal conflict, eschews destructive competition with the maker, taking the original as a point of useful, relatively unconflicted departure.

3. The original, as signet of paternal potency and maternal unavailability-refusal, incites the remaker's unalloyed negativity. This precipitates a savage, contemptuous attack upon the original, in which its significant elements are erased, disfigured, and/or parodied.

4. The remaker, simultaneously worshipful and envious of the maker, enters into an ambiguous, anxiety-ridden struggle with a film he

both wishes to honor and eclipse. Caught up in contested homage, he eclipses his own native gifts—one ventures that this was the case with Spielberg in *Always*—dwindling to a hopelessly compromised raider of the lost text.

NOTES

1. Michael B. Druxman's *Make It Again, Sam: A Survey of Movie Remakes* remains the most comprehensive investigation of Hollywood remaking practice to date. Druxman views remaking as a function of industry pragmatism, variously undertaken because of "product" shortages; the cost effectiveness of recycling previous scripts; the profit potential of deploying new stars and techniques in proven vehicles, et cetera. He describes the transformation of some thirty films at length and cites many other remakes briefly. His approach is avowedly more anecdotal than hermeneutic.

The following common remake categories are based upon Druxman's work, and my overview of the subject:

The acknowledged close remake: The original film is replicated with little or no change. Advertising and press book material may inform viewers of the remaker's intention to hew to the previous movie's narrative and characters. Verisimilitude often constitutes a strong selling point. Notable examples are found in the Biblical epic subgenre (e.g. *Ben Hur,* 1907, 1925, 1959).

The acknowledged transformed remake: Transformations of character, plot, time, and setting are more substantive than in the acknowledged close remake. The original movie is openly, but variably, mentioned as a source, and mention ranges from a small screen credit to significant promotional foregrounding. Remakes in this category during the past two decades include *A Star Is Born* (1976), *Heaven Can Wait* (1978), *Stella* (1990), and *Always* (1990).

The unacknowledged, disguised remake. Major alterations are undertaken in time, setting, gender, or—most particularly—genre. The audience is deliberately uninformed about the switches. Disguised remaking peaked roughly from the thirties through the early fifties—the heyday of the studio system, when the relentless demand for new films, wedded to a perennial lack of fresh "material," compelled frequent reuse of earlier screenplays. Any list of disguised remakes would be formidable. See Druxman, particularly pp. 13–24, for examples.

2. The second volume of William Luhr and Peter Lehman's study of Blake Edwards's oeuvre (*Returning to the Scene*) undertakes an elegant inquiry into the complex, usually unacknowledged aesthetic and ideological premises of remaking. Edwards is cited as a consummate improviser who refuses to valorize the original as a historically fixed, forever completed project. He assays "not so much . . . to remake the film as . . . to replicate the conditions that allowed the film to be made . . . [returning] to the creative moment when the original film could have developed in any number of directions" (209–210). Again, his "remakes often question the premises of what they reprise, and often attempt to reformulate the mainstream cinema of which they are a part . . . " (224).

Corollary to Luhr and Lehman's theories, Robert Eberwein suggests that a remake always exists under the sign of erasure, effecting "a kind of reconstruction of the original. . . . Erasing it [presents] an opportunity to recuperate the voyeuristic lack we experience in our viewing of the original . . . " ("Remakes Writing under Erasure," presented at the Florida State University Conference on Literature and Film, 1988, 3). Eberwein suggests that the remaker's efforts invade implicitly forbidden territory, analogous to the child's "invasion" of the primal scene.

Allusions to material from previous films have been escalating in American cinema since the seventies. In effect, these comprise remakes in miniature, embedded *pars pro toto* in the "parent" film's associative matrix. Noël Carroll's authoritative study of allusions provides valuable insights into the remaking of an entire film, as well as the citation of its parts (51–81).

3. Spielberg's production team consulted with government and private firefighting agencies during the making of *Always*. The film's numerous departures from fire-fighting realities thus do not proceed from ignorance, but rather seem to have been dictated by a combination of melodramatic license (for instance, had Pete actually dropped chemicals from his craft upon Al Yackey's burning plane, the latter would most certainly have crashed), the director's penchant for hyperbole, and sexism. Holly Hunter's Dorinda is one of a few female personnel at the fire-fighting station and related locales, whereas the percentage of female smoke jumpers actually ranges from twenty-five to thirty. Pilots, however, are exclusively male as of this writing. (Information supplied by Arnold Hartigan, Public Affairs Officer, Boise Interagency Fire Center, 3905 Vista Avenue, Boise, ID 83705).

4. In *A Guy Named Joe*, Pete is still subject to military discipline after his death. His squadron of ghostly "advisers" is commanded by an anonymous general (Lionel Barrymore), probably modeled after Billy Mitchell. He rebukes Pete for letting his jealousy affect his tutelage of Van Johnson, with a stirring homily about making the world safe for democracy. Corollary to its transformation of *Joe's* protagonists into New Age post-Reaganites, *Always* metamorphoses the squadron and its commander into Hap, a female angel-cum-EST facilitator (played with tooth-grinding sweetness by Audrey Hepburn). She gently chides Pete for his samsaric attachments with no-brainer epigrams that could have been culled from the back of Celestial Seasons tea bag packages.

5. I am indebted to Professor Krin Gabbard for these observations.

6. Robert B. Ray explores the tutoring of the American "loner" in films like *Casablanca* and *Air Force* (1943) on the communitarian values required for winning the war.

7. Ariel Dorfman comments tellingly on the trend toward infantilization in the mass culture of late-twentieth-century capitalism (145–53). Dorfman's arguments are exceptionally pertinent to Spielberg's oeuvre as director and producer in recent years.

8. "Pastiche is . . . the imitation of a peculiar or unique style, the wearing of a stylistic mask, speech in a dead language . . . " (Jameson, 16).

" . . . [I]n a world in which stylistic innovation is no longer possible, all that is left is to imitate dead styles, to speak through the masks and with the voices of the styles in the imaginary museum . . . " (18).

9. "[T]he very style of nostalgia films [is] invading and colonizing even those movies today which have contemporary settings: as though . . . we are unable today to focus on our own present, as though we have become incapable of achieving aesthetic representations of our own current experience . . . an alarming and pathological symptom of a society that has become incapable of dealing with time and history. . . . [W]e seem condemned to seek the historical past through our own pop images and stereotypes about that past, which itself remains forever out of reach" (20).

10. "American political life has never been a consistently reliable source of sustenance; and most people who grew up in the '50s and '60s have come to count, for their sense of value and style and even identity, on the ambient culture that has given postwar American life its special richness. . . . [T]his culture seems to have reached a very high level of technical accomplishment, and then to have run out of anything fresh to say. . . . [It] seems thrillingly vacant. The wonderful package has nothing inside. . . . There is a genuine aesthetic *frisson* in emptiness . . . " (22).

11. I am indebted for this transliteration to Zachary Bayer, chief librarian of the YIVO Institute for Jewish Research, 1048 Fifth Avenue, New York, NY 10028.

12. Inter alia, above interviews; Mott and McAlister Saunders; Smith, 135–45.

13. According to the history supplied by *Indiana Jones and the Last Crusade* (1989), Professor Henry Jones is a noted medievalist caught up with proving the historical reality of the holy grail. The death of his wife left him to raise his son. His scholarly obsession and unremitting criticism made the latter revolt against his authority. During his teens, Indy left home to pursue his own peculiar archaeological ambitions. The stormy relationship of Jones Senior and Junior echoes the fractiousness of Adam and Cal Trask in *East of Eden,* previously cited by Spielberg in describing the signatory moment of rebellion against his own father.

The Last Crusade openly portrays angry division between father and son as in no other Spielberg film to that date. The Joneses' search for the grail is a rather heavy-handed symbol of their quest to heal their rift. Their mutual competitiveness is enormous; vis-à-vis the oedipal motif in *Always,* the film has Indy unknowingly sleep with the same woman his father had bedded in aid of finding the grail.

14. In *Hook,* business pressures and the strain of repressing his fabulous past have diminished Peter Pan—now Peter Banning—to a dim shadow of his former self. He is specifically estranged from his latency-age son, whom Hook woos after kidnapping him with promises of being a better father.

In an overview of Spielberg's career, I noted that every privileged Spielbergian psychological theme is folded into *Hook:* childhood as paradise, heart over head, the middle-class family menaced from without and within—and chiefly a father who has to rise above his failings to save the day. I further speculated that Spielberg may have identified both with Banning-Pan and the son, insofar as *Hook* was meant to rescue the director himself from a midlife creative stall. The film arguably afforded him an opportunity to continue the project of *Indiana Jones and the Last Crusade:* to process again a variety of youthful traumata, including his parents' divorce, and, centrally, to heal the narcissistic wounds caused by the failure of *Always* with another blockbuster success (44–48, 80, 83).

15. Such as, for instance, a preoedipal-oral relationship between the remaker and the original film, informed by primitive wishes for incorporation by, and fusion with, the "materialized" source. In this regard, see Holland's analysis of the reader's oral relationship with the literary text (63–103).

16. My remarks are obviously pitched at the oedipal relationship between a male remaker and his subject, predicated upon the industry-driven reality that virtually all remaking has been done by men of films made by other men. I have so far been unable to discover remaking of a "male" original undertaken by a female director or other key female cinema figure (and I welcome information on this subject). In the highly unlikely circumstance of a woman remaking another woman's film, the elaboration of an Electra configuration around the source movie, corresponding to the male oedipal dynamic, seems plausible.

17. The articulation between neurotic conflict and artistic effectiveness must be viewed as exceptionally problematic. It is analytically naive to suppose that in every instance a serious oedipal conflict related to the original film would necessarily compromise the aesthetic effectiveness of the remake. For instance, an oedipally motivated hostile "defacement" of the source film could still be accomplished through great art, if in a spirit of great contempt.

18. Since emerging as a major force in Hollywood, Spielberg usually wields this sort of influence over the pictures he directs. While in most cases he has not written the screenplays of his films (*Close Encounters* was a notable exception), crucial conceptual, narrative, and visual elements often reflect his choices. He is intimately bound up with script selection, then rewriting and/or interpretation during film production. Thus it may reliably be assumed that, much like Hitchcock, the salient psychodynamics of the screenplays he chooses to process closely reflect his own preoccupations.

WORKS CITED

Barthes, Roland. *The Pleasure of the Text.* New York: Hill and Wang, 1975.

Bloom, Harold. *The Anxiety of Influence: A Theory of Poetry.* New York: Oxford University Press, 1973.

Carroll, Noël. "The Future of Allusion: Hollywood in the Seventies (and Beyond)." *October* 20 (spring 1982).

Dorfman, Ariel. "The Infantilizing of Culture." In *American Media and Mass Culture: Left Perspectives,* edited by Donald Lazere. Berkeley and Los Angeles: University of California Press, 1988.

Druxman, Michael B. *Make It Again, Sam: A Survey of Movie Remakes.* New York: A. S. Barnes and Co., 1975.

Greenberg, Harvey R. "8 1/2: The Declensions of Silence." In *The Movies on Your Mind: Film Classics on the Couch from Fellini to Frankenstein.* New York: Saturday Review Press/E. P. Dutton, 1975.

———. "On the McMovie: Less Is Less at the Simplex." In *Screen Memories: Hollywood Cinema on the Psychoanalytic Couch.* New York: Columbia University Press, 1993.

———. "Spielberg on the Couch." *Movieline,* December 1992.

Holland, Norman N. "The 'Willing Suspension of Disbelief.' " In *The Dynamics of Literary Response*. New York: Oxford University Press, 1968.

Jameson, Frederic. "Postmodernism and Consumer Society." In *Postmodernism and its Discontents: Theories, Practices,* edited by E. Ann Kaplan. New York: Verso, 1988.

Kael, Pauline. "Review of *Always.*" *The New Yorker,* 8 January 1990.

Luhr, William, and Peter Lehman. *Returning to the Scene: Blake Edwards, Vol. 2.* Athens: Ohio University Press, 1989.

Margolis, Herbert, and Craig Modderno. "Interview with Steven Spielberg." *Penthouse,* February 1978.

Menand, Louis. "Don't Think Twice: Why We Won't Miss the 1980s." *The New Republic,* 9 October 1989.

Mott, Donald R., and Cheryl McAllister Saunders. *Steven Spielberg.* Boston: Twayne, 1986.

Ray, Robert B. *A Certain Tendency of the Hollywood Cinema, 1930–1980.* Princeton, N.J.: Princeton University Press, 1985.

Smith, Dian G. "Steven Spielberg." In *American Film Makers Today.* Dorest, Mass.: Blandford Press, 1983.

Spielberg, Steven. "The Autobiography of Peter Pan." *Time,* 15 July 1985.

Steranho, Jim. "Behind the Camera: A Candid Conversation about the Past and Future Films of Steven Spielberg," *Prevue* (November 1981): 46.

Tallmer, Jerry. "Jawing with Steven Spielberg." *The New York Post,* Entertainment Section, 28 June, 1975.

EIGHT

Double Takes:
The Role of Allusion in Cinema

John Biguenet

When, with the corpse of Agamemnon sprawled at her feet, the vengeful Clytemnestra confesses his murder, the unrepentant queen compares to morning dew the blood that spattered her as she struck the mortal blows against her husband: "I exulted as the sown cornfield exults / Drenched with the dew of heaven when buds burst forth in Spring" (1391–92). The bitter irony of the image would have echoed for Aeschylus's fellow Athenians far more innocent lines in the *Iliad* (Garner, 180): "And Menelaos was refreshed at heart / as growing grain is, when ears shine with dew, / and the fields ripple" (23.597–99).

For well over twenty-five hundred years, Western writers have invoked the authority of earlier works through the trope of allusion. Though the etymology of *allude* (deriving, of course, from the Latin *ludere*) may suggest a certain playfulness in the exercise of this device, the function of allusion has most often served the essential task of investing a work of literature with a lineage, a tradition, quite literally a context, within which an interpretation may be grounded. Thus provided, the reader will discover in the transposition of the old, known text onto the new, unknown text a dialectic of correspondences that will illuminate both works, demonstrating the relevance of the old and confirming the authority of the new.[1] Allusion is, therefore, one of the primary mechanisms by which authors themselves establish and maintain the canon.

However, the richness of the Western tradition poses its own problem. Working in genres that have existed for millennia, the contemporary author faces a dilemma similar to that of which Italian poets complain—everything rhymes. It is virtually impossible today to pluck a note on the poet's lyre that will not reverberate all along our three-or four-thousand-year-old tradition.

The filmmaker, however, working in a medium barely a century old, does not dance among so many graves. Though we speak of "classic" films, the adjective has far less resonance than in older art forms; cinema, after all, is in its infancy. So it is especially surprising to discover how common are allusions in films and how diverse is the taxonomy of cinematic strategies of alluding.

Though one might expect the construction of visual images to serve as the fundamental mechanism of alluding in films, the various forms of literary allusion are frequently employed. In fact, direct references to classic literary works, such as the Bible, are common. But gaining in frequency with the growth of mass media are allusions to popular culture. Music, both classical and popular, serves as another means of buttressing a film with an earlier work of art. But, far and away, cinematic allusions most frequently point to other films. Whether it be a direct reference by title or the inclusion of an actual clip from another film, a similarity to a famous character or a repetition of a classic shot, an imitation of a well-known scene or an allusion to an entire film genre, filmmakers demand of their audiences a knowledge of the history of cinema.[2] These subtle strategies of creating a subtext in a film through allusion constitute, in a very literal sense, the briefest form of "remaking."

As just noted, the filmmaker has the opportunity to use allusions of both literary and visual varieties. The visual arts have an ancient tradition of their own in the use of allusions. In the twentieth century, a tradition of "appropriations" has been established, running back at least to Marcel Duchamp's 1919 *L.H.O.O.Q.,* his famous altering of the Mona Lisa with a goatee and mustache. Is it mere vandalism or is it allusion writ large? Eschewing Duchamp's impudent wit, Francis Bacon demonstrated in his 1953 *Study after Velazquez' Portrait of Pope Innocent X* just how serious a work of art appropriation could engender. In fact, in the entire series of paintings Bacon completed based on the Velazquez portrait, we discover something of the same relationship of the contemporary to the classic as we do in film remakes.

However, the visual allusion often results in the creation of an icon, which, as Peter Wollen explains in paraphrasing Charles Sanders Peirce, "is a sign which represents its object mainly by its similarity to it; the relationship between signifier and signified is not arbitrary but is one of resemblance or likeness" (122).

From André Bazin to Christian Metz to Erwin Panofsky, the defense of realism as the vocation of cinema has been waged at the expense of the significance of iconography in cinema. Along with Roland Barthes, they castigate any attempt to employ imagery as a rhetorical strategy (Wollen, 147). Essentially, the visual is impugned as primitive. As Wollen notes, "[F]rom the early days of the film there has been a persistent, though understandable, tendency to exaggerate the importance of analogies with verbal language. The main reason for this, there seems little doubt, has been the desire to validate cinema as an art" (140). This argument finds its origins in the criticism of Baudelaire, who condemns photography to serve as the mere "handmaid of the arts" (297). But it is obviously self-delusion to minimize the visual in hopes of equating film with literature by asserting that it is fundamentally an extension of the verbal tradition. Wollen concludes his argument with an enthusiastic defense of imagery: "The film-maker is fortunate to be working in the most semiologically complex of all media, the most aesthetically rich. We can repeat today Abel Gance's words four decades ago: 'The time of the image has come' " (154).

If we are willing to join with Sergei Eisenstein and Josef von Sternberg in affirming the visual as a legitimate vocabulary and grammar in its own right, then we must not stop with verbal allusions in film but instead examine those images that convey references to other works of cinematic art.

But let us at least begin with the strictly literary allusions that are offered in films. Here, as elsewhere in a consideration of allusions, we are engaged in a meditation on the obvious. However, a patient examination of the obvious sometimes yields the unexpected.

The bitter prologue of Wolf Biermann's poem at the beginning of Lina Wertmuller's *Seven Beauties* (1976) is so integral to the work that it might not even be considered an allusion. However, the references in *My Own Private Idaho* (1991) to Shakespeare's *Henry IV* (as well as to Orson Welles's *Chimes at Midnight* [1967] seek to lift the small story of a band of male prostitutes into the company of such immortal tales of love and betrayal as Shakespeare's. Here literature is at its most useful to the filmmaker, elevating the merely sad to the tragic.

Similar in function are cinematic allusions to popular culture. In *Honeymoon in Vegas* (1992), Jack Singer, the mark in a gambling con, wins a pot with a full house of aces and eights, the "dead man's hand" that Wild Bill Hickok was holding when he was shot in the back; the attentive viewer will anticipate the ill fortune about to befall the young man. If one misses the allusion, which goes unremarked in the film, little is lost. But in *Children of Paradise* (1945), a similar reference to popular culture will soon require a footnote for its viewers. In the police inspector's questioning of Garance, there is an exchange about playing the violin like Monsieur Ingres. Jean-Auguste-Dominique Ingres was a fine painter, but his pretensions as a violinist were the joke of nineteenth-century France. Just as Jack Benny is still remembered for his wretched fiddling, poor Ingres was still invoked in scornful reproach of dilettantes in the first half of our century. Unfortunately for Marcel Carné, he hitched his wagon to a dying horse. With each passing year, those lines of the film become ever more obscure. Whenever an allusion on which a scene depends fades from memory, a lacuna spreads across the screen like a hole burning in a jammed frame.

Another nonvisual strategy, the self-consciously false elevation of light material through musical allusions, is the source of much parodic humor. How many times since the hero of *Rocky* (1976) first climbed the steps of the Philadelphia Museum of Art has the audience of another film endured his trumpet theme? Similarly, when the Big Kahuna rides a monster wave in *Back to the Beach* (1987), is anyone surprised to hear the march from *Raiders of the Lost Ark* (1981)? However, though an allusion to classical music rather than to another film, the use of Beethoven's setting of Schiller's "Ode to Joy" in *Die Hard* (1988) when the German terrorist succeeds in opening the vault perhaps offers a bit of comic relief in the intense action adventure.

But the most obvious method of cinematic allusion is literally mentioning another film. In *Truly, Madly, Deeply* (1991), the company of affable ghosts who invade the flat of a former lover of one of the deceased argue about whether to watch *Five Easy Pieces* (1970) or *Fitzcarraldo* (1982) on the VCR. Here the good taste of the departed goes a long way in establishing a new and modern characterization of ghosts. In *My Blue Heaven* (1990), Vinnie Antonelli, resplendent in a white suit, passes in front of a movie marquee advertising *White Hunter, Black Heart* (1990) as he escorts an attractive district attorney and her two sons to a baseball game. Always in question in the film is Vinnie's sincerity, so when the viewer sees him hauling the proceeds from a charity drive under the marquee a few days later, with only "Black Heart" visible overhead, the likely conclusion is drawn. Of course, the happy ending of the film contradicts our expectations, which have been established in part through the allusion to the title (rather than the film itself) of the current offering at the local movie house. As is often the case, these simplest allusions are directed to some narrow aspect of the film mentioned.

Some films employ a kind of cinematic quotation by working in clips from other films, a form of alluding only slightly less obvious than actually naming the other works. In *The Grey Fox* (1982), Bill Miner, an outlaw fresh from a stretch in the penitentiary for the robbery of a stagecoach, is inspired to change with the times when he sees his first movie, *The Great Train Robbery* (1905). In *Home Alone* (1990), clips from *Miracle on 34th Street* (1947) and *It's a Wonderful Life* (1946) (dubbed in French) fail to transform the hugely successful film into a Christmas movie. Though John Hughes does work in a sentimental holiday reunion of an old man and his estranged son, the film follows traditions that are very different, as I will argue below, from those in the classic holiday movies to which it alludes.

A film that uses a clip, among other strategies, in the development of a highly allusive structure is Mario Van Peebles's *New Jack City* (1991). Following an opening sequence that begins with the Statue of Liberty, Van Peebles introduces a thematic motif through allusions to I Corinthians 6:9–10 (edited to exclude the "effeminate" and the "covetous" from the iniquitous whom Saint Paul condemns). The Biblical verses, painted on the side of a ghetto building shown just after the opening sequence, return midway through the film in the sermon of the preacher at a police informer's funeral and again on the lips of an avenging old man in the conclusion. While Van Peebles works hard to demonstrate the morality of his message (even prefacing the video version with a monologue about the film's good intentions), he seems much more interested in placing his work in the long tradition of American gangster films. As Gee Money, the gang leader's lieutenant, crows after his discovery of crack cocaine, "Brother, we gonna come off like the mob."

The most unmediated allusion Van Peebles employs (in which an interpolated clip of another film functions as a kind of Greek chorus counterpointing the hero's hubris) is a private exhibition of *Scarface* (1983) in the midst of a New Year's Eve party. As Nino Brown and his gang watch the Marielito refugee and cocaine king Tony Montana in his final shoot-out, the woman who will eventually prove the gang's undoing assures Brown that "[t]he world is yours, Nino. Only you won't be as careless as Tony Montana." As he dances with the woman, who has now begun a striptease in front of the screen, the image of the dying Montana flits across Brown's shirt as he repeats, "The world is mine."

After his drug empire begins to crumble following police infiltration, he calls his lieutenants together. In a clear homage to Brian De Palma's *The Untouchables* (1987), Van Peebles seats the gang at a large table as Brown circles with a dog chain and cane, trying to establish blame for the disaster. In a sequence similar to a scene in which Al Capone beats one of his lieutenants to death with a baseball bat in retaliation for the loss of one of his illegal operations, Brown suddenly turns on his own responsible underling. But instead of continuing the allusion to *The Untouchables,* Van Peebles switches to one of the most famous scenes from *The Godfather* (1972). Drawing a sword from the cane, he drives it through the hand of his unfortunate accountant; then, as the surprised man writhes, Brown wraps the chain around his neck and is prevented from strangling his terrified victim only by the other gang members. The attack clearly mimics the murder of the Godfather's devoted bodyguard.

Finally, in the most explicit allusion to the tradition of gangster films, Brown exults, as he frolics in a huge indoor pool, that his life has turned into "some George Raft, some James Cagney type shit." Van Peebles is obviously quite anxious to drape *New Jack City* in the distinguished Hollywood mantle of the immigrant-turned-gangster tradition. Thus the film closes with a shot that flees the Manhattan skyline and leaves behind the Statue of Liberty, as if to reject the immigrant dream promised in the opening shot of the film.

In yet another motif developed through allusion, Van Peebles uses camera angles to enforce a sheer verticality in some of his shots. In the opening sequence, following a bird's-eye view of skyscrapers, the viewer witnesses Brown execute a man by having him dropped from a bridge. When Brown finally falls in the end, he is seen sprawled at the bottom of a spiraling staircase, in a shot reminiscent of *Vertigo* (1958). Through internal allusions to earlier shots, Van Peebles is able to suggest the rise and fall of Nino Brown.

The possible allusion to *Vertigo* raises the interesting question of whether certain shots become so well known that they cease to serve as allusions and become mere conventions. Hitchcock's film has little to do with *New Jack City,* and up to this point in his film, Van Peebles has chosen his allusions very carefully. It makes little sense to insist upon every boom shot of a spiral staircase as an allusion to *Vertigo*.

Many apparent allusions may, in fact, fulfill quite different functions. *Dream On,* a situation comedy on HBO, intercuts very brief clips from cinema and television to comment on the action or to dramatize the hero's thoughts. Serving as a kind of Greek chorus (as in *New Jack City*), these clips are actually closer to the metaphoric device developed in *Morgan!* (1966), where encounters with humans engender images of animals in the mind of the hero (a device that harks all the way back to Eisenstein's *Strike* (1924)). If the reference does not invoke the subject of the work itself or at least its title, it makes little sense to describe it as an allusion. Thus, the singing kitchen boy in the vast, vertical sets of *The Cook, the Thief, His Wife & Her Lover* (1989) cannot be said to allude to a similar singing boy and high sets in the little-seen *Scrooge* (1935). Nor can the Paula Abdul music video *Cold Hearted* (1989), whose choreography echoes the dance staged in the rehearsal hall for nervous investors in *All That Jazz* (1979), be said to allude to that film. Although the two highly erotic dance sequences are similar in the use of scaffolding, pilot's hats, group groping, and flustered spectators, the music video is interested only in the choreography, not the subject, of the Bob Fosse film. Perhaps it is best to consider such coincidences a homage to the earlier work rather than an allusion.

A similar problem presents itself when a filmmaker alludes to his or her own work. In *A Clockwork Orange* (1971), Stanley Kubrick impishly includes the sound track to his own *2001: A Space Odyssey* (1968) in the rack behind Alex when the nasty teenager picks up two girls in a record store midway through the film. Though clearly meant as no more of a joke than Hitchcock's brief appearances in his own films, the sharp-eyed viewer will not find the distraction a positive contribution to the film. Less disruptively, in

A Little Romance (1979), George Roy Hill hides his young lovers, awaiting their chance to kiss at sunset beneath the Venetian Bridge of Sighs, in a movie theater playing *The Sting* (1973), his earlier hit. Also, the film's opening montage includes Hill's *Butch Cassidy and the Sundance Kid* (1969) along with clips from films starring Humphrey Bogart, Burt Reynolds, and John Wayne. Movie allusions are so much a part of the characterization of one of the two children that the director may be forgiven for slipping in his own films. Another of such self-references appears in *Cat's Eye* (1985), based on a trio of Stephen King stories. When a father returns from tucking in his daughter, who is troubled by bad dreams, his wife is reading King's *Pet Sematary*. The humor of the inside joke leavens the horror of the tale by hinting at a kind of self-deprecating irony.

Since a sequel is, by nature, a self-referential allusion to an earlier work, it is not surprising to find numerous references to the first film included in the second. In fact, promotional materials for a sequel invariably focus on such allusions. The well-known signature line of Tobe Hooper's successful *Poltergeist* (1982) is the whining "They're he-ere!" Early trailers for the sequel, *Poltergeist II* (1986), began with the cute face of the same little girl who had been the object of the poltergeists' affections in the first film turning away from the static of a television set to inform us, "They're ba-ack!"

Steven Spielberg demonstrates a more innovative approach to allusion in his sequel to *Raiders of the Lost Ark*. In *Indiana Jones and the Temple of Doom* (1984), the eponymous hero is confronted by a pair of adversaries who approach him with a dazzling display of swordsmanship in assuming an *en garde* position. Jones, smiling, reaches for his revolver, as he had done to dispatch a similar virtuoso of the sword in the earlier film. This time, however, there is no gun: his holster is empty after he has bounced through a death-defying roller coaster ride in a coal hopper. So, with a smirk that he shares with the audience, the hero is forced to fight the two swordsmen. The pleasure of Jones's simple solution to the problem of an untutored modern man facing a master of a centuries-old martial art delighted viewers the first time but would have bored them if repeated. The second time around, the joke has to be on Jones. (It is tempting here, but mistaken, to suggest an allusion to the death by gunfire of the master swordsman in *Seven Samurai* [1954]. The melancholy image of the exquisite world of the samurai shattering in a burst of gunpowder is Kurosawa's nostalgic lament for a time when a master of an art could not be overcome by a ruffian with superior technology. Untroubled by melancholy, Spielberg knows it is unlikely that a Western audience, devoted as we are to such technology, will pause in our laughter over the corpse of the elegant and well-schooled swordsman of *Raiders of the Lost Ark* to consider what it is, precisely, that we applaud.)

Few contemporary filmmakers have so reveled in the use of cinematic allusion as Brian De Palma. Throughout his career, he has yielded to this device over and over again, thus presenting an excellent test case to see cinematic allusion in action.

There certainly can be no doubt about De Palma's intentions in his use of a baby carriage tottering on the broad marble steps of a railway station as federal agents shoot it out with mob goons in *The Untouchables*. Those viewers with even the vaguest notion of film history will recognize a homage to Eisenstein's most famous montage from *The Battleship Potemkin* (1925). While Eisenstein uses the Odessa Steps sequence to indict the cruelty of Czarist troops against the Russian people, the allusion in *The Untouchables* demonstrates the bravery and compassion of the state's representatives as they defend citizens against ruthless mobsters (who, in the first scene of the film, murder a child in the bombing of a shop). In both instances, the filmmakers wish to portray the unbridled savagery of a cruel regime—whether led by Nicholas II or Al Capone—and to imply that their own, current governments, in having opposed these earlier regimes, prove the morally superior authority. Though the villains are reversed—in one case the state and in the other the enemy of the state—the motive remains the same, and so the allusion succeeds.

However, when, in the more recent *Raising Cain* (1992), De Palma repeats the allusion to Eisenstein (and—ironically, one must suppose—to his own earlier use of the image in *The Untouchables*), its function is far more problematic. Detached from its original context and treated more as parody than as allusion, the baby carriage ceases to resonate as an image of society in jeopardy. Instead, the director's clumsy, self-conscious handling of the carriage destroys the suspense of the film's climax. In fact, it is difficult to explain the maniac's movement of a baby carriage, not down stairs but on an elevator, as anything other than a kind of in-joke for cineastes.

In De Palma's two homages to Eisenstein, the double edge of allusions is revealed. When an appropriate reference to an existing work is knit seamlessly into the fabric of a new film, the director invokes a context that enriches the film. But when the allusion is merely a wink and a nod to knowledgeable viewers, the effect is likely to undercut the narrative line of the film through the self-consciousness of the device. At its worst, it is a condescending gesture on the part of the director to acknowledge that he or she is superior to the material being presented: it becomes a snide joke for the elite.

Eisenstein's imperiled infant finds a brother, of sorts, in another endangered child of the cinema. In this film, however, both structure and subject depend upon allusions. The enormous success of this box-office hit suggests how fundamental allusions can be in the creation of a film.

In *Home Alone*, writer and producer John Hughes (in collaboration with his director, Chris Columbus) tells the story of an abandoned child who is menaced by two larcenous adults. Such a tale obviously descends from both a literary genre, the fairy tale, and a cinematic genre, the cartoon. In both traditions, the archetypal story recounts the adventures of a small and vulnerable creature who is imperiled by a large and fierce predator. To draw upon the rich psychological resonances of the fairy tale and the comic visual strategies of the cartoon, Hughes quite rightly resorts to allusion.

Kevin McCallister, the child who angrily wishes away his family and wakes to find his wish fulfilled, is typical of the young and resourceful heroes of "Hansel and Gretel" and "Jack and the Beanstalk." Facing the monstrous villainy of wicked adults, the children, separated from their parents, must save themselves by wit alone. The fate awaiting these innocents, once they are properly fattened by the warty witch or slobbering giant, is cannibalism. The profoundly dark intimations of a story in which adults feast on children need not be dredged up for examination in this discussion; it is enough to note that, as the climax of *Home Alone* approaches, the infuriated villain lifts the child's hand to his mouth to make good his threat to bite off the boy's fingers, one by one.

Having invoked the tradition of the fairy tale through such structural allusions, Hughes turns to the most famous endangered child of the genre, Little Red Riding Hood, to save Kevin from the devouring jaws of the wicked burglar. In both "Hansel and Gretel" and "Jack and the Beanstalk," the children effect their own escape from the clutches of their evil captors. But the moral lesson embodied in the tale of a self-sufficient child, superior to adults and fully prepared to survive without his family, might trouble parents (and they, after all, are the ones who pay for the tickets to the movies). So Hughes rather gracelessly hands over Kevin to his enemies, to sport with the boy according to their vile whims. Hung from a peg, Kevin endures a terrifying recitation of how the villains plan to punish his temerity in opposing them. But at the very moment they are about to take their revenge on the helpless child, an old neighbor, whom Kevin has earlier encouraged to reunite with his estranged son, brings his snow shovel down on the heads of the robbers. Like the woodsman who slaughters the voracious wolf in "Little Red Riding Hood," an adult bursts in at the climactic moment to save the imperiled child. Thus Kevin is restored to the bosom of his family, and (at least until the sequel opens) everyone lives happily ever after.

The joyous conclusion of the film masks a much darker drama that has been played out between child and tormentor. Hughes might very well be accused of exploiting the molestation of a child by evil adults in order to titillate an audience that has been primed by a decade of hysteria about child abuse. To escape such an indictment, the filmmaker demonstrates an awareness of the implications of his story through a stylization of its violence that is drawn from animated cartoons. In the process of buffering his

Figure 17. Macaulay Culkin as Kevin McCallister performs cartoon–like antics in Chris Columbus's *Home Alone* (1990). Photograph by Don Smetzer.

audience from the frightening potential of his subject through obvious al-lusions to the slapstick sources of his mayhem, he subtly points to another film against which *Home Alone* can be understood as a serious, if subtle, exploration of the child as prey. Through this brief allusion, Hughes suc-ceeds in placing his comedy in a context that transforms our understanding of the film.

The booby traps with which Kevin bedevils the efforts of the burglars to gain entrance to his house are likely to remind many members of the audience of those children's cartoons in which an intended victim, such as the Road Runner, turns the tables on a hapless villain, such as the forlorn Wile E. Coyote. The key moments of each episode involve the plotting of the villain's nefarious plans, the intended victim's reversal of those plans, the attack (which the audience already knows is doomed), the close-up in which the villain's face reveals his late recognition that the violence pre-pared for the victim is about to engulf the perpetrator himself, the act of violence accompanied by exaggerated sound effects, and the exasperated retreat of the foiled villain, who hobbles away bearing the visible mutila-tions of the violence—only to return in the next scene for yet another varia-tion on the same theme. (See figure 17.) Hughes's careful choreography and editing of the burglar's assault on the McCallister house clearly invoke this animated tradition. In doing so, he displaces the horrendous violence to a stage on which we know that no scar is ever permanent, no wound is ever fatal, and—as with contemporary versions of fairy tales—no villain ever prevails.

Though there are many examples from which to choose, one scene adheres, virtually without variation, to the traditional form of the cartoon. Having blindly yanked an overhead string, Marvin, the luckless assistant of the evil mastermind, Harry, is caught in close-up as he peers up a laundry chute at a heated iron that is plunging toward him. After he is struck (with appropriately enhanced sound effects), we discover that his whiskered, hangdog visage has been branded by the hot metal; as he stalks off, he carries the impression of the iron on his face. From the close-up recognition of impending doom to the crushing injury to the visible mutilation—the hapless Marvin reenacts the fate of all cartoon villains.

Hughes' allusions to two genres in which violence against the vulnerable is safely contained—the fairy tale and the cartoon—are certainly of use in defusing the explosive ramifications of his subject. However, in the midst of constructing these concurrent systems of allusion, Hughes refers to a classic film that provides a context through which we might come to a much more serious view of his work.

Kevin has cleverly heated his house's monogrammed doorknob with a charcoal lighter. When the nasty Harry grasps the knob to enter the McCallister house, he burns his hand. Leaping back down the steps, he plunges his hand into the snow, and then holds up his palm to his face. Branded into his flesh is the letter "M." Even the least imaginative student of film will recognize Hughes's allusion to Fritz Lang's masterpiece, *M* (1931), the story of Hans Beckert, a child murderer.

Kevin McCallister shares similarities with Beckert's first young victim, Elsie Beckmann, and all the other children who have been menaced by adults in the history of cinema. But, unlike Lang, Hughes holds out the happy possibility that the innocent may prevail. Though the brief allusion succeeds in counterposing *Home Alone* to *M*, it also serves to darken the character of Harry by suggesting a parallel to him in Hans Beckert. Thus, Hughes hints that Kevin is in greater jeopardy than first supposed, increasing the suspense for the sophisticated viewer of the film. Finally, the allusion to *M* attempts to lift the film from the humble ranks of popular culture to the ethereal realms of serious art, where even a boffo box-office bonanza like *Home Alone* is self-conscious of itself as a work of art.

But what if the *M* on the doorknob were unintentional, a mere coincidence?[3] And if it were unintentional, would it even be an allusion? John Hollander, echoing Quintilian, insists that "one cannot in this sense allude unintentionally—an inadvertent allusion is a kind of solecism" (64). We need look no farther than the sets of Hollywood productions to find evidence of such inadvertence. As John Bailey, the distinguished cinematographer of such films as *Ordinary People* (1980) and *Mishima* (1985), complains, "[I] have to worry whether or not I should mention to this director that this scene is similar to a sequence in *Beauty and the Beast* or *A Man Escaped*" (Schaefer, 70).

If one is merely trope hunting, it is difficult to distinguish the intentional from the accidental. But if the allusion underscores elements buttressed elsewhere in the film through other allusions or related devices, then intentionality becomes irrelevant. Are we limited in our interpretation to those relationships that the director consciously wove into the fabric of the film? It seems a rather simpleminded stance, and one that most artists would reject. A perhaps apocryphal anecdote about Robert Frost circulated for years at the Bread Loaf Writers Conference. According to the story, a woman had objected to a critic's elaborate explication of a poem, demanding to know whether Frost had actually intended all the meanings ferreted out by the ingenious critic. The curt old poet assured her, "Madam, if he read it, I wrote it."

Similarly, the diversity of cinematic modes of alluding and the sheer number of allusions themselves in films ought not to be ignored merely because intentionality cannot be proved. Rather, acknowledging the fundamental role of allusions in cinema, we should remember, as Flaubert reminds us, that "even Homer had his Homer" and seek out the intertextualities of films that do indeed demonstrate the relevance of the old and confirm the authority of the new.

NOTES

1. The audience's perception of the interplay between a new text and an older text to which it refers is examined in Peter J. Rabinowitz's " 'What's Hecuba to Us?': The Audience's Experience of Literary Borrowing."

2. For a discussion of the emergence of an American audience literate in the history of cinema (and of the implications for filmmakers), see Noël Carroll's "The Future of Allusion: Hollywood in the Seventies (and Beyond)."

3. In fact, Hughes's sequel, *Home Alone 2: Lost in New York* (1992), confirms the filmmaker's intention to place the series in the context suggested above by repeating, when the criminals first confront Kevin, the image of the "M" branded into Harry's palm. Even more telling is a detail in the film's opening. In establishing the sequel's premise, a newspaper's front page announcing "Wet Bandits in Daring Escape" is blown against the McCallisters' door. Beneath the photos of the two escaped convicts are the captions "Marvin Murchins" and "Harry Lyme." Equal to Hans Beckert in the extent of his wickedness toward children, Harry Lime, the villain of Carol Reed's famous mystery, *The Third Man* (1949), supplies hospitals with stolen and diluted penicillin for children infected with meningitis, who consequently suffer brain damage or die after administration of the adulterated

drug. Identifying Harry Lyme, Kevin's nemesis, with both Beckert and Lime, John Hughes leaves little doubt that he wishes the *Home Alone* series to be understood in terms of a classic cinematic tradition of children imperiled by adults.

WORKS CITED

Aeschylus. *Agamemnon.* In *The Oresteian Trilogy,* translated by Philip Vellacott. Harmondsworth: Penguin, 1959.

Baudelaire, Charles. *Selected Writings on Art and Artists.* Translated by P. E. Charvet. Harmondsworth: Penguin, 1972.

Carroll, Noël. "The Future of Allusion: Hollywood in the Seventies (and Beyond)." *October* 20 (1982): 51–81.

Garner, Richard. *From Homer to Tragedy: The Art of Allusion in Greek Poetry.* London: Routledge, 1990.

Hollander, John. *The Figure of Echo: A Mode of Allusion in Milton and After.* Berkeley and Los Angeles: University of California Press, 1981.

Homer. *The Iliad.* Translated by Robert Fitzgerald. Garden City: Doubleday, 1974.

Rabinowitz, Peter J. " 'What's Hecuba to Us?': The Audience's Experience of Literary Borrowing." In *The Reader in the Text: Essays on Audience and Interpretation,* edited by Susan R. Suleiman and Inge Crosman. Princeton: Princeton University Press, 1980.

Schaefer, Dennis, and Larry Salvato. *Masters of Light: Conversations with Contemporary Cinematographers.* Berkeley and Los Angeles: University of California Press, 1984.

Wollen, Peter. *Signs and Meaning in the Cinema.* Bloomington: Indiana University Press, 1972.

PART TWO

Distant Relatives:
Cross-Cultural Remakes

NINE

The French Remark:
Breathless and Cinematic Citationality

David Wills

I am not, it seems, in the cinema. Not even in the video. This all comes at a complicated series of removes. At some point I could have said, "I am in the cinema," and left the ambiguity at play between the theater room and the film on the screen. The metonymy works for theater and cinema, but not for video. Yet this is the position I am in, watching a film on video years after its commercial release. In fact, since I was only six in 1959, I was never in the cinema of *A bout de souffle;* it has always come to me by means of a series of detours. But the metonymic ambiguity of being in the cinema allows for that, and a more general detour mechanism allows even for the current state of affairs whereby I am watching the American remake of *A bout de souffle* (*Breathless,* 1983) before I take another look at the original. The chronological wires are crossed: the first thing I watch is a remake.

So it seems I am really not in the cinema. Not even in the video. I am here uttering these things to you the reader, having been there, various versions of "there," writing them. Everything I utter has a complicated play of quotation marks about it, not just because this reading is something of a recital of what I have previously written, but because in a more irredeemable fashion everything I write refers back to a "there"—a film, an experience of watching it, over and over—it refers back to an act of detaching, operations of excision and grafting, functions of de- and recontextualization. That which is a necessary fact of any reading, what we can call the "quotation" or "citation" effect, becomes even more explicitly the case once we come to talk about remakes.

But perhaps I am in the cinema. Perhaps even in the film. Perhaps, even as I write this in front of a screen—a cinema screen, a TV-video screen, a word processor monitor screen, a page—and even as this gets repeated like some sort of screen in front of its submobile and visually stimulated, if not scopophilic, reader, I am more than ever in the cinema. I say that because as viewer and reader myself I am automatically and inevitably involved in the grafting or (de)recontextualization process just referred to. But I by no means initiate such a process. The film was never an intact and coherent whole offered up for my consumption. It was always, one might say, in the process of writing itself. Quoting, one might say "always already." Always writing and quoting itself. Remarking and remaking itself. Thus what is being commonly and communally referred to here as the remake, the possibility that exists for a film to be repeated in a different form, should rather be read as the necessary structure of iterability that exists for and within every film. That, at least, is my hypothesis, drawn of course from Derrida in work such as "Signature Event Context" (1982) and "The Law of Genre" (1980). First, "every sign . . . can break with every given context, and engender infinitely new contexts, in an absolutely nonsaturable fashion"; but second, as a corollary to that "the possibility of citational grafting . . . belongs to the structure of every mark" and "constitutes every mark as writing" (1982, 320), that is to say, as iterable mark, as remark, as remake. And the cinematic mark is no exception. The slightest mark is being remarked or remade even as it is being uttered or written, to the extent that it cannot make itself as full presence, as intact and coherent entity. It constitutes itself as reconstitutable, at least it must do so in order to function, that is to say, in order to make sense.

Thus what this book refers to as the remake—the essays demonstrate that as soon as we investigate the category its edges begin to blur—is but a particular case of what exists within the structure of every film. The remake has its own codes and practices and by means of them it is able to distinguish itself from another category of films: those not remade in the same set of varied institutional forms. But what distinguishes the remake is not the fact of its being a repetition, rather the fact of its being a precise institutional form of the structure of repetition, what I am calling the "quotation effect" or "citation effect," the citationality or iterability, that exists in and for every film.

The particular case of the remake that I remark upon here is that of the French film reconstituted as Hollywood product. Now, given that something like the Hollywood film or the "classic narrative film" seeks to erase the traces of its own production, and given that, as I have just maintained, after Derrida, the form of production of any mark can be called, between quotation marks, "writing," then it stands to reason that what a Hollywood remake would seek to erase from a French film would be precisely the traces of writing. For purposes of economy, shortly to be explained, I shall concentrate that idea by proposing the following self-evidence: what the Hollywood remake seeks to have erased from a French film is quite simply the subtitles. I can hear the reproach that my argument, quoted from

Derrida, for an idea of "writing" as trace that belongs to every mark, is negated or at least rendered seriously reductive by this recourse to writing in the literal sense of words upon the screen representing a translation of what can be heard on the sound track. However, my strategy has its own logic, namely, that it is the particularly explicit and privileged manifestation of the structure of writing that is the subtitle that enables me to develop the sense of the remake and remark, and that for the following reasons.

First, the subtitles do not—or at least the same ones do not—appear in the "original" foreign language version. When they do appear, as for instance in the English-language version, they show the film "in process," in production if you will: in the process of being transposed, translated, exported. They show that in being exported the film explicitly reveals its supplementary structure, its iterability, its (de)recontextualization. As a result the film might be said to come apart at a most basic level of cinema, namely, in the combination of image and sound tracks. Once subtitles are added the sound track reveals its difference from the image track—the seamlessness of spoken dialogue and moving lips is rent—but it does so on the level of the image track such that the seamlessness of the image track itself as coherent or intact reproduction of the real, as uniform visual surface and depth, is also rent.

Second, as I have noted (and I am saying nothing but the obvious here, nothing that has not already been observed or said, for I am quite simply quoting), the subtitles offer a translation of what is heard on the sound track, and as such they repeat the spoken sound track and so repeat the structure of iterability of the film. For in writing itself and in automatically being rewritten, the film translates itself, repeats itself with a difference, recontextualizes itself to a foreign place within itself. But the repeating effect is redoubled as it is reflected in the inversion[1] of the translated subtitles. The subtitles provide an abyssal form of that iterability by being inserted into the film or inscribed on the surface of the film; by appearing at the bottom of the screen they cause the bottom of the film to fall out.

Last, the translation that is the subtitles renders explicit the particular form of transposition that the Hollywood remake of a foreign film involves, namely, its removal to a more familiar place—a tramp falls into a Beverly Hills swimming pool instead of the Seine (*Down and Out in Beverly Hills* [1985], *Boudu sauvé des eaux* [1932]), a Las Vegas petty criminal falls for a French architecture student instead of a French existentialist hero falling for an American student and would-be journalist (*Breathless* [1983], *A bout de souffle* [1959]), three men are reset with their baby in America (*Trois hommes et un couffin* [1985], *Three Men and a Baby* [1987], like the cousins in love (*Cousin, cousine* [1975], *Cousins* [1989], like the recidivist female punk heroine called in to work for this government (*La Femme Nikita* [1991], *Point of No Return* [1993]), and so on. The remake neutralizes the otherness of the foreign film, in general, but in no way more clearly than by effacing the subtitles. However, the paradox is that in erasing the effects of otherness, in removing the subtitles, Hollywood is duped into believing it has restored the seamlessness of a coherent, intact, and consumable image (and sound). It is unaware that it is working within the structure of the supplement and adding to, rather than subtracting from, the play of differences. The film Hollywood produces becomes enfolded into the abyss that is the subtitles of the original film. As a translation and transposition of the foreign original, it takes the place of the explicit form of that foreignness that inhabits the subtitles, it inscribes itself within the structure of noncoherence and nonintegrality, and, in transferring the film to a familiar context, however much it might presume to erase those effects of difference, it simply carries them over into the new product. That is, in any case, my contention, and I would like to explore it further through the remaking of Godard's *A bout de souffle* into Jim McBride's *Breathless*.[2]

Godard's film is quite obviously a privileged object for this discussion. It is a film that is less obviously concerned with the erasure of the traces of its own production than many others, although more so than other Godard films. And it is a film that has been given a thoroughly Derridean reading by Marie-Claire Ropars in her exemplary article "The Graphic in Filmic Writing: *A bout de souffle* or the Erratic Alphabet." But for these same reasons it is a highly unusual candidate for a Hollywood remake. Given the level of its "invention" when it appeared in 1959, its use of the jump cut, its borrowings from film noir and Hollywood, its self-reflexivity in general, it would seem to present a number of quandaries for whomever sought to make it over in the early eighties, inevitably raising the questions of neutralization and domestication. Dated as a revolutionary film, as one of a group of films that brought in the New Wave, but also dated by that historical reference, it could not but represent a problem of transposition, the problem of transposition and translation, the problem of the remake as remark. Although the film was made by a director known for his independence, and although McBride argued strongly for the right to remake the film and fought hard to produce something worthy of the original (cf. McBride, 1983), the American *Breathless* met with a lukewarm critical reception on both sides of the Atlantic, being dismissed as academic and certainly "not Godard."

However, I find what results to be particularly interesting: on the one hand McBride's film demonstrates the practical compromise of a film that has retained something of the "hip" quality of Godard's film but privileges the narrative structure more than does the French original, while on the other hand it reveals that what I have just called a "compromise," putting the word between quotation marks, is a fact of any film and any remake: it

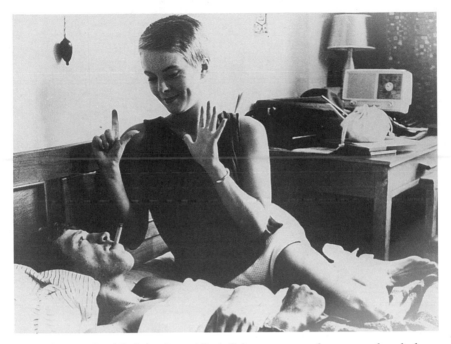

Figure 18. Jean-Paul Belmondo and Jean Seberg capture the cross-cultural play-fulness of postmodern young love in Godard's *Breathless* (1959).

necessarily both covers and fails to cover the discontinuities or incoherences that structure it; it can only ever repeat itself as difference and inscribe those differences in the process of its writing. In other words, because of the multiple play of otherness that works so explicitly through *A bout de souffle*, two things occur: the first is another self-evidence, simply that not all the otherness gets neutralized; the second is the other side of that, namely, that otherness can never be neutralized, it will only ever reinscribe itself. *Breathless* is something of the dilemma those ideas represent.

In *A bout de souffle* small-time gangster Michel Poiccard (Jean-Paul Belmondo) has had a brief affair with the American student, newspaper girl, and aspiring journalist Patricia Fracchini (Jean Seberg) on the Côte d'Azur. (See figure 18.) He halfheartedly kills a policeman, returns to Paris in order to fetch Patricia and flee to Italy, but is held up by her tergiversations and a check he can't cash and is finally killed by the police after she denounces him. In *Breathless* Jesse Lujack (Richard Gere) has an affair with French architectural student Monica Poiccard (Valérie Kaprisky) in Vegas, even more "accidentally" kills a highway patrolman and returns to Los

Figure 19. Richard Gere and Valerie Kaprisky pause while on the run in Jim McBride's reverse-role remake of *Breathless* (1983).

Angeles to fetch her and head for Mexico. (See figure 19.) She also denounces him and he is presumably shot, although, as we shall see, the final frame does not show it.

One could discourse at length on the slight and not-so-slight differences between the two versions. Here are some of them: whereas Poiccard wants to be Bogart, Lujack wants to be Jerry Lee Lewis or the comic-book hero the Silver Surfer; whereas in the French version there is a long "seduction" scene in the cramped quarters of Patricia's Paris apartment, in the American version this scene takes place between the large rooms and swimming pool of a Los Angeles apartment block; whereas the Paris detectives say *"[O]n ne plaisante pas avec la police parisienne"* ("[O]ne doesn't kid around with the Paris police"), the American says "Don't F-U-C-K with the L-A-P-D"; whereas in Godard's film it is Godard himself who plays the part of a passerby who recognizes the gangster from a newspaper photograph, I have no idea whether the tramp on the steps of a church who does the same is Jim McBride; whereas it is the American woman who introduces the Frenchman to William Faulkner's work in Godard's film, it is the Frenchwoman who introduces the same to the American in *Breathless*. On the basis of those differences one might begin to make an argument concerning

McBride's adaptation of Godard's film, his domestication or neutralization of it. One might refer to the less marginalized, more institutionalized female figure that has the effect of making the narrative less psychologically convincing—Monica seems much "straighter" than Patricia, less likely to be seduced by Jesse, who appears in turn as more of a boor than Michel; or to the compromise required by changing standards of cultural literacy—Faulkner is considered to be enough of a foreign reference for an American audience without having recourse to some canonical example from French literature. But the explanations for such differences would have, somehow, to collaborate with that which they sought to describe or critique, to some extent explaining away the differences by taking into account the "practical" considerations of adaptation: changes in history as well as geography (De Gaulle's France on the cusp of the sixties versus Reagan's eighties); the desire for a psychological contrast that has Monica fascinated and seduced by someone totally opposite; the importance of the quotation from Faulkner in its own right ("Between grief and nothing I will take grief"). In other words in accounting for these sorts of differences one would get caught up precisely in the question of differences between one film and another, reaching down to the smallest details of the texts but overlooking for the most part the matter of differences within the text, its intrinsic remarkability.

In one respect the differences just referred to would lead us to such a remarkability, namely, in respect to what has been called the self-reflexivity of Godard's *A bout de souffle,* its constant reference to matters cinematic. However discussion of such references does not necessarily remove us from the framework of complicit explanation just referred to. While it is true that Bogart has been replaced by Jerry Lee Lewis, and film posters and young people selling cinema journals do not appear in or out of the background of *Breathless,* Hollywood can never be far from the foreground of a fantasy romance set in Los Angeles. And in any case references to cinema are not absent from McBride's film: there is an Antonioni-like frame of Monica standing at a bus stop that advertises the Hollywood Wax Museum, in front of a military cemetery; the final scene takes place in the ruins of Errol Flynn's "Pines"; and there is the sequence in the movie theater, much more developed than in Godard's film, that I shall return to shortly. The argument is easily made that it would not be a good artistic choice for a film made in the eighties to be self-conscious in the same way as one that was like a new wave breaking in 1959. Similarly, Godard's signatory appearance in his own film in fact says little. Presumably he was no more recognizable to a 1959 French audience than Jim McBride would have been to us in 1983. And what would a contemporary audience raised on Hollywood's permanent fear of self-recognition do with a camera jerking across the sky to the sound of gunshots as Godard's Michel pretends to shoot, like a converse of Camus's outsider, at the blinding sun, or with a Michel who turns to the camera as he drives to say, "If you don't like the sea, if you don't like mountains, if you don't like cities, then go and get fucked!" (["allez vous faire foutre!"]—this last invective already sanitized by a milder translation in the subtitles)? These things have attained historical inscription as marks of Godard's filmmaking practice that can not easily be translated.[3] So the discussion would bring us back to questions of compromise and problems of translation without, for all that, allowing us to think the questions through very far.

Yet if we read such references less as self-consciousness or self-reflexivity and more as self-iterability, as cinema quoting itself, drawing attention to itself as effects of writing, such things come to form the basis for another level of dislocations that, as I have suggested, turn the question around. The film doesn't just say "I am a film, I am an object-in-construction being presented to you as a self-constituted commodity," it also says: "I am a series of images within images, sounds within sounds, subject to constant recontextualization. The images that constitute me are constantly undercut, in the process of their constitution, by their inability to define themselves as presences without at the same time falling prey to effects heterogeneous to those presumed definitions. Thus I am a series of images within images that are never just or never completely images, never untouched by radical difference, and never purely pictorial without also being graphic. There is never the immediacy of perceived objects without also the presence of hieroglyphic labyrinths; thus I am always graphic in two senses, that of the pictorial and that of the written." The still image of Bogart on the poster of *The Harder They Fall* and of Michel imitating the way Bogie passed his thumb across his lips becomes not just an image of a poorly formed identity, a petty criminal with personality problems trying to be a larger-than-life celluloid hero, but a type of freeze-frame that arrests the narrative flow, a silence within the noise and music of the continuous images, a problem of identity for the images themselves. The image of Bogart has inscribed upon it like a title or a signature the image of Poiccard, and vice versa. Similarly, when Godard playing a man on the street looks at a photograph in the newspaper he is reading, then looks at Michel, then back at the newspaper photograph, then crosses the street to show the same photograph to two policemen, Godard doesn't just sign his film and wink at the audience in the manner of Hitchcock. He transfers the question of identity posed at the level of the image—and repeated here by means of the competing images of Michel, still and moving, arrested and passing, here and there, past and present, print and celluloid, written and pictorial—he transfers that question of identity to the level of his film as a whole. Once Godard is in it, on its surface, it can no longer simply be a film he has made; nor does it become instead performance art; rather his appearance as a character pointing at an image in another medium, inscribing his body or his finger on its surface, is like a name written across his whole film that erases its wholeness and renders it irredeemably heterogeneous. Any translation or transposition of the film will henceforth necessarily be a translation of that heterogeneity, a translation from foreignness to foreignness.

In her article, Marie-Claire Ropars has traced such effects through the play of language in *A bout de souffle,* especially the play of the written word within the image. Although she in no way limits the idea of writing to these chance or designed appearances of the written word, her strategy enables her to develop the notion of an image constantly worked upon and over by its others. It is her conclusion that I have used as the basis for my argument here, namely, that what the film offers in the final analysis is a question about translation, a problem with translation. All the way through, *A bout de souffle* keeps coming back to the matter of inter- or translinguistic usage. And it would be incorrect to presume that that is all a function of a relationship between a less-than-bilingual American woman and a Frenchman. Patricia does get her French wrong from time to time, but Michel also corrects the usage of another woman, presumed to be French, whose apartment he visits in order to steal some money. And he himself resorts more than once to the Swiss usage for the numerals seventy and eighty (one could hear that as another signing by Godard, who is of Swiss origin). There is no pure French in the film, but always effects of translation, within a language, between languages.

However, it is in the final exchange of the film that, as Marie-Claire Ropars points out, the matter becomes concentrated, bringing with it a complicated thematics of misogyny that has the female bear the weight of linguistic otherness (156–58). *"Tu es vraiment dégueulasse"* ("You are really shitty," my translation), Michel says as he lies dying. When Patricia asks the policeman what he said he replies *"Il a dit: 'Vous êtes vraiment une dégueulasse'"* ("He said: You are really an arsehole" ["bitch" in subtitles]). This is no simple quotation of Michel's words by the policeman. First, he gives the effect of reported speech and so changes the familiar "tu" to the formal "vous," but at the same omits the *"que"* ("that") so that syntactically his words amount to a quotation of direct speech. But his quotation is a misquote, for he inserts an indefinite article before *"dégueulasse"* so that that adjective becomes a noun with a stronger sense—"shitty" becomes "arsehole" or something similar, just as *"con"* ("stupid") as adjective becomes "cunt" as a noun. Patricia is left asking *"Qu'est-ce que c'est 'dégueulasse'?"* ("What does *'dégueulasse'* mean?"), a question that receives no response, except in the subtitles of the English-language version where many of the preceding subtleties take on quite different nuances.[4]

In McBride's *Breathless* there are of course similar linguistic transpositions. First of all Monica has a foreign version of the French name "Monique."

LIVERPOOL JOHN MOORES UNIVERSITY
LEARNING SERVICES

She has to have Jesse explain to her what *jinxed* means, and what a desperado is, although in the latter case the word should be evident enough to a speaker of a Romance language. She refers to Jesse as *"taré,"* another word that can alternate between an adjective and a noun—"It means crazy, a disgusting person, jerk," she explains—and he appropriates the word for his own use. But in the American film, as in the French, the most interesting linguistic play occurs in the more precise form of the misquotation, in terms of a translation that occurs more strictly within the space of the same.

The first example comes from the scene in the cinema. Here, the characters enter the space behind the screen and watch the images in mirrored form playing in black and white before them. This is first of all, it seems to me, a more radical *mise en abyme* of the cinematic than anything in *A bout de souffle.* There are competing cinematic surfaces, inscribing their differences, on almost the same visual plane—this isn't just characters in a film watching a film. The images seen on the screen, from Joseph H. Lewis's *Gun Crazy,* occur as an inverse background, a sort of subtitle or translation, to the film *Breathless*—Lewis's characters are speaking of the high stakes in their relationship as Jesse and Monica begin to make love in the moments after a close escape from the police. But that effect is inverted again when Jesse and Monica in turn inscribe themselves within the film they are watching, back to front, especially by means of Monica's quoting of the woman within it. She repeats the words we have just heard from *Gun Crazy*—"I don't want to be afraid of life or anything else"—to which Jesse replies, "You don't have to be afraid of nothing."

What the quotation has set up here is something quite different from a repetition, a transposition of words from one mouth to another. It is rather a recontextualization radical enough to amount to a reversal, an inversion, according to what I shall call, for reasons that the rest of what I have to say will explain, a logic of the chiasmus.[5] It reoccurs quite clearly at the end of *Breathless.* After Monica returns to inform Jesse she has denounced him to the police, she tells him to leave so as not to be apprehended. He wants to stay, because he loves her, and believes her to love him. "Do you love me?" he asks, then demands that she reply: "Say it!" When she doesn't, he turns the logic around and at the same time demands that she quote him: "Say you don't love me and then I'll go." She replies and quotes him: "I don't love you," but unconvincingly enough for it to be read by Jesse as meaning the opposite: "Liar!" he declares, and deciding that she loves him, rushes off to pick up the money from Berrutti and return to flee or be with her. Thus the translations and quotations run to and fro within the structure of iterability to the extent that the repetitions become inversions, *contresens.* Something similar happens in *A bout de souffle* as Patricia reverses the position of the adjective in the name of the street, *Rue Campagne Première,* when she denounces Michel, making the correct linguistic assumption that "premier" as adjective precedes the noun, occurring in the weak position, whereas in this case it follows. Her error works as a corollary to her attempts to fathom the logic of her feelings for him, with her finally settling on the inverted formula of "Since I am mean to you I am not in love with you."

Once iterability or the remarking effect comes into play, and it does so from the beginning and never stops doing so, then any translation or trans-position—that which occurs in and from the beginning as much as that occurring in the case of a remake—involves the sorts of cross-purposes just outlined. Translation necessarily occurs as a chiasmus between the homogeneity of a single sense and the heterogeneity of a divided sense: like the homogeneity of a self-evident image and the heterogeneity of that same image crossed over and crossed out by things supposedly foreign to it. There can never be a faithful remake, and not just because Hollywood demands compromises or because things get lost in translation or mistakes occur, but because there can never be a simple original uncomplicated by the structure of the remake, by such effects of self-division.

In the final analysis it no longer comes down to a question of what *Breath-less* tries, or doesn't try to do with *A bout de souffle*, or even what it does or doesn't do with it. Thus in returning to the final and perhaps most impor-tant divergence between the two films, *Breathless'* choice of a musical subtext over the French film's use of cinema, Jerry Lee Lewis instead of Bogart, I wish above all to emphasize once more the idea of chiastic self-division that renders the American film irretrievably different from the French one, and that, paradoxically, in spite of any attempts by Hollywood to produce a more domesticated version of Godard, renders it irretrievably different from itself and eminently Godardian. On one level it comes down to the impressive work of Jack Nitzsche on the sound track and his association of a Philip Glass theme with the female character as a counterpoint to Jerry Lee Lewis for Jesse. But I doubt whether the title of that theme, "Openings," from Glassworks had anything to do with his choice. However it is by means of the musical openings produced on the sound track that McBride's *Breath-less* breaks with Hollywood in favor of something more like Godard at the same time that it comes together as a film.

Although Godard's use of sound always recognized its force as an other-ness "within" the visual field of film, in some of the films that marked his return to commercial cinema in the early eighties, contemporaneous with *Breathless,* the work on sound became concentrated in terms of music. That was so for *Sauve qui peut (la vie)* (1979 [*Every Man for Himself*]) and more explicitly for *Prénom Carmen* (1983 [*First Name Carmen*]).[6] The effect is to seriously disrupt the distinctions between layers of the sound track on the one hand, and sound and image tracks on the other hand. A version of the same thing occurs with the sound track at the end of *Breathless.* The French ending that has Michel shot in the back by the police and running for his life but to his death at the end of the *Rue Campagne Première* is replaced by a Jesse pausing over a gun on the ground, being urged not to pick it up by a frantic Monica and by the police who have their guns trained on him. He suddenly turns to face the police and breaks into a mimed rendition of Jerry Lee Lewis's "Breathless." The sound track music, which during this scene has used an increasingly syrupy strings rendition of Glass's minimalist piano piece "Openings," is interrupted by the beat and melody of the Lewis song; then the two compete in a melodic and rhythmic crisscross as Jesse's mime veers into a sort of expressionistic limbo. The Lewis song reasserts itself with Jesse facing Monica and singing the word from its title and the title of the film before stooping to pick up the gun and again face the police and his death.

By foregrounding the music in this way, *Breathless* goes beyond the self-consciousness of Jesse's worship and imitation of Jerry Lee Lewis and in a very Godardian fashion brings the music track from its offscreen position into the narrative and onto the screen. Conversely, the visual track is crossed by the sound track and the narrative is frozen in a ghostly mime. Whereas the Glass theme has been used as a pensive "feminine" contrast to the impulsive and macho Lewis songs, presumed to be never more than background, here the counterpoint suddenly takes itself literally, leading to the chiastic effect of this climax. If one wanted, one could read in the word "counterpoint" precisely such a musical and graphic chiasmus by translating it or transposing it as follows: the word "point" would come to be the musical or rhythmic equivalent of the word "trait," privileged by Derrida (1980, 1987) to express the heterogeneity of the line (the French word *trait* means both brushstroke and stroke of the pen), the divisibility of the pictorial by the graphic and vice versa. "Point" would then mean both "dot" and "beat," and "counterpoint" would express the crossing of one by the other. The counterpoint of Glass's "Openings" would then become the punctuating effect of music upon the narrative and visuals in general that occurs as that piece struggles against the beat of Jerry Lee Lewis in the final shots. It would be like the rudimentary writing effect that is the dot inserting itself as foreign otherness on the screen and on the film. As a result the film is frozen in a composition—the climactic halting of the narrative flow—that is also a transposition or translation: the crossing of the two musical themes and their imposition upon that narrative. The final sequence of *Breathless* thus works as an opening onto a cinematic process—an opening of the film onto itself and a crossing of the film by itself, a remaking of the marks of cinema—that can be read as far more radical than anything in *A bout de souffle*.

The story of the remaking of Godard's groundbreaking New Wave film is not finally about how faithful the American copy manages to be or how original it manages to be, two paradoxical qualities requested or required of a remake. It is rather about how any film, from the explicitly Brechtian to the most seamless Hollywood product, works as a quotation of itself, the repetition or rehearsing of its own differences. The story of *A bout de souffle*, carried over to *Breathless* is, after all, about a problem with a check, a check that can't be cashed, a written promise that can't be immediately fulfilled in the form of hard currency. It is therefore about a problem with different media within a system of exchange, like the visual and audio media of cinema, and also a problem with signatures. The problem Michel faces is that although the check is made out to him, it is crossed, made nonnegotiable, requiring it to be processed through the institutional rigors of a bank account. It has lines drawn or written across it and needs more writing and stamping on the back before it can be of any use to him. It is also crossed in the sense suggested by the French word *barré*, meaning blocked, immobilized. In the American *Breathless* the problem is similar, although it is the check itself, as written monetary form—or written monetary form different from cash, since there is no nonwritten form—that holds Jesse up and allows the police to close in on him. Either way, the check requires some form of endorsement, a structure that can be called—especially since this is a check that travels to a foreign land, like a traveler's check—that of the countersignature. But, as Derrida (1982, 1984) has shown, what the countersignature does in reaffirming the authenticity of the original signature is subvert that very authenticity by showing the presumed singular and idiosyncratic event of the signature—what makes it mine and the written code for my proper name—to be repeatable and thus subject to the same decontextualizations, in this case especially forgery, as any sign or line. The countersignature is a repetition of the same that ushers in the structure of difference; it is a quotation of the original that is a translation and transposition of it.

The American film *Breathless* might be read as an attempt to cash in on the credit established by Godard's film, to cash it and at the same time process it through the Hollywood institution, an institution concerned with nothing more than what is bankable. But the check stays crossed, the film remains written, for it cannot be otherwise. On the other side, once it has crossed the Atlantic, in spite of the translations and inversions, there are more crossings, there is more writing. Whichever film one reads first, whichever version is taken to be the original, the heterogeneities of cinema continue to cross both ways; the countersignature divides itself in a play of writing. *A bout de souffle*, *"Breathless"* the subtitled version, *Breathless* the American version, and "Breathless" the song by Jerry Lee Lewis, as well as all the versions that I have quoted in writing about it here, are caught up like so many stolen cars, in such a complicated interchange, something of the shape of which this article has sought to outline.

NOTES

1. The spoken words "appearing" in the mouths of the characters in the top half of the screen or "off" to the side might be said to be inverted in the written form at the bottom. *Une version* is French for a translation into the mother tongue, as well as being, as in English, the expression that distinguishes different forms, especially different language forms of a given film (e.g., *version originale, version française*).

2. For a lengthy comparison of the two films, see Falkenberg.

3. However, McBride's film has the very Godardian shot through a large doughnut that gives the appearance of the iris that Godard uses for some of his fades, and during which the word "nuts" appears briefly.

4. The differences between French dialogue and English subtitles are worth repeating. First of all, as Ropars points out, Michel's dying words remain somewhat inaudible, but the difficulty is not with the word "dégueulasse," which is heard quite clearly, but rather in the difference between *"C'est vraiment dégueulasse"* ("It's really shitty") and *"Tu es vraiment dégueulasse"* ("You are really shitty"). That is relayed into English by an ellipsis, as follows:

> *Michel: Tu es (C'est) vraiment dégueulasse.*
> You . . . are really.
> *Patricia: Qu'est-ce qu'il a dit?*
> What did he say?
> *Policeman: Il a dit: "Vous êtes vraiment une dégueulasse."*
> He said you are really "a little bitch."
> *Patricia: Qu'est-ce que c'est 'dégueulasse'?*
> A little what? I don't understand.

5. For discussion of the chiasmus, see Derrida (165–66).

6. For further discussion of this, see Wills, 1986 and 1991.

WORKS CITED

Brunette, Peter, and David Wills. *Screen/Play: Derrida and Film Theory.* Princeton: Princeton University Press, 1989.

Derrida, Jacques. "The Law of Genre." In *Glyph* 7, 202–29. Baltimore: Johns Hopkins University Press, 1980.

———. "Living On / Borderlines." In *Deconstruction and Criticism*, edited by Harold Bloom et al., 75–176. New York: Seabury Press, 1979.

———. *Signsponge/Signéponge.* Translated by Richard Rand. New York: Columbia University Press, 1984.

———. *The Truth in Painting.* Translated by Geoff Bennington and Ian McLeod. Chicago: University of Chicago Press, 1987.

Falkenberg, Pamela. " 'Hollywood' and the 'Art Cinema' as a Bipolar Modeling System: *A bout de souffle* and *Breathless.*" *Wide Angle* 7, no. 3 (1985): 44–53.

McBride, Jim. "Sortie des Marges: entretien avec Jim McBride." *Cahiers du cinéma* 350 (1983): 31–34, 64–66.

Ropars-Wuilleumier, Marie-Claire. "The Graphic in Filmic Writing: *A bout de souffle,* or the Erratic Alphabet." *Enclitic* 5, no. 2; 6, no. 1 (1981–82), 147–61.

Wills, David. "Carmen: Sound/Effect." *Cinema Journal* 25, no. 4 (1986): 33–43.

———. "Representing Silence (in Godard)." In *Essays in Honour of Keith Val Sinclair,* edited by Bruce Merry, 180–92 Townsville: James Cook University, 1991.

TEN

The Spring, Defiled:
Ingmar Bergman's *Virgin Spring* and
Wes Craven's *Last House on the Left*

Michael Brashinsky

*Nothing, neither among the elements nor within the system, is anywhere ever simply
present or absent. There are only, everywhere, differences and traces of traces.*
JACQUES DERRIDA, "POSITIONS"

In 1972, *Cries and Whispers,* Ingmar Bergman's thirty-fourth film, was released to universal acclaim, followed by a foreign-language Academy Award. The same year, Wes Craven, a neophyte, made *The Last House on the Left,* a picture that even today, after the near disappearance of drive-ins, can be found in selected video stores only under the category "Drive-In Horror." If merely for this utter coincidence, the two names would never meet on the same page of film history. But they do, for, incredibly, *The Last House on the Left* is a remake of *The Virgin Spring,* a film Bergman had made thirteen years earlier.

This fact, while widely publicized in film literature from Gerald Mast's *Short History of the Movies*[1] to popular video guides,[2] goes unannounced in *The Last House on the Left.* Instead the legend reads, "The events you are about to witness are true. Names and locations have been changed to protect those individuals still living."

Why deceive us? Or is it really a deception? In the realm of doubling visions and mutating images, which is precisely what the culture that favors the remake should be, the question, Why wouldn't a filmmaker admit to remaking a classic? could be only another way of phrasing the questions, Why remake classics at all? and What is the remake?

The remake is not a genre, nor is it a kind of film. It is neither a newly filmed old script nor a new script based on an old one. It is nothing but a film based on another film that is itself a system of narrative and cinematic properties.

As such, the remake can be seen among aesthetic expressions built on reinterpretation and engaged in a "trialogue" with nature and a culture other than their own. But unlike the stage production of a play or the film adaptation of a literary work, the remake interprets the work of the same medium and thus bares its own secondariness.[3] It skips the act of meta-aesthetic transition in which, according to the widely accepted modernist prejudice, originality begins. This, of course, is what the remake should be praised rather than blamed for. It provides us with countless clues to the medium, the culture, and ourselves that would be eclipsed by the study of what the original material has gained or lost in passage from one medium to another.

Indeed, *Hamlet* and *Medea* would not be classics had they not offered a vast scope of options for interpretation. We have seen Hamlet-poets and Hamlet-impotents, Hamlet-soldiers and Hamlet-nerds, Hamlet-rebels and Hamlet-fascists. In Shakespeare's play, theater sees a literary "empty space" (to use Peter Brook's famous formula) to be filled with a new theatrical content, and the magic of this space is that its shape, size, and texture seldom say no to new meanings. But plays are intended to be reinterpreted on stage. Films are not made to serve as sources for other films, just as books are not written to be rewritten, unless by Pierre Menard, the father of all remakes, who resolved to compose *Don Quixote*—not just "another *Don Quixote*," but "*the Don Quixote*"—as if it had never been done before.

The gap between the worlds of the remake and other aesthetic translations is not as technological as it is cultural. Stage and screen adaptation existed from the beginning of their respective arts. The remake has become the most explicit gesture of a culture that finds its psyche in the Other and cannot express itself through anything but a quote. In this culture's tired eyes, life does not imitate art—art has replaced life. Michelangelo and Fellini, Bach and Picasso *are* there, just as the air and the trees, and there is no pretending otherwise. Trying to avoid *Oedipus* when telling a story of a man who tried to avoid his fate would be as senseless today as setting up a camera in a bathroom and dismissing Hitchcock's eye in the drain. Culture, that Ortega y Gasset's window separating an artist from the garden, has become a garden of its own, and its flora, all those *fleurs du mal*, leaves of grass, and rose tattoos beat the natural vegetation. Similarly, *The Virgin Spring* is as "real" for the postmodern imagination as any other spring, and Wes Craven is as telling as he is teasing when he suggests that his film is based on "a true story."

This story *is not true*, and not only because it is too implausible and contrived to seem real. *The Last House on the Left* is in fact an uncredited remake ("a rip-off," according to Leonard Maltin[4]) of *The Virgin Spring*, and the first evidence it offers to us is, clearly, the narrative.

Stripped of all imagery and magic down to an austere plot, the *Last House* narrative is, in fact, closer to its source than those of such admitted remakes as *Scarface* (1932, 1983), *Cat People* (1942, 1982) and *The Fly* (1958, 1986).

In both films, an innocent teenage girl, the only child of loving parents, leaves home for a weekend excursion, accompanied by a shrewd confidante. On the road, she is brutally raped and murdered by a gang of criminals. (In *The Last House on the Left,* the girlfriend is similarly attacked and killed, providing one of the few notable deviations from the original). Fleeing the scene of the crime, the killers stumble upon their victim's home and stay overnight (a coincidence equally unmotivated in both scenarios) only to meet a merciless retribution from the girl's father.

If this is a story of crime and punishment, then neither film is about its story. Nor is it about the young, the girls on whom each picture centers briefly only to liquidate them and move on. Here the narrative parallels between films end.

As if it were a western, the black-and-white *Virgin Spring* is ruled by dichotomy. It juxtaposes the virgin, Catholic, and blonde Karin, who is killed on her way to mass, with the pregnant, pagan, and brunette Ingeri, who survives to lament and possibly to convert. Preoccupied with moral (and other) dilemmas, Bergman gives his pain and lens to the father, who is played by the then-thirty-year-old Max von Sydow as an ascetic warrior undergoing a tremendous internal turmoil. He is torn between the pagan God he has renounced and the Christian God he does not understand. The killers are godless, but so is the father's eye-for-an-eye revenge. A hero of a classical tragedy, seen through a prism of modern culture—Kierkegaard, Dostoyevsky, Camus—he kills because the God he has chosen has not only left him but has also left him no choice. Ultimately, *The Virgin Spring* becomes a story of a shattered faith redeemed in repentance.

In *The Last House on the Left,* Dr. Collingwood, played by the unforgettably bland Gaylord St. James, is all but faceless compared to his "paternal" model. He also takes over the initiative in the end, yet not because his self is tragically conflicted but because it is his turn to be violent. Violence in Wes Craven's films is the measure of all things; it is the last "means of communication" left for his characters to respond to the cruelty of the others and the world.[5] Rape and murder and then revenge—these climactic eruptions of violence, so crumpled and clumsy in *The Virgin Spring* that the attackers and not the victims seem to be suffering from the mess—are what *The Last House on the Left* dwells on. Not off to the church and not "after the rainbow," as the song on the sound track suggests—the girl is after a rock band called "Blood Lust," and the film insinuates that the director made it to the concert while his heroine didn't. Unlike moralist Bergman, for whom any savagery is senseless, the post-Vietnam "immoralist" Craven provides the world's violence with a cause as appalling as its absence in *The Virgin Spring:* "We're gonna have some fun," promises the Mansonesque killer before he rapes. Conversely, where Bergman takes great pains to establish motives for the father's revenge, Craven throws his doctor into a whirlpool of unwarranted cruelty and gives him a hand only when it comes to choosing a weapon simply because there is nothing else left for him to do.

Just as *The Virgin Spring* was a tale of faith, *The Last House on the Left* becomes a tale of havoc. Order returns at the end of *The Virgin Spring;* it never does at the end of *The Last House.* But isn't it the incentive of every remake to tell the same story with a different meaning?

The otherness of the meaning, of course, is visible only to the informed. Clearly, one must be familiar with the original to understand what the remake alludes, or bids adieu, to. Like one of those tricky airport billboards that reads "Welcome" or "Have a Good Flight," depending on the passenger's direction, the remake says one thing when read as an original work and another when seen in retrospect, through the lens of its source.

The Last House is as full of hidden (and not so hidden), playful (and straight-faced) allusions to its prototype as its landscape is full of springs. Just like the coquettish blonde Karin, who insisted on the white Sunday dress that was a bit too immodest for a medieval Swedish maid, the coquettish blonde Mary Collingwood argues with her parents about clothing. She puts on an outfit to which her father remarks, "What, no bra?! You can see nipples!" propelling a lengthy discussion on "tits." Later, the delinquent kid—or "little toad," as his fugitive parent refers to him—says he wants to be a frog. The character does not mean what Wes Craven does: in *The Virgin Spring,* a toad, squashed by the ill-natured Ingeri into a loaf of bread, is found by the boy. Having latently recognized himself in the amphibian, the urchin repents, just as his offspring in 1972 will. Neither one lives to see the end of his film.[6]

Here, at the stage of narrative interaction, many remakes would stop. But what would do in the screenwriter's heaven of Hollywood mainstream, where remaking a film is often synonymous to retelling the story, was not good enough for Wes Craven, a pioneer of rediscovery and a rebel with a cause to dare the guru of European film auteur.

If *The Virgin Spring* were a tapestry it would be made of canvas, the coarseness of which would only be highlighted by its artist's translucent style. Canvas and wood are two basic materials this universe is made of. Fire and water are two elements that combat one another here for man's soul. Sven Nykvist's camera, solemnly frontal, creates an image as pure and minimalist as the world it depicts. This world does not know any middle ground, just as its inhabitants are unaware of compromise. If it's raining here, watch for the Deluge; if it's hurting, await a bloodshed. In this world, the woods are teeming with ravens and goblins. The ravens caw; the goblins see "three dead men riding north"; both prophesy ill. Everything is an omen here,

Figure 20. One of the most startling film rituals ever: we see the father's sacred cleansing before the sacrificial killing. Max von Sydow and Brigitta Pettersson star in Ingmar Bergman's *The Virgin Spring.*

and nature speaks to man. Pagan Ingeri begs Karin to turn back, for "the forest is so black." Karin doesn't listen, and pays for it.

There is nothing this world values more than a ritual. A film whose legendary time spans from dawn to dawn, *The Virgin Spring* begins with Ingeri starting a fire while conjuring up the god Odin and ends with the father's invocation of the Lord. In between, there is one of the most startling film rituals ever: the father's sacred cleansing bath before the sacrificial killing. (See figure 20.) The father wants to be Christian, and this world—pagan, primitive, fossil—does not make it easy for him. Another word for this world would be mythic, which seems to entirely match with Bergman's conception, inspired, according to the opening credit, by the fourteenth-century Swedish legend. In the realm of myth, all dimensions of *The Virgin Spring*—thematic and formal—coincide and intersect in an ultimately tuneful order.

The remake's bond with cultural mythology is as solid as it is basic. What a serious, conscious remaker sees in the source film is an individual expression of the myth to be remade. From the narrative, through the filmic properties, to the underlying cultural myth lies the trajectory of any remake that is of interest to thinkers and not just to financiers.

Of course, there are myths, and then, there are myths. The kind of myth-making in which the remake is involved is "low" and popular, not "high" and classical. But what is the difference? What is the difference between Orestes and James Bond? Both are great spokesmen for their times. Both are serial heroes. Neither can breathe outside the genre structure.[7]

There was nothing that popular culture, this spoiled and prodigal off-spring of romanticism, would seize more eagerly from its classical parent than the notion of genre: genre as a formula and genre as a model channel, or conductor, for myth. The convenient beauty of the genre is that its for-mulaic and mythical qualities are not discrepant. Genre in fact does in cul-ture what no individual genius could: it formulates myths.

This is why most remakes are genre films. The self-conscious, referential culture of the remake, constantly in search of codes, finds a dual code in the genre film to make over: the code of the individual source and the code of its genre. (Martin Scorsese's *Cape Fear,* for example, was not only a re-make of J. Lee Thompson's picture but also of the thriller formula as a whole.) Even more significantly, genres do for remakers what sieves did for gold miners: they sort and retain, they distill the myths of the time.

When the myth of a genre (the frontier naïveté of the western, or the apocalyptic dread of the disaster film) does not match the myth of the time, the genre fades away. For the same reason some ideally formulaic genre offerings fade away untapped by remakers (the western in the 1980s, the "invasion film" after the end of the cold war).

But if the secret of a successful remake is chiefly in finding a perfect match between the genre and the epoch (which is true about many re-makes, all based on genre films), this secret was of no use for Wes Craven in remaking *The Virgin Spring,* a film without a genre. Yet Craven, a director dressed to head the A list of B moviemaking, knew perfectly well what he was doing when he picked one of the most mythical films ever as his pro-totype. He found exactly what he wanted: a different kind of myth, a mod-ernist myth, unscratched by popular culture. In Bergman's pure, distilled, and culturally virgin myth, Craven had a perfect spring to defile.

What in 1959 was the fourteenth century, becomes 1972 in 1972. And what in fourteenth-century Sweden was primeval forest, the realm of basic ele-ments and instincts, in 1972 becomes an American suburb. (See figure 21.) Typically peaceful and sweet, typically boring and dull, typically middle class, it is decorated with integrally standard facades (on the outside) and requisitely moderate "abstract" prints (on the inside). Here, what looks like wood is actually Formica; what could be canvas is really nylon.

Yet Craven does not reduce the poetry of myth to mythless prose. Rather,

Figure 21. The fourteenth-century primeval forest (*The Virgin Spring*, 1959) has became an American suburb (*The Last House on the Left*, 1972) in Wes Craven's remake of Bergman.

he embarks on a dimension no less mythological than Bergman's, but with different kinds of myths.

Suburbia, the citadel of normality in American culture, is where the myth of family values found refuge from society's nervous breakdown. An isolationist haven (ours is *the last* house on the left, which also could be *the first* house on *the right*), the suburb is a mutation of urban and rural mythologies. Neither city nor country, it appropriates (in the collective subconscious of its inhabitants) the best and the safest of both.

Never a paradise, but always a target, the suburb is a perfect setting for the bizarre, more so against the backdrop of nauseating and often fake familial serenity. In the 1950s, the suburb was the most sacred site that the rootless body snatchers could possibly invade; its invasion, therefore, was the scariest. In the early 1980s, the suburb, an ideal metaphor for neoconservatist mentality, returned as a favorite location for science fiction and horror films, a scene most appropriate for the invasion of alien (Steven Spielberg's *E.T.* [1982]) or supernatural (Tobe Hooper's *Poltergeist* [1982]) forces. A few years later, David Lynch, the poet of provincial void, romanticized suburban evil by demolishing the suburban myth in *Blue Velvet* (1986).

The Last House on the Left, with a rock sound track that sounds as if it were

borrowed from *Easy Rider* (1969), is one of the first ventures into the reno-
vated, postradical myth of the 1970s. It is also one of the first reactions to
the defeat of the 1960s, coming from inside the generation that lost. A film
with plenty of violence, it is also a film without suspense. It is not meant to
frighten us or in any way involve us emotionally—something suspense cannot do without. A surgeon rather than a lyricist, Craven, who will return
to suburbia in the more baroque but less personal *Nightmare on Elm Street*
(1984), gives us nobody to identify with and maintains his own distance.
What he sees is a society that has fallen asleep (or was put to sleep), a
desensitized society to which Philip Kaufman in 1978 will find a perfect
metaphor in the 1950s' *Invasion of the Body Snatchers*. This society is crushed
here by the hippielike killers and, even more so, by its own chain-saw defense. That this chain saw belongs to another story and a different, "anti-
suburban" myth is precisely what *Last House on the Left* is about.

Hitchcock was only kidding when he began *Psycho* with a tale of theft
that led nowhere. Craven's play is less elegant but more candid. In the opening, he also promises a different kind of movie, a "sweet sixteen" melodrama, with a fruity birthday cake, cute neighbors, and the indispensable
generation gap, expressed in conflicting approaches to brassieres. These
promises are as vain as they are essential for suburban utopia, absurdly solid
and solidly absurd.

The wishful destruction crushes this sleepy world with a savage energy
that makes Bergman's violence look like figure skating, just as Craven's
handheld camera and jerky editing make Bergman's frontal grandeur look
like an old master's frescos. When Mary's mother, a housewife with facial
features all but washed out, bites off the assailant's penis, there can be no
mistake: something went awry in this world. When Mary's father, who looks
like the Reverend Billy Graham, splatters the rapist's brains all over his
tacky furniture we know sweet suburbia is no more. Violent frenzy has invaded the myth of normality as it took over intellect in Sam Peckinpah's
Straw Dogs (1971). Similarly, George Romero's crazed zombies snatched the
bodies of loyal citizens.

In 1959, Ingmar Bergman made a film about a tragedy that inevitably
accompanies the shift of mythologies, the passage of cultures. So, in 1972,
did Wes Craven. Only his is a kind of tragedy that could be written not
by Shakespeare but by Shakespeare's Fool: ruthlessly cynical and painfully
funny.

As a postmodern artist has no other way to "interview" reality but through
an interpreter of another culture, it is hard to imagine a remake made
within the same cultural tier as the original. The cultures must vary, either
in time, as is the case in *The Thing* (1951, 1982), *The Fly* (1958, 1986), *Cape
Fear* (1962, 1992), and most other notable remakes, or in space, as it hap-

pens between *Yojimbo* (1961, Japan) and *A Fistful of Dollars* (1964, Italy), *Seven Samurai* (1954, Japan), *The Magnificent Seven* (1960, USA), and even George Cukor's *Adam's Rib* (1949, USA) and its Bulgarian remake (1956), and Rambo's *First Blood* (1982) and the Russian response to it, currently in production, in which an Afghan war vet comes out of his drunken oblivion to fight the evil of the world.[8] In any case, the remake remains a metacultural medium that has to cross borders, temporal or spatial, in order to connect.

The Last House on the Left at least tripled the shift. It switched from the 1950s to the 1970s, from European to American sensibility and, last but not least, from a militant, genreless auteurism to an excessively personal style of a B slasher movie before the genre went mainstream. Wes Craven's film met its prototype and interlocutor on the terrain of myth and proved that only mythless times will not be remade. If only one could imagine times like that. And if only one could believe that times like that deserved a remake.

NOTES

1. See Gerald Mast, *A Short History of the Movies,* 5th ed. (New York: Macmillan, 1992), 547.

2. See *Roger Ebert's Movie Home Companion,* 1993 ed. (Kansas City: Andrews and McMeel, 1992); Leonard Maltin, ed., *Leonard Maltin's TV Movies and Video Guide* (New York: Signet, 1992); Steven H. Scheuer, *Movies on TV* (New York: Bantam, 1987).

3. Unless a readaptation of a literary work refers to the previous adaptation(s) and not directly to the written source, the readaptation should not be considered a remake. Thus, Martin Scorsese's *Cape Fear* (1991) and Werner Herzog's *Nosferatu: Phantom of the Night* (1979) are remakes, but Francis Ford Coppola's *Bram Stoker's Dracula* (1992), Kenneth Branagh's Hamlet (1996), or any other recent Shakespeare production is not.

4. Ibid., 1254.

5. A shocking variety show of vengeance, elaborately schemed and painstakingly executed, is one of Craven's trademarks, seen, for example, in *A Nightmare on Elm Street* (1984), *Deadly Friend* (1986), and *Shocker* (1991). God left Craven's world, and left it without a blueprint; the revenge with shaving cream spread on the floor, invisible strings attached to murderous hammers, chain saws, short circuits, etc., is the only plan possible in the total chaos.

6. Narrative, verbal, stylistic, casting, and other references to the source are precisely what should decisively distinguish a remake from a "rip-off" (Maltin). Thieves conceal and pretend to not have taken what they took—something that neither Wes Craven, nor any other true remaker, credited or uncredited, ever does.

7. No one could claim the absence of differences between the classical and the pop culture for reasons other than polemical. Thus, for example, the authorship of the popular myth is more "anonymous" than that of the classical myth. Orestes

belongs to Aeschylus and 007 to . . . well, not exclusively Ian Fleming, but maybe because of this James Bond is even more mythical than Orestes. Myths emerge from the existential anonymity and, having passed the stage of individual expression, should lead back to anonymity, this time cultural.

8. Between 1992 and 1995, several Hollywood remakes of the relatively recent European productions—*Scent of a Woman* (*Profumo di donna,* Italy, 1975), *Sommersby* (*The Return of Martin Guerre,* France, 1982), *The Vanishing* (Netherlands, 1988), *Point of No Return* (*Nikita,* France, 1990), and *My Father, the Hero* (*Mon Père, le Héro,* France 1992)—were released; several more are currently in production. While a short temporal gap is caused directly by the "exploitation" aspect of remaking a successful (or potentially commercial) feature, these remakes could not have been done if the source films did not originate overseas. A scenario in which Joe Dante, John Carpenter, or Walter Hill are remaking a Jim Jarmusch, a Jon Jost, or a Henry Jaglom picture yet remains in the realm of fantasy.

ELEVEN

Cinematic Makeovers and Cultural Border Crossings: Kusturica's *Time of the Gypsies* and Coppola's *Godfather* and *Godfather II*

Andrew Horton

I think that the concept of border suggests something very subversive and unsettling. . . .
[I]t means recognizing the multiple nature of our own identities.
HENRY A. GIROUX, *DISTURBING PLEASURES*

DEDICATED TO GYPSIES, FILMMAKERS, AND BORDER CROSSERS EVERYWHERE.

"Yes, this is a Gypsy *Godfather*," wrote the *Time* reviewer Richard Corliss in 1990 when *Time of the Gypsies,* by the Bosnian-born Yugoslav director Emir Kusturica, was released in the United States after it won for him the Best Director award from the Cannes International Film Festival the previous year.

The reference to Coppola's 1972 hugely successful Mafia family epic based on the Mario Puzo novel and screenplay is more than an American critic's effort to interest a home audience in a quality foreign film. For Kusturica's gypsy tale, based on actual newspaper stories, turns out to be not only a transfixing glimpse at a "parade of ethnic eccentricity" (Hinson), but a hymn to world cinema at a time when television has become the more dominant form of presenting moving images. Finally, this Balkan recasting of Coppola's *Godfather* and *Godfather II* (it was made before *Godfather III* appeared) also manages to go beyond such intertextuality and international border crossings to emerge as a "Yugoslav" text reflective of the cinema of that troubled country that tragically no longer exists in any discernible form. In this essay I use Kusturica's captivating film as a case study in a larger consideration of cinematic remakes viewed from the triple perspective mentioned above: how a film from a non-English-speaking, third world country may drastically remake a Hollywood film (films in this case), how such a film can also allude to the cinemas of other nations and thus in some way announce itself as a member of the discourse of "world cinema" while maintaining its own cultural integrity as, in part, seen by its allusions to the cinema of its own nation. Not all elements of such a complex case of border crossing, as cultural-cinema critics such as Henry A. Giroux have explored the term, can be thoroughly illustrated in such a short piece as this. But it is my hope that this essay furthers cross-cultural cinematic studies.

Rather than remake *The Godfather* in any overt sense, however, Kusturica, a Bosnian filmmaker from Sarajevo, has made over Coppola's work to reflect Kusturica's own personal and cultural (Yugoslav) interests. In fact, Kusturica has often used *The Godfather* more to point to contrasts than parallels, culturally and cinematically.

Most attention paid to cinematic remakes involves Hollywood films, which we can consider either from the purely capitalistic urge of the industry to make more profit on a proven product or, as Leo Braudy has suggested in his remarks in this collection, the larger view of movie remakes as metaphorically reflecting "the history and culture of this self-made and self-remade country" (330). But I wish to look into that area of cinematic remakes, mentioned above, that has received little critical scrutiny: what I call the cross-cultural makeover. If Hollywood is indeed the acknowledged dominant cinema in the world, the ways in which minority cultures appropriate and make use of that dominant discourse can prove instructive for both narrative film studies and cultural studies. Taken all together, this investigation should reinforce Victor Shklovsky's keen observation that "[i]n the history of art, the legacy is transmitted not from father to son, but from uncle to nephew" (49).

Narrative in any form is, as Edward Branigan reminds us, "[o]ne of the most important ways we perceive our environment" (1). But, as he also notes, narrative depends on building story structures "based on stories already told." In Branigan's useful analysis, narrative is studied both for the process of generating stories and for the act of comprehension. In either case there is the need for a level of experience that recognizes patterns of storytelling and thus the sense of a backlog of "stories already told" that are shared by storytellers (authors, filmmakers) and audiences. In most cases, of course, recognized patterns do not suggest a direct adaptation of a set tale but rather a range of similarities. In such a manner, we could, for instance, identify one kind of story "already told" as belonging to a "coming of age" pattern. As Branigan notes, " '[M]eaning' is said to exist when pattern is achieved" (14).

We recognize the remake as a more intensified and self-conscious form of the narrative process described by Branigan. Within the territory of the remake, "meaning" involves the knowledge of specific texts, not only for their patterns but for their characterization, tone, texture, and point of view. Even more so than other forms of narrative, the remake announces itself as negotiating a self-conscious balancing act between the familiar and the new or the familiar "transformed."

Finally, what I will term the "makeover" is a particular form of remake that purposely sets out to make significant changes in what is either acknowledged or perceived as a prototype or important precursor to the film in question. Seymour Chatman has distinguished between overt and covert narration depending on the "degrees of audibility" of narrators (196). This distinction can also be applied to remakes. Films that clearly announce themselves as remakes in one or multiple ways are "overt" recastings, while the makeover is constructed to be more covert (by varying degree) in its audibility for the viewing audience. Makeover as a term will help us to emphasize the characteristics and strategies, overt and covert, of difference that the film in question presents in terms of previous texts while also noting possible levels of connection, similarity, continuity beyond various borders, geographic, intellectual, imaginative, and cinematic. Jean Renoir was fond of saying that he was not able to become a filmmaker until he realized his love for von Stroheim, Chaplin, Griffith, and Keaton had to be transformed into his own French "language," cinematic and linguistic, since he was, after all, French (Durgnat, 9).

MAKING OVER NARRATIVE: FAMILY BUSINESS

At the core of the fabula, or story, of both *Godfather* films is what Coppola's characters call the twin peaks of their lives: the personal ("family") and "business." Building on Puzo's novel, Coppola managed to infuse the Hollywood gangster genre with a richly textured double dose of the Italian American immigrant experience in the United States and the importance of family life to that experience. As Peter Cowie has observed about the first part of the trilogy, "[T]he film is really a paean, not so much to the Mafia as to the pioneer spirit that enabled generations of Italians to sail to the USA, settle, and establish a new caste of ironclad proportions" (53). (See figure 22.)

Note to what degree Coppola's two films exist not as prototypes for *Time of the Gypsies* but as complex examples of stories "based on stories already told." On the most immediate level, *The Godfather* is an adaptation of the novel with the added connection that the script was written by the novel's author. And *Godfather II* thus appeared as a sequel. A further exploration, however, would have to discuss Coppola and Puzo's "rewriting" of the cinematic genre of the crime film. It is just as important to our understanding of Coppola's films to know what kind of border crossing Coppola has done between the various films that make up the genre of previous mob-crime

Figure 22. The godfather, Marlon Brando (with Al Pacino), takes the role of the gangster patriarch far beyond the genre stereotypes of the past in *The Godfather* (1972).

films as it is to study the process of adaptation from Puzo's written page to Coppola's moving images. Noting such a complexity in speaking about Hollywood cinema, Raymond Bellour has observed that "in the classic American cinema, meaning is constituted by a correspondence in the balances achieved. . . . Multiple in both nature and extension, these cannot be reduced to any truly unitary structure or semantic relationship" (99).

Acknowledging such a pluralistic state of balances and meanings within

Figure 23. A Balkan family portrait: Perhan (Davar Dujmovic), far right, standing next to his beloved grandmother (Ljubica Adzovic), is the young Gypsy who later becomes a gypsy Mafia member in Emir Kusturica's *Time of the Gypsies* (1989), a makeover of Francis Ford Coppola's *The Godfather.*

Coppola's texts as, to one degree or another, makeovers of previous crime films as well as adaptations of a novel, we can now turn to *Time of the Gypsies* and the even more complex nature of the makeover.

Kusturica's saga follows a similar story-subject perspective—that of business and family. *Time of the Gypsies* is an epic chronicle of a young Serbian gypsy, Perhan (Davor Dujmovic), from awkward adolescence through puberty, young love, travel, involvement in a godfather-controlled crime network in Italy, and on to his eventual marriage, fatherhood, godfatherhood, downfall, and death.[1] (See figure 23.) Perhan's struggle, like that of *The Godfather*'s Michael Corleone, is between his strong sense and need of family and the pressures on him to go into the "business," in this case a crime empire dedicated to selling gypsy babies and exploiting cripples, dwarfs, and women (via prostitution) across the border in Italy (all based on true accounts of over thirty thousand gypsy children "sold" into such slavery by their parents and other relatives, a practice that has not ended). Beyond these plot and thematic similarities to the Coppola films, the differences mushroom in the fertile soil suggested by *The Godfather* and *Godfather II*.

For our purposes, I shall focus on both the cinematic (including narrative) and cultural differences that Kusturica's text evokes, with the addition of an extra observation: Part of the pleasure of Coppola's trilogy is that of watching the high level of professional acting, in many cases by actors such as Marlon Brando and Al Pacino, who began their film careers with impressive stage backgrounds. Kusturica, in contrast, has gone in absolutely the opposite direction, using predominately nonprofessional gypsies to play themselves, though the roles of Perhan and Ahmed especially are played by well-known actors.

If we embrace the totality of *difference* served us by Kusturica and his screenwriter Goran Mihic,[2] we could describe the fabula-plot of this Balkan makeover in the following way: *Time of the Gypsies* is a dramatic-comic tale told with both realism and dreamlike fantasy, full of cinematic references, concerning an Eastern Orthodox Serbian orphan gypsy with certain telekinetic powers who is raised within a matriarchal culture by his grandmother. He becomes a gypsy godfather but ultimately fails to mature due to the lack of a proper father figure. He finally tries to resolve his personal crises by murdering his adopted "godfather"-father and is in turn murdered by the godfather's latest bride. His dying expression, however, is not one of pain but is instead a satisfied smile as he sees a vision floating above him suggesting his dead mother, wife, and beloved pet turkey. Rather than a sense of loss, Perhan's death has brought him a deeper peace and seeming understanding. On a deeply spiritual level, he has been fulfilled.

Let us now explore more closely the nature and implications of Kusturica's makeover, beginning with the level of the cinematic border crossing.

MAKING OVER COPPOLA'S GODFATHERS

Style: Gothic Realism vs Magic Realism

Coppola's style in the trilogy might be termed "gothic realism"—a blending of realistically based scenes shot in deep expressionistic tones and shades, with no flights of fantasy or dreams within the narrative. In strong contrast, Kusturica's film is, as I shall discuss more fully, dream oriented. Perhan's trickster figure Uncle Merdzan tells him at one point, "I see life as a mirage," and so do we for two hours as Kusturica treats us to frequent dream sequences and fantasy-like realities heavily influenced, according to Kusturica, by Gabriel García Márquez and the South American tradition of "magic realism."

The impermanence of gypsy life is more than one of physical mobility: it is a condition of the spirit, a perception of the universe, which Kusturica captures in his overall style and approach to his narrative. The gypsies, he told a *New York Times* interviewer, "move . . . easily from reality to illusion to dream, as in a Gabriel García Márquez novel. *Time of the Gypsies* belongs entirely to the world of García Márquez and other Latin American writers who built their art on the irrationality and poverty of their people" (Insdorf). Thus, while a study of Coppola's films should, as we have noted earlier, incorporate a stylistic and narrative study of the American crime film genre, Kusturica's film could also be fruitfully studied in relation to the tradition of literary magic realism, suggesting once more the plurality of meanings Bellour alludes to in "reading" films.

Cinematic Tone: The Tragic vs the Joyfully Comic

Coppola's vision, especially when taking the trilogy as a whole, is one of tragedy, of loss, of a falling apart as he himself has commented (Goodwin, 161–93). Kusturica's gypsy epic is one of what he calls "joy," a term that embraces "happiness and sorrow." This double vision is particularly reflected in the Charlie Chaplin motif worked throughout the film, including the final image of Uncle Merdzan, who has consciously acted out Chaplin for the amusement of the family earlier. We see him leave Perhan's funeral and run off through mud, wind, rain, his back to the camera, coat clutched, a cane in hand à la Chaplin. One could argue that Chaplin's solo endings in his films actually push us finally into melodrama rather than the comic. But the memories we have of Chaplin and of Kusturica's work is one tinged more with the comic than the tragic, though we are aware in both cases that the comic embraces pathos as well as laughter (Horton, *Comedy/Cinema/ Theory*, 5).

KUSTURICA'S SALUTE TO WORLD CINEMA IN AN AGE OF TELEVISION

Coppola's *Godfather* films build on the whole American tradition of crime genre films. But Kusturica cuts a much larger territory of cinematic border crossing with direct and indirect references to over forty directors, ranging from the surrealism of Luis Buñuel to the straightforward, clean, narrative visual style of John Ford. Part of Kusturica's cinematic makeover strategy in *Time of the Gypsy* results in an anthology of allusions and homage to Yugoslav and European cinema, as well as to classical Hollywood movies. When Perhan becomes a godfather and dons the appropriate looking clothes, he winds up appearing remarkably like Al Pacino. At one moment, he stands in front of a movie theater playing *Citizen Kane*. As Perhan goes to light his cigar, he sees a still of Orson Welles with an unlit cigar in his mouth. Before lighting his own cigar, Perhan holds the match up to Orson Welles's Havana in a double allusion and tribute to Welles and, we can add, to François Truffaut, who staged a similar Wellesian homage in his first feature, *400 Blows* (1959), as well as in his later hymn to filmmaking itself, *Day for Night* (1973). Thus, while the overriding nod in *The Time of the Gypsies* is to Coppola's two films, Kusturica is at pains for us to understand that he is involved in a much larger cinematic world of influences and allusions.

It is significant that two of the most important European films of 1989 concern a double interest in the odyssey of young males trying to come of age and in the presentation of their narratives within a cinematic context that pays homage to, and asks for authentication from, a tradition of world cinema. I am speaking, of course, of *Time of the Gypsies* and the Italian-French Oscar-winning production of Giuseppe Tornatore's *Cinema Paradiso*. Like Perhan, the young boy in *Cinema Paradiso* must grow up without a father. But unlike his gypsy counterpart, the Italian boy has a grandfather figure in the character of a small town movie projectionist played by Philippe Noiret.

Even more striking, however, is the way in which both films embrace through allusions, film clips, and cinematic quotations their respective national film traditions and that of classical Hollywood and world cinema. Of course, in casting a narrative around, and in, a movie theater, *Cinema Paradiso* allows for a more overt dialogue on cinematic homage and a simultaneous need for authentication. But before discussing particular cinematic influences contained in Kusturica's makeover, we need to understand that both of these European films announce themselves as *nontelevision* at a time when television has not only supplanted cinema as the major entertainment form but has done so in an age when cinema has, in order to survive, in many ways become television. Kusturica wishes to celebrate particular masters of the cinema and their works—Yugoslav, Hollywood, and European—but he is also necessarily making it clear that he wishes to be authenticated and included in their company, in the family of national (Yugoslav) and world cinema.

The dilemma of world cinema today is well captured by Todd Gitlin when he notes: "More and more, movies themselves have turned into coming attractions—fodder for TV (and radio) morning shows, local and national TV news, syndicated shows like ENTERTAINMENT TONIGHT, national magazines from PEOPLE to VANITY FAIR, USA TODAY and the newspaper style sections, novelizations, comic books, theme song records, toys, T-shirts, and, of course, sequels. The sum of the publicity takes up more cultural space than the movie itself" (15–16). *Cinema Paradiso* might more aptly be retitled *Cinema Nostalgia,* and *Time of the Gypsies* as *Time of the Filmmaker as Gypsy.* For in every way, Kusturica's film announces itself as a film and not as television. The allusions starting with Coppola and *The Godfather* are many, but 99 percent are to cinema and not the tube. And they may be called hymns to the movie-going cinema experience as well, for it is more than a sense of narrative closure that requires in *Cinema Paradiso* the blowing up of the local cinema (and thus the main character's youth) to build a parking lot: a way of life has gone and the age of video and television has triumphed. Similarly, the very beginnings of love and sexual awakening take place in Kusturica's film as Perhan and Azra watch an important Yugoslav film (Rajko Grlic's *The Melody Haunts My Memory* [*Samo Jednom Se Ljubi*, 1980]) in a makeshift open-air cinema and try to imitate the passion on the screen while Perhan's pet turkey looks on.

Thus in our post-postmodern media times, when even American presidential candidates communicate with their audiences via television by mentioning television in the form of shows such as *Murphy Brown, The Simpsons,* and *The Waltons,* Kusturica places his Balkan-Hollywood film (produced and released through Columbia Pictures during the closing days of David Puttnam's reign) squarely within a realm of reference that champions the cinematic experience for filmmakers and viewers alike.

Within this context, Kusturica's vision is one that includes both a realist and a surrealist tradition: thus does John Ford meet up with Luis Buñuel within this gypsy cinematic caravan. These extreme borders go beyond individual filmmakers, of course, for to mention Ford and Buñuel is also to embrace the classical Hollywood tradition and the anarchistic European avant-garde at the same time.

Kusturica has often spoken of his love of Ford's films.[3] And there are many scenes in Kusturica's films that share a general set up of straightforward dramatic confrontation with simple camera work reminiscent of Ford's approach. Furthermore, there are direct allusions to Ford's work, as in the closing scene of Kusturica's first feature, *Do You Remember Dolly Bell?* (*Sjecas Li Se Dolly Bell?* 1981). In the final shot, a Bosnian family is loaded into an open truck with all of its belongings, and they begin to drive toward a new home. The direct reference to *The Grapes of Wrath* is not just cinematic but thematic as well: the family has suffered but will survive, despite all odds.

There is much in *Time of the Gypsies* that echoes the playful surrealism of Buñuel. We can sense something of Buñuel's spirit in much of the absurdity that Perhan encounters, in the use of dreams and visions, in the unexpected plot twists and digressions (Buñuel, "Digression Seems to Be," 166), and in an atmosphere of magic realism in which forks fly and whole houses can be pulled from their foundations by a simple pickup truck. Kusturica, like a gypsy, has stolen from everyone, including from his native Bosnian and Yugoslav tradition for folk surrealism and magic realism (Horton, "Oedipus Unresolved," 68–74). Remember, for instance, the appearance of the Virgin Mary a few years ago in the little town of Medjugorje in Bosnia, an appearance that may well owe just as much to folk surrealism as to religion.

At heart, however, there is more of John Ford's style in Kusturica's work than there is of even Coppola, Buñuel, or any other cinematic father figure. John Ford's darkly humored acceptance of people goes beyond the sense of tragedy, loss, and alienation pictured in Coppola's trilogy. These words of Ford's could easily be Kusturica's: "The situation, the tragic moment, forces men to reveal themselves, and to become aware of what they truly are. The device (a small group of people thrust by chance into a dramatic situation) allows me to discover humor in the midst of tragedy, for *tragedy is never wholly tragic. Sometimes tragedy is ridiculous*" (Gallagher, 81; italics my own).

Taken together, all of these intertextual, Hollywood, European, and other national cinematic "quotes" strongly suggest that Kusturica wishes his film to be taken as a member of a club that includes not only Hollywood but world cinema itself.

THE YUGOSLAV FILM CONNECTION

Coppola managed to stamp a decidedly Italian American mark on one of Hollywood's most popular genres. Kusturica, however, announces himself as both an heir to Yugoslav filmmaking—ironically only a few years before such a label no longer had meaning for a country and an industry deconstructed by strife, war, and rebellion—and also to world cinema. Within this tradition, Kusturica's homages are numerous. For the title and subject matter of the film—gypsies—the filmmaker is indebted to Alexander Petrovic's *I Have Even Met Happy Gypsies* (1967), the film voted the best Yugoslav film ever by a hundred critics in the 1980s and winner of the Best Film award at Cannes in 1967. Kusturica owes much of his tone and atmosphere—emotional and locational—to Petrovic's pioneering tale of the rough life of Yugoslav gypsies in their ambiguous relationship, at the time, to a communist-socialist state.

Among the twenty or so other Yugoslav films alluded to in *The Time of the Gypsies,* one feels Kusturica has most clearly nodded to Zivojn Pavlovic's *When I Was Dead and White* (1967), which was co-written by Kusturica's screenwriter, Goran Mihic. In that film, for instance, the main character is shot to death in an outhouse with his pants down, much as the godfather's assistant is gunned down by Perhan in *Gypsies.*

There is also Goran Paskalovic's *Guardian Angel* (1987) which treated the same story as Kusturica's film but two years earlier: the true story (widely reported in the press and on television) of Yugoslav gypsy children being sold into slavery. Also incorporated, directly this time, is Rajko Grlic's *The Melody Haunts My Memory,* a clip of which is shown in the film (see below). And the use of magic realism to express the reality of those who have died echoes a similar use of the technique in other Yugoslav films, most clearly in Srdjan Karanovic's *Petria's Wreath* (1980).

All of these Yugoslav film allusions are lost, of course, on viewers not familiar with Yugoslav cinema, which is to say most world viewers. But that is not the point. What is significant is that within the context of world cinema, Kusturica's text suggests how a film can embrace multiple connotations aimed at a variety of audiences. David Bordwell speaks about the "degree of communicativeness" in a film narrative (59) and notes that such a degree can be judged "by considering how willingly the narration shares the information to which its degree of knowledge entitles it." By making over many of the elements of two Hollywood films—Coppola's texts— Kusturica's film provides an overall wide degree of communicativeness or access to his Yugoslav story. But in his allusions to Yugoslav cinema, he has purposely built in a "home culture" element that speaks to those who know, without detracting from the pleasure and involvement the film has set up for the non-Yugoslav audiences. We are aware that such narrative layering is common in many forms. For example, Groucho Marx's asides are missed by many and a great pleasure to those who "get" them, but the existence of the asides themselves does not detract from the overall impact of a Marx brothers' comedy. Similarly, but on the level of cross-cultural, cross-cinematic tradition, Kusturica's border crossings speak to multiple audiences simultaneously.

MAKING OVER ONE'S OWN CAREER: CROSS MY GYPSY HEART

Kusturica has, finally, made over his own themes and narrative concerns in *The Time of the Gypsies*. When asked by his son at the train station if he will return, Perhan looks at him and promises, "Cross my gypsy heart." Of course, like everyone else in the film, he breaks his promise. The complexity of the oedipal situation is thus passed from Perhan to the next generation, setting us up for the conclusion in which the son steals the gold coins off his father's eyes during the funeral.

In his essay on Spielberg's *Always* in this collection, Harvey Greenberg has explored clearly the oedipal implications of the cinematic remake. For recasting a film that another "father" has produced is both the son's effort to replace the father and, in choosing to use the same text, a nostalgic wish to hold on to childhood and the past. Kusturica's nods to Coppola's films are both a challenge and a form of asking for a blessing by striving to be a member of the cinematic family and business, both within his culture (the former Yugoslavia) and beyond: Hollywood, Europe, and the world.

In addition to such a traditional oedipal situation, however, exists the effort of the filmmaker to remake himself. Thus, we conclude that beyond Coppola and world cinema, Kusturica has "made over" his own films as well.

Thematically all three of his features have been male coming-of-age stories. This is particularly true of the film previous to *Time of the Gypsies, When Father Was Away on Business,* which won the Best Film award at Cannes in 1985. In that film we see a similar use of magic realism and dreams of flight as the main protagonist manages to "fly" over Sarajevo in his dreams and, perhaps, in reality as well in this tragicomic view of the post-Stalinist 1950s in Yugoslavia, when the boy-protagonist's father is not away on business but in prison on trumped up political charges. Also present in *When Father* is the actor Davor Dujmovic, who stars as Perhan in *Time of the Gypsies.* Furthermore, in his first film, *Do You Remember Dolly Bell?* (1981), Kusturica presents a tale involving sexual initiation of a young male who is in conflict with a number of father figures who surround him, a motif also reflected in *When Father* and *Time of the Gypsies.*

MAKING OVER CULTURE: FOUR LEVELS

Beyond the cinematic, the makeover calls attention to multiple cultural differences. As a Bosnian-Yugoslav making a film about gypsies in the gypsy language with Hollywood studio money, Kusturica was clearly involved in a "multicultural" project. Moreover, the echoes to Coppola's films serve to delineate more sharply, as reviews of the film have shown, the differences of cultures, turning all audiences into border crossers. Four cultural dimensions are studied here.

Making Over Theme: The Stolid vs the Impermanent

While the thrust of the Puzo-Coppola trilogy is toward assimilation and the legitimization of their Italian American immigrants and their descendants, Kusturica's gypsies are shown to exist as they always have and, supposedly, always will: on the fringe, outside any traditional European cultures *by choice.* As Richard Corliss noted, these gypsies are "a Third World nation of wanderers, displaced and dispossessed in the midst of European bounty" (82). The opening ten minutes of *The Godfather* projects an overwhelming sense of solid, stolid immobility: the men in Don Corleone's study seem rooted to the heavy furniture and deep shadows. Kusturica's film reflects the impermanence of gypsy life itself. Within the cinematic frame, all is motion. And between cuts, characters constantly drift between Yugoslavia and Italy and back again. But there is more: the dominant motifs of Kusturica's film are of floating—people, animals, ghosts, objects including houses— and of the sound of the wind. It blows through the entire film, much as Gabriel García Márquez's wind blows through *One Hundred Years of Solitude.*
A key image is that of Perhan's house being literally pulled off its foun-

dations during a thunderstorm by his drunken Uncle Merdzan (it seems unlikely that the "merd" is an accident of naming). Merdzan has tied one end of a thick rope to the roof and the other to his mini-pickup truck and simply yanked away. That the security of home can so easily be destroyed becomes a lasting image for the film's audience.

The border crossing in this case is one of culture. Clearly Kusturica could have tried to make a film that did not consciously (even covertly) echo previous Hollywood texts, but in the realm of cultural discourse we realize that, by making over a familiar movie text, Kusturica is able to use his border crossing to highlight "different contexts, geographies, different languages, of otherness" (Giroux, 167).

Making Over Patriarchs into Matriarchs

The Godfather trilogy is heavily patriarchal. By contrast, *Time of the Gypsies,* like gypsy culture itself, is strongly matriarchal. Even what could be called the theme song—a haunting gypsy Orthodox hymn to Saint George's Day—is sung by a young woman. The gender implications that radiate from such a makeover of Coppola's crime classics are profound, indeed. Kusturica's opening shot is of an unhappy bride and an unconscious (passed out drunk) groom. The gender pattern is immediately established: women survive and grieve while men pass out, leave, disappear, die.

Almost literally we feel in Kusturica's film that the center of Perhan's universe is his grandmother, Hatidza (played with poignant intensity by a gypsy, Ljubica Adzovic). She is a mountain of a woman who embraces her grandchildren with tears, laughter, advice, strength and who, of course, has a cigarette constantly dangling from her lips. Gypsy life is a kind of impermanent dream-myth, and it is Hatidza who is the mythmaker as well as the possessor of special powers. Perhan's odyssey toward becoming a godfather is set in motion when Hatidza is summoned by the current gypsy godfather, Ahmed (played with Brando-like expressions and gusto by Bora Todorovic, the all-time leading star of Yugoslav cinema)[4], to save the life of one of his relative's sons. When she does so, Ahmed offers to take on Perhan as an apprentice in the "business" (Perhan does not yet know that it involves selling and exploiting Gypsy children).

Hatidza as healer, mediator between local quarrels, grandmother, substitute mother/father figure, and myth weaver embodies gypsy culture itself. In the "lift high the roof" scene already mentioned, Hatidza comforts a frightened Perhan and his sister by telling them this creation myth: "Once upon a time the Sky and Earth were man and wife. They had five children: Sun, Moon, Fire, Cloud, Water, and between them, they created a fine place for their children. The unruly Sun tried to part the Earth and the Sky, but failed. The other children tried too but failed. But one day the Wind lunged at them and the Earth was parted from the Sky." Dream, reality, myth, and motherly concern all blend together at such a moment. Kusturica's film grows out of the reality of gypsy life and crime today, but it also embraces the mythic creation of the earth itself. Within the particular narrative of the film, the damage done by a man (the uncle) is handled by Grandma. The pattern continues throughout till we see Perhan's corpse laid out in the same home, with Hatidza mourning and yet carrying on as she must.

Fatherly Blessings Given and Absent

Building on the previous point, the parallel journeys of Michael Corleone and Perhan Feric as young males differ greatly. Michael's odyssey is one of growing into adulthood, as the Don "blesses" him while passing on the godfather role to him. Perhan, in contrast, is an orphan who never knows his father or mother. In fact, given Hatidza's mythmaking powers, there is no proof that the story she tells Perhan about his parents—that his mother was a very beautiful woman who died in childbirth and his father a handsome Slovenian soldier—is true. Either way, Perhan has no true father to pass on the "blessing" that commentators such as psychiatrist Peter Blos note is necessary for any boy to become a male adult (32). On a psychological level, therefore, Kusturica's protagonist and film are "frozen" in the world of a male adolescent who cannot come of age.

Coppola and Puzo's Michael Corleone has the task of accepting his father's blessing, making sense of his ethnic family and business heritage, and renegotiating these elements within a changing American culture. The male-centeredness of Coppola's trilogy is well captured in the opening sequence of *The Godfather.* While it is quickly established that the wedding of Don Corleone's daughter is taking place outside on a bright sunny day, the center of attention is the group of men gathered in the Don's darkly lit study. The strong sense of the father never leaves *The Godfather* trilogy and, we might add, culminates in *Godfather III* with the father figure of the pope as a significant image.

Perhan's world in *Time in the Gypsies* is quite the opposite. The film's opening shot of the unhappy fat bride has already been mentioned. From this shot on, Kusturica surrounds Perhan with women. He cares, for instance, for his sick sister (his initial reason for leaving home with the gypsy godfather is to help heal his sister).

But most important, his life intertwines with his true love, Azra (Simolicka Trpkova). It is with Azra that he first experiences love, sex, and companionship and, ultimately, marriage, the birth of a son (which may or may not have been fathered by his uncle), and death, as Azra dies in Italy. Perhan's conflicted feelings for Azra—should he believe that her son is his?—are, of course, another expression of his failure to find an appropriate father figure to help him grow into maturity.

In an earlier scene, however, there are no conflicts at all. Kusturica orchestrates one of the most hauntingly beautiful scenes of sexual initiation ever to reach the silver screen. The moment happens immediately after Perhan's grandmother has described his parents to him. The scene is presented as a dream, as we see Perhan float through the sky clutching his beloved pet turkey on Saint George's day as a hymn to Saint George plays throughout on the sound track. As Perhan (and the camera) come down to earth, we see a river scene. Hundreds of gypsies with torches are gathered by the river to celebrate Saint George's day. On the river is a small wooden boat floating with Perhan and Azra, bare-chested, lying next to each other, playfully involved with each other.

Desire, religion, ritual, nature, music, and magic realism (dreams) all flow together in one "mirage" of sexual awakening. It is a joyous scene, the happiest moment of the film. Everything else in Perhan's life becomes a falling away from this moment of union with the woman he loves.

Nothing similar exists in the *Godfather* films. Men in Coppola's male-centered world exhibit no such pure joy in the presence of women, ritual, religion. Diane Keaton's "outsider's" role as Kay Adams is that of a proper Mafia wife and mother, with no sexuality presented or explored. Something much closer to the world of *Time of the Gypsies* is hinted at, of course, in the Sicilian romance and marriage scene as the young Michael courts a Sicilian beauty who is finally killed by a car bomb meant for Michael. But we never feel the completely embracing sense of women of all types that we feel in Kusturica's gypsy world.

Finally, for Perhan's female-centered universe we should mention the influence of his long-dead mother. She is represented by a wedding veil that trails through the sky at several points in the film. As Perhan dies, shot in the back by the godfather's new bride ("You ruined my wedding, you bastard!"), he looks heavenward and sees a combined image of the veil and his dead turkey, an image that unites his mother, Azra, and his pet.

Thus, much of the poignancy of Kusturica's film is that of a young male unable to become a man who both appreciates (loves) and fears the power and mystery of women.

Catholicism vs the Orthodox Faith

Coppola's trilogy draws a deeply ambivalent portrait of the Catholic Church and uses Catholic ritual as an important structuring device within the films. Kusturica's film, similarly uses church ritual and custom throughout, but it is the Orthodox faith of the Balkans (more specifically, the Serbian Orthodox tradition). The prime example is the one just given: Perhan's sexual initiation takes place within the comforting frame of a traditional religious holiday, Saint George's Day. Religion for the gypsies is tied together with family, tradition, custom, culture, and personal identity.

It is not so in *The Godfather.* Clearly, one can map out *The Godfather* according to the Catholic rituals of a wedding, funerals, and, finally, a baptism. But Coppola introduces Catholicism in order to undercut it ironically (Hess, 84). For it is during a baptism that the baptism of blood takes place in parallel editing, as Michael has ordered a shooting of all rivals at the very moment he is at his sister's child's baptism. For Coppola's gangsters, Catholicism is omnipresent. But it is simply part of being "Italian American," rather than a spiritual force capable of guiding individuals in their lives. John Hess speaks well of Coppola's critical view of the church: "Religion is still an important prop of bourgeois ideology, and the church also represents a community of sorts. But by juxtaposing it with its opposite— murder, hatred, brutality—Coppola implicates the Church in this activity. By showing the Church's inability to comfort anyone, Coppola shows its impotence. It is one more bourgeois ideal that does not work" (87).

Godfather III caps all of Coppola's ambivalent feelings about the church, of course, as even the Vatican is drawn into mob activity.

Religion, finally, for Kusturica and his gypsy culture, is tied strongly to folk mysticism as the dreamlike magic realism scenes of floating veils and the floating pet turkey viewed in death, as well as the whole motif of Perhan's telekinetic powers, suggest. For the gypsies, *Time of the Gypsies* suggests, are part pagan, part Christian, part believers, part passionate hedonists. As in their lives, so in their faith: they live within a sense of multiple possibilities.

STOLEN COINS: CROSSING ALL BORDERS

Leo Braudy puts it well in his remarks in this collection when he speaks of remakes as a form of "unfinished cultural business." The ending of Kusturica's gypsy narrative, with the young boy who may or may not be Perhan's son stealing the coins off Perhan's permanently sealed eyes before his burial, leaves us with a key to survival for gypsies: steal and run.

It is the perfect closing scene for a film about a culture that has survived because it exists beyond the cultural, political, spiritual, and economic borders of more stolid cultures by being itself perpetually "unfinished," impermanent, and in motion.

Finally, then, Kusturica's film is a survivor too because it refuses, like the gypsies, to be assimilated and identified completely with any one cinematic tradition. The perpetual state of making over cinematic texts and allusions, with Coppola's *The Godfather* and *Godfather II* being the primary object of plundering, locates Kusturica in the "unfinished" state of being a Bosnian-born filmmaker who has gone beyond the borders of geography, politics, language, and regional culture (though he does strongly represent these as well) to "steal" from the international currency of cinema.

This "gypsy-" like approach to narrative and cinema is not the only one available to filmmakers from minority non-English-speaking cultures, of course. Theo Angelopoulos of Greece and Andrei Tarkovsky of Russia, for instance, created internationally praised films by turning away from classical Hollywood and European narrative traditions, cinematic and otherwise.

But *Time of the Gypsies* is a vibrant example of how the more recognized border crossing represented by Hollywood remaking the films of other cultures can be reversed with imaginative cinematic and provocative cultural implications.

Our parting shot takes us outside of cinema itself.

It is tragically ironic that Kusturica's first film *Do You Remember Dolly Bell?* ends with a tracking close-up of the main character, our young male rock 'n' roll singer, who, in voice-over as he rides in the back of a truck headed for a new apartment building, says, "In every way, every day, things are getting better." That same skyline in 1995, as this essay is completed, has been blown apart, and millions of the people have been left homeless, almost three hundred thousand murdered, and many others raped and tortured. The all-embracing range of Kusturica's cinematic vision has, in reality, become a nightmare of ethnic hatred that the darkest Hollywood war or crime genre film could not envision.

We can only hope that cinema itself can prove to be one form of border crossing beyond the boundaries of hatred, violence, and death.

NOTES

1. Since the Perhan figure echoes the Al Pacino character in Coppola's trilogy, we can say that Kusturica presents in one film what Coppola develops in three, recognizing once more that *Godfather III* came out after *Time of the Gypsies*.

2. Mihic is one of the most if not the most prominent of Yugoslav screenwriters. For many years, it was not uncommon to see in an industry that produced no more than thirty or forty films, three or four films with Mihic scripts. This fact alone means that in choosing to work with Mihic, Kusturica was embracing the creator of many of the most memorable Yugoslav films.

3. Emir Kusturica, interview by author, Moscow, July 1989.

4. For Kusturica to use Bora Todorovic in the role of the godfather was itself a significant piece of casting. As the Brando and John Wayne of Yugoslavia rolled into

one, Todorovic has been the Partisan Hero of hundreds of films, the playboy-bad guy you love to hate in many more, and even a star of *light comedies as well. Todorovic *is* Yugoslav cinema! Certainly Brando's casting was important for the moody "method" actor implications Brando has always carried with him. And Coppola builds on this Brando persona. Kusturica likewise capitalizes on Todorovic's seemingly unbound energy, gusto, flexibility.

WORKS CITED

Bellour, Raymond. "The Obvious and the Code." In *Narrative, Apparatus, Ideology,* edited by Philip Rosen. New York: Columbia University Press, 1986.

Blos, Peter. *Son and Father: Before and beyond the Oedipus Complex.* New York: Macmillan, 1985.

Bordwell, David. *Narration in the Fiction Film.* Madison: University of Wisconsin Press, 1985.

Branigan, Edward. *Narrative Comprehension and Film.* New York: Routledge, 1992.

Breskin, David. "Francis Ford Coppola: The Rolling Stone Interview." *Rolling Stone,* 7 February 1991, 60–66.

Buñuel, Luis. "Digression Seems to Be My Natural Way of Telling a Story." In *My Last Sigh: The Autobiography of Luis Buñuel,* translated by Abigail Israel. New York: Alfred A. Knopf, 1983.

Chatman, Seymour. *Story and Discourse: Narrative Structure in Fiction and Film.* Ithaca: Cornell University Press, 1978.

Corliss, Richard. "A People Cursed with Magic," *Time,* 19 February 1990, 82.

Cowie, Peter, ed. "Francis Ford Coppola." *Film Guide International* (1976): 50–59.

Durgnat, Raymond. *Jean Renoir.* Berkeley and Los Angeles: University of California Press, 1974.

Gallagher, Tag. *John Ford: The Man and His Films.* Berkeley and Los Angeles: University of California Press, 1986.

Giroux, Henry A. *Disturbing Pleasures: Learning Popular Culture.* New York: Routledge, 1994.

Gitlin, Todd. "Down the Tubes." In *Seeing through Movies,* edited by Mark Crispin Miller, 15–48. New York: Pantheon, 1990.

Goodwin, Michael, and Naomi Wise. *On the Edge: The Life & Times of Francis Ford Coppola.* New York: William Morrow, 1989.

Hess, John. "*Godfather II*: A Deal Coppola Couldn't Refuse." In *Movies and Methods: An Anthology,* edited by Bill Nichols, 81–90. Berkeley and Los Angeles: University of California Press, 1976.

Hinson, Hal. "Drifting in the World of Gypsies." *Washington Post,* February 21, 1990, p. D4.

Horton, Andrew, ed. *Comedy/Cinema/Theory.* Berkeley and Los Angeles: University of California Press, 1991.

———. *"Do You Remember Dolly Bell?"* In *Magill's Survey of Cinema: Foreign Language Films,* 486–50. Los Angeles: Salem Press, 1985.

———. "Oedipus Unresolved: Covert and Overt Narrative Discourse in Emir

Kusturica's *When Father Was Away on Business.*" *Cinema Journal* 27, no. 4 (summer 1988): 64–81.

———. "Yugoslavia: A Multi-Faceted Cinema." In *World Cinema since 1945,* edited by William Luhr, 639–660. New York: Ungar, 1987.

Insdorf, Annette. "Gypsy Life Beguiles a Film Maker," *New York Times,* 4 February 1990, pp. 18, 25.

Mast, Gerald. *A Short History of the Movies.* 4th ed. New York: Macmillan, 1986.

Pachasa, Arlene. "Time for Kusturica." *American Film* (January 1990: 40–44.

Shklovsky, Victor. Quoted in Wallace Martin, *Recent Theories of Narrative.* Ithaca, N.Y.: Cornell University Press, 1986.

TWELVE

Made in Hong Kong:
Translation and Transmutation

Patricia Aufderheide

Just as the comparison between *Boudu Saved from Drowning* (1932) and *Down and Out in Beverly Hills* (1986) comments on the differences between Jean Renoir's Paris and Paul Mazursky's Los Angeles (Morgan, 1990), so other films that move along less predictable cultural pathways also reflect the cities in which they are made. Since those pathways arc usually cut along the lines of the flow of power—economic, political, cultural—differences also refract those realities through a creative prism. In Hong Kong, a city where economic growth and political anxiety mix headily, a flourishing, unabashedly imitative cinema inescapably comments on surrounding social and political tensions in the choices of its adaptations.

In national and subcultural cinemas worldwide, issues of cultural autonomy, cultural and national identity, and resistance to international cultural domination are all familiar and intertwined themes (Armes, 1987; Cooper, 1989). Also familiar is the criticism of the exoticization of foreign cultures in international entertainment, as was done in *Indiana Jones and the Temple of Doom* (1984) (Shohat, 1991). At the same time, the entertainment appeal and market success of dominant international cinema is undeniable and, to many filmmakers, enviable.

Humor, irony, parody and flamboyant imitation can be seen as strategies to express both resistance to and fascination with dominant cinema (and culture). Within the U.S. mainstream tradition, one might point to Robert Townsend's 1987 *Hollywood Shuffle*, a send-up of many black film roles and racist film clichés. In Brazil, whose film industry has often struggled to compete with U.S. product (Aufderheide, 1987), wry and sometimes self-deprecating parodies have long been a staple. For instance, *High Noon* (1952) was parodied in *Kill or Run* (1954), in which the hero role is buffoonish and cowardly; *Jaws* (1975) called forth the raucous comedy *Codfish*

(1976) (Vieira, 1982, 259, 262). In Nigeria, James Bond's 007 has been one-upped, at least numerically, by a local hero, "009." The spoofing of Hollywood reflects a simultaneous chafing at and admiration for at least some aspects of internationally dominant film culture, and it carries distinctive regional and national implications.

Hong Kong is a case in point. The postage stamp–size British crown colony, poised uneasily for integration into China in 1997, has a complex history in which East met West, fought, and eventually did business. Its post–World War II political history has been powerfully affected by tensions with mainland China, which resulted in pervasive and enduring censorship, earlier marked by anticommunism and more recently censorship of films that might antagonize China (Elley, 1988, 203). Culturally, it has been a place where different international currents of pop culture come together. It has also been marked by an international trading economy in perpetual high gear, which among other things has generated an elaborate underworld whose money laundering has benefited the film industry.

Hong Kong film has been a favorite with the locals since the 1930s, and widespread anxiety over 1997 has apparently only fueled "moviemaking fever" (Elley, 1992, 185; O'Brien, 1992, 39). It is a rare case of a small national cinema where local productions outsell imports at the box office. Helping the financial situation is the fact that the Hong Kong market extends not only throughout the Pacific Rim but worldwide, although violent fluctuations in the market are common. Wherever there are Chinatowns, there are devotees of Hong Kong superstar Chow Yun-fat. But it is also a remarkable testimonial to Hong Kong's cultural uniqueness that national cinema has always been commercially successful.

A distinctive and long-standing feature of Hong Kong film—perhaps one indicator of Hong Kong's unusual positioning as an international business crossroads—is its voracious appetite for imitation, most boldly of Hollywood material but also of anything that has had international commercial success. Hong Kong movies as a whole constitute, for critic Geoffrey O'Brien, "a single metanarrative incorporating every available variant of sentimental, melodramatic and horrific plotting set to the beat of nonstop synthesized pop music" (9).

Some of the most popular Hong Kong films have been remakes, takeoffs or simply steals of popular American movies. Hong Kong–based film critic Paul Fonoroff notes that both in Shanghai and Hong Kong, Charlie Chan knockoffs were made in the 1930s and 1940s, starring a Chinese actor who resembled Hollywood's (Caucasian) Charlie Chan, Warner Oland. Other instantly imitated films include *Some Like It Hot* (1959; *Every Cloud Has a Silver Lining* [1960]), *City Heat* (1984; *All the Wrong Clues* [1984]), and *Police Academy* (1984; *Naughty Cadets on Patrol* [1986]) (Fonoroff, 1988).

The past is also fertile territory for rifling; a Jackie Chan hit of the 1989–

90 season was a period film set in the 1930s, *Mr. Canton and Lady Rose,* a remake of Frank Capra's *Pocketful of Miracles* (1961) (Elley, 1991, 188). Imitation does not restrain itself to one major source, either. An early success by Vietnamese-born, Texas-trained, Hong Kong–based (and now Toronto-based as well) Tsui Hark, *Butterfly Murders* (1979), drew different elements from a Chinese novel, a Japanese thriller, Hitchcock's *The Birds* (1963), and George Lucas's *Star Wars* (1977).

In addition, the Hong Kong film industry is notorious for seizing upon a working formula (for instance, John Woo's high-violence gangster drama *A Better Tomorrow* [1986]) and then working it to death. (*A Better Tomorrow* generated two sequels and many imitators.) Its own movie traditions instantly become grist for remakes, parodies, and transformations. The post–World War II history of Hong Kong film is the rapid rise, flourishing, exhaustion, and transformation of genres—such as the evolution of the martial arts drama from origins in a kind of Eastern western (bad guys attack the village) into swordplay films, kung-fu comedy, and "spectacular mega-comedy" (Lent, 1990, 115–16; Hong Kong International Film Festival, 34 and passim).

The brazen and catholic imitation of Hong Kong films permits, ironically, a kind of cultural autonomy over the material. Like genre work generally, imitation emphasizes treatment, style, and selection rather than originality of raw material, and it positively values entrepreneurial opportunism. The attitude mirrors and even plays with prevailing stereotypes of Hong Kong commercial culture.

A recent Hong Kong action film by the renowned comic and producer Samo Hung, *Eastern Condors* (1986), provides an intriguing case of the tongue-in-cheek remake. The film, a commercial failure on its release despite its all-star cast and star director, has become a cult classic. Set in postwar Vietnam, it replays the characters, themes, and plot of *The Dirty Dozen* (1967), with touches of *Rambo* (1985), *The Deer Hunter* (1978), and *The Guns of Navarone* (1961). The film also draws on traditions of Chinese opera–style acrobatics and martial arts films to entertain audiences entirely aware of genre expectations in at least two cultures.

Samo Hung is the person to weave together these expectations. Born in Hong Kong circa 1950, he studied traditional Chinese singing, acrobatics, and martial arts for Chinese opera as a student, becoming a child star. Working first as a martial arts instructor for the hugely successful Golden Harvest studio, he went on to become a major Hong Kong star and film producer, making his first film in 1977. His films have been marked by a zesty reworking of traditional entertainment forms, both Eastern and Western (Hong Kong International Film Festival, 1980, 173–74; Overby, 1987, 177).

In *Eastern Condors,* Samo Hung cheerfully mixes and matches from East and West to produce an action drama with comic overtones. As in *The Dirty Dozen,* each of a group of convicted "Asian American" felons in U.S. jails—a buffoon, a stutterer, a coward, a grizzled cynic, and so on, each a major star—is offered a chance at suicidal heroism in exchange for a clean slate and two hundred thousand dollars if he survives. (Samo Hung himself plays the intrepid second in command and eventual leader of the survivors.) The mission, evocative of *The Guns of Navarone,* is to destroy a U.S. arsenal of 2 million pounds of explosives left behind in Vietnam by the Americans. The enemy is the fat-cat Vietnamese military bureaucracy; the allies are Cambodian women guerrillas. On the eve of departure, the colonel (also Asian American) tells the commando team leader, "Just do the job and don't get killed." However, he also asks him to rescue his brother, trapped in a Vietnamese village, if possible.

Upon parachuting into Vietnam (the jump is midway when the mission is canceled, but the leader proceeds anyway, following his men), the ragtag bunch falls in with the guerrillas, who acrobatically dazzle their enemies and rescue the fallen parachutists. One team member doesn't make it; the stutterer has taken too literally the leader's command to "count to twenty" before opening the chute, and is still on "sixteen" when they find him on the ground. This mixture of buffoonery and gore is typical of the film's tone (although Hong Kong audiences reportedly found the humor far too subtle [S. C. Dacy, personal communication, 28 December 1992]).

Vietnamese troops on river patrol surprise a team member urinating in a field, mortally wounding him and triggering a battle. They escape with the wounded man. "It's only a bruise," his buddy tells him with false bravado, as he gazes appalled at the ghastly chest wound. "We won't let you die," he says, as the man expires.

Anger at the leader's silence on the purpose of the mission leads to a walkout. National pride turns the situation around, when a friend runs up to a deserter and says, "It's ok for a Vietnamese [referring to another deserter] to leave, but it's a disgrace for us Hong Kong men." He returns "for the dignity of it."

A handful of the men proceed to the colonel's brother's village—it's a Vietnamese military stronghold, of course—and there find both the brother (played by Haing S. Ngor, who had won an Academy Award for his role in *The Killing Fields* [1984]), apparently deranged, and a cheerfully apolitical but extremely entrepreneurial peddler (the renowned Hong Kong actor Yuen Biao). Both perforce join the team in the ensuing confrontation.

The group is reunited when the guerrilla women show up on the peddler's motor scooter, and they flee to the forest where another urination scene triggers a battle and their capture.

In camp, the heroes are put in tiger cages; one is tortured and hard-eyed local children force the POWs to play Russian roulette. The team deploys acrobatics and martial arts once again, dodging and setting explosives as well, in their escape. One soldier dies at the hand of one of the hard-eyed kids, after refusing to kill him.

In the forest, the latest casualty's brother grieves loudly, saying he prefers to die in place with his brother if he cannot know the reason for the mission. Just as the leader is about the reveal it, one of the guerrillas is discovered to be a spy and is executed by her fellow guerrillas.

Hotly pursued by the Vietnamese, the commando team must cross a heavily defended bridge; the crossing leaves two mortally wounded. They stay to stave off the tanks with explosives. (The grizzled cynic says he doesn't mind "dying in the East," since "my daughters are all married.") "Uncle, see you down below," says the younger man, grunting in pain. "No, up above," assures the other as his vision fails him.

When the heroes finally encounter the weapons arsenal—an underground set looking, as producer S. C. Dacy (personal communication, 21 December 1992) has noted, like a low-rent steal from a James Bond film— the scene is set for the final encounter, which involves close shooting, running up and down ladders, and explosions. Our heroes are in competition with the wounded Cambodian guerrilla leader, who lays claim to the arms for her cause. She dies, but takes a bad guy with her. The remaining heroes—the second in command, another soldier, and the local peddler— escape through the (polluted) sewer as the entire top of the mountain is blown away, plunging over a (cleansing) waterfall to (Western) freedom.

The film borrows in a cheerfully catholic way from all available traditions. Martial arts traditions as they had evolved into fantastic and showy displays by the 1970s (the period in which Samo Hung was a martial arts instructor) are of course fully exploited. So are story lines and characters. For instance, the peddler character draws from a Hong Kong slapstick comedy tradition of the little guy who lives by his wits and wisecracks (Hong Kong International Film Festival, 1980, 34; Rayns, 1992, 22).

East and West mix and match. For instance, the guerrillas conform to a stereotype, evolved in Chinese opera and backed by a long literary tradition, of the aggressive heroine, often disguised as a boy, who confronts the enemies (Eberhard, 1972, 6–7). At the same time, the execution of the spy by her comrade, after the commando team members hesitate, echoes a scene in *The Guns of Navarone*. In it, Gregory Peck hesitates to kill a woman who betrayed them; she is then killed by another woman partisan.

The Dirty Dozen gleefully inverted some basic elements of the World War II combat film by portraying the group as tainted from the start, making its mission questionable, and celebrating the antihero (Basinger, 1986, 202–13). Critics called it "a glorification of the dropout" (Sarris, 1970, 296), "irresponsible" (Drummond, 1967, 445), and "a studied indulgence in sadism" that encouraged "hooliganism" (Crowther, 1967). It went on to become one of the biggest box office hits of the year, appreciated for its high-intensity war action by some, and for its sly anti-authoritarianism and underlying commentary on the savagery of warfare by others.

Eastern Condors builds on and plays with this legacy of anti-authoritarianism and ragtag heroics, by now itself a cliché. The conventions are the object of knowing irony—there's a "Hey guys, it's only a movie" quality to the whole film. The comic banter, the slow motion shots to let the viewer savor the spectacular action (a staple technique of Hong Kong action films), and of course visual jokes clue the viewer to the fact that the framework of reference is familiar. For instance, as a night scene begins the good guys are seen in infrared rifle sights, backed by ominous music; suddenly we see that some members of the team are spying on others, to see if anyone's involved in hanky-panky with the guerrillas. The conventions, however, simply facilitate the action plot. Thus, *Eastern Condors* can be read as a simple action thriller or as an arch, sophisticated send-up of the form.

The Dirty Dozen was widely seen as, if not an antiwar film, at least a product of the Vietnam era and its cultural conflicts. *Eastern Condors* might be seen as a product of the 1997 era, using the past as a metaphor for the perils of the future.

Eastern Condors, like several of its sources, pits an unstructured fighting unit against minions of a hostile state, led by an arrogant and dandified officer. Its digs against the Communist Vietnamese government are unsubtle. Like *The Deer Hunter,* the film enthusiastically uses tiger cages and Russian roulette as emblems of the monstrosity of the regime, even though the South Vietnamese government had been better known for tiger cages than the Communist Northern government that eventually ran the country, and Russian roulette games appear to have been a product of media imagination. It too celebrates guerrilla military actions, while at the same time linking them to feminine wiliness.

As in *Rambo,* misunderstood heroes are refighting the Vietnam war, against the odds. But these heroes do not have or need the peculiarly American chip on the shoulder, Rambo's smoldering resentment against an authority that he trusted and that betrayed him, his will to rewrite his own country's history with his muscles (Aufderheide, 1991). These heroes are aware that they are cleaning up the mess someone else—the Americans—left behind, a mess the Americans could be expected to make.

The Americans are untrustworthy from the start, on a personal and cultural basis. The white, U.S. military officer briefing his men at the outset snarls, "Well, we lost the goddamn war." The Americans' pusillanimous vacillation is shown by the last-minute (but rejected) cancellation of the mission. The jailer who releases the criminals who will become the commando team says, leering, "Take ten, take a hundred . . . and if that's not enough, no problem. I can always arrest more." So these men fight not to vindicate America, and not even, in the end, for their release from jail and cash reward, but for their own reputations as "Hong Kong men."

The resentment generated by the Americans' perceived contemptuous attitude, especially in light of American incompetence, is demonstrated at the story's outset. In the opening scene, as the commando team's future leader is being driven past a military post, a hapless U.S. soldier is trying to raise the U.S. flag. But the flag is stuck, and so the bugles keep tooting while the soldier yanks. "Why are foreigners so stupid?" says his Asian American colleague. The officer jumps out of the jeep, shinnies up the flagpole, releases the catch, shoots down, and smartly salutes the flag. The superiority of the Chinese hero over the creaky imperial military machine has been deftly demonstrated, as has his therapeutic contempt.

Clearly, the United States, as the military power that created the problem our heroes have to solve, is the most powerful, if behind the scenes, geopolitical force in the story. As the conclusion makes clear, it is also the most powerful cultural force, a focus of desire as well as rage and contempt.

The three survivors stagger away from the waterfall, onto a plain where they wonder if the plane will arrive. One soldier, now free but stunned by his travails, rails to the skies, "So those Americans brought us this. Fucking America, God damn America!" "Where will you go if the plane arrives?" asks the stalwart. "America, of course!" he replies.

Thus, as in the Brazilian parody genre, *Eastern Condors* pays tribute to an enduring love-hate relationship with a culture whose movies provide not merely entertainment but promotions for a way of life. (Not for nothing is Jack Valenti at the Motion Picture Association of America proud to call Hollywood America's ambassador to the world.) It also reflects an uneasy and censored concern with the power of its neighbor and soon-to-be-owner, China. It indirectly alludes to the flight fantasies of many Hong Kong residents uneasy about the 1997 transition—as the closing song asks, "How to get out?" *Eastern Condors*' pointedly negative references to communism, its celebration of the entrepreneurial spirit, its portrayal of Hong Kong as the cleanup crew for the bungling imperial power, all bolster the final reference to flight.

In these allusions to 1997, and in their very indirectness, *Eastern Condors* is at one with much recent Hong Kong work ("Hongkong's Film-makers," 1990; Elley, 1991, 185; Rayns, 1992, 21–22) marked by "a fearful undertone of geographic precariousness" (O'Brien, 1992, 43). Many in the Hong Kong filmmaking community have either invested or actually relocated—as has Samo Hung himself—overseas. But reference to 1997 and flight has been encoded or treated in what critic Tony Rayns calls a "frivolous" way (Rayns, 1992, 21), because of the combination of political censorship and the drive for box office popularity. Tsui Hark's bold, dark 1980 experiment in imagining a post-1997 future, *Dangerous Encounters—First Kind,* was a box office flop. By contrast, his 1986 *Peking Opera Blues,* with clear and intended parallels between the early twentieth-century period of warlord rule in China and the immediate future, was a hit. Filmgoers appear to like their anxiety refracted through an entertainment matrix.

Perhaps it was the entertainment threshold that *Eastern Condors,* with its anti-imperial grace notes, did not clear on its release, when Hong Kong audiences initially dismissed it (S. C. Dacy, personal communication, 28 December 1992). One common reaction, apparently, was to reject the film's premise—the commando team—as being too Western, a military action that was simply unbelievable in a Chinese context, with Chinese stars. The film, under this logic, simply deviated too far from the martial arts origins of Hong Kong action films. At the same time, it was that very setup that permitted the expression of chafing under cultural colonialism that marks the film and that has contributed to its cult success.

The choices for imitation and transformation in *Eastern Condors* bespeak the peculiar historical conditions of the Hong Kong colony in a moment of anxiety-laden transition. It would be interesting to pursue the question of genre parody in other cross-cultural permutations, to see what is fashioned when Hollywood, seen as a cultural dominator, is remade in one's own image.

In addition, the Hong Kong film industry may be pioneering a new phase in global cinema. In the nineties, Hong Kong films became filmfest fashion in the West, and Hong Kong directors—notably John Woo—have won U.S. studio contracts. Hong Kong cinema, itself a pastiche product, may now become the inspiration for tomorrow's Hollywood hits.

WORKS CITED

Armes, Roy. *Third World Filmmaking and the West.* Berkeley and Los Angeles: University of California Press, 1987.

Aufderheide, Patricia. "Brazil." In *World Cinema since 1945,* edited by William Luhr, 70–85. New York: Ungar, 1987.

———. "Good Soldiers." In *Seeing through Movies,* edited by Mark Miller, 81–111. New York: Pantheon, 1991.

Basinger, Jeanine. *The World War II Combat Film: Anatomy of a Genre.* New York: Columbia University Press, 1986.

Cooper, Scott. "The Study of Third Cinema in the U.S.A. Reaffirmation." In *Questions of Third Cinema,* edited by Jim Pines and Paul Willemen, 218–222. Bloomington, Indiana: Indiana University Press; London: British Film Institute, 1989.

Crowther, Bosley. *"The Dirty Dozen* (June 16, 1967)." In *New York Times Film Reviews.* New York: New York Times and Arno Press, 1970.

Drummond, G. *"The Dirty Dozen." Films in Review* 28, no. 7 (August–September 1967): 445–446.

Eberhard, W. *The Chinese Silver Screen: Hong Kong and Taiwanese Motion Pictures in the 1960's*. Taipei: Orient Cultural Service, 1972.

Elley, Derek. "Hongkong." In Cowie, Peter, ed., *International Film Guide*, 200–204. New York: New York Zoetrope, 1988.

———. "Hongkong." In *Variety International Film Guide*, edited by Peter Cowie, 185–189. New York: Samuel French, 1991.

Fonoroff, P. "Orientation." *Film Comment* (June 1988): 52–56.

Fourth Hong Kong International Film Festival. *A Study of the Hong Kong Martial Arts Film*. Hong Kong: Hongkong International Film Festival, 1980.

"Hongkong's Film-makers and 1997: The Shadow of the Square." *The Economist* 315 (12 May 1990): 93–4.

Lent, John A. *The Asian Film Industry*. Austin: University of Texas Press, 1990.

Morgan, J. "From Clochards to Cappuccinos: Renoir's Boudu Is 'Down and Out' in Beverly Hills." *Cinema Journal* 29, no. 2 (winter 1990): 23–35.

O'Brien, Geoffrey. "Blazing Passions." *New York Review of Books*, 24 September 1992, 38–43.

Overby, D. "Eastern Horizons." *Festival of Festivals* [catalog]. Toronto: Twelfth Toronto International Film Festival, 1987.

Rayns, Tony. "Hard Boiled." *Sight and Sound* (August 1992): 19–23.

Sarris, Andrew. *Confessions of a Cultist: On the Cinema, 1955–1969*. New York: Simon and Schuster, 1970.

Shohat, Ella. "Imagining Terra Incognita: The Disciplinary Gaze of Empire." *Public Culture* 3, no. 2 (1991): 41–70.

Vieira, J. L. "From *High Noon* to *Jaws*: Carnival and Parody in Brazilian Cinema." In *Brazilian Cinema*, edited by R. Johnson and R. Stam, 252–269. London: Associated, 1982.

THIRTEEN

Modernity and Postmaternity:
High Heels and *Imitation of Life*

Lucy Fischer

REMAKING A REMAKE

Reappropriating existing representations . . . and putting them into
new and ironic contexts is a typical form of postmodern . . . critique.
LINDA HUTCHEON, *THE POLITICS OF POSTMODERNISM*

Pedro Almodovar's *High Heels* (*Tacones Lejanos,* 1991) is a work that might be placed within the emerging genre of "postmodern" film. In fact, a review of it by Roger Ebert notes how "the writers of New York weeklies" regularly link that term to the film's director. As Linda Hutcheon makes clear, one of the hallmarks of the postmodern aesthetic is its radical intertextuality—its tendency to quote and recycle tropes and thematics from the discursive past.

Almodovar has acknowledged this inclination. He has deemed himself a creative "mirror with a thousand faces" that "reflect[s] everything around [him]" (Morgan, 28). While admitting a penchant for homage, he notes his citations are not the "tributes of a cinephile." Rather, they arise "in a lively and active way" as organic features of the text (Morgan, 28).

It is within this framework that we might envision *High Heels* as a remake of Douglas Sirk's canonical film, *Imitation of Life* (1959). Many have recognized Sirk's influence on Almodovar's style. The latter bemoans the devaluation of melodrama and calls Sirk a "genius" (Morgan, 29). To characterize Almodovar's theatrical mode, Roger Ebert deems it "inspired" by Sirk (44). Dave Kehr sees, in the Spaniard's "bold, ironic use of color," a tribute to the Hollywood legend (F7).

Clearly, however, there are specific aspects of *High Heels* that solicit a comparison to *Imitation of Life*.[1] Both films take a female performer as their heroine. *Imitation* traces a decade in the life of Lora Meredith (Lana

Turner), an aspiring actress who eventually achieves success on Broadway and the silver screen. *High Heels* follows the character of Becky Del Paramo (Marisa Paredes), a singer who is already a star when the narrative begins. In both cases, the protagonist has a tense and troublesome relationship with her daughter. In *Imitation*, Susie (Sandra Dee) accuses Lora of parental neglect and becomes enamored of her mother's lover—a circumstance that brings the women's conflict to a head. In *High Heels*, Rebecca (Victoria Abril) similarly accuses Becky and marries (then murders) her mother's former lover, Manuel.

In both texts, there is a subplot involving another parent-child dyad. In *Imitation*, it involves the family of Lora's maid, Annie Johnson (Juanita Moore). In *High Heels*, it concerns the menage of Judge Dominguez (Miguel Bose), the man investigating Manuel's homicide.[2] In both cases, the child involved in the subplot is a performer whose vocational choice mocks that of the heroine. In *Imitation*, Sarah Jane (Susan Kohner) becomes a burlesque dancer; in *High Heels*, Dominguez goes "under cover" as a female impersonator. In both instances, the parent in the subplot is involved with the star performer. In *Imitation*, Annie serves as Lora's backstage confidante and dresser. And in *High Heels*, Senora Dominguez keeps a fan album of clippings on Becky's career.

At times, the parallel between the films is even tighter. Both open with sequences involving a beach locale and a lost child. In *Imitation*, Lora frantically searches a Coney Island boardwalk for Susie, who has disappeared. In *High Heels*, as Rebecca awaits the arrival of her mother's airplane, she recalls running away as a youth during a seaside vacation. Both films end in heart-wrenching deathbed scenes. In *Imitation* it is that of the black domestic; in *High Heels* it is that of the heroine.

High Heels' status as a remake is made more complex by the intricate "genetics" of *Imitation*. Originally written by Fannie Hurst in 1932 as a piece of serialized magazine fiction, it was published as a book in 1933. It was first adapted for the screen by John Stahl in 1934, then later refashioned by Sirk. Hence, *High Heels* constitutes a remake of a remake, a copy of a copy, an imitation of an *Imitation*. (See figure 24.)

A POSTMODERN SIMULACRUM

Rather than a mere expression of nostalgia,
postmodernism may be seen as an attempt to recover the
morphological continuity of specific culture. The use of past styles
in this case is motivated not by a simple escapism, but by a desire
to understand our culture and ourselves as products of previous codings.
JAMES COLLINS, "POSTMODERNISM AND CULTURAL PRACTICE"

Aside from its citation of *Imitation*, there are other reasons why Almodovar's film constitutes a *postmodern* remake. Its intertextual vision is highly parodic—filled with (what Hutcheon has termed) "self-conscious, self-contradictory, self-undermining statement" (1). In the Sirk film, melodramatic moments often border on comedy (as when the telephone rings for Lora with a job offer each time she is about to kiss her lover, Steve [John Gavin]). This nascent farce (just below the histrionic facade) was apparent to Rainer Werner Fassbinder—whose films were also modeled on Sirk's. Here is an excerpt from Fassbinder's tongue-in-cheek summary of *Imitation* (which he calls a "great, crazy movie about life and death . . . [a]nd . . . America"): "[The characters] are always making plans for happiness, for tenderness, and then the phone rings, a new part and Lana revives. The woman is a hopeless case. So is John Gavin. He should have caught on pretty soon that it won't work" (Fischer, 1991A, 244–45).

In *High Heels* the ironic and melodramatic modes are nearly indistinguishable. When Becky and Rebecca are first reunited, they embrace. At that heightened instant, Rebecca's earring becomes caught in Becky's hair. When Judge Dominguez asks Becky whether she has killed Manuel, she replies, "You don't do that before an [theatrical] opening." Later, as Becky is taken away in an ambulance, she tells her homicidal daughter, "Find another way to solve your problems with men."

Beyond its conjuration of *Imitation,* the film's cinematic references are quite extensive. With Almodovar's focus on maternal melodrama, there are intimations of *Mildred Pierce* (1945). That film also depicts an incestuous triangle in which a daughter kills her mother's lover. Like Becky, Mildred attempts to assume responsibility for her offspring's crime. (Interestingly, Roger Ebert sees the performance of Marisa Paredes in *High Heels* as "inspired . . . [or inhabited by] Joan Crawford" [44]). While *Mildred Pierce* is never mentioned in Almodovar's film, Ingmar Bergman's *Autumn Sonata* (1978) is. That film (which concerns a woman's struggle with her renowned pianist-mother) is cited by Rebecca to explain how she is plagued by Becky's fame. Other quotations issue from Dominguez's pose as a female. As he sings in a nightclub, members of the audience duplicate his every gesture (like spectators of *The Rocky Horror Picture Show* [1975]). When Dominguez confesses his love to Rebecca and she rebuffs him for cross-dressing, he replies, "Nobody's perfect." That line replicates one spoken by Osgood (Joe E. Brown) in *Some Like it Hot* (1959) when he learns that the woman he adores is a man.

While *High Heels* circulates in elitist film markets, its citations often derive from mass culture—a fact that distinguishes postmodernist from modernist works. As Almodovar, himself, has stated: "I think you can look at genre . . . without making those 'exquisite' divisions of art cin-

Figure 24. Lana Turner struts her stylish stuff in Douglas Sirk's *Imitation of Life* (1959), a remake of the 1934 version with Claudette Colbert.

ema [and] popular cinema" (Morgan, 28). That his quotations are often from American movies, testifies to the hegemony of Hollywood film in the world economy, as well as to America's more "egalitarian" vision of the arts.[3]

Aside from deconstructing the binaries of high and low culture, the postmodern work has been said to relax the boundaries between fact and fiction. Hutcheon sees the form as enacting a process of hybridization "where the borders are kept clear, even if they are frequently crossed" (37). *High Heels* slyly suggests the "real" in its invocation of a controversy that surrounded the making of *Imitation:* the fatal stabbing of Lana Turner's lover by her daughter, Cheryl Crane, in April of 1958 (Fischer, 1991A, 216–18). In *High Heels,* this fact reenters (with a vengeance) in Rebecca's twin murders: her childhood killing of her stepfather (by switching his medications) and her later shooting of Manuel.[4] While this subtext can be excavated from *Imitation,* it is on the surface in *High Heels,* which makes crime the central axis of the drama (Fischer, 1991A, 21–8). Thus, *High Heels* partakes in a dual homage: to the fictional narrative of Sirk's film and to the documented tragedy of Turner and Crane. As though to suggest the infamous 1958 tabloid expose, Almodovar makes Rebecca a newscaster who confesses her offense during a broadcast. He also has Becky write her memoirs, a fact that alludes to the autobiographies penned by Turner and Crane. If Marisa Paredes reminds us of Joan Crawford, thoughts of *Mommie Dearest* (1981) cannot be far behind.

While *High Heels* accesses the "real" of a Hollywood scandal, it relinquishes the theme of race so prominent in *Imitation,* figuring it only in a flashback of the "natives" who populate the island of Rebecca's childhood vacation. If "passing" is at issue in the film, it is devoid of racial overtones and attends to Judge Dominguez and his feminine disguise.[5]

As *High Heels* intermingles fact and fiction, so it crosses genres—much as Judge Dominguez crosses dress. (Almodovar himself states that he does not "respect the boundaries of . . . genre" but "mix[es] it with other things" [Kinder, 1987, 38]). Hence, *High Heels* is a "hybrid" of the melodramatic, satirical, and film noir modes. The film's myriad references to cinema, publishing, and television tap into another postmodern theme: the overwhelming presence of *media* within contemporary culture—producing a vision of existence as the transmission of synthetic images. For Jean Baudrillard, we live in an age in which "production and consumption" have given way to "networks" through which we experience an "ecstasy of communication" (1983, 127). Significantly, the life dramas in Almodovar's film are enacted on TV. Manuel is a network executive. Not only does Rebecca break down during a televised program but her mother and Judge Dominguez learn of her wrongdoing by watching the show. Likewise, it is by viewing TV that Rebecca discerns her mother is ill. Finally, a narrative twist arises when Rebecca claims the wrong set of prints from a photographic lab—as though to symbolize the rampant confusion of images in the world. Clearly, the issue of artificiality is already apparent in *Imitation,* whose title and theatrical setting unavoidably elicit the theme (Affron, Stern).

Other aspects of *High Heels* reveal a postmodern bent. At times, the drama suffers "lapses" at odds with its overall continuity. (David Kehr, for example, complains of the film's "strange displacements.") When Rebecca is jailed and sent to the prison courtyard, several inmates enact a bizarre, choreographed "production number" reminiscent of those in a Hollywood musical. On another occasion, when Rebecca reads the television news, she laughs as she reports the weekend traffic fatalities (as though to reference Jean-Luc Godard's *Weekend* [1968]). In both cases, the diegesis is ruptured through homage. At other times, the slippage is produced by an excess of emotion rather than by an ironic gap. As Becky sings in a theater (distraught over Rebecca's incarceration), she kisses the stage floor, whereupon a tear drop falls and lands on her bright red lip print. It is an unlikely moment that functions as a pure icon of sentimentality (like a bird on a branch in a D. W. Griffith film).

"SIGN CRIMES AGAINST THE BIG SIGNIFIER OF SEX"

Nothing is less certain today than sex.
JEAN BAUDRILLARD, *SEDUCTION*

Perhaps, the most postmodern aspect of *High Heels* is its presentation of gender. Postmodernism has been known for its decentered and negotiable engagement of subjectivity: both that of its dramatis personae and of its audience. (As Hutcheon explains, subjectivity "is represented as something in process" [39]). Privileged in this regard is the genre's depiction of sexuality. According to Arthur Kroker and David Cook, a "reversible and mutable language of sexual difference" is a yardstick of postmodern discourse (20). Elsewhere, they describe the postmodern creator as "committing sign crimes against the big signifier of Sex" (21).

In *High Heels*, this authorial "larceny" (which duplicates Rebecca's) arises in a variety of ways. Clearly, one of the most transgressive aspects of the narrative is the figure of Judge Dominguez who allegedly goes "under cover" as "Femme Lethal" (a female impersonator), in order to solve the case of a transvestite's murder. (As Barbara Creed has noted, the androgyne is a signal figure in today's mass culture [65]). While we assume that Rebecca knows that Lethal is a man when she follows him into his dressing room, she seems shocked as he disrobes—perhaps, because he has a mole on his penis. While the two become amorous, he does not use his genitals for their erotic caper. Rather, in a more gender-neutral manner, he performs cunnilingus as she hangs from the rafters. What is not revealed at this time is that Lethal is Judge Dominguez (though an astute viewer can surmise it). But when this is disclosed, along with his professional rationale for cross-dressing, we are not convinced that it "explains" his behavior. Rather, we suspect that his real reasons are "under cover" too. Perhaps, he is not (what Chris Straayer would term) a "temporary transvestite," but one with a more permanent commitment [36]). Recalling the parallel subplots of *Imitation* and *High Heels*, we are reminded that Dominguez "stands in" for Sarah Jane—also a nightclub performer—thus, accomplishing yet another gender crossing.

To make this issue more slippery, there is a second sexually enigmatic character in the film. When Rebecca is jailed, she meets Chon, an inmate who seems atypically large for a woman. One considers whether she is a male in drag, but rejects this theory due to her exposed, prominent, (and seemingly "natural") breasts. Evidently, however, for the Spanish audience the situation is less perplexing. Chon is played by a notorious Spanish transsexual, Bibi Andersson—ostensibly named for the Swedish movie star (Morgan, 29). (Curiously, while writing this paper, I happened upon an edition of *The Maury Povich Show* entirely dedicated to the plight of imprisoned transsexuals—which indicates that the situation goes beyond one of Almodovar's campy plot devices.)[6]

The question of gender instability seems encapsulated in an exchange within the film. When Manuel asks Lethal if he is male or female, the latter replies, "For *you,* I'm a man." Clearly, Lethal's drag performance highlights another element within postmodern discourse—a penchant for the carnivalesque. For Brian McHale, "[P]ostmodernist fiction has reconstituted both the formal and the topical . . . repertoires of carnivalized literature" (173).

In all these cases, the notion of gender is presented as something flexible rather than fixed; it is one more Truth that postmodernism can dismantle. And the cinema is especially adept at executing such a masquerade. For, as Parker Tyler once noted, "With its trick faculties and gracile arts of transformation, the film's technical nature makes it the ideal medium for penetrating a mask, physical or social, and thus for illustrating once more that . . . things are not always what they seem" (210).

For Almodovar, however, the nature of Dominguez's protean sexuality has broader political ramifications: "[F]or me, there is ambiguity in justice and that's why I have given it to the character of the judge. I don't know what the face of justice is—sometimes it's masculine, sometimes it's feminine" (Morgan, 29). Curiously, in his last remark, Almodovar implies that masculinity and femininity exist as static and oppositional poles—rather than as the fluid continuum the film seems to imagine.

Beyond remaking a man as a woman, *High Heels'* postmodernist remake casts Lethal as counterfeiting the theatrical persona of Becky. It is *her* appearance he conjures at the cabaret, and *her* signature musical number that he performs. He later even apologizes to her for his "imitation." This plot device has numerous connotations. It foregrounds the power of the female star as a "role model" not only for women but for men. Specifically, it invokes the gay camp mimicry of such figures as Judy Garland, Barbra Streisand, Cher, Mae West, Joan Crawford, and Lana Turner. For, as Rebecca Bell-Mettereau has noted, "The homosexual impersonator's desire is to imitate a woman of power and prestige, a professional performer rather than a 'real woman' " (5). Lethal's simulation also reveals what many theorists have observed about "femininity" within patriarchal culture: that it requires a masquerade even of biological women—a performance not all that different from drag (Doane, 1990; Johnston). Judith Butler, in fact, sees the engagement of gender as *requiring* a failed imitation of an elusive prototype: "[T]he repetitive practice of gender . . . can be understood as the vain and persistent conjuring and displacement of an idealized original, one which

Figure 25. Ana Lizaran, Marisa Paredes, and Victoria Abril star in Pedro Almodovar's hilarious and timely Spanish update of *Imitation of Life* (1959), *High Heels* (1991).

no one at any time has been able to approximate" (2). Significantly, she sees the narrative of *Imitation* as exemplifying this process, through its focus on the hyperfemale, Lora Meredith.

But the more intriguing element of Lethal's approximation of Becky is that it places him within the *maternal* position: after all, it is Rebecca's *mother* whom he ends up "being." Rebecca even acknowledges this. When she encounters a poster for Lethal on the street (see figure 25), she tells Becky that she had gone to see him when she missed her. Thus, in reproducing himself as a female, Dominguez also becomes the human capable of corporeal reproduction: woman. This facsimile of motherhood becomes more resonant when one recalls that, earlier in the film, Rebecca had accused Becky of merely "acting" her parental role—a charge also issued by Susie to Lora in *Imitation*.[7]

But what are the implications of this narrative move, as regards the film's overall sexual politics? Typical of postmodernism, a multiplicity of readings and subject positions are offered to us. On one level, the device seems to raise questions about the relationship between a heterosexual woman's adult desire for a man and her infantile love for her mother. According to the prescribed psychiatric script, if a girl is to become heterosexual, she must "shift" her affection from her mother to a male. While in the traditional literature, this turnabout is likened to a substitution, recent views have cast it as a supplementation. While the girl does not relinquish her affection for her mother, she "widens" it to allow for a man. As Nancy Chodorow observes, "[A] girl develops important Oedipal attachments to her mother *as well* as to her father" (127). The drama of *High Heels* enacts this move by cementing mother and lover in Dominguez (a man attached to his *own* mother).

It further complicates this odd arrangement by implying that Dominguez may be gay (given his penchant for drag, and his mother's mention of AIDS). That he chooses a female love object (in Rebecca) is not entirely incompatible with that reading. For, as Kaja Silverman has remarked (in paraphrasing Marcel Proust), "[T]here are two broad categories of homosexuals—those who can love only men, and those who can love lesbian women as well as men" as both occupy a same-sex "feminine psychic position" (381). Interestingly, such homosexuals identify strongly with their mothers—enclosing "a woman's soul . . . in a man's body" (Silverman, 339–88). For Lethal, that soul spills over onto his exterior, in the form of his female attire. Within this framework, Rebecca is a repressed lesbian—a woman who can only want a man who appears to be a woman—the primal woman at that. For Marsha Kinder, Rebecca's conduited maternal desire is liberatory: "This film . . . boldly proclaims that mother love lies at the heart of all melodrama and its erotic excess" (1992, 40).

The film further investigates the problematic rapport between mother and daughter. If Rebecca is haunted by a nostalgia for the Imaginary, so is Becky (whose signature torch song is entitled "You'll *Recall*"). She returns to Madrid specifically to acquire the basement flat in which she was raised. At the end of the film the two women's regressions merge. As Becky lies in her childhood apartment dying, Rebecca pulls the curtains of the high window that faces the street above. As pedestrians stroll by, she watches their legs and feet. She remembers how, as a child, when Becky went out, she would anxiously await the sound of her mother's high-heeled footsteps returning (hence, the literal title of the film: *Distant Heels*).

Though this scene is poignant, it is undercut by earlier parodic moments of the film. Within the context of the myriad "perversions" the text invokes (patricide, transvestitism, incest), the notion of foot fetishism unavoidably comes to mind—a syndrome signaled in the work's title. For Freud, this symptomology is tied to the young boy's shock at seeing his mother's lack of a penis. As Freud notes, "[W]hat is possibly the last impression received before the uncanny traumatic one is preserved as a fetish. Thus the foot or shoe owes its attraction as a fetish . . . to the circumstance that the inquisitive boy used to peer up the woman's legs towards her genitals" (217). In *High Heels*, Lethal's platform shoes are very visible in his cabaret number— an act that imagines a mother *with* a penis. And, when he and Rebecca

make love in his dressing room, she is afraid to jump from the rafters because she is wearing high heels. These ironic moments (involving shoes)
"infect" the denouement, giving Rebecca's yearning for her mother's footsteps a masculine and "unnatural" cast. Significantly, she looks up, from a
basement window, at people walking by on the street—as though to liter-
alize Freud's vision of the male fetishist-to-be, gazing up women's skirts.

Given Becky's desire to return home, Rebecca's melancholy and nostalgic angst seem a remake of her parent's—adding to the problematic ten-
dentious portrayal of mother-daughter symbiosis. But Rebecca is a replicant
on more levels than one. Her name seems a variant of her mother's: hence
"Re-Becca" remakes "Becky." She marries her mother's former lover and
then considers wedding her mother's male doppelgänger. Furthermore,
during the course of the film, Rebecca becomes pregnant (by her maternal look-alike), thus approaching the matrilineal position herself. Hence,
within the film, "the reproduction of mothering" goes berserk. But its ver-
tiginous chain of duplication should not surprise us, for, as Hutcheon notes,
"commitment to doubleness or duplicity" is a benchmark of postmodernism. *High Heels* engages this trope both within the style and thematics of
the film: it is a remake about the process of remaking.

POLYMORPHOUS PERVERSE

The postfeminist play with gender in which differences
are elided can easily lead us back into our "pregendered"
past where there was only the universal subject—man.
TANIA MODLESKI, *FEMINISM WITHOUT WOMEN*

While the mutable world of postmodernism has been applauded in some
critical circles and heralded for its progressive thrust (Hutcheon, 141–68),
in other arenas it has been treated with suspicion. Feminists have been
loathe to relinquish the category of "woman" for fear that the act subverts
their analysis of patriarchal culture. E. Ann Kaplan notes that "much of
what people celebrate as liberating in . . . postmodernism is . . . an attempt
to sidestep the task of working through the constraining binary opposi-
tions, including sexual difference" (43). And Barbara Creed observes that
the "postmodern fascination with the . . . 'neuter' subject may indicate a
desire *not* to address problems associated with the specificities of the oppressive gender roles of patriarchal society, particularly those constructed
for women" (66).[8]

It is clear how this debate might inform the case of *High Heels*. It is a film
that, no doubt, entails gender fluidity, but (we might inquire) fluidity
for whom? Ultimately, it is *man* who has that prerogative, not woman.
Almodovar can dabble in the "woman's picture." Dominguez can imitate a

female. And Chon can "become" one. The only hint of movement in the opposite direction is the androgynous demeanor of Marisa Paredes as Becky. But what she resembles is not so much a man, as a man impersonating a woman—like Dominguez as Lethal. Hence, what passes for difference is, ultimately, the same—like Luce Irigaray's notion of the Freudian "Dream of Symmetry."[9] B. Ruby Rich makes a similar point in her observations on postmodernism: "In all the talk about transvestitism and transsexualism there's little acknowledgment that even the world of gender-bending is male dominated—it's just that here men rule in the guise of women" (73).

There is also a fetishistic strain to *High Heels* that works against the film's claims for an unconventional vision of sexuality (despite Kinder's deeming such fetishism "fetching" [1992, 41]). Aside from shoes, the theme privileges the prop of earrings: pendulous objects seen to hang from a women's body, as though in "compensation" for that which does *not*. In the opening scene of the film, as Rebecca awaits Becky's arrival, she remembers that her mother bought her earrings on a childhood trip. We learn that they were made of horn—a substance associated with *male* animals. It is this jewelry that Rebecca fondles and wears on the day of her mother's return—that gets tangled in Becky's hair. Later, when Rebecca takes her mother to the nightclub, Lethal and Becky exchange mementos: she donates one of her earrings (a stand-in for the lost penis) and he offers one of his "tits." In the later scene of Becky performing on stage, she wears huge, dangling earrings that graze her shoulders. In all these cases, Becky seems linked to a fetishistic object that "substitutes" for the male genitalia. This bespeaks a masculine view of woman as signifying a distressing, physiological "lack." Only a man like Dominguez (in drag) can constitute a woman who is "fully equipped."

Rebecca, too, seems haunted by a phallic lack, which is overcome by her appropriation of a gun (a familiar symbol). In the film's opening credits, drawings of high heels and guns are juxtaposed—linking the two fetishistic items. Furthermore, a *Sight and Sound* cover (announcing a review of *High Heels* inside) reads "Almodovar's *Stiletto* Heels"—again coupling shoes with a phallic weapon (this time a knife). Significantly, Rebecca hides the gun in the chair in which Manuel used to sit—emphasizing the physical and semiotic proximity of the firearm and the phallus. It is this gun that she delivers to the dying Becky, so that her mother might mark it with her own fingerprints and false guilt.

In forcing the gun on Becky, she turns the latter into the archetypal Phallic Mother—a classic figment of the male child's imagination. Sigmund Freud referred to this fantasy in 1928, while discussing the fetishist's inability to accept his mother's genital "omission." But, in discussing this phenomenon, Freud implies that the fabrication is present in *normal* masculine development. As he notes, "[T]he fetish is a substitute for *the . . . (mother's) phallus which the little boy once believed in* and does not wish to forego" (215). Thus, Rebecca is placed in the position of a "transvestite" daughter—whose psychic essence is male. Obviously, she finds the ultimate Phallic Mother in Lethal and his masquerade as Becky.

Clearly, this fantasy is equally powerful for Dominguez, who, in his role as cross-dresser, makes a similar maternal disavowal (Kulish, 394). His problematic relation to his own bedridden mother surfaces in scenes in which he is depicted in her home. The narrative context is unclear, but it is entirely possible that they still live together.

But need the fetishistic drift of the film be read as masculine? While some feminists have raised the possibility of *female* fetishism, it bears a different cast than the male variety. In an article on lesbianism, Elizabeth A. Grosz makes the point that, rather than disavowing the "castration" of their mothers, young girls may deny their *own* (47). It is *this* disavowal that is translated into female fetishism. The "narcissistic" woman may compensate for her own perceived "lack" by vainly making a fetish object of herself (through excessive costume, makeup, jewelry, etc.). The "hysterical" woman will compensate by selecting a part of her body for fetishistic "disabling" (e.g., paralysis). The "masculine" woman will dissociate herself from femininity by seeking out women with whom she can act "like a man" (47–52). None of these cases of alleged female fetishism are dominant in *High Heels*—where women are linked to phallic objects—a configuration more closely tied to men.

Significantly, we find the same male bias in the writing of a critic who pioneered discussions of transvestitism and film: Parker Tyler. In *Screening the Sexes*, he sees male cross-dressing as replicating the symbolism of sexual intercourse, which he describes from a masculine perspective: "When, with the surrogate of his penis, a man penetrates a woman, *he wears her body.* The penis dons the vagina via the vulva and wears the womb as a headdress. . . . In dynamic terms a curious kind of transsexuality has taken place" (217).

Hence, male cross-dressing is appropriate, as he already "wears [a woman's] body" (like some hatted Ziegfeld girl) in coitus. (In the world of the 1990s, the notion of a man "wearing" woman's body has disturbing associations to *The Silence of the Lambs* [1991]). When Tyler talks of conception, his metaphors are somewhat modified: "In 'planting the tree' of his body, the male *transplants* it . . . duplicates his own penis in the opposite direction. . . . [T]he woman, as the penetrated one, herself senses this exchange of penis orientation as a transference, or 'transvestitism.' Hence at the crux of the act of potency, *she* becomes the penised one and, as such, one who wears, has donned her own vagina" (217–18).

Thus, it is only through access to man's penis that the woman can "wear" her own organs—which are, otherwise, worn by him.

In many ways, *High Heels* replicates Parker's scenario. It is Dominguez who makes love to and "wears" Rebecca's vagina in the dressing room of the club in which he cross-dresses. It is he who will later implant his "tree" and "seed" in her—thus, "permitting" her to wear her own sexuality.

POSTMATERNITY

The writer is someone who plays with his mother's body . . .
in order to glorify it, to embellish it, or in order to dismember it.
ROLAND BARTHES, QUOTED IN SUSAN SULEIMAN, *SUBVERSIVE INTENT*

Clearly, *High Heels* remakes *Imitation* and the star scandal surrounding it. But how does it reproduce motherhood? Elsewhere, I have shown how the Sirk film charts the impossibility of female parenting: if Lora is damned as uncaring, Annie is guilty of overprotecting; if Lora is faulted for putting profession before home, Annie is chastened for making a career of domesticity. While the narrative begins by establishing Annie and Lora as good versus bad mothers, it ends by equalizing them in failure (Fischer, 1991A, 14–21). Whenever the women have troubles with their daughters, Steve steps in. When Lora departs on a film shoot, Steve is left in charge of entertaining Susie. When Annie wishes to pursue Sarah Jane, Steve makes the travel arrangements. "It's so nice to have a man around the house . . . "

While this masculine takeover is subtle in *Imitation,* it is strident in *High Heels,* which adopts (what we might deem) a "postfemale" stance. Clearly, this position requires the figure of Dominguez—a man who imitates and supplants a woman. Jean Baudrillard has argued that "[t]he strength of the feminine is that of *seduction*" (1990, 7, my italics). This act is based on "artifice" and stands in opposition to the masculine reality principle. As he writes, "The only thing truly at stake" in seduction "is mastery of the strategy of appearances, against the force of being" (1990, 10). If femininity is associated with surface (as distinct from masculine "depth"), it follows that the female body holds no particular truth or weight. As Baudrillard states, seduction knows "that *there is no anatomy . . .* that all signs are reversible" (1990, 10). According to this logic, the *transvestite* (like Lethal) becomes the ultimate "woman" because of his exaggerated play with the codes of femininity: "What transvestites love is this game of signs, . . . with them everything is makeup, theater, and seduction" (1990, 12–13). While championing this mimicry, Baudrillard admits that it may bear a critical tone: "The seduction . . . is coupled with a parody in which an implacable hostility to the feminine shows through and which might be interpreted as a male appropriation of the panoply of female allurements" (1990, 14). In *High Heels,* this translates into a cruel joke on the negation of anatomy as destiny.

Beyond valorizing a postfemale world, *High Heels* offers a "post-*maternal*" one—envisioning a universe in which men (like Dominguez) make the best Moms (as Tootsie once made the best feminist). For, it is he who functions as maternal hero(ine) or surrogate mom—a role vacated by Becky through her parental ineptitude. It is he who loves and comforts the hysterical Rebecca, who arranges for a rapprochement within her family, who finesses her release from jail, who bares the maternal "breast" (albeit a "falsie"). Meanwhile, all that Becky manages is to reproduce her neuroses in her daughter and to visit her maternal sins upon her child.

Hence what we find in *High Heels* is the kind of questionable "male mothering" so prevalent in contemporary cinema—a phenomenon that I have critiqued elsewhere (Fischer, 1991B).[10] While, superficially, this trope seems to express a benign male nurturant impulse—it arises at the *expense* of woman—causing her to feel a monumental postpartum depression.

In writing on the film, Kinder notes that Almodovar's project began as a narrative about two sisters who kill their mother. In Kinder's interview with him, Almodovar claims that "[w]hen you kill the mother, you kill precisely everything you hate, all of those burdens that hang over you" [1987, 43]). While Kinder admits the misogyny of Almodovar's abandoned scenario, she sees the final film as an "inversion" of that paradigm, in which "the . . . goal [is] no longer to destroy the maternal but . . . to . . . empower it" (1992, 39). Elsewhere, I have used the term "matricide" for the male diegetic appropriation of maternal space ("Sometimes"). Unlike Kinder, I find it applicable to the fate of Becky in *High Heels*—a fate that indicates a return to Almodovar's original theme. For, Becky's demise seems linked as much to Lethal's "voodoo" *replacement* of her as to Rebecca's heinous behavior. As Baudrillard observes, "To seduce is to die as reality and reconstitute oneself as illusion" (1990, 69). As Becky expires, Lethal triumphs as the seductive maternal imago.

In cataloging various attacks on postmodernism, Hutcheon notes that its contradictory and multifarious discourse has been found "*empty at the center*" by critics who decry the vacuity of its myriad interpretive scenarios (38).[11] This image of the *void* might well apply to Dominguez—who can emulate the maternal surface but never be "fully equipped" at the maternal core or corps. It might also to apply to Almodovar, who "empties" *Imitation* of its maternal weight.

Curiously, for Baudrillard, it is masculinity that is aligned with "production" and femininity with its absence: "All that is produced, be it the production of woman as female, falls within the register of masculine power. The only and irresistible power of femininity is the inverse power of seduction" (1990, 15).

What this vision accomplishes is to deny any mode of female agency. It negates production as maternal *reproduction*—once again declaring woman's body null and void. Furthermore, it deems man (like Adam) the creator of "woman as female"—leaving her entirely out of the semiological and biological loop.

One suspects that Almodovar chose the name "Femme Lethal" to highlight the cultural cliché of the femme fatale. (Since *High Heels* invokes film noir, this archetype is especially apt.)[12] According to Mary Ann Doane, the stereotype arose with the Industrial Revolution—at "the moment when the male seems to lose access to the body which the woman then comes to *overrepresent*" (1991, 2). By 1991, however, the female is underrepresented, and her being subsumed by the allegedly "disembodied" male. For Doane, the femme fatale is "the antithesis of the maternal—sterile or barren, . . . produc[ing] nothing in a society which fetishizes production" (1991, 2). In this sense, the figure finds her true incarnation in the *corpus manquée* of Lethal. Hence, while Almodovar (in feminist drag) may have meant to mock female stereotypes with the name "Femme Lethal," we can also read his epithet "against the grain." Perhaps it reveals that the postmodern posture may be "lethal" to the women who deem it progressive, who are "seduced" by it. Doane wisely remains skeptical of the femme fatale as a "resistant" figure: "[I]t would be a mistake to see her as some kind of heroine of modernity. She is not the subject of feminism but a symptom of male fears about feminism" (1991, 2–3).

Elaine Showalter once observed that "[a]cting as a woman . . . is not always a tribute to the feminine" (138). Ultimately, what is "under cover" in *High Heels* is not only a male judge but a male *judgment* latent in the euphoric "polymorphous perversity" of the postmodern pose.

NOTES

1. Thompson is the only critic I have found to actually compare *High Heels* and *Imitation of Life,* and he only does so in passing.

2. The character Dominguez is also known as Eduardo (in addition to posing as Lethal). Hence it is also possible that he is masquerading as the judge. There is no stable baseline of identity from which to operate.

3. Morgan discusses the strict distinction between high and low culture in Spanish society (28).

4. David Kehr also noticed the parallels between the narrative of *High Heels* and the details of the Turner-Crane-Stompanato scandal.

5. Thanks to Chris Holmlund for pointing out to me the fleeting appearance of the racial theme in *High Heels.*

6. The show aired on October 8, 1992.

7. The parallels between the dialogue in *Imitation* and *High Heels* were also noted by Thompson (62).

8. See also the article (cited below) by Kristina Straub for a discussion of the dangers of postmodernism for feminism.

9. In talking of the "old dream of symmetry," Irigaray is characterizing Freud's constant tendency to imagine female development as parallel to and/or "symmetrical" with that of the male.

10. See also Modleski, 76–89.

11. Though Hutcheon catalogues the objections to the appropriation of postmodernism by feminism, she ultimately rejects that position.

12. Thompson mentions the film noir atmosphere in *High Heels* (62).

WORKS CITED

Affron, Charles. "Performing Performing: Irony and Affect." In Fischer, *Imitation of Life,:* 207–15.

Barthes, Roland. *The Pleasure of the Text.* Translated by Richard Miller. New York: Hill and Wang, 1975.

Baudrillard, Jean. "The Ecstasy of Communication." In *The Anti-Aesthetic: Essays on Postmodern Culture,* ed. by Hal Foster. Port Townsend, Washington: Bay Press, 1983: 125–134.

———. *Seduction.* Translated by Brian Singer. N.p.: Editions Galilée, 1979; New York: St. Martin's, 1990.

Bell-Mettereau, Rebecca. *Hollywood Androgyny.* New York: Columbia, 1985.

Butler, Judith. "Lana's 'Imitation': Melodramatic Repetition and the Gender Performative." *Genders,* no. 9 (fall 1990): 1–18.

Chodorow, Nancy. *The Reproduction of Mothering: Psychoanalysis and the Sociology of Gender.* Berkeley and Los Angeles: University of California Press, 1978.

Collins, James. "Postmodernism and Cultural Practice." *Screen* 28, no. 2 (spring 1987): 11–26.

Creed, Barbara. "From Here to Modernity: Feminism and Postmodernism." *Screen* 28, no. 2 (spring 1987): 47–67.

Doane, Mary Ann. *Femmes Fatales: Feminism, Film Theory and Psychoanalysis.* New York: Routledge, 1991.

———. "Film and the Masquerade: Theorizing the Female Spectator." In *Issues in Feminist Film Criticism,* edited by Patricia Erens, 41–57. Bloomington: Indiana University Press, 1990.

Ebert, Roger. "Story Looks Stylish in *High Heels.*" *Chicago Sun Times,* 20 December 1991, p. 44.

Fassbinder, Rainer Werner. "Six Films by Douglas Sirk." Translated by Thomas Elsaessar. Excerpted in Fischer, *Imitation of Life,* 244–249.

Fischer, Lucy, ed. *Imitation of Life.* New Brunswick, N.J.: Rutgers University Press, 1991.

———. " 'Sometimes I Feel Like a Motherless Child': Comedy and Matricide." In *Comedy, Cinema, Theory,* edited by Andrew S. Horton, 60–78. Berkeley and Los Angeles: University of California Press, 1991.

Freud, Sigmund. "Fetishism." In *Sexuality and the Psychology of Love,* edited by Philip Rieff, 214–9. New York: Colliers, 1974.

Grosz, Elizabeth A. "Lesbian Fetishism?" *differences* 3, no. 2 (summer 1991): 39–54.

Hurst, Fannie. *Imitation of Life.* New York: Collier and Son, 1933.

Hutcheon, Linda. *The Politics of Postmodernism*. New York: Routledge, 1989.

Irigaray, Luce. *Speculum of the Other Woman*. Translated by Gillian C. Gill. Ithaca, N.Y.: Cornell University Press, 11–240.

Johnston, Claire. "Femininity and the Masquerade: *Anne of the Indies*." In *Psychoanalysis and Cinema*, edited by E. Ann Kaplan, 64–72. New York: Routledge, 1990.

Kaplan, E. Ann, ed. *Postmodernism and its Discontents*. London: Verso, 1988.

Kehr, David. "Almodovar Takes a Melodramatic Turn in *High Heels*." *Chicago Tribune*, 20 December 1991, p. F7.

Kinder, Marsha. "*High Heels*." *Film Quarterly* 45, no. 3 (spring 1992): 39–44.

——. "Pleasure and the New Spanish Mentality: A Conversation with Pedro Almodovar." *Film Quarterly* 41, no. 1 (fall 1987): 33–44.

Kroker, Arthur, and David Cook. *The Postmodern Scene: Excremental Culture and Hyper-Aesthetics*. New York: St. Martin's, 1986.

Kulish, Nancy Mann. "Gender and Transference: The Screen of the Phallic Mother." *International Review of Psychoanalysis* 13 (1986): 393–404.

McHale, Brian. *Postmodernist Fiction*. New York: Methuen, 1987.

Modleski, Tania. *Feminism without Women: Culture and Criticism in a 'Postmodernist' Age*. New York: Routledge, 1991.

Morgan, Rikki. "Dressed to Kill." *Sight and Sound* 1, no. 12 (1992): 28–9.

Rich, B. Ruby. "Gender Bending." *Mirabella*, December 1992, 71–75.

Showalter, Elaine. "Critical Cross-Dressing and the Woman of the Year." *Raritan* (fall 1983): 130–49.

Silverman, Kaja. *Male Subjectivity at the Margins*. New York: Routledge, 1992.

Stern, Michael. "*Imitation of Life*." In Fischer (1991): 279–88.

Straayer, Chris. "Redressing the 'Natural': The Temporary Transvestite Film." *Wide Angle* 14, no. 1 (1992): 36–55.

Straub, Kristina. "Feminist Politics and Postmodernist Style." In *Image and Ideology in Modern/Postmodern Discourse*, edited by David B. Downing and Susan Bazargan, 273–86. Albany: State University of New York Press, 1991.

Suleiman, Susan. *Subversive Intent: Gender, Politics, and the Avant-Garde*. Cambridge: Harvard University Press, 1990.

Thompson, David. "*High Heels*". *Sight and Sound* 1, no. 12 (1992): 61–2.

Tyler, Parker. *Screening the Sexes: Homosexuality in the Movies*. Garden City, N.Y.: Doubleday, 1972.

FOURTEEN

Feminist Makeovers:
The Celluloid Surgery of
Valie Export and Su Friedrich

Chris Holmlund

What constitutes a remake? How far, and in what ways, can the boundaries of "remake" be stretched, "made over," before a new "original" emerges? What, in particular, can be made of experimental film's fondness for recycling fragments of sounds, images, and story lines from earlier movies of all kinds? In this age of mechanical reproduction and celluloid surgery, are there any essential elements that allow us definitively to distinguish a remake from an original? Or are there just spare parts?

Marjorie Garber's discussions of the ways transsexuals, transvestites, and makeup or makeover artists trouble gender categories seem analogous. She finds the case of Renée Richards, born Dick Raskind, particularly instructive, though she is also intrigued by the transformations of cultural icons like Michael Jackson. With Renée, "it is the cutting off, by surgery, of the name and identity of 'Dick'—in effect the quintessential penectomy, the amputation of male subjectivity—that enables the rebirth of Renée" (Garber, 1992, 104). Yet for all the hormone injections, electrolysis, implants, amputations, and more, surely somewhere within Renée "Dick" lives on.[1] And even though everyone agrees that, despite plastic surgery, powder, and makeup, Michael is still Michael, he looks more and more like Diana Ross and more and more white.[2] Indeed, the controversy around Michael's hit single "Black or White" was generated as much by the man as by his message: "I'm not going to spend my life just being a color."

Such controversy is not surprising: artificial alterations of gender, sexuality, and race like those practiced by Renée Richard and suspected of Michael Jackson are hotly debated. Horrified if titillated talk-show audiences protest such changes are both against nature and anti-social; cultural critics gleefully proclaim surgical modifications cut away at and/or reshape privileges predicated on visible—and not so visible—differences. To my knowledge, however, as yet no one has combined these arguments with questions about the status of experimental makeovers vis-à-vis Hollywood or experimental film originals.

In order to examine celluloid surgery together with plastic surgery, therefore, I want to compare two experimental films by Valie Export and Su Friedrich with the two mainstream originals they make over. What each borrows, and how and why it borrows it, varies, but both manage to blur the boundaries separating film from literature, painting, sculpture, and video by chopping up earlier cinematic sources, then stitching them together with yet other material. In the process, I will argue, each creates films that jeopardize "natural" or "essential" definitions of gender, sexual preference, or race.

Valie Export works within and against a range of philosophical, literary, and artistic traditions. Since the 1960s she has explored several different media and written a number of critical articles and books about her own and others' work. The director of several short and three feature films,[3] Export is best known in Austria and elsewhere as a feminist performance artist practicing what she calls "action art." No matter what medium she uses, however, she is always concerned with the impact of gender on art and art on gender. Her first feature, *Invisible Adversaries* (*Unsichtbare Gegner,* 1976), has been called a feminist *Invasion of the Body Snatchers* (Siegel, 1956, and Kaufman, 1978).[4] But Export's film contains more than one makeover: there are several references to Buñuel and Dali's 1929 *An Andalusian Dog* (*Un Chien Andalou*),[5] to famous paintings, and to Export's own previous performance pieces. As a result, *Invisible Adversaries* is visually rich, entertaining, striking, but also demanding.

Su Friedrich's experimental narrative films are more accessible, though equally transgressive. Primarily a filmmaker, with a long list of shorts and several full-length films to her name,[6] Friedrich has a history of involvement with the New York experimental and feminist art worlds. She describes herself as a lesbian-feminist-experimental filmmaker who reaches various audiences by what she calls "ghetto hopping."[7] But though Friedrich speaks from and for several at times overlapping, at times disparate, positions, her work has consistently been concerned with contesting heterosexual assumptions and broadening what is seen and desired as "lesbian."[8] Nowhere is this truer than in the 1987 *Damned If You Don't,* with its reframing of Powell and Pressburger's 1946 acclaimed melodrama, *Black Narcissus,* and lesbian feminist written and oral histories.

From different angles, then, both these experimental makeovers snip away at sources and clip up centers, demonstrating in the process that "new definitions of identity, the subject, gender [and I would add sexual and racial] roles and reality . . . are a possible consequence of the age of electronic signs" (Export, 1992, 27). I will explore in conclusion just what these new definitions of identity, roles, and reality may be and ask one last time whether there are any essential elements, or just spare parts, in cinema or society.

OF CLONES AND MEN: *INVASION OF THE BODY SNATCHERS* AND *INVISIBLE ADVERSARIES*

Thanks to technology, which transforms and dissolves the body itself, "man has, as it were, become a kind of prosthetic God," says Freud in *Civilization and Its Discontents*. But, asks Valie Export in "'The Real and Its Double: The Body,"[9] does Freud mean man in the generic or the specific sense, or both? What of woman?

Invisible Adversaries offers partial, and contradictory, answers to these questions as it rewrites and transforms Siegel's *Invasion of the Body Snatchers* through cinematic injections, implants, alterations, and amputations. Both films share the same narrative premise: aliens from outer space have invaded and are replacing human beings. They are so successful that real people are almost indistinguishable from clones, called "pods" in *Invasion of the Body Snatchers* and "hyksos" in *Invisible Adversaries*. Both movies weave love stories together with this basic invasion plot. Both indict authority figures like psychiatrists and policemen for collaborating with and even becoming the enemy, and both suggest mass communication networks distort as much as they report. A strong fear of totalitarianism thus subtends both narratives, though what constitutes totalitarianism differs. *Invasion of the Body Snatchers* is typically discussed with reference to communism, McCarthyism and/or fascism,[10] whereas *Invisible Adversaries* targets the Austrian right and center left, naming the neo-Nazis and the SPO (Austrian Socialist Party) while, more broadly, linking Western governments to imperialist wars.[11]

Nevertheless, unlike the 1979 Hollywood version of *Invasion of the Body Snatchers*, *Invisible Adversaries* cannot really be called a remake. In her descriptions of her film, Export never mentions Siegel's movie, though neither does she comment on the plethora of other visual and written citations she cuts into and adds onto the "main" hyksos story.[12] Critics, too, often overlook the similarities between *Invisible Adversaries* and *Invasion of the Body Snatchers*,[13] in part because *Invasion of the Body Snatchers* is carefully structured,[14] whereas, as Marita Sturken says, the " 'hyksos' plot . . . gets rapidly lost in the experimental vignettes" (Sturken, 1981, 18). Export alters her protagonist's gender and occupation from male small town doctor to female big city photojournalist. The relative importance accorded psychoanalysis and the mass media shifts in consequence, and the meanings assigned to voyeurism and paranoia within the film's visual and audial structures, vary as a result as well.

The misogynist gender politics of *Invasion of the Body Snatchers,* like its antitotalitarian stance, remain for the most part below the surface. Yet for Dr. Miles Bennell (Kevin McCarthy) the ultimate moment of terror is linked to the absence of female passion: hiding from the pods in a cave with his fiancée (Dana Wynter), he kisses her and she does not respond. From the time and space of the film's frame story, set in a mental institution, he confesses in voice-over, "I'd been afraid a lot of times in my life, but I'd never known the real meaning of fear until I kissed Becky. A moment's sleep and the girl I loved was an inhuman enemy bent on my destruction."[15]

Invisible Adversaries, in contrast, begins by highlighting the importance of gender and leftist politics to its narrative, while expressly calling attention to the roles played by mass media and art in modern society in general and 1970s Vienna in particular.[16] In the first sequence, a male broadcaster warns through static of an invasion by alien hyksos: "Anyone can be a hyksos and not know it. You are contagious. You are alone." The other news items he reports are factual, yet they too revolve around violence, aggression, and contagion. The camera zooms in to a close-up of a newspaper headline with the film's title, then pans the body of a sleeping woman, and finally moves out her apartment window to scan the rooftops of Vienna. At one point, another male voice interrupts the first to quote action artist Georges Mathieu. The voice thereby provides an explanation for the hyksos's presence (radiation) while describing their mission (the destruction of the earth).[17]

It is as if Export had amputated the first two-thirds of Siegel's narrative. She begins with the last third of his film, with much of the world already under hyksos control. She also performs a kind of cinematic sex change on *Invasion of the Body Snatchers,* rewriting it from Becky's point of view at the very moment when she is about to mutate. The film style is correspondingly chaotic, with jump cuts, 360-degree pans and elaborate montage sequences suggesting disturbance and alienation, perhaps even translating the trauma of the cinematic alterations. Siegel's film, in contrast, is characterized by straightforward point-of-view shots and subtle cinematographic hints of abnormality.[18]

What are the implications for gendered subjectivity when faced with the cutting room floor?[19] Repeatedly Export asks whether it is possible that women in general, and the protagonist Anna (Susanne Widl) in particular, have always been hyksos, never humans? The second sequence certainly suggests as much, showing Anna framed in a doorway, then framed and reflected in a mirror. Her reflection takes on a life of its own, applying lipstick as she watches. Fascinated and horrified by what she has seen in the mirror and heard on the radio, Anna sets out to observe and document her own, her lover Peter's (Peter Weibel), and others' transformations into aliens.

Since Anna is a photographer and video artist, her voyeurism is, quite literally, mediated. Newspapers, photography, video, film, tape recorders, and radio serve as her allies and tools, not—or not primarily, as in *Invasion of the Body Snatchers*—as her enemies. Miles's voyeurism is, in contrast, direct. He relies on the naked eye, peering into or from windows at his nurse as she prepares to turn a crying baby into a peaceful pod, or down on the triangular town "square" where the aliens have assembled to carry out the takeover of surrounding communities.

With her media helpers Anna finds, and fashions, doubles everywhere. In a videotape entitled "Silent Language," she examines women's body language in art and daily life, documenting a lack of change from Renaissance paintings to the present: Michelangelo's *Pietà*, for instance, dissolves into a woman holding a vacuum cleaner. Later she runs around cardboard cutouts of people she has placed beside a fountain in a plaza, then, back home, outlines her silhouetted reflection in pins on a wall. A larger-than-life-size photo of herself, hair slicked back rather than down, decorates her refrigerator; inside is a kind of future "double," a baby.

For all Anna's and *Invisible Adversaries'* emphasis on female doubles, however, the central question Anna asks in one of her tapes, "When is a human being a woman?" is never clearly answered, either in her own videos or photographs or in the film itself.[20] Caught in a web of representations, woman is always a body determined by others: "the natural body of the woman doesn't exist" (Export, 1988, 7). Yet woman is not just a body. As Export says in "The Real and Its Double," woman "views her own body from outside as alien. . . . The ontological experiencing of the body by woman is the simultaneous experiencing of the personal and the alien" (1988, 12–13). Woman is both split and doubled, simultaneously subject and object, eye and "I."

Throughout the film the schizophrenia of Anna's positioning as both hyksos and Anna, alien object and alienated subject, is made visible on and through the body. Overcome by angst after talking to Peter about the spread of the hyksos, she slides down the glass walls of a phone booth. In the street she rearranges herself to fit her environment, wrapping herself around a curb, or cramming herself into corners. At home she suddenly starts to shake. A bit later she unpacks her groceries and starts to cook, only to have a rat run across the table, then a live bird and fish appear. In a rapid and highly surreal montage sequence she decapitates these animals one after another, then goes to the bathroom to photograph feces floating in the toilet, develops the pictures, and finally goes to bed.

Many of these sequences recreate Export's performance pieces from 1972–76, described as "the pictorial representations of mental states, with the sensations of the body when it loses its identity" (Hofmann and Hollein, 1980, 13). An early dream sequence, for example, implants one of her 1972 explorations of the physical and emotional effects of bodily constraints into the "main" hyksos narrative.[21] A screen with black-and-white images of Anna wearing ice skates and walking through Vienna appears over color images of her sleeping. In the black-and-white film the scene changes with each step, echoing the nonsensical temporal and spatial editing of *An Andalusian Dog,* as also Maya Deren's *Meshes of the Afternoon.* At the end of *Invisible Adversaries* Anna enacts another piece from this same set of experiments, going to bed in a mountaineering outfit, woolen hat, gloves, and boots as the radio recounts still more tales of violence and horror.

By stitching this particular performance piece into the main film body, Export makes it clear that the paranoia, angst, and isolation Anna experienced at the beginning of the film have worsened: no trace remains here of the final guarded optimism of *Invasion of the Body Snatchers* where the psychiatrists finally believe Miles and call the FBI in to help. Instead invisible adversaries are everywhere, and they are both internal and external. Peter, Anna's leftist lover, grows increasingly hostile. "Women are parasites," he tells her at one point, to which she has a woman in her videotape respond, "Men are dwarfs." The playfully perverse heterosexual sex we see so much of at the beginning of the film comes to seem threatening, especially since other couples around Peter and Anna quarrel and fight as well. Peter himself maintains love is worthless, impossible: "This disgusting longing for love is an emotional plague," he tells Anna; "love is a transparent prison." What he says echoes what the pod psychiatrist tells Miles in *Invasion of the Body Snatchers:* "Love, desire, ambition, faith—without them life is so simple. . . . There's no need for love. Love doesn't last."

In contrast to the relatively major part accorded *Invasion*'s psychiatrist, Anna's psychoanalyst plays a relatively minor role and appears only near the end of the film. He first suggests she have her eyes checked, then diagnoses her as schizophrenic and prescribes pills. The pictures Anna takes of him reveal he is a hyksos but, unlike Miles, Anna does not particularly care. The men and boys she encounters masturbating and fighting in the streets pose more serious threats to her psychic and physical well-being. These images are often intercut with newspaper, film, and TV images of rocket launchers, burning trucks, and napalmed children, effectively linking violence in the third world to violence in the first, and distancing Export's makeover still further from Siegel's original.

Near the end of *Invisible Adversaries,* Anna goes to see a war movie. "Help in the search!" ("Suchen Sie mit!"), urges the male narrator over the black-and-white and color images of destruction. Anna looks anxiously at herself and the audience in a pocket mirror. Siegel's film was to have ended similarly, with a close-up on Miles's frightened gaze as he tries to convince motorists on the L.A. freeway "You're next!" Whether or not Export is intentionally parodying *Invasion of the Body Snatchers,* her injection of yet another film within her main film speaks not just to Anna, but also and more broadly to the spectator of *Invisible Adversaries*. Export's, Anna's, and other women's reflections on the position and positionings of women open outward, to include us as well.[22] "My visual art is for me a monologue . . . a dialogue with an invisible partner," says Anna in her videotape "When Is a Human Being a Woman?" Unlike *Invasion*, which encourages our identification by playing on our desire to *see*, or, better yet, by fueling "our urge to gain access to the meeting ground between the specular and the blind" (Telotte, 1990, 152), *Invisible Adversaries* proposes "an 'aesthetic of reception' . . . [wherein] [t]he signifying practices of cinema are deployed as an element of a de/re/construction not only of genre film, but also of its spectators. . . . [T]he film makes sense (narratively, technologically) only in feminist terms" (Cranny-Francis, 1990, 225).[23]

For all the implants and injections, amputations and alterations that characterize Export's self-reflexive celluloid surgery, however, her film doubles do not guarantee a way out of the double bind in which women find themselves in patriarchal cultures. Nevertheless these "stagings of the body" do make more obvious the extent to which woman is defined as body "by an alien ideology" (Export, 1992, 33). As Export says of feminist action art in general, "[O]nly knowledge prevents contagion" (1989, 73).

In her writing, Export recognizes that tapping the tendency of technology "to transform and dissolve the body itself" is risky: (1988, 2) in a world where woman equals body, "deconstructing the body can lead to extinction." Yet, she continues, "since . . . the increased prosthesis-like quality arises from the progress of civilization, we cannot refuse disembodiment" (1988, 17–18). In *Invisible Adversaries* she even has Anna devise her own prosthesis, cutting her pubic hair and using it as the basis of a temporary sex change wherein she makes herself over into a mustachioed man. For a moment, the artificiality of gender is very much apparent, as it is in *An Andalusian Dog* where, through the miracles of editing, a woman's armpit hair is transformed into a man's beard.

At times Anna's de- and reconstructions of femininity provide the basis for solidarity among women. At times they unsettle masculinity as well. But Anna's, and Export's, critiques of gender remain tenuous, hampered and hobbled, for, as Export says, "the battle of the sexes has always already been won by men" (1989, 72). Inevitably so, I would argue, since Export never broaches the question of homosexuality in *Invisible Adversaries*, even though heterosexuality is obviously in crisis.[24] As long as heterosexuality remains an uncopiable original, in trouble yet intact, what Marjorie Garber terms "the twin anxieties of technology and gender" (1992, 108) remain in place, and the dualistic or binary frame that positions women as irremediably inferior and inalterably Other survives and proliferates as well. Export's implants and additions may make us forget the amputations and subtractions she performs on *Invasion of the Body Snatchers,* and may thereby jeopardize the notions of cinematic or artistic original, but they stop short of demonstrating once and for all the constructedness of gender.

MUCH ADO ABOUT NUN-THINGS:
BLACK NARCISSUS AND *DAMNED IF YOU DON'T*

By shifting the central organizing perspective of her science fiction film from male to female, Valie Export begins to "rewrite gender within genre" (White, 1987, 84). But, as Judith Butler argues, sex, gender and desire are not necessarily synonymous: "Gender can denote a *unity* of experience, of sex, gender and desire, only when sex can be understood in some sense to necessitate gender—where gender is a psychic and/or cultural designation of the self—and desire—where desire is heterosexual and therefore differentiates itself through an oppositional relation to that other gender it desires. . . . This conception of gender presupposes not only a causal relation among sex, gender, and desire, but suggests as well that gender reflects or expresses desire" (1990, 22).

As "the narrative form that takes desire as its subject" (Lang, 1989, 12), melodrama offers a more logical site than science fiction for cinematic investigations of the connections and disjunctures among sex, gender, and desire. *Damned If You Don't,* Su Friedrich's makeover (and more) of *Black Narcissus,* successfully adopts this strategy, highlighting how much *Black Narcissus* and melodrama in general are predicated on the assumption that all desire is heterosexual. Snipping up, then reconstructing Powell and Pressburger's original tragedy of unrequited (white) heterosexual love, madness, and death, Friedrich instead proposes a narrative with a happy ending for lesbians: for once the (Latina) girl, not the boy, gets the (white) girl, and no one dies or goes insane.[25] By the end of *Damned If You Don't,* lesbianism is no longer a sickly copy of a healthy heterosexual original. (See figure 26.)

The same spirit pervades both *Black Narcissus* and *Damned If You Don't.* Both make nuns the central characters of stories where, as Friedrich pointedly puts it, "the chaste are chased" (Hanlon, 1982–83, 81). Both are highly sensual, though, as Michael Powell says of *Black Narcissus,* "it is all done by suggestion" (1987, 584). Unlike Export, moreover, Friedrich is quite willing to acknowledge her debts to and appreciation of *Black Narcissus,* even as she manipulates and criticizes several of its basic premises. Like Export, she includes a variety of other material in her film, thereby altering the shape of the original.

But where Export's celluloid surgery of *Invasion of the Body Snatchers* is ongoing and multiple, *Damned If You Don't*'s relationship to *Black Narcissus* is like a single large implant: for the most part the *Black Narcissus* makeover is confined to the first eight minutes of *Damned If You Don't,* although a few

Figure 26. Lovers embrace in Su Friedrich's *Damned If You Don't* (1987), a transgressive retake on Powell and Pressburger's 1946 melodrama, *Black Narcissus*.

Black Narcissus images reappear briefly at the end as well. Even within this implant, however, Friedrich sets other more minor alterations in motion, then further amplifies and modifies these alterations in the rest of the film. Cinematically, within the *Black Narcissus* sequence and indeed elsewhere as well, *Damned If You Don't* is more restrained than *Black Narcissus,* though no less compelling. Narratively, the two films differ in three key and overlapping areas: 1) how they portray the two lead female characters; 2) whether and how they represent male characters; and 3) how they inscribe racial and ethnic difference.

Rather than contrast virility and femininity, repression and expression, West and East as Powell and Pressburger do, Friedrich takes a different tack. For the most part *Damned If You Don't* excises *Black Narcissus*' imperialist fantasies. Gone are the lush but artificial settings created in British studios through matte shots, glass shots, and painted backdrops or, as in the case of the subtropical gardens filled with "cedars, deodars, rhododendrons and azaleas," literally transported from India to England by retired "merchant princes and pro-consuls" (Powell, 1987, 562).[26] Gone too is the incessant drumming of the natives, and gone is almost all reference to any "Indian" characters. Except for one brief shot of Sister Clodagh (Deborah Kerr) and Kanchi (Jean Simmons), the "sexy little piece who attracts the eye of the young Prince" (Sabu) (Powell, 1987, 576),[27] the Malays, Indians, Gurkhas, Nepalese, Hindus, and Pakistanis Powell and Pressburger indiscriminately cast as Indians have been cut from Friedrich's film.[28] In the stripped-down, stitched-up version of *Black Narcissus* she offers, the principal characters are known only as the Good Nun (Deborah Kerr), the Bad Nun (Kathleen Byron), and Mr. Dean (David Farrar).

The offscreen female narrator of the *Black Narcissus* sequence (Martina Siebert) only mentions the Orient twice, in passing. Each time she mocks the racism signaled so blithely in the very title of Powell and Pressburger's film: "Black Narcissus" is the name of the cheap perfume the young prince wears.[29] In *Black Narcissus* the young prince proudly tells the nuns his perfume comes from the Army Navy Stores of London. "I'll call him Black Narcissus," Sister Ruth, the Bad Nun, says when he leaves. "He's so vain, like a peacock. A fine black peacock." "He's not black," another nun replies. "They all look alike to me," Sister Ruth retorts.

In *Damned If You Don't*, in contrast, Siebert's offbeat voice-over—which includes, for example, such lines as "[the nuns] forgive [Mr. Dean] for arriving naked, given the state of emergency"—makes the melodrama she recounts seem more like a comedy. Rather than talk of the need to "humanize" the natives, as Mr. Dean and the nuns do, Siebert says flippantly that the nuns "work hard, day and night, bringing aspirin and the English language to Indian peasants." The flatness of her delivery detracts from any exoticism that might attach to her German accent. She also directly links racism to sexism: "[The Good Nun] asks [Mr. Dean] why the local people can't be more disciplined, which somehow raises the question of whether or not she likes children." The *Black Narcissus* sequence she refers to is more overtly racist, but it disguises sexism as flirtation: wearing shorts, a shirt, and a hat, Mr. Dean crosses and uncrosses his hairy legs and glances "meaningfully" at Sister Clodagh, all the while insisting that the "natives" are "primitive people . . . like children, primitive children."

At only one moment does Friedrich incorporate text from *Black Narcissus*. The Good Nun says, "If you have a spark of decency left in you, you won't come near us again." Then Friedrich interrupts Siebert's narration to sing Mr. Dean's song herself: "No I won't be a nun, no I shall not be a nun, for I am so fond of pleasure, I cannot be a nun." The pastiche is doubly gender bending: first, because a man sings a song "only" a woman should sing since "only" women can be nuns;[30] second, because a woman, Friedrich, sings a song "originally" sung by a man. Only at the end of the segment do we hear Mr. Dean himself sing the song. Now, however, he does so over medium two-shots of the Good and the Bad Nuns. (See figure 27.)

Figure 27. The nun in Su Friedrich's experimental makeover, *Damned If You Don't* (1987), raises questions of identity and gender.

Friedrich performs other more minor surgical operations on her eight-minute *Black Narcissus* segment as well. Roll bars flicker across the screen since she has taken the images from a television broadcast without standardizing them to film. Periodic cutaways show a woman who will become one of the main characters of Friedrich's primary narrative (Ela Troyano) pouring herself a glass of wine, then settling in to watch Powell and Pressburger's film on TV, and finally falling asleep.

Friedrich's reshaping of the *Black Narcissus* implant leaves no doubt about what the lesbian character of her main narrative finds to like in Powell and Pressburger's melodrama. She abbreviates and reframes several shots in order to insist on the exchanges of looks between the Good Nun and the Bad Nun. As a result, the force of their desire and rivalry for Mr. Dean imperceptibly acquires another, lesbian, layer.[31] As Martha Gever says, Friedrich "tells . . . the story of passionate relationships between women within the film's male-centered narrative—by concentrating on the key moments in the rivalry between two female characters" (1988, 16). With the amputation of Kanchi and the young general from the *Black Narcissus* segment, happy heterosexual love disappears entirely from *Damned If You Don't,* leaving only what Friedrich calls "the sexual hysteria at the core of the film" (MacDonald, 1992, 304).

In the final analysis, however, Friedrich's makeover is more a reverent restatement than an outright rejection, as much the enhancement of secondary celluloid characteristics as the castration of primary ones. Friedrich says she appreciates, for example, "the really high drama of *Black Narcissus.* . . . Powell and Pressburger used lighting to such great effect and created a lot of expression in the faces, which is all you have to work with when you're dealing with characters who are completely covered" (MacDonald, 1992, 304). *Damned If You Don't* translates this drama into its own terms, using black and white instead of color. For the most part, Friedrich's reconstruction of *Black Narcissus* refuses the canted angles, extreme long shots, dramatic framing, superimpositions, dissolves, and flashbacks of the original. Instead Friedrich insists on meter and tempo, editing "the rhythm of gestures within the shot . . . with the rhythm of the roll bars, [and] . . . the cadence of the speech at the moment" (MacDonald, 1992, 304–5).

Friedrich admits that "what I felt I was doing by beginning with the *Black Narcissus* material was saying, "Okay, you want a narrative, here, take it: you can have it. And you can have it just for its high points, you don't have to slog through all the bullshit, all the transitions" (MacDonald, 1992, 306). Yet *Black Narcissus* functions not only as hook but also as model for the rest of *Damned If You Don't,* in that Friedrich's film remains a dramatic narrative, though Friedrich adds "god forbid, a happy ending" (Friedrich, 1989–90, 123).

In many ways, therefore, Friedrich's implant of *Black Narcissus* becomes the basis for the new celluloid body that is *Damned If You Don't.* The woman (known only as the Other Woman) who watched Powell and Pressburger's film at the beginning of *Damned If You Don't* adapts elements from the former to fit her own devious designs. At one point she even buys a needlepoint head of Christ as a gift for the next door neighbor, the Nun (Peggy Healey), whom she desires. Friedrich carries on Powell and Pressburger's emphases on framing and costuming as well, insisting as they do on the sensuality of spirituality. On an outing to the New York City Aquarium, for example, the Nun watches white whales swim within their tank. Her black robe and white face visually echo their white bodies on the black water. Later images of her in her tiny room or behind grillwork make it clear that she too is a prisoner. The Other Woman's restless movements, dark good looks and flamboyant clothes (black bolero pants, tight tops, a lowcut and diaphanous black party dress), offer a conspicuous contrast to the Nun and combine eroticism and exoticism just as Sister Ruth and especially Kanchi did in *Black Narcissus.*

Except for the offscreen voice of a priest, there are no male characters at all in the main story of *Damned If You Don't.* All the watching, all the desiring that occurs in the constant shot/reverse shots, point-of-view shots and eyeline matches takes place between women. Finally the Nun gives in to desire and decides to love her neighbor as herself. The Other Woman slowly unveils her, and the two make love in silence—a major shift from *Black Narcissus'* operatic climax, where "music, emotions, images and voices are blended together into a new and splendid whole" (Powell, 1987, 583) as, mad with jealousy and grief because Mr. Dean has rejected her, Sister Ruth tries to kill Sister Clodagh by pushing her off a cliff. Instead she slips and falls to her death. The final credits of Friedrich's film unfold, appropriately enough, to the lascivious lyrics and raucous tune of Patti Smith's "Break It Up."

Two other subnarratives, both of which reinforce the main story's emphasis on the virtues of lesbian love, are grafted onto the sound track of *Damned If You Don't*. The first set of grafts is excerpted from Judith Brown's *Immodest Acts*, a study of a nun found guilty of "misconduct" in Renaissance Italy and imprisoned for thirty-five years in prison within her convent.[32] Friedrich also interrupts the first of the two selections she includes. An offscreen narrator (Cathy Quinlan) reads Sister Crivelli's testimony that, as she watched, Jesus removed Sister Benedetta's heart and replaced it with his own. Quinlan chuckles as she says, "How can I live without a heart now?" "Well, why not?" Friedrich's voice responds. Stepping completely out of character, Quinlan says, "You know what? I just had the funny idea that Sister Crivelli said this millions of times too. At a certain point she was just reading the fucking testimony." The second selection, which describes a series of lesbian sex acts in graphic detail, is uninterrupted.

By grafting sections from *Immodest Acts* onto and into her main story, Friedrich implicitly reclaims past lesbians for the present. Periodically, if more parenthetically, a second set of grafts tells of other lesbian love stories. At one point an anonymous voice on the sound track asserts that the nuns she had crushes on as a child were lesbians. Onscreen we see still other nuns framed in two-shots or three-shots. By association they too become lesbians, or at least potential lesbians.

Each and every element of Friedrich's film, including her implant of *Black Narcissus*, thus hints at the persistence of lesbian desire through time and across cultures, despite silencing and persecution. By the end of *Damned If You Don't*, heterosexual melodrama has, in effect, been "lesbianized." The moral of Friedrich's film is quite unequivocal: here you're only "damned if you don't."

But while the moral of *Damned If You Don't* is unequivocal, its address and its referents are not. Who is the "you" in the title? Who will be "damned if they don't?"[33] Only women? Only lesbians? Only white and Latina lesbians? Friedrich's decision to focus on the role played by sexuality in melodrama, like Export's decision to focus on the impact of gender on science fiction, pushes questions of racial and ethnic difference to the background. Even though each acknowledges in passing that such differences exist— Friedrich through her ironic commentary about *Black Narcissus* and casting of Troyano and Healey; Export through the offscreen news stories and the documentary images of destruction and disaster in third world countries— "white" remains the dominant, and hence the invisible, color in both films.

IN STITCHES: CUTTING UP AS SERIOUS BUSINESS

Both Export and Friedrich question profoundly what might constitute copy or serve as source. Though neither operates primarily on racial or ethnic differences, the celluloid surgeries both perform demonstrate the extent to which "the original, like the author and the real are themselves constituted as effects" (Butler, 1991, 146). Each stretches and pads, clips up, and cuts together more than one original. As a result, their fantasies, like Foucault's phantasms and, much earlier, Plato's "bad copies," "brea[k] down all adequation between copy and model, appearance and essence, event and Idea" (Young, 1991, 82).

Are there, then, any essential elements that might allow us to distinguish copy from original, makeover from model? Or are there just spare parts?

Of course more than textual politics is at stake in and around these films, for their indeterminate status as remakes or originals is matched by their offhand insistence on the ineffability of subjectivity. Since identity is predicated on difference, each film to some extent places identity in jeopardy because each, though differently, makes it difficult to *see* difference, and therefore difficult to *tell* the difference: in Export's case, between men, women, and hyksos; in Friedrich's case between nuns and lesbians. This does not mean, however, as Barbara Christian argues in another context about such postmodern politics, "that reality does not exist, that everything is relative, that every text is silent about something—which indeed it must necessarily be" (1990, 43). The point must also be made, I think, that since each film overlooks or downplays some differences, each leaves some identities untouched and intact. It is imperative we acknowledge, for example, that both these films leave race largely unexamined. We could, indeed we should, imagine makeovers of *Invasion of the Body Snatchers, Black Narcissus,* or any one of a number of other Hollywood or experimental films, which would foreground and fragment the "security" of identities predicated on racial, ethnic, or national origins as well, much as Michael Jackson's multiple makeovers confuse neat categorizations not just of gender and sexuality but also of race and age.[34]

The extent to which identities are interlocking, not additive, and not unitary, only emerges when the various celluloid surgeries these experimental filmmakers employ are evaluated each against the other, and both against still other films made from yet other political perspectives. Collective participation and cross-pollination are crucial. Abdul JanMohamed and David Lloyd put it well: "Just as it is vitally important to avoid the homogenization of cultural differences, so it is equally important to recognize the common basis of . . . struggle" (1990, 10).

The more serious question then, politically speaking, is not *whether* there are essential elements or just spare parts, but *who* asks such questions, how, and why. As critics, artists, and activists, then, let us openly acknowledge, eagerly expect, and diversely desire different answers.

Taken together, though, I would argue that these two films do begin to shake up "the inevitability of a symbolic order based on a logic of limits, margins, borders and boundaries" (Fuss, 1991, 1), even as they trouble an aesthetics of origins and a metaphysics of identity—at least where gender and sexuality are concerned. Given how much "the twin anxieties of *visibility* and *difference* . . . mobilize . . . all of the culture's assumptions about normative sex and gender roles" (Garber, 1992, 130)—and, again, let us not forget race—it may be a very good thing, therefore, if what Marjorie Garber says of essential elements versus spare parts applies equally to cinema and to sex: "The boundary lines . . . never clear or precise . . . are not only being constantly redrawn but are also receding inward . . . away from the visible body and its artifacts" (1992, 108).

Thanks to Lucy Fischer, Chris Straayer, and Su Friedrich for their insightful suggestions for revision.

NOTES

1. The number of operations and other procedures Richards underwent in her changes from man to partial woman to man to woman is mind-boggling. In addition to those I have already mentioned, Garber also lists the removal of Raskind's Adam's apple and breast reduction surgery: after initial hormone treatments Raskind married a woman and found himself embarrassed by his large breasts. The whole cycle began all over again three years later with the end of the marriage. The final stage of Raskind's change to Richards included a penectomy and the construction of a vagina using penile tissue. See further Richards's autobiography.

2. In passing, Garber comments that Jackson's age has become increasingly indeterminate, in part as a result of his operations but primarily thanks to his androgynous, ageless, and "raceless" performances. See Garber, 1992: 185.

For years pulp magazines and newspapers have tried to "explain" Jackson's androgyny in order to capitalize on his appeal. According to the weekly magazine *For Women First*, for example, Jackson "owns up to two nose jobs" but "sources close to [him] number his rhinoplasties as high as seven." The magazine goes on to cite a medical expert, identified as "David Alessi, MD, clinical assistant professor at UCLA," who claims Jackson "looks as if he's had cheek and chin implants, lip reduction and skin lightening. . . . He may have also had liposuction under the chin" ("Plastic Surgery under Fire," 1992: 23).

On an Oprah Winfrey special aired February 10, 1993, Jackson vehemently denied such allegations. He maintained that he had only twice undergone plastic surgery, though he refused to say what had been altered. He also revealed that he suffered from a skin disease that made areas of his skin "white," and said he used powder and makeup to even out the blotches.

3. I have only seen Export's three feature films—*Invisible Adversaries* (*Unsichtbare Gegner,* 1976), *Menschenfrauen* (1978) and *Practice of Love* (*Praxis der Liebe,* 1984)—on video. All are available for rental or purchase from Facets Multimedia, 1517 West Fullerton Ave., Chicago, IL 60614 (800–331–6197).

4. See, for example, Lyon, 1991, and Mueller, 1983.

5. Export claims the surrealists are precursors of Viennese action art and Western feminist performance art. See Export, 1989.

6. Friedrich's longer films—*The Ties That Bind* (1984), *Damned If You Don't* (1987), and *Sink or Swim* (1990)—are available from Women Make Movies, Canyon Cinema, and the Museum of Modern Art. Three of the shorts—*Cool Hands, Warm Heart* (1979), *Gently down the Stream* (1981), and *First Comes Love* (1991)—are distributed by Women Make Movies and Canyon Cinema. Canyon Cinema distributes a fourth short, *But No One* (1982), as well.

7. The term comes from Friedrich's presentation at the 1992 MLA feminist film session I organized, entitled "Lesbian Tongues Untied."

8. See Holmlund, "Fractured Fairytales and Experimental Identities."

9. The title of Export's article is, of course, itself a makeover of Antonin Artaud's *The Theater and Its Double.*

10. In interviews, Siegel maintains only that "the majority of people in the world . . . are pods, existing without any intellectual aspirations and incapable of love" (Braucourt, 1972: 75). See also Kaminsky, 1991: 154–57. LaValley, however, argues that Siegel was also critical of conformist right-wing 1950s America, though his critiques in *Invasion* were less pointed than those scripted by left-leaning screenwriter Daniel Mainwaring. See LaValley, 1991: 911. For other interpretations, see, for example, Biskind, 1991: 193–97; Kaminsky, 1991: 178–81; Laura, 1972: 71; LaValley, 1991: 3–17; Rogan, 1991: 201–5; Sayre, 1991: 184; Sobchak, 1987: 123; Steffen-Fluhr, 1991: 206–21; and Warren, 1982: 287.

11. As the film opens, an offscreen news broadcaster reports that Chancellor Kreisky's SPO is engaging in "Watergate methods" in its hunt for left-wing radicals. A bit later this same broadcaster mentions Henriette von Shirach, wife of the Nazi youth leader, in connection with a story on the rise of neo-Nazism in Austria. Later mention is made of the prevalence of corruption in the Second Republic.

12. See, for example, the description Export offers in Hofmann and Hollein, 1980: 108.

13. See Couder, 1984, and Lukasz-Aden and Strobel, 1985: 249.

14. See Warren, 1982: 284; Laura, 1972: 72; and LaValley, 1991: 11.

15. Steffen-Fluhr reads the film as more overtly misogynist than I do. For her, the film's major theme is "a dialectic between sleep and wakefulness, between deadly 'alien' passivity and passionate human activity (i.e. between stereotypical female and male modes. [*sic*]) This dialectic is further complicated because, in *Invasion*, 'to sleep' is linked to the euphemism for sexual intercourse, 'to sleep with' " (Steffen-Fluhr, 1991: 214).

16. Because Export repeatedly shows the effects imperialist wars have on people of color, one might argue that she also calls attention to the racial politics which, Robert Eberwein maintains, underpinned the original *Invasion of the Body Snatchers*. See Eberwein's essay in this volume.

17. Unlike the first and last sequences of *Invasion of the Body Snatchers*, which Siegel had to add on to satisfy test audiences and his producers, Export's opening sequence is not part of a frame story, although the principal elements it incorporates are repeated again, with modifications, at the end.

18. An old man looks ominous, for example, even though he is just mowing the lawn, because we see him from behind or suddenly in extreme close-up in the foreground of a shot. Since Siegel has hidden the man's face and/or unsettled three-dimensional space, we cannot be sure of his "humanity."

19. In the last section of her chapter "Spare Parts," provocatively titled "Postscript: The Transsexual on the Cutting Room Floor," Garber explores a related question: how transsexuals have been represented in recent mainstream and independent films. She does not discuss experimental films or examine the relationships between experimental makeovers and mainstream originals, however. See Garber, 1992: 110–17.

20. The related question, "When is a woman a human being (in patriarchal societies)?" is never articulated, though it is obviously the starting point for Export's analysis. Thanks to Lucy Fischer for this observation.

Similarly, Elizabeth Lyon argues that Export inverts the question that Miles asked himself when confronted with the pod Becky's entreaty to "sleep" with her. For Lyon, Export thereby "shift[s] the ground from telling the difference between alien and human to posing the question of the relation between sexual identity and the body" (Lyon, 1991: 1).

21. Export's second feature film, *Menschenfrauen*, incorporates still other performance pieces from this time period.

22. Helke Sander talks about her own feminist filmmaking in one of Anna's videos, and the end of *Invisible Adversaries* quotes Rahel Varnhagen, a nineteenth-century Austrian writer recently rediscovered by feminists.

23. Joanna Kiernan makes a similar point about some of Export's short films: "[T]he audience is a necessary part of the transference and the polemic" (Kiernan, 1986–87: 185)

24. *Menschenfrauen* does briefly take up lesbianism. The ending is especially telling: the two main female characters, both pregnant by the same man, leave him for each other.

25. MacDonald maintains that Friedrich made *Damned If You Don't* as a response to the taboo on cinematic and narrative pleasure imposed by certain 1980s feminist filmmakers, because she views such a strategy as a dead end. She says, "I like

films that are both sensual and entertaining, that engage me emotionally as well as intellectually. . . . [With *Damned If You Don't*], I wanted to make something I (and viewers) would enjoy" (MacDonald, 1992: 295 and 299).

26. From the start, Powell insisted that "the atmosphere in this film is everything. . . . Wind, the altitude, the beauty of the settings—it must all be under control" (Powell, 1987: 562–63).

27. How much the association of the exotic and the erotic, the Oriental and the feminine, is destined for a Western *male* gaze is clear in the anecdote Powell provides about his friend Stewart Granger's infatuation with Jean Simmons as Kanchi: "When Stewart . . . saw Jean eating a squashy fruit with a ring through her nose, he went straight out, proposed to her and married her. I always said it was the baggy umbrella she carried. It was the final erotic touch" (Powell, 1987: 585).

28. Powell and Pressburger cast fancifully clad British actresses as the most important female Indian characters. May Hallatt played Ayah, the old guardian of the brothel-nunnery and Jean Simmons played Kanchi. Yet as Antonio Rodrig points out, for all Powell and Pressburger's imaginative re-visioning of the Orient, in *Black Narcissus* "India is not just a decor or a visual backdrop. The natives possess many faces . . . " (Rodrig, 1985: 5). Translation mine.

29. Henry Sheehan argues that Powell and Pressburger's title is itself a self-reflexive send-up of racism. For him "the pair's unconsummated flirtations with kitsch" represent "self-conscious depictions of the reality that lurk[s] beneath analysis" (Sheehan, 1990: 39).

30. On the attraction of habits for transvestites, see Garber, 1992: 210–23.

31. Katharina Sykora makes a similar comment, writing that Friedrich "filters out the erotic connotations through the editing of single frames, revealing the commonality in the women's rivalry, namely, the function 'Man' as the means of confirmation and understanding of their own sexuality" (Sykora, 1989: 100). Translation mine.

32. See Brown, 1984 and 1986.

33. As I show in another article on Friedrich's work, "Fractured Fairytales and Experimental Identities: Looking for Lesbians in and around the Films of Su Friedrich," reviewers of *Damned If You Don't* disagreed profoundly on these questions. Martha Gever took an implicitly separatist stance, arguing that Friedrich "introduces a male character in order to exile him from her story" (Gever, 1988: 15). MacDonald insisted, in contrast, that Friedrich is "willing to share . . . pleasure with men (her use of a male and female tightrope walker to announce the love making suggests that the sexual pleasure of women need not be confined to women)" (MacDonald, 1992: 287).

34. As one example of such imaginings, see my discussion (in "Displacing Limits of Difference") of Marguerite Duras's experimental makeover, *Her Name of Venice in Deserted Calcutta* (*Son Nom de Venise dans Calcutta désert* (1977), of another of her experimental films, *India Song* (1976), itself reformulated from a novel (*The Vice Consul* [*Le Vice Consul*]) and also staged as a play. The two films share the same sound track and setting, and both deal with imperialism and racism, but *Her Name of Venice* voids the screen of any and all characters, making it impossible for specta-

tors to verify racial or ethnic identity. At one point two actresses appear, motionless, in silhouette, but they are clearly not characters.

I only wish that Roswitha Mueller's intriguing study of Valie Export's work, *Valie Export: Fragments of the Imagination,* had been available when I wrote this essay in 1992, for it is extremely pertinent to the arguments I advance here.

WORKS CITED

Biskind, Peter. "Pods, Blobs, and Ideology in American Films of the Fifties." In *Invasion of the Body Snatchers: Don Siegel, Director,* edited by Al LaValley, 185–197. New Brunswick: Rutgers University Press, 1991.

Braucourt, Guy. "Interview with Don Siegel." In *Focus on the Science Fiction Film,* edited by William Johnson, 74–77. Englewood Cliffs, N.J.: Prentice-Hall, 1972.

Brown, Judith. *Immodest Acts.* New York: Oxford University Press, 1986.

——. "Renaissance Lesbian Sexuality." *Signs* 9, no. 4 (summer 1984): 751–758.

Butler, Judith. *Gender Trouble.* New York: Routledge, 1990.

Christian, Barbara. "The Race for Theory." In *The Nature and Context of Minority Discourse,* edited by Abdul JanMohamed and David Lloyd. Oxford: Oxford University Press, 1990.

Couder, Martine. *"Unsichtbare Gegner."* *Skrien Filmschrift* 137 (September–October 1984): no page available.

Cranny-Francis, Anne. "Feminist Futures: A Generic Study." In *Alien Zone,* edited by Annette Kuhn, 219–228. London: Verso, 1990.

Export, Valie. "Aspects of Feminist Actionism." *New German Critique* 47 (spring–summer 1989): 69–92.

——. "Persona, Proto-Performance, Politics: A Preface." *Discourse* 14, no. 2 (spring 1992): 26–35.

——. "The Real and Its Double: The Body." *Working Paper No. 7 (1988), Center for Twentieth-Century Studies:* 1–20. Reprinted in *Discourse* 11, no. 1 (fall–winter 1988–89): 3–27.

Friedrich, Su. "Radical Form: Radical Content." *Millenium Film Journal* 22 (1989–1990): 118–123.

Fuss, Diana. "Inside/Out." In *Inside/Out: Lesbian Theories, Gay Theories,* edited by Diana Fuss, 1–12. New York: Routledge, 1991.

Garber, Marjorie. *Vested Interests: Cross-Dressing and Cultural Anxiety.* New York: Routledge, 1992.

Gever, Martha. "Girl Crazy." *Film and Video Monthly* 11, no. 6 (July 1988): 14–18.

Hanlon, Lindley. "Female Rage: The Films of Su Friedrich." *Millenium Film Journal* 12 (1982–1983): 79–86.

Hofmann, Werner, and Hans Hollein. *Valie Export: Dokumentations-Ausstellung des Osterreichischen Beitrags zur Biennale Venedig 1980.* Vienna: Bundesministerium für Unterricht und Kunst, 1980.

Holmlund, Chris. "Displacing Limits of Difference: Gender, Race, and Colonialism in Edward Said and Homi Bhabha's Theoretical Models and Marguerite Duras's

Experimental Films." *Quarterly Review of Film Studies* 13, no. 1–3 (May 1990): 1–22.

———. "Fractured Fairytales and Experimental Identities: Looking for Lesbians in and around the Films of Su Friedrich." *Discourse* 17, no. 1 (fall 1994): 16–46.

———. "When Is a Lesbian Not a Lesbian?: The Mainstream Femme Film and the Lesbian Continuum." *Camera Obscura* 25–26 (November 1991): 96–119.

JanMohamed, Abdul, and David Lloyd. "Introduction: Toward a Theory of Minority Discourse: What Is to Be Done?" In *The Nature and Context of Minority Discourse*, edited by Abdul JanMohamed and David Lloyd, 1–16. Oxford: Oxford University Press, 1990.

Kaminsky, Stuart M. "Don Siegel on the Pod Society." In *Invasion of the Body Snatchers: Don Siegel, Director,* edited by Al LaValley, 153–157. New Brunswick: Rutgers University Press, 1991.

———. "The Genre Director: The Films of Don Siegel." In *Invasion of the Body Snatchers: Don Siegel, Director,* edited by Al LaValley, 177–181. New Brunswick: Rutgers University Press, 1991.

Kiernan, Joanna. "Film by Valie Export." *Millenium Film Journal* 16–18 (fall–winter 1986–87): 181–187.

Lang, Robert. *American Film Melodrama*. Princeton, N.J.: Princeton University Press, 1989.

Laura, Ernesto G. *"Invasion of the Body Snatchers."* In *Focus on the Science Fiction Film*, edited by William Johnson, 71–73. Englewood Cliffs, N.J.: Prentice-Hall, 1972.

LaValley, Al. *"Invasion of the Body Snatchers.* Politics, Psychology, Sociology." In *Invasion of the Body Snatchers: Don Siegel, Director,* edited by Al LaValley, 201–205. New Brunswick: Rutgers University Press, 1991.

Lukasz-Aden, Gudrun, and Christel Strobel. *Der Frauenfilm*. Munich: Wilhelm Heyne, 1985.

Lyon, Elizabeth. *"Invisible Adversaries,* or Body Doubles." Paper presented at the Modern Languages Convention, 1991.

MacDonald, Scott. *A Critical Cinema*. Vol. 2. Berkeley and Los Angeles: University of California Press, 1992, 283–318.

Mueller, Roswitha. "The Uncanny in the Eyes of a Woman: Valie Export's *Invisible Adversaries.*" *Sub-Stance* 37–38 (1983): 129–139.

———. *Valie Export: Fragments of the Imagination*. Bloomington and Indianapolis: Indiana University Press, 1994.

"Plastic Surgery under Fire." *For Women First* 4, no. 23 (8 June 1992): 14–25.

Powell, Michael. *A Life in Movies*. New York: Alfred A. Knopf, 1987.

Pulleine, Tim. *"Black Narcissus."* *Films and Filming* 377 (February 1986): 31.

Richards, Renée. *Second Serve*. New York: Stein and Day, 1983.

Rodrig, Antonio. *"Black Narcissus."* *Cinématographe* 109 (April 1985): 5.

Rogin, Michael Paul. "Kiss Me Deadly: Communism, Motherhood, and Cold War Movies." In *Invasion of the Body Snatchers: Don Siegel, Director,* edited by Al LaValley, 201–205. New Brunswick: Rutgers University Press, 1991.

Sayre, Nora. "Watch the Skies." In *Invasion of the Body Snatchers: Don Siegel, Director,* edited by Al LaValley, 184. New Brunswick: Rutgers University Press, 1991.

Sheehan, Henry. *"Black Narcissus."* *Film Comment* 26, no. 3 (May–June 1990): 37–39.

Sobchack, Vivian. *Screening Space.* New York: Ungar, 1987.

Steffen-Fluhr, Nancy. "Women and the Inner Game of Don Siegel's *Invasion of the Body Snatchers.*" In *Invasion of the Body Snatchers: Don Siegel, Director,* edited by Al LaValley, 206–221. New Brunswick: Rutgers University Press, 1991.

Sturken, Marita. *"Invisible Adversaries." Afterimage* 8 (May 1981): 18.

Sykora, Katharina. "When Form Takes as Many Risks as Content." *Frauen und Film* 46 (February 1989): 100–106.

Telotte, J. P. "The Doubles of Fantasy and the Space of Desire." In *Alien Zone,* edited by Annette Kuhn, 152–159. London: Verso, 1990.

Warren, Bill. *Keep Watching the Skies!* Jefferson: McFarland, 1982.

White, Patricia. *"Madame X of the China Seas." Screen* 28, no. 4 (autumn 1987): 80–95.

Young, Robert. *White Mythologies: Writing History and the West.* New York: Routledge, 1990.

FIFTEEN

Nosferatu, or the Phantom of the Cinema

Lloyd Michaels

When Georges Méliès's camera jammed on that famous, if probably apocryphal, afternoon at the Place de l'Opéra, transforming the bus he had been shooting into a hearse during projection, he glimpsed for perhaps the first time the ghostly quality of the cinema's particular mode of representation. That phantom image of the hearse has proven to be an evocative symbol of film's unique way of simultaneously deceiving and enthralling the spectator by substituting an illusory presence for an absent referent, rendering as "undead" a lost object by animating projected shadows and light, often revealing the disturbing contours of familiar shapes. Filmmakers and audiences ever since have been attracted to the depiction of spirits and monsters that not only seem to express certain imperfectly repressed human desires but that also may reflect the idiosyncratic signifying process of the cinema itself. Certainly Mary Shelley's monster, Robert Louis Stevenson's Mr. Hyde, and Bram Stoker's Count Dracula now seem rather long-winded intellectuals compared to their original movie incarnations. Is it because as the offspring of uncontrollable technology, doubles of unstable wills, or fleeting creatures of darkness these celluloid characters exhibit something of the intrinsic nature of film?

Among the gallery of screen monsters, the vampire may be especially well suited to portray both the parasitical quality of the film artist's manipulation of the audience and the elusive, insubstantial nature of the film image.[1] Unlike the grotesque, omnipotent, larger-than-life creatures of most horror movies, the vampire remains a *phantom*—a vision of uncertain substance—rather than a certifiable *monster.* (See figure 28.) Christian Metz and John Ellis, among others, have elaborated on how the signifier in film must always reproduce a phantom of its referent. "The cinema image is marked by a particular half-magic feat in that it makes present something

Figure 28. The shadow of Max Schreck, perhaps the most frightening vampire to hit the big screen, looms in F. W. Murnau's *Nosferatu* (1922).

that is absent. The movement shown on the screen is passed and gone when it is called back into being as illusion. The figures and places shown are not present in the same space as the viewer. The cinema makes present the absent; this is the irreducible separation that cinema maintains (and attempts to abolish), the fact that objects and people are conjured up yet not known to be present" (Ellis, 58–59). Metz makes much the same point by contrasting cinema with the theater, noting how the screen presents not the real objects and persons on stage, but only an "effigy, inaccessible from the outset, in a primordial *elsewhere,* infinitely desirable (= never possible)" (61). Thus, the movie spectator "pursues an imaginary object (a 'lost object') which is . . . always desired as such" (59). The vampire frightens us with its shadow rather than its substance; it is not larger than life but rather "undead"; it evokes not merely revulsion but also desire. As a paradigmatic creature of the cinema, especially in Murnau's *Nosferatu: A Symphony of Horror* (*Nosferatu, eine Symphonie des Grauens,* 1922) and Herzog's remake, *Nosferatu, the Vampyre* (*Nosferatu, Phantom der Nacht,* 1979), the vampire on film represents the imaginary so effectively because it *is* the imaginary (Metz, 41).

In addition to these German versions of the vampire myth, there have been innumerable American and British adaptations, the most noteworthy of which include Tod Browning's *Dracula* (1931), Terence Fisher's *Horror of Dracula* (1958), and John Badham's *Dracula* (1978), not to mention the dozens of sequels, spin-offs, and parodies. During 1992, a fashionable year for vampire revivals, *Buffy the Vampire Killer* and Francis Coppola's *Bram Stoker's Dracula* appealed to widely diverse audiences. Each of the five major retellings to date, starring Max Schreck, Klaus Kinski, Bela Lugosi, Christopher Lee, and Frank Langella in the title role, has sufficiently revitalized the power of the original novel to refute Alain Resnais's oft-cited rejection of adaptations as "warmed over meals." Murnau's and Herzog's *Nosferatu*s, however, remain more resonant and compelling than the other Dracula movies for two related reasons: first, they present the count as a complex, even sympathetic character rather than the evil monster of Stoker's novel; second, they suggest a linkage between this indefinable characterization and the phantom images created by the cinematic apparatus. Their modernity, in short, derives from a certain self-reflexiveness missing in the other versions. Unlike their English-speaking counterparts, Schreck and Kinski manage to signify elusiveness rather than presence, lack rather than excess, entropy rather than lust. Their Draculas are less the doubles of perverse creative energy than the phantoms of the cinema itself.

Because it follows so closely the visual design of Murnau's original—essentially copying the costuming, makeup, plot structure, and performance style, borrowing some of the dialogue ("What a beautiful throat your wife has!") and camera angles, even shooting the very same buildings in Lubeck that Murnau had employed—Herzog's *Nosferatu* is a true remake rather than an adaptation, despite its creator's claims. While Herzog has said, "We are not remaking *Nosferatu,* but bringing it to new life and new character for a new age" (33), his film, unlike the others, cannot be fully appreciated without knowledge of its source (his title indicating that source to be Murnau's film and not Stoker's book), allowing the audience to reexperience many sequences by his employment of nearly identical compositions and blocking. The total aesthetic effect goes far beyond the usual allusions to certain images (rats, cut fingers, ruined castles, abandoned ships) or dialogue ("I never drink . . . wine"); instead, Herzog has conceived every moment with the original in mind, "bringing it to new life" as the "undead" inspiration—the unseen presence—behind his own creation. The parallel between his own art and his protagonist's vampirism could not have been far from his mind.

In contrast to Fisher's, Badham's, and Browning's adaptations, all three of which project an animated, elegant, raven-haired, black-caped protagonist—the mass marketed version of Dracula so familiar in cartoons and Halloween masks—Herzog's Nosferatu duplicates the somnambulistic, emaciated, bald-pated figure first incarnated by Max Schreck. Kinski's performance thus brings to life a phantom of a phantom, a doubled double for the eternal melancholy and mystery of human character that the cinema, with its particular mode of representing "lost objects," seems uniquely equipped to represent. Whereas Murnau's silent film projected the deceptive, disturbing, and evanescent aspect of human character through such relatively new cinematic "tricks" as superimposition and negative shots, Herzog employs more subtle self-reflexive strategies to adumbrate the affinities between his central character and his medium. The result, as Lotte Eisner predicted after observing the shooting of *Nosferatu, the Vampyre,* extends the definition of a remake to something like Murnau's film "reborn" (Andrews, 33).

Through the vagaries of film history, *Nosferatu, A Symphony of Horror* had already been reborn—or at least restored—before Herzog undertook the project. According to John Barbow, the original negative of Murnau's classic has been lost; thus, the existing prints (now widely distributed in 16 mm and video format) are *copies,* all of them incomplete, reproduced from Murnau's shooting script and commentary (82). This circumstance compounds the usual ontological status of the film image as a "lost object" and a figure of the "undead." Even the original characters have been displaced: Murnau's shooting script changes the names from Stoker's novel (for example, Dracula is called Count Orlock, Renfield is Knock), and different names are used in different prints of the film (for example, Jonathan's wife may be called Ellen or Nina).

In loosely adapting Stoker's novel to the screen,[2] Murnau simplified the social concerns while significantly expanding the role of the count, making him the dominant character. "Stoker's novel tells of a serious struggle between human systems. The ending is a paean not only to the good and moral but also to the enlightened, social, domestic, and scientific culture of late nineteenth-century England" (Todd, 200–201). Probably influenced by Freud and certainly by German Expressionism, Murnau's concerns are more psychological than social, as is evident in two ambiguous cuts between Nina and the far distant count. In the first of these, while sleepwalking from her bedroom in Bremen, Nina calls out to Jonathan, who lies prostrate before the menacing shadow of the count in his Carpathian castle. An intertitle says that Jonathan heard her warning cry, but the crosscut shows only Dracula retreating in apparent response. In a second sleepwalking sequence, Nina awakens to announce, "He is coming! I must go to him!" but her reference is ambiguous since it follows a shot, not of Jonathan returning by stagecoach, but of Dracula's ship at sea. Earlier, she had kept a vigil on the beach, supposedly for her husband (who left Bremen by land), further suggesting that the film's truest marriage is between herself and the vampire. Indeed, Murnau's other principal transformation of the novel (aside from expanding the count's role) involves making Nina, not van Helsing,

Nosferatu's main antagonist. Whereas in the novel, the woman must be saved from the monster, in the film she willingly sacrifices herself to become his destroyer. Van Helsing, however, is reduced to offering ineffectual lectures on Venus flytraps. The many remaining minor characters in the book are similarly simplified or eliminated. In comparison to Stoker's extended social morality play, Murnau's *Nosferatu* becomes essentially a tragedy with three characters.

In another departure from the novel, Murnau's count casts a menacing shadow as he stalks first Jonathan and later Nina. Stoker's Dracula, of course, casts no shadow or reflection. While striking in their abstraction of the vampire's horrific threat, these magnified shadows on blank walls also serve as reminders of the cinema's mode of representation. Sabine Hake has noted how early German film before Murnau was marked by "a kind of promotional self-referentiality that draws attention to the cinema and foregrounds its means" in order to "show audiences how to appreciate the cinema and its increasingly sophisticated products, how to deal with feelings of astonishment and disbelief, and how to gain satisfaction from the playful awareness of the apparatus and the simultaneous denial of its presence" (37–38). Murnau continues this tradition from the previous decade, although the self-reflexivity of *Nosferatu*, like that of the earlier films Hake describes, has little to do with a modernist questioning of the medium. Instead, Murnau explores the technical means available for representing the phantom of character that, for him, lies at the center of the story. In his film, the sources of Dracula's alienation and depravity remain unfathomed: nothing is to be learned of his ancestry, his philosophy, or his personal feelings. The mystery shrouding his character can only be approached through indirection, as in the grotesque shadows that signify his presence.

Murnau's use of other special effects—particularly the negative shot of the coach taking Harker through the forest to Dracula's castle and the superimpositions (double exposures) of the vampire's sudden spectral appearance—can be understood as similar demonstrations of the affinity between the cinema's process of signification involving the play of presence/absence and the ambiguous character of the film's protagonist. The negative image of the stagecoach, with its shrouded windows and horses, extends the haunting effect of Méliès's phantom hearse; the superimpositions seem to defy human corporeality and privilege the uncanny. Even the vampire's ultimate extinction, his dematerialization as conveyed through stop action and a puff of smoke, suggests by metonymy the spontaneous combustion that threatens the film's own nitrate stock. Of course, such subtle implications may have been far from the director's conscious design, but it seems significant that Murnau employs a quite different repertoire of stylistic devices—notably camera movement and depth focus—when he comes to portray a more ordinary, "realistic," though equally fascinating, character in *The Last Laugh* (1924).

In setting out to adapt Murnau's *Nosferatu,* Herzog has retained the basic plot and misc-en-scène while refining the reflexive and expressionistic elements. Despite one reviewer's description of *Nosferatu, the Vampyre* as "simply Murnau with colour and sound" (Strick, 127), Bruce Kawin has more precisely noted how "no more than three shots are exactly the same in both films (allowing for the fact that Herzog's are in color)" (45). Paradoxically, this homage to the history of German cinema and to the director Herzog considers his country's greatest remains the most personal of all the Dracula films. While remaking Murnau's masterpiece, Herzog has also managed to remake Herzog, exploring the signature themes and stylistic elements that have defined his place as that of one of the seminal artists of the New German Cinema.

Although it is difficult to conceive of a more "faithful" remake, *Nosferatu, the Vampyre* also alters and even subverts Murnau's original in some significant ways. The most prominent changes involve both foregrounding the collapse of civilized society in the face of Nosferatu's invasion and elaborating the vampire's personal history and psychological motivation. The primary effect of these changes is to reverse the theme of Stoker's novel, the triumph of good over evil, and to undercut the sense of closure in Murnau's film. In Herzog's romantic, subversive ending, Nosferatu lives on in the vampirized character of Jonathan Harker, who flees from the bourgeois town of Wismar (actually Delft) into what Metz might call a "primordial *elsewhere,*" announcing that "I have much to do." Like the epilogue Polanski attaches to his version of *Macbeth,* this added scene expresses the director's personal reconception of the thematic implications of the original, an updating of the classic text in response to the exigencies of modern culture. The restoration of order in Shakespeare's and Murnau's work has been superseded by Polanski's and Herzog's vision of chronic malignancy.

Herzog's specific transformations of Murnau's *Nosferatu* may be organized according to a tripartite taxonomy of adaptation strategies broadly derived from Vladimir Propp: simplification, expansion, substitution (Crabbe, 47). By eliminating the original diary frame (the account of the plague in Wismar by one John Cavillius), Herzog excises the voice of rational authority over the progress of the story and replaces it with the mysterious choral accompaniment of Popul Vuh on the sound track.[9] Similarly, Dr. Van Helsing's scientific lectures have been cut, further subverting any "objective" explanation for the film's irrational events. Herzog's expansions chiefly involve the development both of Dracula's more sympathetic character and of Wismar's more stifling, ineffectual society. Murnau could only suggest the count's enervated, alienated existence through Schreck's performance and occasional crosscutting; Herzog adds dialogue expressing

Figure 29. Horror and sexuality blend in Herzog's *Nosferatu, the Vampyre* (1979) as the vampire (Klaus Kinski) approaches Lucy, played by the beautiful Isabelle Adjani.

the vampire's world weariness after witnessing centuries of sorrow, and Kinski speaks in a labored whisper, as if he were breathing through a respirator. Most notoriously, Herzog expands the representation of pestilence by importing thousands of laboratory rats and turning them loose in the streets of Schiedam (after the mayor of nearby Delft had prohibited their release). He also expands the sense of decadence by shooting new sequences of chaos in the town square (antithetical to Stoker's reaffirmation of bourgeois society and quite different from Murnau's orderly scenes showing crosses being painted on quarantined houses and coffins being carried through the streets). In preparation for his pessimistic ending, Herzog substitutes an ominous prelude for Murnau's initial images of domestic bliss (Jonathan picking flowers, Nina playing with her kitten). Thus, the credit sequence of *Nosferatu, the Vampyre* begins with a sustained tracking shot in a cave of contorted mummies, accompanied by a medieval dirge sung by Popul Vuh and followed by slow-motion images of a bat in flight. In the film's first diegetic scene, instead of tenderly receiving a bouquet from her husband, Lucy Harker awakens from a nightmare.

These transformations confirm Herzog's assertion that he is not simply remaking *Nosferatu* but revivifying it. As in all previous versions, however, there remains at the very center of his film the haunting figure of Dracula himself, the mysterious object of both fear and desire. Only in Victor Erice's evocation of James Whale's *Frankenstein* (1931) in *The Spirit of the Beehive* (1973) is the monster treated with such ambivalence. Reflecting another crucial change from its precursors, the climax of *Nosferatu, the Vampyre* depicts Lucy drawing the vampire back to her neck as he begins to withdraw with the arrival of dawn. The bedside tableau clearly portrays the erotic subtext left imperfectly concealed in most versions of the story.[4] (See figure 29.) In this moment, Dracula transcends his previous incarnations as moral monster to become the double of Harker (who first appears whispering words of comfort into his frightened wife's neck as she awakens from her nightmare), the alter ego of Herzog (who identifies with the vampire's romantic restlessness), and the phantom of the cinema.

There are phantoms everywhere in Herzog's text. In addition to the presiding spirit of Murnau, and Kinski's reincarnation of Schreck, *Nosferatu, the Vampyre* conjures up the ghost of Stoker by restoring his original characters' names and echoes Bela Lugosi's famous line from Browning's *Dracula* when the count responds to the cry of wolves: "Listen! The children of the night make their music." Roland Topor's performance as Renfield, which drew a mixed response from reviewers, seems more comprehensible when understood as an allusion to the stylized appearances of Peter Lorre in dozens of horror films. Herzog thus evokes the history of what Eisner called Germany's "haunted screen," in addition to referring to German painting (Caspar David Friedrich's mountain landscapes and ruined castles) and music (the Wagnerian sound track). Finally, Herzog resurrects the ghost of Herzog in a number of ways that reflect his own earlier films: the repertory company of collaborators, including Kinski, Popul Vuh, and cinematographer Jorg Schmidt-Reitwein; the time-lapse landscape shots as the clouds move over the mountains, from *Heart of Glass* (1976); the panning shots of Nosferatu's raft on the river, from *Aguirre, Wrath of God* (1972); the slow-motion depiction of the bat's flight, from *The Great Ecstasy of the Woodsculptor Steiner* (1974); the alienated protagonist and impotent bureaucrats, from *The Mystery of Kasper Hauser* (1974). By such varied means does the film continually inscribe presence/absence as a way of representing the spirit of the vampire.

Noël Carroll has questioned the significance of presence/absence as a paradigm for distinguishing film from other fictional narrative forms such as the novel or stage play. "Once we are considering the realm of fiction," Carroll writes, "it makes no sense to speak of the differences between cinema and theater in terms of what is absent to the spectator. In both fictional film and theatrical fiction, the characters are absent from the continuum of our world in the same way." Therefore, "Shylock is no more present to

the theater spectator than Fred C. Dobbs is present to the film viewer"
(38). But Carroll's point holds true only for the referent—the reader's or
viewer's mental construct of a character—and not for the signifier of that
referent, in this case the actor. That is, Olivier is actually present on stage
in the role of Shylock, while Bogart is not in the movie theater. The issue
Metz and others have raised concerns not *what* the cinema signifies, but
how. Moreover, the paradigm seems especially relevant to the reception of
a remake, when the spectator remains continuously aware of the existence
of a prior model that is both different and (except in the case of inserted
footage, as in *The Spirit of the Beehive*) absent from the present text.

In *Nosferatu, the Vampyre,* Herzog provides several occasions of presence/
absence within the diegesis, discovering more subtle means for depicting a
world of "lost objects" than Murnau's exploitation of stock effects such as
negative shots and stop action. The film's arresting precredit sequence, with
its slow tracking across the stricken faces of the mummified dead, begins
the process of evoking the phantom existence that every film—but especially this film—brings to life. In addition to his relentlessly moving camera,
Herzog employs an expressionist sound track—a mournful two-note chorus
combined with the amplified sound of a heartbeat—to animate the still
images, rendering them as "undead" through the particular signifying processes of the cinema. Similarly, the closing time-lapse shot of Harker riding
off into the distance across a desert landscape accompanied by the choral
strains of Gonoud's *Sanctus* confirms his new identity as a lost soul destined
to wander endlessly in a "primordial *elsewhere.*" But the question of character remains: has his identity been permanently *transformed* by the vampire's
bite, or simply *revealed?*

Another privileged moment that suggests the cinema's potential to
represent the uncanny occurs when Harker seeks transport across the
Borgo Pass to Dracula's castle. Herzog invents a dialogue scene missing
from Murnau's film. While attending his four horses hitched to the stagecoach, the coachman replies to Jonathan's request for passage, "I haven't
any coach." Asked if he will sell a horse for double the price, he answers,
"Can you not see? I haven't any horses."[5] After walking alone for days across
the mountains, Harker is finally rescued by the mysterious appearance
of another coach, whose driver (as in both Murnau and Browning) disappears before they reach the castle. In a third permutation of what might
be understood as a kind of reincarnation of Méliès's phantom hearse, the
stricken Harker is driven back to Wismar in a single-horse rig whose perfectly balanced reflection Herzog mirrors in the adjacent canal. In each
case, the imaginary calls into question, in effect remakes, the real.

In addition to such conventional devices as mirror shots and dramatic
shadows, Herzog often employs formal composition within the frame to
create the presence of absence, most clearly in the domestic scenes in

Figure 30. The "Last Supper" in Herzog's *Nosferatu, the Vampyre* (1979), manages to mix humor and horror in depicting the decay of civilized society.

Wismar after Harker's return. In one shot-in-depth, for example, Lucy reads about Dracula in close-up while her enervated husband can be glimpsed in the background slumped in a chair, now truly a lost object barely distinguishable from the furniture. A more subtle use of mise-en-scène occurs earlier at the mountain inn. Harker impatiently demands his dinner so that he can be on his way to the count's castle. At the mention of Dracula's name, the gypsies all suddenly stop eating, and the composition becomes a virtual freeze-frame. In the foreground with his back to the camera, Jonathan confronts the silent, crowded room, with diners on either side of the frame and a triangular shadow in the middle ground pointing toward an empty window at the vanishing point. In this possible allusion to Renaissance paintings of the Last Supper, Herzog emphasizes not the presence of the Savior but the absence of communion. Jonathan remains estranged from both the innkeeper behind him (and the camera) and the guests before him; there is no chalice, no food, nothing in the window but a foreboding vacancy. Herzog follows this sequence with more obvious parodies of the Last Supper: first, when Jonathan dines with Dracula at the castle and later when the rats replace the bourgeois party consuming "their last supper" in the ruined town square. (See figure 30.)

These various phantom figures—the transmogrified mummies, the uncertain coaches, the debilitated husband, the empty window—all suggest a connection between the vampire's elusive existence and the cinema's presentation of character. As Nosferatu drains his victims of blood, the film image deprives its referent of the materiality it once possessed when it appeared before the camera. Every object, every actor becomes a ghost in the moment of projection, but no object seems as slippery, duplicitous, and evanescent as human character, which must remain both partially hidden (character as a signified, a matrix of emotional, moral and cognitive traits) and subject to change. Herzog, a filmmaker conversant with contemporary critical theory, compounds the spectator's awareness of this "lost object" status of film through a number of self-reflexive moments, some of which have already been described. The prominent mirror images, for example— Lucy's reflection in the water during her sleepwalking, the horizontal tracking shot of the coach returning Jonathan to Wismar, and the powerful scene when Dracula first visits Lucy as she sits before her dressing mirror—serve as reminders of the camera's mimetic function as well as the Lacanian basis ("the mirror stage") for Metz's theory of the cinema's imaginary signifier. Following Murnau's example in defying Stoker's conception of Dracula as casting no shadow, Herzog's Nosferatu is virtually defined by the darkness in which he lives and which he casts over others. In a brilliant stroke, Herzog displays only the count's shadow entering Lucy's bedroom and reflecting in her mirror, the door opening as if by itself; as he advances on her frightened form doubled in the glass, he casts no reflection of his own. Like Lucy, then, the spectator becomes terrified by the *framed reflection of a shadow*. What has been signified in this tableau, the irreducible nature of Dracula's character (he begs only to share Lucy's love), has been perfectly matched by the cinematic signifier.

At times, in fact, Nosferatu almost stands in for the cinema itself. In the memorable long shot of his phosphorescent skull glimmering in the darkened upper window of his Wismar mansion—a shot borrowed directly from Murnau—he resembles the light from the projection booth, casting his gaze on the community he holds in thrall. This association also occurs earlier at the castle when the count serves Harker a midnight supper. Dracula sits above and behind his visitor, his white bulb of a head surrounded by darkness and framed by a window, his labored breath like the sound of the projector mechanism, his attentive guest increasingly menaced by his mesmerizing presence. Judith Mayne has aptly described how Nosferatu here occupies "a literal 'no man's land' " (126) in the black background of the composition, the same uncharted region Harker himself will traverse in the film's concluding vision when he becomes, in effect, the remake of his master.

Perhaps the sanctification of the vampire's continuing mission as enunciated in the finale by Gonoud's chorus should not be regarded as simply ironic. Like Herzog remaking Murnau, the new Nosferatu has not only escaped the quotidian realm that first oppressed him ("These canals that go nowhere but back on themselves," as Jonathan described Wismar) but also transcended his mentor's fate. No wonder, then, that Herzog seems to celebrate his disappearance into myth, to be reborn again as the phantom of the cinema.

NOTES

1. Ingmar Bergman employs images of vampirism—neck biting and blood sucking to powerful effect in *Persona* (1966), his most self-reflexive film.

2. Not loosely enough: Stoker's widow successfully prosecuted Murnau, which may account for the disappearance of the original negative.

3. Herzog's simplification of the narrative frame has the same effect as would eliminating the frame story from *The Cabinet of Dr. Caligari,* thereby restoring the screenwriters' original subversive intent.

4. Badham's *Dracula* also foregrounds the sexual themes, with Lucy portrayed as an early twentieth-century feminist who openly responds to the count's seduction.

5. This scene recalls many similar hallucinatory moments in Herzog's work, most notably the response of the raftsman in *Aguirre, Wrath of God* first to seeing a ship atop a tree and then to being shot by unseen natives: "That is no ship. That is no forest. This is no arrow."

WORKS CITED

Andrews, Nigel. "Dracula in Delft." *American Film* 4, no. 1 (1978): 32–38.

Barbow, John D. *German Expressionist Film.* Boston: Twayne, 1982.

Carroll, Noël. *Mystifying Movies.* New York: Columbia University Press, 1988.

Crabbe, Katharyn. "Lean's 'Oliver Twist': Novel to Film." *Film Criticism* 2, no. 1 (1977): 46–51.

Ellis, John. *Visible Fictions.* Boston: Routledge and Kegan Paul, 1982.

Hake, Sabine. "Self-Referentiality in Early German Cinema." *Cinema Journal* 31, no. 3 (1992): 37–55.

Kawin, Bruce. "Nosferatu." *Film Quarterly* 33, no. 3. (1980): 45–47.

Mayne, Judith. "Herzog, Murnau, and the Vampire." *The Films of Werner Herzog,* edited by Timothy Corrigan, 119–32. New York: Methuen, 1986.

Metz, Christian. *The Imaginary Signifier.* Bloomington: Indiana University Press, 1982.

Strick, Philip. "Nosferatu—the Vampyre." *Sight and Sound* 48, no. 2 (1979): 127–28.

Todd, Janet. "The Classic Vampire." *The English Novel and the Movies,* edited by Michael Klein and Gillian Parker, 197–210. New York: Ungar.

SIXTEEN

How Many Draculas Does It Take to Change a Lightbulb?

Ira Konigsberg

He ought to be left in peace. We keep exhuming him from his musty tomb, trying to set him going again, animating him so that he will continue to rise from the coffin from his own volition. But his volition is really our volition. So much has been written about this dark, enigmatic, seductive figure in recent years that the mind boggles, nausea overwhelms as one again confronts the subject, speculates on the story's popularity. So much has been written on both the book and the films—we can not consider them apart since all the criticism seems concerned with the same basic myth. And yet the book and films will not cohere—each cinematic treatment seems another attempt to get it right, to put the book on film or, at least, to find in the book what is the heart, the center, the significance of the myth. We can certainly think of each filming as a reinterpretation to fit a changing time and culture, but we still wonder at the large number of remakes, at the popularity of the story, at the commitment of director after director to put the story, all over again, on film. We are after bigger game, deeper insights. If Bram Stoker had not invented him, Dracula would have existed anyway.

We are dealing here with more than the subject of remakes: we are dealing with a preoccupation, an obsession. I count seven film versions of the novel—nine, if we consider two television adaptations of some ambition.[1] But the Dracula myth is also an articulation, a configuration of larger themes—I notice a recent publication that describes 372 vampire films in general (Flynn). The Dracula myth, though, is certainly the most eloquent, the most stirring, and the most popular articulation of the vampire motif in contemporary culture. We must, therefore, approach this book and its filmic adaptations as the embodiment of forces that transcend this specific configuration, but we must see this configuration as the most accessible means in our culture of reaching for these transcendent meanings; and we must see each film adaptation as itself a different interpretation of these transcendent significations or, at least, as a different focus on them. What I should like to explore, ultimately, in this essay is the possibility that all of these versions may be seen as an attempt to push deeper into the heart of the myth, an attempt to unlayer the palimpsest.

We see a compulsion to repeat in each of these films: the monster keeps reappearing and he continues to perform his unspeakable acts until the film must close and we must rejoin the daylight world. But the repetition compulsion is also evident in the constant remakes of the film, in telling the story over and over, in trying, finally, to understand and master it. Sometimes the pretense is to get the actual novel on film, to be true to Stoker's vision,[2] but even if we acknowledge the virtual impossibility of adapting a novel to film with any degree of accuracy, we must still be struck by the way in which filmmakers consciously and even waywardly seem to try so ardently not to get the novel on film. The novel, finally, seems a pretext, a legitimization of some other effort, of an attempt to develop something inherent in the novel and earlier films and hence to develop away from the earlier versions. Each telling is not so much a reshaping to fit a new time period as each time period allows a retelling that takes the film one step further, that repeats while doing more than repeating.

Freud goes beyond pleasure in *Beyond the Pleasure Principle* (1920) to explain the repetition compulsion. He attempts to explain the phenomenon in biological and evolutionary terms. He puts us on the edge of a new vista by suggesting that "all instincts tend towards the restoration of an earlier state of things" (26). Why not push further and see psychoanalysis itself as part of an evolutionary process? Why not take the step and think anthropologically, as Freud himself did on this occasion. In this context, then, film becomes something more than film. In this context Francis Ford Coppola's most recent version of the story, *Bram Stoker's Dracula* (1992) can take us farther into the heart of darkness while not being a satisfactory cinematic work—in fact, its weaknesses as a film may be inextricably linked to its success in penetrating back into our biological and evolutionary history. (See figure 31.) We shall proceed with this discussion, finally to arrive at such an interpretation of *Dracula*'s latest remake.

As Coppola's film is both successful and not successful, it is also both a horror film and not a horror film. It is a horror film since it deals with themes that have traditionally been dealt with by this genre, but not one because it no longer deals with these themes horrifically. Horror films seem to have gone as far as they can legitimately go in horrifying people—the nadir has been reached and the genre, for all intents and purposes, is on its last legs. Violence had become so exploitative that the exploited in the audience have become immune to their own exploitation; sex has become

Figure 31. Gary Oldman is convincing as Dracula in Francis Ford Coppola's no-holds-barred, visually arresting retelling of *Bram Stoker's Dracula* (1992).

so violent that violence has become totally sexualized. What Coppola has created is a work strangely divided between its romantic and horrific elements. We saw this turn of events coming with John Badham's 1979 *Dracula,* with the romanticization of Stoker's story to such an extent that the film seems less like *Dracula* and a horror film than all the previous versions.[3] (See figure 32.) Coppola took from the old horror film that which was still salvageable and developed it in the only logical way that he could— as an erotic dream, creating a work more erotic and dreamlike than even Badham's film. Coppola himself admits his attempt to create "almost a

Figure 32. Frank Langella's fine stage presence is lost in the mist of special horror effects in John Badham's overblown recasting of *Dracula* (1979).

dream state" through "a kind of evocative, poetic use of imagery" that he finds in the symbolist movement of the late nineteenth century, clearly referring to the paintings of such figures as Klimt and Moreau (Coppola and Hart, 70). Coppola unleashes the fantastic and sends us hurling into psychic space. The irony here is that he is able to do so only because he has so little vision of his own, because he is such an excellent reader of past films and can derive his own work from all the understated and yet most compelling dark corners of earlier *Dracula* films and other films of fantasy as well.[4] All

Figure 33. Max Schreck chills us to the bone, silently, in F. W. Murnau's *Nosferatu* (1922).

Figure 34. Klaus Kinski stars in Werner Herzog's *Nosferatu, the Vampyre* (1979).

those homages and references to earlier films, as well as the scene in the cinematographic parlor, are but a recognition that this is a film about films and, as such, a dream about dreams.

The equation of the Dracula story to a dream is apparent in Murnau's early silent film of 1922, *Nosferatu, A Symphony of Horror* (see figure 33), with its primitive attempts to achieve this quality through such special effects as accelerated motion and negative images, but also through the characters' references to dreaming as well as Ellen's somnambulism and sleepwalking. Both this film and Werner Herzog's effective and stylistic remake in 1979, *Nosferatu, The Vampyre* (see figure 34), photograph a number of their scenes in the outdoor world, but both films are impressive as a result of their intrusion of the supernatural dimension into this reality. Basing his film on the stage version by Deane and Balderston and focusing on Bela Lugosi's otherworldly performance (see figure 35), Tod Browning confines his 1931 film mostly to the studio, creating a work singularly slow and spatially limited even with the opening sequence at Castle Dracula and the closing one in Carfax Abbey, creating a somnambulistic and dreamlike state to his entire work. Whereas the colorful, bold, but unsubtle film made in England in 1956 by Hammer Film Productions and directed by Terence Fisher gave the count an earthly power and zest through Christopher Lee's perfor-

Figure 35. Bela Lugosi's most memorable screen performance was that
of the count in Tod Browning's *Dracula* (1931).

mance (see figure 36), and Badham's version places much of his story in
an outdoor setting, Coppola insulates his characters and world from any
hint of reality, shoots the whole thing in the enclosures of a studio, breaks
down any semblance of real time and space, and uses performers who seem
themselves totally unreal—there is not enough of the real world in this film
to make events seem threatening either to the characters on the screen or
to the audience. But this is a film that explores and exploits the dream
quality of all previous *Dracula* films, that makes hints of the unconscious

Figure 36. Christopher Lee plays the title role in Terence Fischer's *The Horror of Dracula* (1956). Lee also played the same role in Jesse Franko's *Count Dracula* (1970).

even more visible and recognizable.[5] And in being so focused on the unconscious, Coppola falls into the pit and goes spinning right past the oedipal and preoedipal stages, hurling down our genetic line.

The analogy between watching a film and dreaming is almost as old as film criticism itself, and the concomitant connection between the horror film and a nightmare almost a cliché at this point in time. In recent years the regressive quality of viewing a film, film's ability not only to penetrate into the unconscious but to reawaken early infantile experiences, has received considerable attention (for example, in the writings of Baudry and Metz). The *Dracula* films envelope us in a world already dreamlike and unreal, with their closed bedrooms and dungeons, with their logistics of doors and windows, with their nighttime intruders and sleeping, passive victims, with their intrusion of the dead into the world of the living. Lloyd Michaels, in another essay in this collection, refers to the suitability of film, with its illusion of reality—of a world that seems to be here but is actually not—to portray the phantom presence and nonpresence of the vampire. The point is well taken in relation to Coppola's realization that the year of the novel's publication, 1897, was the same time as the beginning of projected motion pictures and his staging of an early scene between the count and Mina in a cinematography parlor. But I wish to take this point in yet another direction and consider the film image from both a psychoanalytic and phenomenological viewpoint, a consideration that takes us to a major issue in the book as well as in all the films. For me the issue is about perception and representation, a subject closely related to presence and absence (by "perception" I mean the image we perceive and by "representation" the object as it is represented outside of us). Baudry makes the cogent point that "the cinematic apparatus is unique in that *it offers the subject perceptions 'of a reality' whose status seems similar to that of representations experienced as a perception*"—a confusion between perception and representation "characteristic" of both the primary process and dream (120). But whereas Baudry's point is that cinema returns us to an infantile phase in which perception and representation were not yet differentiated, my own point is that this confusion reinforces the drama of the characters' and our own interaction with the vampire figure—a point that Coppola nicely underscores with his film's self-reflexivity, but one that he knows to be inherent in all the films before him. We may relate this notion to the most fundamental aspect of the horror film, the fact that what we see is originally a product not of reality but the mind's reality, that what is dramatized before us is some form or shape of mental configurations that we all share in our dream and fantasy lives. What we have, then, are representations of perceptions mistaken for representations. What we have within the films themselves are stories of characters who must be forced to take as representations what we unconsciously sense as our own perceptions. In a major way, these characters act out our own issues of denial and acceptance, of fear and desire; these films are so uncanny because they actually represent what has heretofore been hidden as our own perceptions.

Recall Van Helsing's speech in Stoker's novel about belief and disbelief: "Do you not think that there are things which you cannot understand; and yet which are; that some people see things that others cannot? That there are things old and new which must not be contemplated by men's eyes, because they know—or think they know—some things which other men have told them" (197). It is interesting that he discourses on what people believe in terms of their seeing and not seeing, in terms of what they will see and will not see, especially since he soon urges Jonathan "[t]o believe in things that you cannot" (198). Let us recall that it was Jonathan's strange adventures in Transylvania that unleashed the unholy forces in the novel; that it was Jonathan who could not see, or would not see, that one of the three female vampires who sought to attack him, the one with blonde hair, seemed so familiar to him because she reminded him of his Mina; and that Jonathan is still, at this point in the novel, suffering from myopia. It becomes clearer and clearer that he and the other characters will not see because they do not want to see, because they do not want to have their subjective perceptions proved to be actual representations. In his *Studies in Hysteria*, Freud refers to the "peculiar state in which one knows something and at the same time does not know it" (117), a description that well fits the human characters in the *Dracula* myth and that will take on even more significance in the latter part of this essay. But we must always remember that these characters are our own surrogates in these films, acting out our own resistance and final submission to the monsters that we see on the screen.

The theme of belief and disbelief runs throughout all the films. Van Helsing tells us in Browning's 1931 film, "The strength of the vampire is that people will not believe in him," emphasizing the fact that people will not believe in the vampire because they do not wish to. In Jess Franco's film, Harker himself asks Van Helsing, "Then why did you not believe what I told you about Count Dracula?" and the wise man responds, "I cannot tell you. I dare not." He dares not because of what he knows about himself and the vampire, that Dracula indeed is the manifestation of some part of himself. Later he says, about Dracula, "I feel as though I know him better than my own soul." All of these films, like the novel, have the same plot wherein a group of people must be convinced of the existence of this nighttime horror; until they are convinced, violation follows upon violation. In Terence Fischer's version, Harker knows from the start that Dracula is a vampire, and, in league with Van Helsing, goes to the castle under the pretext of cataloguing the count's books but with the real purpose of destroying him. Although the start to this film seems fabricated and, once in the castle, Harker seems totally incompetent and incapable, the notion of libraries and books is in keeping with the theme of articulation and communication—articulating and communicating the reality of the vampire to others—that runs throughout the first part of the film, a theme also developed through the importance placed on Jonathan's diary and Van Helsing's Dictaphone.

In Herzog's film Van Helsing claims to be a man of science, but he is weak and ineffectual while the heroine, relying on faith, is able to grasp the situation and bring the plague to an end through her sacrifice.

The asylum guard in Browning's 1931 version has two lines he delivers to a female servant that at first appear to be a throwaway comic bit— "They're all crazy except me and you. Sometimes I have me doubts about you"—but consideration, in the light of my present discussion, gives the statement a telling irony. The issue of belief and disbelief is very much tied in with that of sanity and insanity because either an individual will appear insane to the sane if he or she perceives the truth or one may have to transcend what is normally considered sanity to see this reality beyond our everyday reality. After Harker's adventure, which unleashes Dracula upon an unsuspecting civilization, and the boat ride on the *Demeter* that transits the count from one world to the other, Renfield takes on importance as the only one of the characters who knows the nature of the Dracula figure and the only one who knows what is going on in general. The crazy man is crazy because he is in touch with forces that shatter his sanity, but he is thought crazy because he is in touch with a reality that the other characters cannot and will not see.

Badham's 1979 *Dracula* is the first of these films to emphasize the importance of Seward's mental institution, to see it as the proper location for the myth's abnormal acts and forces—all the shots within the institution are in muted colors with dominant grays as if to suggest a documentary credibility to this context. After Lucy (Badham switches Lucy's and Mina's names) has become the lover and advocate of the count, she herself is locked up in the institution, something unthinkable with her corresponding character in the novel and the other films, but fitting in a larger context: like Renfield she now has the vision that removes her from the limited seeing of the everyday world of reality. Whereas the other characters continue to see only the representations that exist outside of them, Lucy now is able to merge her perceptions with the world of representations. Since perception must be a product of desire, she has projected her desires onto the world outside of her. Since perception and representation have merged for her she has, literally, removed herself from the everyday world of the sane and unseeing. To believe in the novel and all the films, to see the truth, is a form of insanity because belief not only removes one from the world of the sane, but it also reshapes the world that one perceives outside of one's self in the image of the dark recesses of the mind. All the films bear this out, with Count Dracula unleashing the hidden desires of the Lucys and Minas, with these women throwing open their arms to welcome the dark midnight intruder and baring their throats to his teeth.

The ultimate question with all these films is what exactly is the perception we subjectively have of the vampire figure—what do we project onto his representation on the screen (and what, finally, do we introject into ourselves)? The answer resists a simplistic reduction. As our mental lives are the creations of layers upon layers of mental stages and experiences, so does Dracula become a repository for all these levels, a palimpsest who entices us to analyze him layer upon layer. The popularity of this figure resides in the complexity of his representation, in the fact that he is always more than what he at first seems. To trace the development of the *Dracula* story in film is to see what aspect or aspects of this figure each filmmaker emphasizes, a focus very much impacted by changes in our culture in general, especially in issues of gender and sexuality, but also by a growing self-consciousness in the arts of psychoanalytic concepts and by changes in the history of cinema, particularly the decline of genre films and an expanding self-reflexivity in film—the fact that genre films have been replaced by films about genre films.

The variations in the focus upon the Dracula figure very much determine what aspects of Stoker's original story are emphasized. We might think of these films according to two grids, a vertical, paradigmatic grid that represents the various choices that each film makes about the characterization of Dracula and a horizontal, syntagmatic grid that represents the sequence of actions chosen to intersect with the vertical grid. The following paragraphs outline the basic sequence of actions and the syntagmatic variations that emerge from the novel and its film versions.

1. Jonathan Harker's visit to Castle Dracula, which is described in the novel by Harker himself as a transition from the modern West to the old-world East, but also a journey into the world of superstition and "some sort of imaginative whirlpool" (12). Browning's film, largely based on the stage play by Balderstone and Deane, has Renfield make the journey, and Fisher's film takes away much of the journey itself and deposits Harker almost immediately at the castle in broad daylight—an emphasis on the this-worldly qualities of Dracula. Badham's 1979 version is the only one of these films totally to ignore the journey and the visit to the castle, erasing the mysterious background of the figure and making him less a creature from our own imaginations than a creation of Hollywood romance.

2. The journey of the *Demeter*, which reminds us that in mythology and literature the crossing of a body of water is often symbolic of a journey from one world to the next. The fact that the ship is named after the earth-mother goddess of the Greeks may well be Stoker's way of suggesting Dracula's birth into the everyday world of nineteenth-century England, but the name also suits the androgynous nature of the figure as discussed toward the end of this essay. The Hammer

film features no such journey, probably because of budgetary considerations; instead the journey from Castle Dracula to Lucy and Mina is a mere coach drive from one neighboring European city to another. Franco's film also eliminates the boat trip for budgetary concerns and has first Harker and then Dracula suddenly appearing at the sanitarium outside of London, which in this case is run by Van Helsing.

3.   Dracula's interaction with Renfield. Much of the action of the middle part of the story is centered on Dracula's interactions with three characters in England: Renfield, Lucy, and Mina. These interactions are themselves paralleled by the relationship of Van Helsing to the three figures, a relationship that develops his own awareness and powers and that culminates in his expunging Dracula from the everyday world of the living. It is clear that the insane Renfield now takes the place of Harker as the bridge between Dracula's world and England: his major function is to invite Dracula into the Seward asylum and home, since the vampire figure cannot enter on his own volition.

4.   Dracula's seduction, destruction, and transformation of Lucy, which is the most explicitly misogynistic and sexually violent relationship in most versions of the story. The character is absent in the *Nosferatu* films (although Herzog, like Badham, uses her name for his Mina character) since the focus of the film is not on sexuality. In the remainder of the films Lucy is the woman drawn to the vampire figure and punished for her sexuality.

5.   Dracula's relationship with and desire for Mina. In the novel Mina is the strong and virtuous woman with a "man's brain" who is forced by Dracula to drink his blood from a self-inflicted gash in his chest. While Mina and Lucy trade names in Badham's film, the character clearly becomes a creature of the 1970s, a liberated woman and law student who willingly takes the count as her lover and enjoys a protracted act of lovemaking and bloodletting. In Coppola's film Mina becomes a reincarnation of Dracula's wife, and the two characters become star-crossed lovers struggling against the onrush of time.

6.   The pursuit of Dracula back to his place of origin, where he is finally destroyed on the threshold of his castle. The only one of the films to come close to the novel in its ending is the most recent version. In both *Nosferatu* films the monster is destroyed in the heroine's bedroom, victim of her sacrifice. Herzog imposes a modern ending on the tale, sending Harker off on a journey, himself now a vampire, carrying the deadly plague that Dracula began. In Browning's film, Dracula and Mina are followed to nearby Carfax Abbey by Van Helsing and Harker where the older man gets rid of Dracula off-

screen while the two young lovers are united. Badham's Dracula is discovered and exposed to the sun on an outgoing ship, but his cape rises high in the air, becoming batlike wings as Mina's tears are replaced by a smile of triumph.

We can find the following themes residing in the Dracula figure in the book and in these films through the way in which the plot is structured and developed. I would argue that all of these themes are inherent in the figure in every treatment, but that different films manipulate the figure differently to focus on one or another of these aspects of his character.

THE DEAD AND UNDEAD

This is probably the most obvious and immediate significance of the vampire figure, especially with its early connection to plagues, inexplicable deaths, and premature burials in eastern Europe, particularly during the seventeenth and eighteenth centuries. The theme is most emphasized in the *Nosferatu* films, with the connection between the vampire figure and the plague of Wisborg in the first film and the plague of Wismar in the second. Melton claims that the term "Nosferatu" derives from *nosufur-atu,* an Old Slavonic word meaning "plague carrier" (435).[6] Some critics have seen the Nosferatu of both Max Schreck and Klaus Kinski as resembling an erect penis (for example, Danoun, 54–55), but such an interpretation seems to me to be the result of a preconceived sexual interpretation of the vampire in general. Certainly both Murnau and Herzog emphasize the ratlike heads and unworldly demeanor of their vampires to link them to the themes of plague and pestilence. One of the most striking scenes in Murnau's film is the long shot of the procession of pallbearers carrying the coffins down the narrow, claustrophobic street from the top part of the frame to the bottom, a scene repeated and widened in Herzog's work with a high-angle shot of three forlorn processions in the town square of Wismar. But all the films to some degree play with this general motif, especially with Dracula's coffin as a central image. Although vampires in eastern Europe were thought to be reanimated corpses, Dracula is often thought of as "undead," and the theme of immortality is stressed in the book and all these films—remember Van Helsing's words in the novel, "The vampire lives on, and cannot die by mere passing of the time" (245). But Dracula is also seen as a creature who is both undead and dead, a transitional figure who moves between the two worlds and, as such, responds also to our fear of the spirits that inhabit the other world and intrude into ours, especially as nighttime creatures. Yet this is often a creature who seems to have had enough of such intrusions and would prefer to remain permanently in his grave. Recall Lugosi's speech in the 1931 film, "To die, to be really dead—that must be glorious," sentiments expressed in some variation by all the figures in the sound versions of these films. Lucy, in most of these films, becomes a vampire creature of the cemetery after her death and is finally put to rest so that she may remain dead.

The novel also emphasizes the physical aspects of death: though Dracula may appear to grow younger and stronger as he feasts on more blood, he always has the stench of the grave and the pallor of the dead. In the films he is too much a seductive lover to have these qualities, but corporeal decay does rise to the surface in Terence Fischer's film with the effective physical decomposition of Dracula at the end of the work achieved by a series of very skillful superimpositions. Coppola's film also adds a contemporary note to the theme of plague and disease so developed in the *Nosferatu* films by subtly relating AIDS to the disease of the blood spread by Dracula. We first meet the Van Helsing character, Professor Bulwer in the film, giving a lecture to his students on "the diseases of the blood" and their connection to "the sex problem." On a deeper level the connection may even be more disturbing, reminding us that the suave count in the sound films is a representative of the seductiveness of death and, as such, a manifestation of our death wish. In this context we must recognize that the heroines of Badham's and Coppola's films are committing an act of necrophilia when they willingly make love to someone who is not alive.[7]

POLITICAL OPPRESSOR AND VICTIMIZER

Although this is the least developed aspect of the Dracula figure in the films, it still remains part of his characterization and is very much evident in the novel. In Stoker's novel, the count gives to Jonathan Harker an account of his warrior's background and his life as a patriot (37–39). Dracula in all his incarnations is a creature of an aristocratic background, and though he may certainly be symbolic of the decay and degeneration of this class, he is also symbolic of this group's oppressive powers. In various degrees and ways all the Dracula figures have a certain regal bearing and disdain for the other characters they confront. The very act of drinking the blood of the living is symbolic of the way in which the aristocracy has fed off and destroyed those beneath them. Coppola's film most develops Stoker's use of the historically real Wallachian figure, Vlad Tepes, also called Vlad the Impaler for his ruthless way of punishing his Turkish enemies, as a background for his count, but the film never develops this political dimension in its rush into sexuality and romance.[8] One must turn to a West German film made by Hans W. Geissendörfer in 1970, *Jonathan,* an allegorical telling of Hitler and his horrors that has only some resemblance to the novel, to see a full treatment of this political aspect of the figure.

THE ANTI-CHRIST AND ANTI-GOD

On the most fundamental level, all the Dracula stories, like so many horror films, are moral allegories depicting the struggle of good against evil, but this particular myth ties itself more directly into the struggle of Christianity against the forces of darkness: Van Helsing says in Badham's film, "If we are defeated, then there is no God." The religious aspects of the story are well-known and frequently a source of great humor for audiences even when filmmakers do not intend them to be funny. Vampires, along with witches and werewolves, were part of the developing folklore in eastern Europe and also Greece that the Christian Church was quick to pick up and exploit in its war against disbelief during the seventeenth and eighteenth centuries.[9] Vampires were sometimes thought to be creatures unbaptized, excommunicated, buried without a proper religious service, or born on Christmas day (Summers, passim). The ways in which Christian symbols are used as a weapon in the novel and films are easy enough to identify, but I must emphasize how much the very notion and nature of the vampire is shaped to be the reverse of Christ, the symbol of goodness and rebirth. Dracula is a creature of the dark, not the light. Dracula is a creature of the body, a soulless fiend who casts no reflection in the mirror, while Jesus takes us beyond the body and offers us an everlasting life of the spirit. While Jesus was permanently resurrected, the vampire must descend into the tomb every day at sunrise. Jesus offers the promise of everlasting life, while Dracula is a creature of the grave who belongs to the undead and offers a state of perpetual longing and need as a member of the undead. Through the Eucharist, Jesus gives us his blood and flesh in an act of sacrifice and holiness, while the vampire tears at our flesh and takes our blood from us. Therefore all things holy and related to Jesus—the cross, holy wafer, and holy water—are anathema to Dracula. The Christian iconography is played down in both *Nosferatu* films because of the ineffectuality of religion to stop the onslaught of the plague, while it becomes a chief means of fighting and controlling the vampire in Browning and Fischer's films. Badham's version undermines the religious element when Frank Langella, as the count, reaches out and ignites a wooden cross with his touch, so strong and powerful has he become through his passionate love for Lucy. When Dracula tells Lucy in this film, "You will be flesh of my flesh, blood of my blood," as they commence their ardent lovemaking in one of the most stylized and romanticized interaction of vampire and female in any of these films, we know that the motif is neither Christian nor anti-Christian but Hollywood romance; indeed, Van Helsing even fears toward the end of the film that the two will go off and create more of their kind, suggesting the possibility of a happy and fruitful wedlock. Coppola's film most dramatizes this religious element, at least at the very start of the film, even suggesting that

Dracula's career as a vampire and as the undead is very much involved with his sacrilegious behavior in the church after hearing of his wife's suicide and the church's refusal to bury her in holy ground. "Is this my reward for defending God's church?!" Dracula shouts in Romanian before he goes into a rampage, impaling the cross and drinking bloody holy water from the sacramental communal goblet as the chapel fills with blood from the wounded cross.

As Jesus is made of the substance of the father and son, so is Dracula as much an anti-God as anti-Christ. In the novel, Renfield quotes Dracula as seeming to say to him, "All these lives will I give you, ay, and many more and greater, through countless ages, if you will fall down and worship me!" (285). As Van Helsing states, "[H]e can, within limitations, appear at will when and where and in any of the forms that are to him; he can, within his range, direct the elements: the storm, the fog, the thunder . . . " (243)—a limited God, but God-like nonetheless, he is more than human. Of course no such impression of the vampire figure is possible from either of the *Nosferatu* films, where he is clearly a figure of death. In Murnau's film, the Renfield character, Krock, may announce, "He is coming. I must go to meet him." But what arrives in Wisborg from the ship is the count carrying his coffin and a host of rats. Budgetary concerns in Browning's, Fisher's, and Franco's films limit the powers of Dracula and make him seem something less than God, though he remains something more than mortal. Although Gary Oldman is a young performer and plays a young Dracula through much of Coppola's film, he gives a striking performance as an older count in the first part, an overpowering, otherworldly figure who dwarfs the inept Harker. But the sense of Dracula's omnipotence and ever-present threat is created in the film largely through Coppola's visual technique and editing, through the shadow of Dracula that falls upon a scene even when he does not seem to be there (a technique anticipated in Murnau's film), through the all-seeing eyes that we view in the sky on the other side of the window of a moving train, through the unnatural crosscutting that seems to distort and finally overcome time and space in order to impose the presence and actions of the count on the characters in England. Though Badham's and especially Coppola's film are able to create a figure more powerful than those in the other films, with greater supernatural abilities, we still remember these figures more for the strength of their human passions than their inhuman powers.

THE UNCONSCIOUSLY DESIRED

Dracula is very much a projection of repressed sexuality who is able to perform his physical acts upon the young people because he is the aggressor and takes responsibility for their violation. Sexual repression is an underlying motif throughout Stoker's novel, a clear product of his own Victorian age. The seductiveness of sin in the guise of Dracula is most related to the female characters who, deep down, are shown to desire the male's physical penetration. This is certainly not the case, though, in both *Nosferatu* films. The heroine is the woman "pure in heart" whose virtue and sacrifice destroy the vampire figure; in both versions the monster drinks her blood in the most repulsive and least erotic scenes of this action in all the films—in both films she lies in bed across much of the horizontal plane of the frame from left to right, with the monster sitting behind her and taking his nourishment by sipping from her neck. In Herzog's film the vampire starts to take up her nightgown, but she guides his head to her throat. The shots of the count lowering his head to the exposed necks of both women in the Browning film is the first filmic statement of the theme of repressed sexuality, which is then made more explicit in Terence Fisher's film where both Lucy and Mina, under the power of the count, allow him into their bedrooms. Van Helsing tells us in this version that "victims consciously detest being dominated by vampires but are unable to relinquish the practice." Although sexuality is forced upon these women by the mesmerizing powers of the count, they must be punished for such a transgression, for the defilement of their bodies, which, on some deeper level, was obviously desired. The theme of repressed sexuality is rampant in all versions after the *Nosferatu* films, growing in explicitness until we have the extraordinary wanton portrayal of Lucy and then her physical destruction in the Coppola film. The first graphic stakings of the female body take place in the 1956 Fisher film, where we see the stake penetrating Lucy's body and the blood surging from her wound—the very punishment itself must remind us of the act of sexual intercourse. Though Lucy, as a prototype of a modern feminist, needs no such punishment in Badham's film, her counterparts in the novel and both Fisher's and Coppola's films are branded by the cross, a wound erased only with Dracula's death—"Unclean, unclean!" shout both women in the novel and Coppola's film version.

But let us not forget Jonathan Harker, who, in Stoker's novel, is masochistically overwhelmed by the three vampire women. Only with Coppola's recent work is repressed male desire pushed to the forefront of a *Dracula* film (the scene between Jonathan and these female vampires is never developed in either Browning's or Franco's film, where the three figures appear only briefly). But once we begin talking about repressed sexuality, especially in relation to sadism and masochism, we are into the subject of desire itself and find ourselves peeling off the layers and going further into the psyche. We must remember, throughout this part of my discussion, that where desire produces conflict, where there is a possibility of retribution for desire, an important defense of the ego is to make that which is desired into a fearsome object; this concept is fundamental to an understanding of the human psyche as it develops in our earliest years as well as to our later emotional reactions to the horror film. This concept also explains the basic rationale for the Dracula figure.

THE OEDIPAL FATHER

Here we bring together our first four themes, discovering that they may, indeed, be splittings and displacements for us of even deeper levels of psychic emotions and configurations. To some degree all of these Draculas are powerful and even God-like figures who threaten the other characters with violent sex and death. The conflation of these qualities suggests something implicit in the novel's count but a little more explicit in the visual images of older men violating younger women in the hidden recesses of their bedrooms in these films. We feel this oedipal resonance most strongly from the image of Bela Lugosi leaning over the throat of Helen Chandler, and Christopher Lee penetrating into the bedrooms of his female victims, in Fisher's and Franco's films, but we feel this level of recognition from all these films. I am referring to Dracula as the oedipal father, sexually desired by both male and female children, but I also wish to suggest that these bedroom scenes of erotic violence are suggestive of the child's fantasies about the primal scene, the imagined sexual violation brought upon the mother by the monstrous and powerful father.

We can take our oedipal reading a little further and see the issue of the son's feared punishment of castration for desiring the mother as relevant to the treatment of both Harker and Renfield—we especially remember the character of Harker in Fischer's film, who first receives two puncture marks on the side of the neck, two bleeding holes, and who is then dispatched by a stake through the heart. If we are willing to see these oedipal configurations in the basic myth, if we are willing to see Dracula as the fearsome oedipal father, then the reading of the story as a version of Freud's theory about the primal horde and the sons' slaying of the father to possess (or repossess) the mother as described in *Totem and Taboo* (141–46) have a certain validity (see Richardson, 428–29), as long as we remember that much in these films deals with the father's control over and intimidation of the young people and that normally only one of the younger generation, along with Van Helsing, is involved in the destruction of Dracula. Coppola's film, however, captures something of the excitement and deeper resonances of the novel as the three young men go in pursuit of Dracula and ultimately overwhelm the gypsy caravan to attack him. Only when the young are banded together under the leadership of Van Helsing, the good father, can the young men slay the evil father and claim the mother, in the guise of Mina. We can see both Dracula and Van Helsing, for children of both sexes, as manifestations of the child's sense of the bad and good aspects of a single figure, as the splitting of the original father into two separate figures at war with one another. However, in Murnau's *Nosferatu* Van Helsing and the adult figures are seen as ineffectual, and in Herzog's remake of that film they are totally inept before the force of death that Dracula represents and that even the heroine's sacrifice cannot abet.

THE PREOEDIPAL MOTHER

We might think of the entire Dracula story as implicitly suggesting a regression from the genital to the oral stage, from desiring pleasure through normal sexuality to the more primitive stage of attempting to satisfy desire through the mouth. The very act of drinking blood from the body, though, is more than an attempt to find satisfaction through the mouth—it is an inverted memory of the child's hungry and sadistic taking of milk from the mother's breast.[10] Beginning with the vampire woman's protruding bosom in the Hammer film directed by Terence Fisher, most vampire films put heavy emphasis on this female part of the anatomy—one need only think of Sadie Frost's bare breast as Dracula puts the bite on her in Coppola's film, or even the elderly and slovenly Van Helsing, in the midst of cold winter before Dracula's castle and in the midst of his crusade to destroy the monster, being tempted in the same film to suck on young Mina's breasts. The movement of the mouth from breasts to neck (a movement literally and physically carried out by all the Draculas since Christopher Lee in 1956) and the change of milk to blood in the underlying fantasy to the *Dracula* myth is the result of an intensification of oral sadism conflated with a later awareness of the relation of blood to the mother's sexuality, primarily though an awareness of menstruation. The oral act has become both destructive and intensely sexualized. The Hammer vampire films were the first, with their vivid and bold color, to put the emphasis on the conjunction of female breasts and bright red blood—a particular lobby poster for *Dracula Has Risen from the Grave* (1968), one of the many spin-offs from the 1956 film, shows a female neck with two bandages rising from a very developed bosom (Twichell, 111).

I suggest, however, that the image of the vampire sucking the blood of his victims conveys something more, conveys another inversion, where the mother becomes herself the sadistic punisher and taker of sustenance from the child. We can see the suggestions of this inversion in Coppola's film with the presence of the three vampire women—their breasts most obvious when they themselves feast off Jonathan Harker—but it is evident in a more direct way in the novel and in all these films when Lucy as a vampire desires

LIVERPOOL JOHN MOORES UNIVERSITY
LEARNING SERVICES

to suck the blood of young children. We must take this argument one step further, to the very chest of the count himself. Recall what Van Helsing and the young men in the novel see when they break into Mina's bedroom: "With his left hand he [Dracula] held both Mrs. Harker's hands, keeping them away with her arms at full tension; his right hand gripped her at the back of the neck, forcing her face down on his bosom. Her white nightdress was smeared with blood, and a thin stream trickled down the man's bare breast which was shown by his torn-open dress. The attitude of the two had a terrible resemblance to a child forcing a kitten's nose into a saucer of milk to compel it to drink" (287–88).

How can this be? Mina drinking blood from the count—and from his chest! I must emphasize once more the palimpsest nature of this figure, the fact that he is a creature of our repressed fantasies with a considerable amount of condensation. He is much more than one thing: he is a composite and configuration of various stages and also various desires and fears in our psychic history and topography. In Browning's film, Mina drinking Dracula's blood is slightly less distressing since she drinks from his arm and describes this dastardly scene as a distant dream. In both Badham's and Coppola's films the drinking is turned into an erotic act in which the heroine willingly imbibes the blood of her lover from his chest so that she will remain with him forever. Undoubtedly Dracula in these films is a highly sexualized male figure, but there is something more, something strongly implicit in his actions that resonates through his masculine facade. In the novel, Mina's drinking from the wound in his chest is an instance where this implicit meaning breaks through the surface. She is like a child drinking her mother's milk, but the gash on his chest also suggests the oedipal child's fantasy of the mother's castration and thus offers another explanation of the conversion of milk into blood.

But the violence of this scene reminds us that Dracula victimizes his partners and takes far more blood than he gives. The gash on the chest giving forth blood, a symbol both of castration and the vagina, must also remind us of the vampire's bloody mouth and fangs sucking the life out of his victims—and both these gashes are also suggestive of the fantasy of the vagina *dentata*, the vagina with teeth, that conveys the fear of the mother's genitals.[11] The image of Christopher Lee, in the early part of Fisher's *Horror of Dracula*, with his blood-dripping mouth torn across his face, made a remarkable impact on audiences of the time. I am suggesting that on some level the blood-drinking vampire is a product of the child's fear of and anger toward the mother, an impression of the woman when she fails to give the child what it wants and so seems to take from it: she is the feared maternal figure who is distinct from the good mother and the later-victimized oedipal mother. The bleeding wound she bares in the mind of the child during the oedipal stage is imposed upon her earlier image as an instrument of destruction and terror. In this context we are on the threshold of also seeing this figure as the parental cannibal that Leonard Shengold finds symbolized by rats and teeth in fantasies of adult patients suffering from the childhood trauma of overstimulation.

The very terror of castration is clearest in the depiction of the Lucys of these films who, once bitten, themselves become biters only to ultimately have their bodies ripped open by the stake through the heart and, in the case of Franco's, Badham's and Coppola's films, their heads severed from their bodies. In these films the fear of castration is compensated for by a displacement onto the female bodies, a displacement that at first fetishizes the female body only to mutilate it next. But each of these women is at first converted into the monstrous creature who imposes such bleeding wounds upon others. All of the vampire women can easily be seen in this context— my argument is that Dracula himself is the most violent and terrifying extension of this figure, violent and terrifying because he ultimately transcends any single sexual identity, because he ultimately victimizes both men and women.[12] We can trace his very roots to the child's fantasy of the mother from a time when she was undifferentiated according to gender but a version of the figure with the child's later oedipal fears imposed upon it.[13] The *Dracula* story, as all vampire stories, is inherently a hidden, and sometimes not-so-hidden, tale of children and parents torn from the terrors of our childhood years.

THE BEAST THAT ONCE WE WERE

We delve deeper into our psyches now, so deep that we go hurling back into our genetic history. What I wish to suggest at this point is a reading of the novel and visual reading of the last *Dracula* film that is as much anthropological as psychological, a reading that Coppola more than all the other directors recognized in the count and his story. Our impression of the young people in the center of the film—the impression we often have of children play-acting at being adult—may destroy the dramatic credibility of the film, but such an impression also intensifies and eases the return to earlier times that we unconsciously feel, to childhood and infantile emotions and imagos, to both oedipal and preoedipal stages but also to a vague sense of a kind of polymorphous sexuality and pleasure we felt in our childhood. We confront in this film something more than sadistic and masochistic desire; we confront a kind of fetishism that lies beyond Freudian fetishism. Here kissing is not confined to the lips: the chest and neck are even more central to pleasure and desire; here the drinking of bodily fluids is an act of nourishment, pleasure, and even fusion. Here one drinks and is drunk. We trace these acts back, then, to our earliest months when we were so much creatures of our bodies, when our fantasies were comprised largely of bodies and physiological functions, when we functioned so much on a basic animal level.

But we must push even further. Recall, if you will, Stoker's insistence on relating Dracula to animal life. Van Helsing tells us at one point, "[H]e can command all the meaner things: the rat, and the owl, and the bat—the moth, and the fox, and the wolf . . . " (243). More than this, Dracula is a shape-shifter and can become certain kinds of animals himself—the bat and wolf, for example.[14] Coppola's film explores this ability, not only allowing Dracula to appear as these last two creatures but also on occasion allowing him to appear in a half-human, half-animal state, emphasizing that with all his human attributes he also is an embodiment of the beast that remains within us.[15] Perhaps the most striking appearance in this state occurs when Mina discovers Dracula mounting Lucy between her legs, described in the screenplay as "a wet man or beast" (71), a description much akin to a similar one in Stoker's novel when Mina is unable to discern whether the figure leaning over Lucy is a "man or beast" (101). There is no question that Dracula in Stoker's novel and at certain points in Coppola's film is more like an animal than a human, that when biting flesh and drinking blood, when sexually violating women, he reminds us more of a beast in heat than a human lover. It seems fitting that sometimes he appears a wolf on all fours because, on occasion, his very act of lovemaking reminds us of our earliest animal state, when we were still quadrupeds, when the mouth had no limitations, when the nose and mouth pushed themselves into all parts of the anatomy of other quadrupeds, when sexuality, appetite, and violation were indistinguishable.

There have been numerous horror films dealing with our repulsion for the animal in us, a repulsion meant to defend against remnants of desire having to do with the animal state. I am reminded of horror films such as *King Kong* (1933) and *Creature from the Black Lagoon* (1954), which deal implicitly with human evolution and which send us back along the evolutionary scale, forcing us to identify, to think that we recognize some earlier stage of animal life—suggesting that such memories and desires still remain residually within us. Perhaps the film that most directly deals with this fear is *Island of Lost Souls* (1933), where animals are turned into humans only to revert to their animal states. There are moments in all the *Dracula* films when something of this regression occurs, when something inside of us is unpleasantly stirred. Dracula is certainly a palimpsest, layer upon layer of psychological stages, a condensation of the very worst we have desired and feared. In some ways Coppola's film offers us the deepest insights into this figure, unflinchingly reducing his hero not so much to the beast that remains within us as to our very bestial origins.

NOTES

1. *Nosferatu, A Symphony of Horror,* (*Nosferatu, eine Symphonie des Grauens,* Germany; F. W. Murnau, 1922); *Dracula* (United States; Tod Browning, 1931); *The Horror of Dracula, Dracula* (Great Britain; Terence Fischer, 1956); *Count Dracula* (*El Conde Dracula,* Italy, Spain, West Germany; Jess Franco, 1970); *Nosferatu* (*The Vampyre, Nosferatu, Phantom der Nacht,* West Germany; Werner Herzog, 1979); *Dracula* (United States; John Badham, 1979); *Bram Stoker's Dracula* (United States; Francis Ford Coppola, 1992). The two television versions are *Dracula* (United States; Dan Curtis, 1973) and *Count Dracula* (Great Britain, United States; Philip Saville, 1977). The names of the characters in Murnau's work were changed from those of the characters in the novel (e.g., Dracula is called Orlok) because the film was made without copyright clearance. The long-standing rumors of the superiority of the Spanish-language version to Browning's film, with which it was made simultaneously, have been discredited by the recent release of that version on videotape. The Spanish version, directed by George Melford, is better edited and lacks some of the gaps in the English version, but it does not have the performances of Lugosi, Frye, and Van Sloan nor the moody atmosphere of Browning's film. Since both films are basically the same version of the Dracula myth, with the same script and sets, I shall discuss only Browning's better known and more effective work. See Waller and Flynn for surveys of the vampire film in general.

2. Franco's *Count Dracula* begins with titles claiming that the film is exactly the way Stoker wrote the novel; Dan Curtis's television version was titled *Bram Stoker's Dracula* on the screen; and both Coppola and screenwriter James V. Hart claim that their version, *Bram Stoker's Dracula,* is the first version true to the book (Coppola and Hart, 3 and 6).

3. Louis Jourdan's understated performance in the 1977 television version, which appeared on *Masterpiece Theater,* anticipates this approach, though his Dracula does not have the same rapturous relationship with Mina.

4. Film buffs will find many filmic allusions not only to the earlier Dracula films and to horror films such as Friedkin's *The Exorcist* (1973) and Kubrick's *The Shining* (1980) but also to Jean Cocteau's surrealistic fantasies *Orpheus* (1949) and *Beauty and the Beast* (1946), not to mention the entire German expressionistic canon.

5. A point made by Coppola himself in an interview (Biodrowski, 34).

6. According to Melton, the common assumption that "Nosferatu" is the Romanian word for the "undead" is wrong (435).

7. Necrophilia plays an important part in psychiatric case histories of vampirism (Noll).

8. Jess Franco's film first suggests this connection, and Dan Curtis's 1973 television version more directly associates its Dracula, played by Jack Palance, with Vlad Tepes. See McNally and Florescu for an extensive discussion of Vlad Tepes and his relationship to Stoker's Dracula. But also see Farson, in his biography of Stoker (127–34), and Ambrogio, who argue against any significant influence of the historical figure on Stoker's characterization of the count.

9. Although polemical and not fully reliable, Montague Summers's *The Vam-*

pire: Kith and Kin, in its opening chapter, gives a fairly good idea of the ways in which ecclesiastic writers usurped the subject of vampires.

10. Karl Abraham sees the oral phase of the child divided into two stages, the first focused upon sucking and the second, the "oral-sadistic stage," which is related to teething, marked by biting and devouring (447–53).

11. Otto Rank claims that the fantasy of the vagina *dentata* is a result of anxiety aroused by the mother's genitals because of the child's "first separation from the libido-object" through the act of birth (48–49). At an earlier point he states that this primary anxiety for the mother's genitals is exacerbated by the father's prohibition of the child's return to the mother and is eventually displaced on other objects (13). Although Rank's analysis of this fantasy clearly makes it applicable to both male and female children, the vagina *dentata* is also a male fantasy that conveys the fear of both sexual intercourse and women. Roth mentions the vagina *dentata* in relation to the devouring woman of the novel *Dracula* (119–20).

12. Gary Oldman says that he sought to make his Dracula in Coppola's film androgynous in order to unnerve people sexually (Abramowitz, 56).

13. Melanie Klein describes the child's fantasy of the "combined parent," a figure possessing a combined vagina and penis (245–46). The image of the vampire's mouth and fangs may also be the projection of such a fantasy.

14. In eastern Europe, a vampire was sometimes thought to be the risen body of a dead werewolf (Summers, 20).

15. Nina Auerbach's total negation of Coppola's film in her recent study of the vampire figure (see especially 209n) seems to explain her general dismissal of "animalism" in "twentieth-century Dracula films" (88).

WORKS CITED

Abraham, Karl. "A Short Study of the Development of the Libido, Viewed in the Light of Mental Disorders." *Selected Papers.* 1924. Reprint, London: Hogarth Press, 1927, 418–501.

Abramowitz, Rachel. "Neck Romance." *Premiere* 6 (1992): 49–58.

Ambrogio, Anthony. "Dracula Schmacula! Misinformation Never Dies." *Video Watchdog* 19 (1993): 32–47.

Auerbach, Nina. *Our Vampire, Ourselves.* Chicago: University of Chicago Press, 1995.

Baudry, Jean-Louis. "The Apparatus: Metapsychological Approaches to the Impression of Reality in Cinema." Translated by Jean Andrews and Bernard Augst. *Camera Obscura* 1 (1976): 104–25.

Biodrowski, Steve. "Coppola's *Dracula:* Directing the Horror Epic." *Cinefantastique* 23 (1992): 32–34.

Coppola, Francis Ford, and James V. Hart. *Bram Stoker's Dracula: The Film and the Legend.* New York: Newmarket Press, 1992.

Danoun, Roger. "Fetishism and the Horror Film." Translated by Annwyl Williams. In *Fantasy and the Cinema,* edited by James Donald, 39–61. London: BFI, 1989.

Farson, Daniel. *The Man Who Wrote Dracula: A Biography of Bram Stoker.* London: Michael Joseph, 1975.

Flynn, John L. *Cinematic Vampires: The Living Dead on Film and Television from The*

Devil's Castle (1896) to Bram Stoker's Dracula (1992). Jefferson, N.C.: McFarland, 1992.

Freud, Sigmund. *Beyond the Pleasure Principle.* Vol. 18, *The Standard Edition of the Complete Psychological Works of Sigmund Freud.* Edited and Translated by James Strachey. 1920. Reprint, London: Hogarth Press, 1955, 3–64.

———. *Totem and Taboo.* Vol. 13, *The Standard Edition of the Complete Psychological Works of Sigmund Freud.* Edited and Translated by James Strachey. 1913. Reprint, London: Hogarth Press, 1955, 1–162.

Freud, Sigmund, and Joseph Breuer. *Studies on Hysteria. The Standard Edition of the Complete Psychological Works of Sigmund Freud.* Edited and Translated by James Strachey. 1893–95. Reprint, London: Hogarth Press, 1955, 2.

Klein, Melanie. *The Psycho-Analysis of Children.* Translated by Alex Strachey. 1932. Reprint, New York: Delacorte Press, 1975.

McNally, Randell, and Radu Florescu. *In Search of Dracula: A True History of Dracula and the Vampire Legends.* Greenwich, Conn.: New York Graphic Society, 1972.

Melton, Gordon J. *The Vampire Book: The Encyclopedia of the Undead.* Detroit: Visible Ink Press, 1994.

Metz, Christian. *The Imaginary Signifier: Psychoanalysis and the Cinema.* Translated by Alfred Guzetti. Bloomington: Indiana University Press, 1982. Part III: 99–147.

Noll, Richard, ed. *Vampires, Werewolves, and Demons: Twentieth-Century Reports in the Psychiatric Literature.* New York: Brunner/Mazel, 1992.

Rank, Otto. *The Trauma of Birth.* 1929. Reprint, New York: Harper Torchbooks, Harper and Row, 1972.

Richardson, Maurice. "The Psychoanalysis of Ghost Stories." *Twentieth Century* 166 (1959): 419–31.

Roth, Phyllis A. "Suddenly Sexual Women in Bram Stoker's *Dracula.*" *Literature and Psychology* 27 (1977): 113–21.

Shengold, Leonard. "More about Rats and Rat People." *International Journal of Psycho-Analysis* 52 (1971): 277–88.

Stoker, Bram. *Dracula.* New York: Signet, New American Library, 1965.

Summers, Montague. *The Vampire: His Kith and Kin.* New Hyde Park: University Books, 1965.

Twichell, James B. *Dreadful Pleasures: An Anatomy of Modern Horror.* New York: Oxford University Press, 1985.

Waller, Gregory A. *The Living and the Undead: From Stoker's Dracula to Romero's Dawn of the Dead.* Urbana: University of Illinois Press, 1986.

PART THREE

Altered States:
Transforming Media

SEVENTEEN

The Superhero with a Thousand Faces: Visual Narratives on Film and Paper

Luca Somigli

The last decade has brought about a somewhat unexpected renaissance of the visual narrative medium known as "the comics,"[1] which toward the end of the seventies seemed to be on its last legs.[2] The comics industry has been shaken by a new awareness of the artistic potential of the medium, facilitated by new systems of production and distribution (especially the independent comics companies and the direct sales system) that have given never-before-experienced creative freedom to writers and artists alike. Yet, comics remain a less-than-becoming medium for serious scholars. Joseph Witek, whose work *Comic Books as History* is one of the few important attempts to examine comics from a theoretically informed perspective, concludes his introduction with a rather candid acknowledgment: "The emergence of comic books as a respectable literary form [with the works of practitioners like Art Spiegelman and Harvey Pekar] in the 1980s *is* unlooked for, given the long decades of cultural scorn and active social repression, but the potential has always existed for comic books to present the same kind of narratives as other verbal and pictorial media" (11). The perception that comics are an inferior narrative medium has hindered not only their own development, as Witek suggests, but also their relationship with those media, such as cinema, that from time to time have turned to them for characters and concepts. Although in the thirties and forties many popular characters, including Flash Gordon, Dick Tracy, Batman, and Captain America, made the transition from paper to film, they were usually relegated to Saturday matinee serials, rather than featured in major productions. It is only recently, with the success of films like *Superman* (1978) and *Batman* (1988) and their sequels, that Hollywood has developed a real interest in the comics as a source of inspiration.[3]

I wish to discuss how cinema and the comics have had to solve similar problems, given their common nature as visual media. Then I will articulate the relationship between the two media in terms of a model that rejects both the notion of remake and that of adaptation in favor of that of myth.

CINEMA AND THE COMICS: TWO VISUAL LANGUAGES

March 22, 1895: the Lumière brothers project their first films to a private audience. February 16, 1896: the "Yellow Kid," the first successful comic strip character, makes his first appearance in the New York newspaper *World*.[4] Born less than one year apart, the two narrative media made possible by the advent of the age of mechanical reproduction then went on to widely different futures. Cinema was to become the only medium dependent upon the technological revolution of the last two centuries to be admitted into the hallowed halls of art (the "tenth muse," as it has been called), whereas the comics remained for most of their history the point at which "Art" turned her eyes with horror, the point of no return beyond which lies the realm of hopelessly and irredeemably "popular" culture. The appropriation of cinematographic techniques by comics artists has been often remarked upon.[5] Nevertheless, the relationship is not necessarily one-way. John Fell has pointed out that early filmmakers and comics artists were confronted with "common problems of space and time within the conventions of narrative exposition" (89), and that the comics developed a highly sophisticated language that in some cases anticipated cinematographic solutions to these common problems. For their part, a number of film directors, including Federico Fellini, Orson Welles, and George Lucas (Inge, xx) have acknowledged an interest in and even a debt to the comics.[6]

Cinema and the comics are both primarily visual languages. Comic writer and artist John Byrne has remarked recently that "good art will save a bad script, whereas good writing can do little to save bad art," a statement especially to the point in regards to recent mainstream comics (particularly the superhero genre) in which an increased aesthetic awareness on the part of artists has been accompanied by an almost opposite trend in plots. Both media construct a story through the juxtaposition of images, so that the relations established among them can convey the illusion of temporal and spatial development. Like cinema, a comic narrative is assembled through the succession of frames; however, whereas in film the quick succession of the frames can give the impression of actual movement, the comics have had to devise other solutions to represent movement and progression. As Daniele Barbieri explains in his excellent structural study of the comics medium, the panel itself is not simply an image frozen in time, but it can be used to represent a duration through a number of different techniques (use of motion lines, repetition of the image as with an overexposed photograph, particular arrangements of the balloons, and sound effects, etc.): "Therefore, we have one image—traditionally corresponding to one instant—within which there is a duration. With the comics, the panel no longer *represents* an *instant*, but a *duration:* just like cinema (230–31)."[7]

If we take this definition of the comic panel, perhaps we can establish a more useful comparison between it and the cinematographic shot as the basic unit of composition of the two media. In film, meaning is generated by the syntagmatic relation of the shots in a sequence: like the combinatory elements of articulated language, the shots are arranged along a space that is "linear and irreversible" (Barthes, 58), the previous shot preparing the viewer for a range of possibilities in the following one. To quote Roland Barthes again, "[E]ach term derives its value from its opposition to what precedes and what follows" (58). Likewise, the panels that compose the comic page, traditionally arranged for reading from left to right, from top to bottom, construct meaning by their relation to one another. However, this syntagmatic reading is paralleled by "a paradigmatic reading of interrelationships among images on the same page" (Collins, 173), allowing for effects that are not available to cinema and that make up for the relatively static nature of the comics.

As an example, let us discuss a page of the comic book adaptation of Francis Ford Coppola's *Dracula* (1992), published by Topps Comics (story by Roy Thomas and art by Mike Mignola). The page reproduces the crucial scene in the frame story of Dracula's origins (so much for *Bram Stoker's Dracula*). In the film, the count stabs the cross on the altar with his sword; from the gash in the wood blood starts pouring out, until it covers the whole floor of the church and submerges the body of Dracula's dead wife, Elisabeta.

The first striking element about the comic book adaptation is the page itself: the border that surrounds the panels is not white, as is common with most comics, but black. (See figure 37.) This technique can be used very effectively to connect the panels, as the borders are not as clearly demarcated. In particular, in the long panel on the bottom of the left half of the page the shadows of the gargoyles blend in with the darkness of the frame so that the latter seems to be an extension of the shadows of the church (this sense of continuity between panel and border is reinforced by the trickle of blood that reaches the edge of the page). Therefore, the smaller panels appear superimposed on this larger one, which comes to include the whole of the page.

The first two panels give a good example of how the illusion of movement can be created through static images. In the first, Dracula dips a cup in the holy water spilled in the previous page. In the next, he is shown raising the cup to his lips. In following the cup from the bottom half of the first panel to the top half of the second, the eye goes through the same

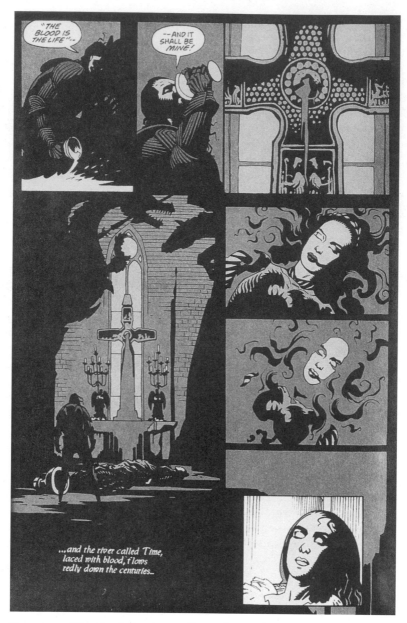

Figure 37. The comic book transformation of Francis Ford Coppola's *Dracula* offers imaginative "takes" on the film. Courtesy of Topps Comics.

movement as the cup lifted from the ground to the count's lips. The illusion of continuity and trajectory is reinforced by the little drops of water splashed in panel one in the direction of panel two.

The next panel presents a frontal close-up of the cross, out of which blood starts flowing. Now, in a syntagmatic reading of the sequence the successive panel is the long left-hand one mentioned above. Here, the "camera" pulls back to a long shot that reveals Dracula facing the cross, his wife lying dead on the steps of the altar on which the cross is mounted. Then follows a close-up of the dead woman's face. However, the third and fifth panel can also be read vertically (a reading encouraged by the vertical thrust of panel four, and by the fact that the following panel, panel six, is directly below five rather than next to it). Thus, the blood gushing out of the cross seems to be pouring directly over Elisabeta's face, partially covering it in panel six, and finally drowning it out in panel seven. In fact, by its very shape, panel seven continues the flow of blood that started four panels above: its top edge and part of its sides are straight lines, but instead of closing into a square, as with a regular panel, they taper into the shape of a dripping red strip of blood, eventually cut off by the edge of the page itself. The blood that in the film covered the whole screen here flows throughout the page, and beyond it. Finally, in a device that may be as close as comics can come to a lap dissolve, an eighth panel is superimposed on the seventh.[8] Through it, we are carried forward in the narrative outside the frame story and into 1897 London, but the panel itself is used to establish a clear link between the two parts of the narrative, since it represents Mina's face in roughly the same position as Elisabeta's in panel five. (As we know, in Coppola's version of the story Mina is a sort of reincarnation of Dracula's beloved wife.)

Although my analysis is concerned with one single page, I would like to point out that, as Witek has suggested, "[t]he largest perceptual unit of comic-book storytelling is the two page spread (20)."[9] In fact, in the first panel of the facing page the "camera" moves back to give a full shot of Mina in a washtub, her face in the same position as in the last panel of the previous page. Above her, Lucy pours water over her head, a gesture that looks back to both Dracula filling the cup with holy water and the blood pouring out of the cross on the opposite page.

ADAPTATIONS HIGH AND LOW

Adaptations of films to comics such as the one discussed above are fairly common, and they show a degree of respect for the original comparable to that of the cinema for its literary sources. However, the translation of comics into films has usually entailed a much more cautious and critical approach on the part of the latter medium. This is to some extent due to the nature of cinema itself. Drawing allows the comic artist a degree of freedom with the visual material that cinema can hardly match since, for better or worse, it must rely on human actors. The partial or total failure of films like Robert Altman's *Popeye* (1980) and Willard Huyck's *Howard the Duck* (1986) is symptomatic. When drawn by Val Mayerik, Howard is an anthropomorphic duck; in the film, he is just a guy in a duck suit.[10] However, even films based on comics centered on human characters can hardly be called "adaptations."

In a paper delivered at the 1992 Modern Language Association Convention in New York City, David Newman, one of the scriptwriters for the first three Superman films, began by emphasizing that a distinction must be made between remake and adaptation but then went on to argue that neither model was applicable to his own approach to translating Superman for the big screen. Rather, he approached Superman as "the most American myth." The use of the term "myth" is remarkable in view of its frequent application to the comics, to which we will turn in a moment. However, the distinction between remake and adaptation is also significant, and the rejection of both deserves some discussion. In an essay in this anthology, Robert Eberwein gives a good working definition of a remake: "A remake is a kind of reading or rereading of the original." In the "Preliminary Taxonomy" of remakes appended to the same essay, he writes: "Even more problematic, the taxonomy itself doesn't address the issue of adaptation: are there any films in the various categories that can claim a common non-cinematic source? If so, is it correct to call a film a remake or a new adaptation . . . ?" As Eberwein makes clear, the crucial issue at stake when dealing with remakes and adaptations is that of the "original." In fact, the definition of the remake as (re)reading seems to me equally applicable to adaptation. What distinguishes the two is the relation between the new reading and the medium of the original: as the term suggests, an adaptation is not simply a matter of retelling a story. Rather, it entails a move from one medium to another and therefore the "adjustment" of the narrative to the expressive language of the target medium (to borrow a term from translation theory). In both cases, however, the existence of a source is assumed and even necessary to make the new work a remake or an adaptation. This observation is not as tautological as it may at first appear: it is obvious that there is some "source" for Newman's Superman, but it stands in a very different relation to the film than, say, E. M. Forster's novel does to Merchant and Ivory's *A Room with a View.*

This is the result of the differential relation that cinema bears to sources from other media. When drawing from canonized texts (in particular, so-called literary texts), from works firmly enshrined within the cultural tradition, the prime concern is faithfulness to the original, seen as a fixed entity complete in itself. A glaring example is Claude Chabrol's recent adaptation of *Madame Bovary* (1991), in which whole *descriptive* passages were lifted out of Flaubert's novel and superimposed through a voice-over on images that actually clashed with them. In order to reproduce the original in the most integral way possible, the language of film was subordinated to that of the literary text. However, when the source is a work of "popular culture," the integrity of the original is not an issue.

As Lawrence Levine suggests in his study of the evolution of the idea of "culture" in America, the very notion of popular culture rests on the openness of the text to outside intervention. The many versions of the story of Count Dracula comprise an index of how elements of a popular narrative may become dissociated from their original source and thus undergo endless rearticulations (Coppola's version, for all its faithfulness to the letter of Bram Stoker's novel, takes remarkable liberties with it, the most significant being of course that Dracula comes to occupy the center of the stage).[11] Even a film that follows fairly closely the plot of its comic strip source, Mike Hodges's *Flash Gordon* (1980), seems to have no problems with changing the background of the characters and transposing the action from the 1930s to the 1980s. Significantly, Nash and Ross (871) consider this film a remake of the 1936 *Flash Gordon* film serial (and a poor one, at that), rather than an adaptation of Alex Raymond's comic strip.

The issue of the status of the original is a central concern of translation theory, and the following comment on nineteenth century approaches to translation can help us understand what is at stake in this differential treatment of the original. According to Susan Bassnett-McGuire, two positions can be distinguished: "[T]he one establishing a hierarchical relationship in which the [source language] author acts as a feudal overlord exacting fealty from the translator, the other establishing a hierarchical relationship in which the translator is absolved from all responsibility to the inferior culture of the [source language] text" (4).

Comics, science fiction, mysteries, and so on belong to the inferior realm of popular culture: therefore, in "translating" them into another medium, what needs to be considered is not the integrity of the original, but that of the target medium, which to some extent elevates the status of the popular culture artifact to its own by adapting it. An *a contrario* proof of this is the fidelity of comic book adaptations of films: as a superior art form, the integrity of the film must be respected by the comic book. The opposite, of course, is not true. Newman argued quite frankly that the main problem with selling the concept of a Superman film to a producer was that of selling it as a "grown-up movie." The relation to its source had to be played down, and even disguised, so that the film could be cleansed of the unfavorable association that the source medium, the comics, carries with it. In a short article on Warren Beatty's *Dick Tracy* (1990), based on the character created by Chester Gould, Patricia Kowal attributed "the simplicity of the story" to "its comic strip origin" (95). While this comment was not meant as a critique (Kowal is generally appreciative of the comic-like quality of the film), it brings out a commonly held belief that comics are simplistic, even naive, narratives that have little to offer more sophisticated media.

After all, cinema has been able to make its bid as a serious cultural medium by emphasizing its association with already canonized cultural formations. As narrative cinema developed in the direction of complex, realistic narratives centered on well-defined characters, all the instruments available to analyze a (by then) traditional literary form, the novel, could be brought to bear on it. There are indeed a number of structural similarities between prose fiction and narrative cinema; for instance, both types of narrative are limited in scope, developing, in Aristotelian fashion, through a beginning, a middle, and an end. The proximity between the two media was reinforced by theorizing cinema in ways that assimilated it to literature and in fact disguised its specific features: the auteur theory developed in the fifties by the *Cahiers du cinéma* school is only the culmination of that process. Ascribing the authorship of the film to the director denies the collaborative effort that goes into its making, but also makes it possible to see it as a homogeneous whole and to construct the critical discourse around it in terms of authorship, coherence of vision, an so on. In the comics, however, we can distinguish two patterns. Again the critics have often tended to approach the medium in terms of the individual genius: therefore, there has been an emphasis on figures like Winsor McCay, George Harriman, Carl Barks, Will Eisner, or, in more recent times, Frank Miller, who have combined functions that in most popular comic books are separate: writer, artist, inker, and even letterer or colorist.[12] However, in mainstream comics, a story is usually the result of teamwork. Typically, the writer is responsible for the plot, which is then drawn by the artist and inked by the inker. The letterer fills in the balloons, and the colorist, not surprisingly, provides the chromatic effects for the story. Furthermore, the Aristotelian pattern applicable to both the film and the novel does not quite work with the comics: even if an episode is self-contained (and this does not happen very often in contemporary comics), it is usually part of a larger narrative that spans the whole of the series of a specific character, and in many cases other series by the same publisher, with plots and subplots carrying over from episode to episode. It is extremely unusual for any member of the creative team to stay with the character for more than a few years, and as comics' characters are passed on from creative team to creative team they are reinterpreted, their story told again and again, so that, while remaining the same, they keep changing their relationship with the public. David Newman's remark that "each generation gets the Lois Lane that it deserves" can be generalized to the whole of comicdom. In a sense, a comic book character is always already a remake.

Thus, we can return to the interpretation of the comics as myth. There are a number of narrative elements that can justify Newman's approach to Superman in these terms. Newman himself mentioned, for instance, Superman's vulnerability to kryptonite, which can be compared to Achilles's heel, or, in a more complex way, his status as a superior being walking among mortals disguised as one of them, which can offer a number of parallels with the central myth of Christianity, Christ's first coming.[13] What to me is significant is that Newman's approach, derived from local details of Superman's story, coincides with a more general approach to popular culture, and comics in particular.[14]

Through myth, the problem of the relation between original and adaptation can be framed in a new way. In his seminal essay "The Structural Study of Myth," Claude Lévi-Strauss argues that with mythological narratives the question of the original cannot be asked: "Our method . . . eliminates a problem which has, so far, been one of the main obstacles to the progress of mythological studies, namely, the quest for the *true* version, or the *earlier* one. On the contrary, we define the myth as consisting of all its versions; or to put it otherwise, a myth remains the same as long as it is felt as such" (217). Now, I would like to argue that myth has been effectively used as a model in discussing a number of popular narratives because it interprets well the way that popular narratives are produced and circulated.

In a 1962 essay entitled "The Myth of Superman," Umberto Eco articulated his critique of superhero comics by comparing them to myths.[15] The limitations of Eco's essay are, perhaps, those of the general approach to popular culture at the time of its writing. Surprisingly for a critic who has always shown a great, and positive, interest in popular culture, Eco here plays the part of the "apocalyptic," falling back on a simplistic critique of popular literature as a means of manipulation and control of the "masses" on the part of "the offices of the great industries, the *advertising men* of Madison Avenue, what popular sociology has called, with a suggestive epithet, 'hidden persuaders' " (*Apocalittici e integrati*, 223). However, some of his comments can be of some use in this context.

After arguing that, in contemporary industrial society, "the positive hero must embody to an unthinkable degree the power demands that the average citizen nurtures but cannot satisfy" ("The Myth of Superman," 107), Eco then discusses the problems that this "archetypal" function of the superhero entails on a narratological level. He contrasts myth and novel as two diametrically opposed narratives: in the former, we have a story that follows an already established pattern; in the latter, the events in the story happen as the story is being told, so that the main concern is on "what will happen next?" According to Eco, comics superheroes are divided between these two forms of narrative: "The mythological character of comic strips finds himself in this singular situation: he must be an archetype, the totality of certain collective aspirations, and therefore he must necessarily become immobilized in an emblematic and fixed nature . . . ; but, since he is marketed in the sphere of a 'romantic' production for a public that consumes 'romances,' he must be subjected to a development which is typical . . . of novelistic characters" ("Myth of Superman" 110).[16] His conclusion that "for precise commercial reasons, . . . [Superman's] adventures are sold to a lazy audience" that "would be terrified by an indefinite development of the events that would keep their memory busy for several weeks" (*Apocalittici e integrati*, 232) is of course part and parcel of the moralizing attitude of early popular culture studies. What Eco misunderstands here is precisely what I have indicated earlier: popular narratives are produced in ways that cannot be assimilated into postliterate classical literature, and the iterative mechanism (as he calls it) of popular narratives need not be only a symptom of mental laziness on the part of both producer and audience. The development of the narrative over time in subsequent retellings and rearticulations does not entail a suspension of memory, a sort of continuous oblivion, as Eco seems to imply, but works more effectively the more the audience is aware of the previous articulation of the narrative that each retelling extends *and* remakes. I suspect that one of the reasons for the lukewarm popular reception of *Dick Tracy* was precisely the fact that, after his heyday in the thirties and forties, the square-jawed detective has not been "retold" for later audiences and therefore has not become as deeply ingrained in American culture as his caped colleagues.

In a later essay on repetition and seriality, Eco himself has come to reexamine the pleasures of iteration in a more positive light, even suggesting the possibility of an "aesthetics of serial forms," whose purpose would be to provide an account of the historical configurations of the dialectic between innovation and repetition ("Innovation and Repetition," 175). From this point of view, it is precisely on the level of myth that remakes and serial forms should be considered: "Every epoch has its myth-makers, its own sense of the sacred. . . . Let us take for granted the intense emotional participation, the pleasure of the reiteration of a single and constant truth, and the tears, and the laughter—and finally the *catharsis*. Then we can conceive of an audience also able to shift onto an aesthetic level and to judge the art of the variations on a mythical theme" (182). The distance between this and the "lazy audience" envisioned in the previous essay is obvious. What is important, however, is the fact that in this "aesthetic of serial forms" the question of the original is bracketed out, and what makes the text successful is its effectiveness as a variation on its theme.

What narrative could pretend to be the original of the Superman film? Of course, we know that in June 1938 the first issue of the comic book *Action Comics* published a story entitled "Superman," written by Jerry Siegel and drawn by Joe Shuster. That story can make the claim to be the (chronologically) "first" version of Superman, but not the original, since the character has profoundly changed in its fifty-year career, and the version that Newman looked at for inspiration was as far from Siegel and Shuster's as that of today's comics is from either. The point was made succinctly by Frank Miller in a recent interview: "Go back to the origins of Superman, before World War II. He was dragging generals to the front of the battles. He was fighting corrupt landlords. He was *not* the symbol of the status quo he's since become" (Sharrett, 39).

Batman has undergone a similar fate: from the grim sometime gun-toting vigilante of the early stories he has gone on to become the wholesome crime-fighter of the mid-fifties and early sixties, the camp Batman of the TV series, and the current "Dark Knight" persona popularized by Frank Miller's *The Dark Knight Returns* (1986) and uncountable comics since then.[17] Even though Frank Miller's reinterpretation of the character has been billed as a return to the original, it had to take into account all the textual elements that the many rearticulations of the story of Batman have gathered in time. It was a propos *The Dark Knight Returns* that Alan Moore wrote: "Yes, Batman is still Bruce Wayne, Alfred is still his butler . . . There is still a Robin, along with a batmobile. . . . Everything is exactly the same, except for the fact that it's totally different."[18] The development of comic book narratives over time can be characterized as sameness with difference, as a reshuffling of a number of narrative elements into new patterns. It is this characteristic that distinguishes comic books (and, in the United States, superhero comics in particular) from most other types of narratives: like soap operas, they are designed to last, to progress over time without the climactic release of the end of a novel or a play or a film. To this must be added the fact that, as Jim Collins has noted, the different versions of the character do not simply follow each other chronologically, but, in a society in which texts can be reproduced cheaply and easily, they also circulate at the same time, so that the "origins" of Batman as told in the original 1939 story, in Frank Miller's *The Dark Knight Returns* and *Batman: Year One*, in Tim Burton's *Batman* film and comic adaptation thereof, and so on, are available to the audience at one and the same time. Each version is perceived as part of the same basic myth, so that the "original," the 1939 story, loses its status and becomes simply one of the many possible ways to articulate the myth.

As an example of this loss in status of the original, let me point out that, according to the Siegel and Shuster version of Superman, our hero did not fly, but could, much more prosaically, "easily leap 1/8th of a mile" (Siegel and Shuster, 19). Yet, flight is one of the powers more closely associated with Superman, and according to Newman one of the aspects of the film that the ad campaign concentrated on was precisely that it showed a man *flying*. Like the myths discussed by Lévi-Strauss, the "myth" of Superman includes all its versions in a number of different media. We can now understand better why the Superman films are not adaptations: like the many rearticulations of the story within the comics medium, they take the basic elements that over time have come to constitute the construction blocks of a Superman narrative and reassemble them in terms of the new medium, to tell a story that adds one more layer to the "myth." Once this new version begins circulating, it becomes one of the many possible stories involving the character named Superman, one of the possible "sources" of any of his future narratives.

This can actually be seen as an asset from the point of view of translating comics into films. In fact, the lack of an urtext gives the creative team more freedom to consider the strengths and weaknesses of the cinematic medium. Tim Burton's film *Batman* provides a useful example. As we have seen, the fact that month in, month out, a new adventure of the hero *must* be published makes the definition of the characters in the book a matter of accumulation of details. Although Batman's archenemy the Joker appeared for the first time in 1940, it was only in 1951 that it was revealed how the criminal "Red Hood," in an attempt to escape Batman, dived into a vat full of a chemical substance that turned his hair green, his lips rouge red, and his face chalk white. Since then, and more so in recent years, Batman and the Joker have developed a sort of symbiotic relationship and are often portrayed as the opposite sides of the same coin: two madmen pursuing relentlessly and single-mindedly their own visions of the world as a place upon which must be imposed absolute order or absolute chaos (the classical texts here are two special volumes, Alan Moore and Brian Bolland's *The Killing Joke,* 1988, and Grant Morrison and Dave McKean's *Arkham Asylum,* 1989).

In Burton's film the problem of the accumulative development of this relationship was creatively solved by changing the origins of the Joker, so that he turns out to have been, before his transformation, the very thief who murdered Bruce Wayne's parents and was therefore responsible for the origins of Batman, just as Batman himself was responsible for the accident from which the Joker was born. Thus, the film establishes an interdependence between the two characters that is comparable to that in the comics, while taking into account the self-enclosed nature of the new medium. At the same time, elements introduced by Burton in the film, in particular the neo-Gothic architecture of Gotham, have been reappropriated in recent comics (*Batman* 474, February 1992; *Tales of the Dark Knight* 27, February 1992; and *Detective Comics* 641, February 1992) through a story specifically designed to change the graphic nature of Batman's environment to that developed by Anton Furst for Burton's movie.

Thus, as this last example makes clear, we must approach the question of the relationship between these two visual media, cinema and the comics, by adopting a new paradigm that is not that of the remake nor that of the adaptation, neither of which fully accounts for the reassemblage of the narrative elements in the move from one medium to the other. The problem needs to be framed in terms that go beyond the question of influence and originality to clarify the unique way in which popular culture texts are appropriated and reconstructed by cinema.

I thank Krin Gabbard for his helpful comments on a previous draft of this essay.

NOTES

1. A basic distinction (all too often neglected) must be made between comic strips, published daily in newspapers, and comic books. Witek (6–10) provides a useful discussion of their difference in terms of narrative structures, production, and reception. It seems to me that the term "comics" itself is extremely problematic, because, pace Thomas Inge, the medium does *not* simply belong "to the great body of humor which Americans cherish in their oral tradition" (Inge, 15). I would like to remark at the very beginning that there is little that is "comical" in the works discussed in this essay.

2. As table I in Parsons (68) shows, comic book circulation reached its nadir in 1979.

3. As Inge notes, "[T]he first of a series of short films based on Frederick Burr Opper's *Happy Hooligan,* which began March 20, 1900, appeared that same year" (143). The crossover between early comic strips and films flourished between 1900 and 1906. It would be interesting to investigate to what extent this was due to the structural and narratological similarities between the two media at this early stage of their history (development over a short period of time, prevalence of humorous situations, etc.). Though naturally limited in scope to its subject, Donald Crafton's biography of French caricaturist and comic strip, animation, and film pioneer Emile Cohl provides an excellent illustration of the close relation between the two media at the turn of the century.

4. The Yellow Kid has sometimes been called the "first" comic strip (Daniels, 2), although, as Couperie et al. (11–21) and Reitberger and Fuchs (11–12) point out, several protostrips in the late 1880s and early 1890s have some claim to the title (for a history of the precursors of the medium, see Kunzle). In using the Yellow Kid as a convenient "point of departure," I follow Boichel's argument that the Kid was "the most notable character of [his] period" (4 5). Incidentally, there is some disagreement over the "birth date" of the Kid, who in 1896 was already a recurrent figure of the cartoon series *Hogan's Alley* (begun by Richard Outcault in 1894). It was not until the character was given a bright yellow nightshirt, from which his name derived, that he became the focus of the series. According to Inge (138), the Kid displayed his nightshirt for the first time on January 5, 1896. Nye (217), Couperie et al. (19), and Reitberger and Fuchs (12) all give the date February 16, 1896.

5. See especially Barbieri, chapter 10. Collins (172–73) and Eco (*Apocalittici e integrati*, 145–67) comment on the problems of reading the language of the comics in terms of film.

6. Apparently Fellini actually worked in the comics industry early in his career, writing stories of Flash Gordon for the Italian publisher Nerbini after Fascism prohibited the importation of American comics. Recently, Fellini collaborated with Milo Manara on a comic version of "Viaggio a Tulum," a script published in the newspaper *Corriere della sera* but never made into a film (Mollica). The first part of "Viaggio a Tulum" (the comic) appeared in *Corto Maltese* 7, no. 7 (1989).

7. Translations from Barbieri and from Eco, *Apocalittici e integrati*, are mine.

8. I compare this effect to a lap dissolve because the panels are effectively juxtaposed one on the other. This is also comparable to a match cut, which establishes a sense of relation between two contiguous but otherwise unrelated shots. To remain within the confines of Coppola's *Dracula*, the effect achieved in the comic book is similar to that of the sudden cut from the scene in which Van Helsing cuts off Lucy's head to the following one, a close-up of a hunk of roast beef. This violent cut was unfortunately not reproduced in the comic adaptation, as the two scenes mark the transition between issues three and four.

9. The two-page spread is the "largest" but not the only perceptual unit. Many comics alternate pages of narrative and pages of publicity, so that often a single page will be the basic unit of composition, the accompanying page having no relation to the story.

10. Of course, animation brings together the best of both worlds. Cartoons starring Popeye have been popular since Fleischer Studios began producing them in 1932 and have helped boost the celebrity of the sailor in America and abroad. Altman's film, however, has practically gone unnoticed.

11. Signet has published a novel based on James V. Hart's screenplay of Coppola's movie and co-authored by Fred Saberhagen and Hart himself. Like the film—and this I find quite amazing—it is entitled *Bram Stoker's Dracula*. In order to distinguish it from Bram Stoker's (no italics) *Dracula*, Signet reissued the latter with the logo "The original classic novel." Now, my question is: "original of *what?*" By the way, let me add that, according to a publicity page that appeared in the comic adaptation, these are the only "two official tie-in novels." From the point of view of copyright, at least, the source (I assume that's what that "Bram Stoker's" is supposed to signify) and the adaptation of a self-acknowledged adaptation have the same status.

12. In this case the distinction between comic strip and comic book is important. The "division of labor" here outlined is seldom seen in comic strips, especially humorous ones.

13. When this essay was written (February 1993), Superman had recently met his untimely demise at the hands of Doomsday in *Superman* 75 (January 1993), an event preceded by a well-organized publicity campaign. His later "resurrection" (see in particular *The Adventures of Superman* 500, June 1993, and *Superman* 82, October 1993) adds a further layer to the Christological parallel.

14. The treatment of comics characters (especially superheroes) as myths is so pervasive as to be almost commonplace. See, among others, Reitberger and Fuchs

(100), Boichel (6 and passim), and Williams (18). Stan Lee, creator of characters like Spiderman and the X-Man, used to compare his activity to the foundation of a modern mythology (one of his creations, the mighty Thor, was lifted out of mythology altogether). John Ostrander, writer of the latest comic book series dedicated to the Spectre, has recently written: "I've always felt that superheroes were the modern equivalent of the stories told in myth and, as in myth, the same element is liable to reinterpretation from storyteller to storyteller. That gives it continuing vitality."

For the discussion of other popular media in terms of myth, see Lozano (soap operas) and the essays in the collection *Media, Myths, and Narratives,* edited by James Carey.

15. A longer version of the essay appeared in Eco's *Apocalittici e integrati,* first published in 1964.

16. The translation of Eco's essay presents some ambiguities. It is clear from the context that he is discussing comic books rather than comic strips (the Italian term, *fumetto,* does not distinguish between the two). Furthermore, the words *romanzo* and *romanzesco* in Italian have a more general meaning than English "romance" and "romantic," employed here, and their meaning is closer to "novel." Again, the context makes it clear that Eco is specifically concerned with popular novels.

17. For an excellent and concise summary of the Batman's career(s), see Boichel.

18. See Uricchio and Pearson for a list and a discussion of the "key components [that] constitute the core of the character of the Batman" (186).

WORKS CITED

Barbieri, Daniele. *I linguaggi del fumetto.* Milano: Bompiani, 1991.

Barrier, Michael, and Martin Williams, eds. *The Smithsonian Book of Comic-Book Comics.* New York: Smithsonian Institution Press and Harry N. Abrams, 1981.

Barthes, Roland. *Elements of Semiology.* Translated by Annette Lavers and Colin Smith. New York: Hill and Wang, 1967.

Bassnett-McGuire, Susan. *Translation Studies.* London: Methuen, 1980.

Boichel, Bill. "Batman: Commodity as Myth." In Pearson, 4–17.

Byrne, John. Reply to the letter of Ryan Day. *John Byrne's Next Men* 10 (1992): n.p.

Carey, James W., ed. *Media, Myths, and Narratives. Television and the Press.* Newbury Park: Sage, 1988.

Collins, Jim. "Batman: The Movie, Narrative: The Hyperconscious." In Pearson, 164–181.

Couperie, Pierre et al. *A History of the Comic Strip.* Translated by Eileen B. Hennessy. New York: Crown, 1968.

Crafton, Donald. *Emile Cohl, Caricature and Film.* Princeton: Princeton University Press, 1990.

Daniels, Les. *Comix: A History of Comic Books in America.* New York: Outerbridge and Dienstfrey, 1971.

Eco, Umberto. *Apocalittici e integrati.* 1964. Milano: Bompiani, 1990.
——. "Innovation and Repetition: Between Modern and Post-Modern Aesthetics." *Daedalus* 114, no. 4 (1985): 161–184.
——. "The Myth of Superman." Translated by Natalie Chilton. *The Role of the Reader.* Bloomington: Indiana University Press, 1979. 107–124.
Fell, John L. *Film and the Narrative Tradition.* Berkeley and Los Angeles: University of California Press, 1986.
Inge, Thomas M. *Comics as Culture.* Jackson: University of Mississippi Press, 1990.
Kowal, Patricia. "Dick Tracy." In *Magill's Cinema Annual 1991,* 92–95. Pasadena: Salem Press, 1991.
Kunzle, David. *The Early Comic Strip. Narrative Strips and Picture Stories in the European Broadsheet from c.1450 to 1825.* Vol. 1 of *History of the Comic Strip.* Berkeley and Los Angeles: University of California Press, 1973.
Levine, Lawrence W. *Highbrow/Lowbrow.* Cambridge: Harvard University Press, 1988.
Lévi-Strauss, Claude. "The Structural Study of Myth." *Structural Anthropology.* New York: Basic Books, 1963.
Lozano, Elizabeth. "The Force of Myth on Popular Narratives: The Case of the Melodramatic Serial." *Communication Theory* 2, no. 3 (1992): 207–220.
Mollica, Vincenzo. "Viaggio a Tulum." *Corto Maltese* 7, no. 7 (July 1989): 8–9.
Moore, Alan. "The Mark of the Batman: An Introduction." *The Dark Knight Returns.* By Frank Miller. New York: Warner Books, 1986.
Nash, Jay Robert, and Stanley Ralph Ross. *The Motion Picture Guide.* Vol. 3. Chicago: Cinebooks, 1986.
Newman, David. "Superman Takes Flight." Paper presented before the Modern Language Association Convention, New York, 29 December 1992.
Nye, Russel. *The Unembarrassed Muse. The Popular Arts in America.* New York: Dial Press, 1970.
Ostrander, John. Reply to the letter of Allan Lappin. *The Spectre* 3 (1993).
Parsons, Patrick. "Batman and His Audience: The Dialectic of Culture." In Pearson, 66–89.
Pearson, Roberta E., and William Uricchio, eds. *The Many Lives of the Batman: Critical Approaches to a Superhero and His Media.* New York: Routledge, 1991.
Reitberger, Reinhold, and Wolfgang Fuchs. *Comics: Anatomy of a Mass Medium.* Translated by Nadia Fowler. Boston: Little, Brown and Co., 1972.
Sharrett, Christopher. "Batman and the Twilight of the Idols: An Interview with Frank Miller." In Pearson, 33–46.
Siegel, Jerry (story) and Joe Shuster (art). "Superman." 1938. In Barrier, 19–31.
Thomas, Roy (story) and Mike Mignola (art). *Bram Stoker's Dracula.* Based on the screenplay by James V. Hart. 1 no. 1 (1992).
Uricchio, William, and Roberta E. Pearson. " 'I'm Not Fooled by That Cheap Disguise.' " In Pearson, 182–213.
Williams, Martin. "About 'Superman.' " In Barrier, 17–18.
Witek, Joseph. *Comic Books as History. The Narrative Art of Jack Jackson, Art Spiegelman, and Harvey Pekar.* Jackson: University Press of Mississippi, 1989.

EIGHTEEN

"Tonight Your Director Is John Ford": The Strange Journey of *Stagecoach* from Screen to Radio

Peter Lehman

Like many commentators on John Ford's *Stagecoach*, Edward Buscombe observes that the journey undertaken by the coach does not conform to the narrative implication that the travelers are going west into Indian[1] country. If the fictional journey has a strange geographical dimension to it, that is not the only strange journey that this fictional coach would undertake. On January 9, 1949, the *NBC Theatre* debuted with a half hour radio version of John Ford's *Stagecoach*. *NBC Theatre* was renamed *Screen Directors Playhouse* and, in 1950, expanded to one hour; it ran until 1951 (Dunning). It featured adaptations of successful films with many of the original stars. The films' directors introduced the programs and chatted about the original film afterward. A version of *Fort Apache*, which was broadcast on August 5, 1949, was the only other Ford film to be included in the series.

Since the shift from film to radio involves a form of adaptation, why consider it in a volume devoted to remakes? Actually, radio adaptations differ significantly from literary adaptations, which are generally the focus of adaptation studies. The author of the original literary work frequently has no creative involvement with the film adaptation and, in the case of many of the most prestigious adaptations, has lived before cinema was even invented. The mere fact that film adaptations included works by Shakespeare, Emily Brontë, and Tennyson created a significant distance between the original creators and the creators of the adaptations. Even when a living author has a role in writing the screenplay for an adaptation, as for example Mario Puzo did with *The Godfather*, such involvement at most seems to imply a likelihood that the adaptation will somehow be more faithful to the original vision of the novel. Such participation is not, however, directly perceived by the film spectator.

The *Screen Directors Playhouse* involved as many of the original stars as possible re-creating their roles. In *Stagecoach,* both John Wayne and Claire Trevor play the same characters they played in the film and, similarly, Henry Fonda and John Wayne play the same central characters in both the film and radio versions of *Fort Apache.* Thus, the radio listener hears the same actor that he or she may have heard in the film, at times even speaking the exact same lines. In some sense, then, there is a more direct remake element at work in the radio programs, if only insofar as the fact that well-known actors are re-creating parts for which they are already famous. This points to yet another significant difference between filmic adaptations of literary works and radio adaptations of films. In the former case, many of the film spectators would not have read the original novels, plays, or poems or, if they had, they might have done so long ago. The *Screen Directors Playhouse,* however, featured recent popular films that many of the radio listeners would have seen. Although it included classics from the early forties such as *Stagecoach,* the 1949 broadcast of the 1947 film *Fort Apache* is much more typical of the series, and some of the programs even featured current films.

Since *Stagecoach* was the first program in the series, the introduction by George Marshall, president of the Screen Directors Guild, included comments about the nature of the new program "in which the directors will personally bring you their favorite film assignments." "Tonight," he tells the listening audience, "your director is John Ford." At the program's conclusion, Marshall returns, "Speaking for the Guild I'd like to express our gratitude to the National Broadcasting Company for the opportunity to better acquaint the public with the work and role of the screen director." Marshall's comments imply a close relationship between the original film and the radio version. Indeed, the public will not only become acquainted with the director who will "personally" introduce the film but also with the function of the film director. Although faithfulness to the original had long been a critical concept applied to film adaptations of novels, such adaptations were generally presumed neither to "personally" acquaint the filmgoer with the novelist nor to educate the film viewer about the role of the author. Even if it was presumed that one might learn about the original novel from such films, it was not presumed that one learned about writing fiction. During the discussion with Ford, Wayne, Trevor, and Ward Bond concluding the program, Trevor reinforces Marshall's point by remarking, "You know, I think it's wonderful that the screen director is being honored like this. He's the fellow that really makes the movie. Ask us actors and actresses."

The *Screen Directors Playhouse* is caught within a bizarre paradox. Sponsored by the Screen Directors Guild, it seeks to promote both the original film and the role of the director in creating that film, but it does so within a medium singularly unsuited to showcasing the talents of a film director. The announcer foregrounds this paradox at the beginning of the program, "Screen Directors Guild Assignment; production: *Stagecoach;* director: John

Ford; stars: John Wayne, Claire Trevor, Ward Bond." After a brief musical interlude, another announcer repeats the film title and actors and adds, "And introducing the director of the film, John Ford." Initially, it sounds as if Ford is the director of this production since he is listed with the stars (one of whom, Ward Bond, was not even in the film version). Moments later, however, we hear the ambivalent announcement that this production will be "introducing" the film's director, John Ford. What then is his role in this production? At the conclusion of the program, the announcer tells us, "Production was under the supervision of Howard Wiley." It sounds at first like Ford is the director of this production, then like he is being introduced to the radio audience in his capacity as the film's director, and finally it becomes clear that he has had no role in this production other than that of brief guest.

This is a strange way either to acquaint the public with the role of the screen director or to honor "him," since, as I will argue, no significant features of the original aesthetic text survive this cross-media remake. Indeed, analysis of the radio remake of *Stagecoach* is helpful in revealing the quite different nature of radio programs and films as texts both aesthetically and ideologically and the quite different status of the director as an author in these two media. Whatever else may have happened on January 9, 1949, the public became acquainted with neither "John Ford's *Stagecoach*" nor the role of a film director.

The notion of "John Ford's *Stagecoach*," as well as the concept of the role of the film director, invokes issues of authorship. I have elsewhere argued in detail that authorship in the arts can be usefully explored within Nelson Goodman's distinction between autographic and allographic arts (Lehman, 1990, 1978). Autographic arts are those, like painting, in which the hand of the artist is crucial in the creation of the aesthetic text. Forgery is thus a crucial issue since to claim that a painting is a Rembrandt is to claim a specific history for that painting—that is, Rembrandt painted it with his own hand, not someone in Tucson in 1992 claiming to be Rembrandt. If the latter is the case, we say that the painting is inauthentic. In an allographic art form, such as classical music, the hand of the artist is not an issue and there is no distinction between an original and a copy. Thus, should someone in Tucson in 1992 rush the stage during a performance of a Beethoven symphony, seize the score, and declare it inauthentic since it was printed by machine in Cleveland rather than handwritten by Beethoven, the poor soul, far from being hailed as having made an insightful discovery, would be led away and declared hopelessly confused.

What accounts for this different status among the arts? Goodman argues that allographic arts are contingent upon the existence of a notational system for the constitutive features of the aesthetic text. That is, whatever constitutes the identity of the aesthetic text must be amenable to notation.

The autographic arts have no such notational system and must be executed by the artist who creates the work. Rembrandt, in other words, could not notate an oil painting and leave it to someone else to paint. Notational systems can be understood by contrasting them with discursive language. In the former case, one and only one thing correctly corresponds to each notated mark within the system. Within classical music, for example, only one sound corresponds to each note. In discursive language, however, a limitless number of things correspond to each unit. There are many shades that correspond to the word "blue," and no matter how many other discursive words we use to qualify it (e.g., bright, extremely bright), this never changes; we can never limit the correspondence to a one-to-one relationship. In my past exploration of issues of autographic and allographic arts in relation to authorship, I have argued that comparing film and theater in particular reveals profound differences between a play script and a film script, as well as a theater director and a film director. It is necessary to briefly summarize those distinctions since I now want to argue that equally strong differences characterize writing and directing in radio and film.

No art forms lie entirely within a notational system. Thus, in classical music, discursive language such as the term "allegro" is used to supplement the notations. If a composer writes such things as "play fast" or "play with passion" on a score, those directions are not constitutive features of the aesthetic work. How one interprets or ignores such directions does not affect the identity of the work; however, playing wrong notes, leaving notes out or adding notes does affect the identity. Notational systems allow the distinction between the quality of the performance and the identity of the work; one can bemoan a poor performance of Beethoven's Symphony No. 5 but still recognize it as Beethoven's work.

In the theater, the dialogue written by the playwright is part of a notational system, but the stage directions are part of a discursive language system. Thus, if someone playing Hamlet says, "Oh, that this too, too solid flesh would melt," he is in compliance with what Shakespeare wrote within the notational system. Only one spoken word corresponds to the notated word. To say, "Oh, that this flesh would melt," is to make a mistake equivalent to leaving out notes in a musical score. It affects the identity of the work rather than the quality of the performance. If, however, the stage directions read "exit stage left quickly" and the actor exits stage right slowly, the identity of the play is not affected. The consequences of this distinction are critical for understanding radio. Within Western theatrical tradition (there are other cultural traditions for theater, music, and all the arts), the dialogue the characters speak creates the fictional world and tells us what the play is fundamentally about. It is for this reason that the same play can bear countless interpretations with widely differing staging and, even more pertinent to our current inquiry into radio, a play can be fully comprehended with a staged reading. That is, the actors can be seated and not in costume. If they speak the dialogue, we can enter the fictional world of the play, understand the characters' actions and the play's themes. We need not see anything in order to identify Shakespeare's "Hamlet," and it is for this reason that we can read, understand, and even evaluate the play without ever seeing a performance of it.

Although we speak of theater and cinema in similar language (e.g., films have a script or screen*play*, actors, and a director), they are in fact quite dissimilar. As with theater, only the dialogue spoken by the actors in a film is part of a notational system; camera directions, descriptions of shots and sets, and so on are discursive language. In the cinema, however, the visual image constitutes the diegesis of which the spoken word is only a small part. Dialogue in cinema, in other words, need not create the characters, describe the situations or even state the themes. Much less of the aesthetic text is amenable to notation in the cinema. It is a question of degree rather than kind, but the degree of difference is so great as to border on being one of kind. In this sense, the common expression that cinema is a director's medium rather than a writer's medium is correct.

Writers and screenplays are not, of course, useless. They occupy an intermediary stage in the process of creation. If a painter uses a photograph or a sketch in creating an oil painting, that prior image has served a useful purpose for him or her. It in no way, however, notates the constitutive features of the oil painting as an aesthetic text, though it may outline or indicate some of its features. Limitless paintings can be made using the same sketch or photograph and they can range in quality from excellent to poor—and they can be good or bad for quite different reasons. Screenplays do not notate the constitutive features of a finished film, though they may provide an outline or indication of some of those features.

The relationship between dialogue and gesture in the theater and cinema is virtually reversed. The dialogue, as we have seen, cannot be changed in the theater without altering the identity of the work. Every director staging "Hamlet" may stage it differently, however, and every actor playing the part may gesture differently than every other actor when delivering a given line. In the cinema, however, the gesturing and placement of the actor frequently are more important in the creation of the aesthetic text than the dialogue he or she speaks. In Ford's *Stagecoach*, for example, a scene occurs where Ringo (John Wayne) asks Dallas (Claire Trevor) to marry him. They stand close to each other, though separated by a hitching post upon which each places a hand. The aesthetic complexity of the moment derives, as we shall see shortly, from both the visual motif of the wooden hitching post and the fact that the characters are positioned on either side of it. The exact wording of Ringo's proposal and Dallas's reply is of lesser importance and, in fact, could be changed without greatly altering the film as a complex aesthetic object. Were the actors to stand in front of a tree, however, the entire meaning and significance of the moment within a complex aesthetic text would collapse. In a very real sense, and in opposition to the theater, this can only be "staged" one way. From the point of view of aesthetics, the same screenplay filmed five different ways is not five performances of the same screenplay, but rather five different films with some similar features of story and dialogue—like five different oil paintings based upon the same sketch of an apple and a pear. It is precisely for this reason that reading screenplays is not analogous to reading play scripts and that a staged reading of *Stagecoach* would be an incomprehensible bore, no matter how much one liked the film. The spoken word in a film script is not a dense, complex aesthetic text as, for example, Shakespeare's "Hamlet" is. It neither creates nor sustains a fictional world, but rather may be a small part of it. The filmmaker, usually the director, fulfills the function of creating the diegesis. Which brings us finally to radio where, among all the media, the situation is once again virtually reversed; the written word does create and sustain the diegetic world and the writer, not the director, creates the aesthetic text. It is within this framework that we can best understand the radio version of *Stagecoach* as well as the paradox of its production by the Screen Directors Guild.

After the introduction, the radio version of *Stagecoach* begins with a cowboy song, then Ford narrating the story's premise about the stagecoach journey in 1885 from Tonto to Lordsburg and the dread of the dangers posed by Geronimo. "It's a story still told by the Indians," Ford says, and the narration then segues to an American Indian narrator who tells of the "mighty white invader" and the city of Tonto, where the "stagecoach stopped to take men to the Westward where Geronimo was leader, chief of the Apaches." The story begins in Tonto, where the stagecoach passengers are warned of the dangers of their journey.

The use of the Indian narrator, who is heard again during and at the end of the story, frames the events quite differently than occurs in the film, where a white narrator tells of the dangers of Geronimo at the film's beginning and is never heard from again. While the brief use of a narrator at the beginning of a film, who then never reappears, is a convention of classical Hollywood cinema, it is important here to note the consequences of the narrational shift in the radio version. The film never claims to have any sympathy with Geronimo or the Apaches; they are simply introduced from the white perspective as a threat to civilization, which is assumed to be synonymous with white culture.[2] In a somewhat bizarre manner, the radio program seems to frame the story as one told from the Apache point of view, something that receives emphasis since it is the last thing we hear Ford tell us. Certainly nothing about the film or the short story upon which it is based seems to justify such a perspective. Why would the Apaches want to tell a story about the journey of whites? Furthermore, in Ford's film, the Apaches receive no development as human beings with their own culture; they are simply a threat synonymous with the wilderness. They emerge from it, attack the coach, and flee back into it. They do not speak and we do not even glimpse their village or way of life. If this radio program is a version of the film, we might very well wonder why the Apache would still tell this story.

The radio version offers no answer. We hear the Indian narrator during the Apache Wells scene as he tells of the gathering Apaches who are about to attack the coach. He returns at the end of the story and, in a totally unexplained manner, celebrates the "brave" white "man's" story: "Thus the story of those brave men, riders of the flying wagon, in the land of Arizona where Geronimo was chief. In the great land in the desert where the flying wagon galloped, that the white men called the stagecoach, bringing brave men to the West." In his initial appearance, the narrator spoke with respect for Geronimo's attempt to stop the "white invader." During the Apache Wells scene, he gives knowledge of what the Apaches are doing, thus at least representing their point of view. At the end, however, he is simply reduced for no apparent reason to celebrating the victory of the enemy of his people. The racism resulting from this narrational strategy is thus of a markedly different kind than that in the film.

The opening scene of the radio program establishes a major aesthetic strategy of this version, a dramatic paring down of the film's characters. Mrs. Mallory, Hatfield, Doc, and Dallas are identified as the sole passengers, with no mention of Gatewood or Peabody. Buck, so effectively characterized by Andy Devine in the film, is a character in name only here, though the sheriff, played by Ward Bond, functions similarly to the film's sheriff. Once the journey gets under way, the coach stops only once, rather than twice as in the film, and there are no characters of even minor significance introduced at the stop. Such a paring down of characters and events is to be expected within the shift from the hour-and-a-half classical Hollywood format to the half hour radio format. As in Hollywood's adaptation of nineteenth-century novels, for example, there are simply too many characters and events in the film to be included in the radio program. Some events, such as when Ringo stops the coach in the wilderness and the sheriff places him under arrest as an escapee, occur in the radio version very much as they do in the film but they take on quite different meanings than in the film.

The manner in which Ringo stops the stage and gets on it in the film has several levels of visual significance. In contrast to all the other passengers who board the coach in town, Ringo is associated with the wilderness in which he first appears.[3] When he gets in the coach, he sits on the floor with his back to the door, the wilderness visible through the window in every shot of him. His position on the floor between the rows of passengers also visually establishes the mediatory function he fulfills: as tensions mount in the coach, rather than take sides he attempts to calm people down. In the radio program, there is no strong association with the wilderness and Ringo sits next to Dallas when he gets on the coach. Their conversation is an abbreviated but similar version of the lunch conversation they have at the first stop in the film; Ringo perceives Dallas as a "lady" and himself as a societal outcast.

At Apache Wells, the travelers learn that Captain Mallory and the troops have been sent ahead to Lordsburg, a vote is taken as to whether to go back or proceed with the journey, Dallas is overlooked in the vote, Mrs. Mallory faints, and Doc Boone is drunk when needed—in short, an encapsulated version of events from the film. Mrs. Mallory gives birth, and Dallas brings the baby to the men. Although the scene seems to parallel that in the film, it serves a different dramatic function since none of the serious divisiveness caused by such things as Gatewood's and Peabody's desire to go back is present in the radio version. Thus, the dramatic counterpoint of everyone gathering together in a rare moment of peaceful unity is absent.

The scene does fulfill the function, however, of bringing the mother/ whore dichotomy into play. We are told euphemistically at the beginning of the program that Dallas is being thrown out of town because she is too "hospitable to the gentlemen." After seeing her hold the baby, Ringo later tells her, "I watched you with that baby today. You looked . . . you looked . . . well, nice." He then proposes to her and she replies, "You don't know me. You don't know who I am." These two moments of the radio program closely follow the film, even repeating dialogue, but once again, the aesthetic and ideological significance varies greatly between the two versions. Classical Hollywood cinema, of course, frequently characterizes women as either nonsexual mothers or sexualized whores, the whore with a heart of gold being a common variant. The iconography of Dallas holding the baby relates to this filmic tradition and operates specifically through point-of-view editing: the spectator, as well as Ringo and the others, is positioned to *see* Dallas as a mother. Furthermore, *Stagecoach* dramatically illustrates the mother/whore polarization within which many female characters were trapped in classical Hollywood: in an instant Dallas goes from one pole to the other and the sight of her holding the baby justifies the reversal. The extremes come dangerously close to baring the device and thus revealing the restrictive limitations of such either/or characterizations.

Similarly, the scene where Ringo proposes to Dallas receives its complexity visually through their positioning around the corral post, described above. The hitching post and the closely related image of the corral post are associated throughout the film with the very civilization that creates such stereotypes as the good mother and the bad whore and then drives the whore out of town. The corral post figures prominently in a shot near the beginning of the film as the coach followed by the cavalry leaves Lordsburg. We see corral posts in the lower foreground of the frame, a butte looming in the center distance, and a dirt road stretching between them. The coach followed by the cavalry enters from the lower right and proceeds along the road on its journey into the wilderness. This highly formal composition, which visualizes the film's dramatic structure of a journey from civilization into the wilderness, prominently uses the corral posts to signify the last vestiges of civilization. The entrances into both of the stagecoach stops are shot in ways that similarly reinforce this post motif with the temporary safety of these isolated places of civilization in the wilderness. Similarly, the horrors of the Indian attack upon Lee's Ferry, the last stagecoach stop, are visualized in images of corral posts left standing in the smoldering ruins. Finally, the hitching post motif appears prominently in Lordsburg as Ringo and Dallas walk along and she fears his reaction when he discovers the truth about her, and as she waits alone in anguish after hearing the sounds of gunshots between Ringo and the Plummers.

It is only in the wilderness that Ringo, who first appears and boards the stage in the wilderness, can perceive Dallas freed from the stigma of her social role, but the post that divides them is a reminder of the realities of the social roles to which they must and do return. When they arrive in Lordsburg and Ringo walks Dallas "home," they once again stand with their hands on a hitching post, this time united on the same side as Ringo resolves to return to Dallas after killing the Plummer boys. In the radio program, there is no complexity to his marriage proposal equivalent to the visual reminder of society's restrictions that Ford's positioning of Ringo and Dallas, and later Dallas alone, provides. Not surprisingly, the same is true at the end of the program when they arrive in Lordsburg. When Ringo leaves Dallas to fight the Plummers, we simply hear him tell her to wait for him. It is a simple event in contrast to the complex culmination of the hitching post motif we see in the film; the way Ringo and Dallas stand with their hands on the post is a profoundly moving moment of the sort that distinguishes Ford's *Stagecoach*.

As in the film, after Ringo proposes to Dallas, she convinces him to escape, saying she will join him later at his ranch in Mexico. As he attempts his escape, however, he encounters Indian smoke signals and goes back to warn the others. The Indian narrator returns and tells of how his nation had to strike "the white man's flying wagon." After the narration, we return to the coach where the passengers mistakenly think they are safe. As in the film, the false sense of security is shattered by the Indian attack.

The scene is interesting in how it uses dialogue to attempt to describe action that we see in the film. "Ringo, look out! That Apache on the painted

Figure 38. Transforming John Ford's *Stagecoach* (1939) to a radio broadcast raises questions about the loss of formal compositional elements.

pony," Dallas screams. We hear a gunshot and Ringo replies, "Got him." "See that Indian on that mustang coming alongside?" Doc asks. "Don't talk, shoot," someone orders and Doc responds by shooting and saying, "Well, now you see him and now you don't." This is the only place in the radio program where we hear an attempt to describe what we see in the film. Indeed, the element of visual detail (e.g., "the painted pony" and the "mustang coming alongside") is forced and out of place. It breaks with the style of the rest of the program where the characters, within the codes of realism, talk as they would in such a situation. Here they talk as if the purpose is to help us visualize the action. It is of note that the effort to supply this type of filmic visualization occurs in an action scene and is never used to recreate any of the film's visual motifs. (See figure 38.)

During the fight scene, Hatfield is killed. Ringo tells Dallas to use the last three bullets on herself, Mrs. Mallory, and the baby so that they won't be captured by the Indians. In the film, in contrast, Hatfield holds the gun to Mrs. Mallory's head as she prays and he prepares to shoot her. He is killed before he can do so and after he slumps over we hear the sound of the bugle indicating the cavalry rescue. Indeed, Hatfield is almost able to kill Mrs. Mallory because Ringo has left the inside of the coach and, in a heroic act, jumped onto the team of horses in an effort to bring them under control. Ringo's active attempt to save the day contrasts sharply with Hatfield's resignation, and it is a contrast that has been richly developed throughout the film.

Both Ringo and Hatfield are men who live by a strong code of behavior: Hatfield is the Southern gentleman and Ringo the westerner. Although their codes are dissimilar, the two men are similar in how they adhere to their codes. Indeed, they are both driven in nearly identical fashion by those codes; Hatfield goes to Lordsburg because his code requires him to protect the Southern "lady" and Ringo goes to Lordsburg because his western code requires him to avenge his brother's death at the hands of the Plummers. In Ford's vision, the crucial distinction between these two men is that one of them enacts a code appropriate to his environment and context and the other applies an inappropriate code of conduct. This is clear in the scene where Hatfield offers Mrs. Mallory a drink out of his silver cup but refuses the courtesy to Dallas. The purpose of social codes is to ease interaction among people, but Hatfield's act merely introduces further discord into the group. Even if his distinction between the two women were valid within an upper-class, genteel Southern tradition, it is hopelessly out of place within this stagecoach in the western wilderness, but Hatfield does not perceive this. Similarly, within Ford's vision, Hatfield's preparation to kill Mrs. Mallory reflects an almost despicable failure of masculine western courage and action. He should be risking his life in battle with the Indians rather than fatalistically preparing to kill a woman. For this reason, it comes as a relief to the film audience when Hatfield slumps over dead. In the radio program, however, Hatfield's death is of little significance, and the way in which Ringo fulfills the function of saving the women from the "fate worse than death" has no more significance in relation to his character.

A description of this scene indicates how the film director can create a dense visual and aural text around a simple narrative event. In one shot, we see Mrs. Mallory praying fervently as a gun from off screen left enters the frame and points at her head. She appears oblivious to her impending death when suddenly the gun drops slowly downward and finally drops out of the frame. Mrs. Mallory continues praying and we hear the sound of a bugle blowing off screen. Her facial expression changes from fear to hope as she realizes the significance of the impending cavalry rescue. Narratively, the moment is not only simple but even clichéd—it is the classic last-minute cavalry rescue. What distinguishes it, however, is Ford's beautiful use of offscreen space. We never see Hatfield as he prepares to shoot Mrs. Mallory or when he himself is actually killed; we infer his death from the dropped gun. This shot begins by being structured visually around offscreen space then ends by being structured aurally around offscreen space: we hear the bugle before we see the cavalry riding to the rescue. A conventional cutting pattern showing Hatfield prepare to shoot Mrs. Mallory, then being hit himself, followed by a direct cut to the cavalry riding to the rescue while we simultaneously hear the bugle would rob this scene of its distinction.

The bugle signals the rescue in the radio program as in the film, and the last scene takes place in Lordsburg. The scene bears careful analysis because it is by far the most aesthetically complex in the radio program, and the nature of that complexity reveals much about the relationship of radio narratives to film narratives. After Ringo tells Dallas to wait for him and goes off to seek the Plummers, Dallas says a prayer. We hear distant shots as her prayer continues, followed by the cowboy song heard at the program's beginning and finally the sound of footsteps heard from Dallas's perspective. Dallas emotionally asks, "Who . . . who's that out there?" and then she happily exclaims, "Ringo!" The scene unexpectedly draws upon the nondiegetic sound element of the cowboy song that had previously been perceived as simple introductory music, as well as draws on elements of diegetic sound perspective from the position of the character around whom the scene is structured, and it further layers those sounds with the foregrounded sound of Dallas's prayer.

The final scene is perhaps the only scene in this remake that achieves a life of its own. Whereas many of the scenes seem to be lesser versions of story elements taken from the original, totally stripped of their visual, thematic, and dramatic complexity—or as in the fight scene, failed efforts to create filmic visual equivalency—the final scene creates an aural density that is, simply put, good radio. Although it takes from Ford's film the idea of Dallas waiting and finally hearing Ringo's footsteps before identifying him, it develops the concept in an original way. In the film, for example, we see Ringo engaged in his fight with the Plummers. Structuring the scene entirely around Dallas waiting intensifies one element of the dramatic structure in the original and makes it the primary organizing principle.

The last scene concludes when Ringo tells Dallas that before dying Luke Plummer confessed that he killed Jed Michael, the crime for which Ringo has been in jail. He is now a free man. Dallas cries in response and Ringo asks despairingly, "Dallas, what are you crying for?" and naively adds "Nothing's happened." On this happy note, the previously discussed narration concludes the program. In the film, Luke Plummer doesn't confess and the sheriff turns the other way to allow the guilty Ringo to "escape" with Dallas to his ranch in Mexico where they will be spared "the blessings of civilization." Since the radio program entirely lacks the film's rich development of the ironic treatment of civilization's blessings, the happy ending makes perfect sense. It is central to Ford's film that Ringo and Dallas have to flee civilization since civilization lacks the flexibility and complexity to perceive them in a different light. They remain the escaped convict and the whore.

Clearly, the radio program does not present "John Ford's *Stagecoach*." Indeed, it is hard to talk about it as either a remake or an adaptation of Ford's film. If anything, it adapts the outline of some of the major story elements and a few fragments of the dialogue but, as I have argued, it is in the nature of film that those elements only constitute a small portion of the finished filmic text. In other words, those are the simple elements that do not create a dense aesthetic text in themselves as they do in theater but that may be used in the creation of such a text. The radio version of *Stagecoach* fails to create a rich aesthetic text not because of anything about the nature of radio, as the exception of the fight scene shows, but because most of this program is content to merely re-present simple story elements from the film. It is also in the nature of radio, however, that if Ford were to have directed this script it would have made little or no difference since the writing creates, shapes, and sustains radio's diegetic worlds. Radio directors have little to do except shape vocal performance and sound effects. If we had five different versions of the same radio script of *Stagecoach* by different directors we would have five different versions of performances of the same work. In contrast to cinema, the identity of the work clearly lies with the writer, not the director.

The Directors Guild seems to have perceived this paradox since the directors did not direct the radio programs. If in fact one wants to present the director to the public, this would be the logical manner. But since the directors would not be involved in an analogous directorial activity, they were simply presented to the public as personalities who introduced the program and reminisced about the original film. The way in which each director is announced at the beginning of the program as the "director" betrays the confusion. Even if they were the directors of the programs, there would, in the filmic sense of the term, be little or nothing for them to direct. The situation would be quite different in the mid-fifties when the Screen Directors Guild became involved with television and the *Screen Directors Playhouse*. In 1955, John Ford directed *Rookie of the Year*. Rather than a remake of a film, the program was an original drama. Both the guild and Ford perceived that in this medium there was a creative role for the film director; he need not simply be briefly presented to the public. Presumably, he was making something rather than remaking something for a different medium. Yet, the guild and the film directors may have seen more commonality between directing in these two media than actually exists. How television directing compares to film and radio directing is, however, another story for another time.

If the Screen Directors Guild's promotion of film directors on radio was a strange aesthetic paradox, from the economic perspective it made good sense. The guild quite correctly perceived that radio, and later television, could be used to promote and stimulate interest in films. The announcer says at the end of the broadcast of "Stagecoach," "John Wayne can soon be seen in John Ford's Argosy Production *Three Godfathers,* and Claire Trevor appears in the soon-to-be-released Amusement Enterprises picture *The Lucky Stiff.* Ward Bond is currently appearing in the Victor Fleming production *Joan of Arc.*"

And one last thing. If the public was not treated to "director John Ford's *Stagecoach*" on January 9, 1949, whose remake was it? During the closing credits of the show, we are told, "Tonight's story was adapted by Milton Geiger." From the point of view of aesthetics and authorship, the announcer should have proclaimed at the beginning, "Tonight your creator is Milton Geiger" rather than "Tonight your director is John Ford." What the significance of that would have been in 1949 is unclear. Unfortunately, given the scholarly lack of interest in radio aesthetics, it is still unclear today.

Special thanks to Warren Bareiss for sharing his knowledge of radio and his resources with me.

NOTES

1. I use the word "Indian" in this essay since my reference is to conventional genre representations and constructs, not Native Americans.

2. The racial ideology of the film is disturbing in more ways than its depiction of American Indians as savages. Buck, the comic, cowardly male character, whines about his Mexican wife, Juliette, and her family, as well as the beans she always feeds him. Although Juliette is never seen in the film, she is characterized with the twin stereotypes of Hispanics: all her family members move in with them and they eat nothing but beans. Even her marriage to Buck contributes to this negative stereotyping: such a woman, the film implies, would not be a fit wife for Ringo, the Anglo heroic male. Chris, the Hispanic proprietor of the second stagecoach stop, is dominated by his Indian wife, whom he cannot control and who turns out to be a thief.

3. Many Ford scholars have commented on this and related points I make about the film. *Stagecoach* contains a number of formal motifs, including one of Christianity that is developed visually with the image of the church in Lordsburg and aurally with the parodic sound track version of "Shall We Gather at the River?"; hats play an important role in visually defining the characters; and the narrative is carefully structured around a day/night patterning. For discussion of these and related aspects of the film, see Place, McBride and Wilmington, Baxter, and Bordwell and Thompson.

WORKS CITED

Baxter, John. *The Cinema of John Ford.* New York: A. S. Barnes, 1971.

Bordwell, David, and Kristin Thompson. *Film Art: An Introduction.* 3rd ed. New York: McGraw-Hill, 1990.

Buscombe, Edward. *Stagecoach.* London: British Film Institute, 1992.

Dunning, John. *Tune in Yesterday: The Ultimate Encyclopedia of Old Time Radio.* Englewood Cliffs: Prentice-Hall, 1976.

Goodman, Nelson. *Languages of Art.* Indianapolis: Bobbs-Merrill, 1968.

Lehman, Peter. "Script/Performance/Text: Performance Theory and Auteur Theory." *Film Reader* 3 (1978): 197–206.

———. "Texas 1868/America 1956." In *Close Viewings: An Anthology of New Film Criticism,* edited by Peter Lehman, 387–415. Tallahassee: Florida State University Press, 1991.

McBride, Joseph, and Michael Wilmington. *John Ford.* New York: Da Capo Press, 1975.

Place, J. A. *The Western Films of John Ford.* Secaucus: Citadel Press, 1974.

NINETEEN

M*A*S*H Notes

Elisabeth Weis

When George S. Kaufman proclaimed that "satire is what closes on Saturday night," he was referring to its ephemeral quality: satire dates quickly. And I would add that political satire dates twice as quickly. Probably because the painful realities it mocks are all too immediate, political satire seems particularly funny while it is fresh. But the intensity of satiric humor is often inversely proportional to its durability. Try looking at the opening monologue from last year's *Tonight Show*. We don't even get the jokes. Or look at any reruns of *Saturday Night Live* that bash then-current presidents. For every political satire that remains funny, there are a dozen that could be called *Saturday Night Dead*.

If satire has a short life span, film is a medium that tends to date almost as quickly. While transcribing a screenplay to film, the camera also records such specifics as hair styles, acting styles, and even cinematographic styles, which permanently fix the film's production in a particular time and place. (Even in historical films, matters of style are kept within the parameters of contemporary fashion—to wit: the stars of *M*A*S*H* were allowed to wear their hair longer than allowed by military regulation for 1950.) By contrast, a play can be updated in performance, through acting style as well as language. Similarly, a novel is regularly transformed by the sensibility of each reader, who supplies much of the mise-en-scène with his or her imagination. But though films are certainly "read" by different viewers in different ways, there is a permanence to the original image that resists reinterpretation.

Hence, as both film and political satire, the 1970 *M*A*S*H* would seem particularly resistant to being remade. Robert Altman's send-up of the American involvement in Vietnam, the military mentality, and the establishment in general, is a movie particularly rooted in the counterculture spirit of its time.

But television is a greedy consumer. So many hours of broadcasting must be produced each day that it acquires properties rapaciously, adapting its varied sources according to its own needs. In a sense television is a gargantuan remaker of texts. It repackages anything from comic strip adventures to home videos for living room consumption. Perhaps it is not surprising, then, that only two years after *M*A*S*H* became the third highest grossing feature film of 1970, the property was remade for television as a situation comedy. What is more surprising is the phenomenal longevity and popularity of a series based on a source that would seem to have offered few elements compatible with standard television practices.

The main reason *M*A*S*H* survived so long is that it underwent constant revision over its eleven seasons (1972–83). In an industry that values predictability, *M*A*S*H* evolved farther from its original form than any other series in television history. In that process it not only revitalized itself but adapted itself to a changing audience. While it never gave up its liberal outlook, the television show became more of a timeless comment on human behavior and less of an overtly political satire rooted in its time. I will discuss a number of factors that influenced *M*A*S*H*'s transformation over its 251 episodes, some of which are unique to *M*A*S*H,* and others of which follow patterns common to most long-running series. One could say that by constantly revising itself, the television series was per se a kind of ongoing remake. At any rate, if we are to study the translation of *M*A*S*H* from film to television, we must also study the continual evolution of the show, since there is a world of difference between the one-hour pilot and the final two-and-a-half-hour episode, a sentimental farewell wrap-up that attracted the largest audience in the history of television to that date.

M*A*S*H originated as a novel that Dr. Richard Hornberger wrote in 1968 under the name of Richard Hooker after serving as a thoracic surgeon in a Mobile Army Surgical Hospital (MASH unit) during the Korean War. The novel was bought for approximately one hundred thousand dollars. It was turned down by fifteen directors before Robert Altman agreed to direct it for Twentieth Century-Fox for a salary of twenty-five thousand dollars (Waters, 48).

The film was extremely popular with the public; it grossed $36.7 million at home (Knight, 82), and it became the first film ever to play twenty-four hours a day in London. It was also admired by industry professionals. It was the first American entry ever to win the Grand Prize at the Cannes International Film Festival and the first American film ever to win Best Picture from the National Society of Film Critics (which had previously favored such films as *Blow-Up* and *Persona*). And the screenplay garnered an

Academy Award for Ring Lardner Jr., who had been blacklisted in the fifties.

The film's style was a revelation. It was the first theatrical film by Altman to manifest the elliptical cutting, the multilayered sound, the refusal to foreground a principal speaker, and the searching camera movements that we think of as the Altman aesthetic. Paradoxically, such a style demands viewer intelligence nearly completely at odds with the oversimplified politics of the film, in which all people are defined by their coolness and the virulence of their railing against establishment rules and regulations. To some extent, there is a connection between form and content: the film is anti-authoritarian, refusing on a stylistic level to assert total control over the viewer. (However, this assertion itself is oversimplified. The case has been made, for example, that Altman's zooms are very controlling [Karp, 25].)

While the film's aesthetic achievements remain impressive, its simplistic attitudes have dated it embarrassingly. Its politics, other than its diatribe against the absurdity of war, seem puerile. The surgeons who are its heroes express themselves in the mode of frat-party antics. Altman seems not only to condone but share their adolescent view of women. For instance, most of the nurses are introduced as they hike up their skirts to get out of a helicopter. Nor are the surgeons much more mature in their relationships with men. Hawkeye and Trapper have all the intolerance of youth: they are equally contemptuous of military martinets, bigots, incompetents, and anyone who believes in God. Those characters who are not hip or cool by the standards of the late sixties are fair targets for ridicule and humiliation. "Cool" could be epitomized by the fact that Hawkeye Pierce (Elliott Gould) has arrived with a jar of olives in his pocket to go with the martini proffered by Trapper John (Donald Sutherland). "Cruel" could be epitomized by the double exposures of Margaret Houlihan (Sally Kellerman) to the public. First, her lovemaking with a married doctor is broadcast over the camp loudspeaker for all to hear. This humiliation is presumably justified by her hypocrisy—her unwillingness to admit to her sexual desire. But then, in order to settle a bet about whether she is a natural blonde, the surgeons reveal her pub(l)ically as she showers. It is a measure of Altman's sensitivity to the situation that he allows the film viewers as well as the diegetical audience to witness her naked humiliation.

The film assumes counterculture values on the part of its audience that we associate with the late sixties. For instance, it exhibits a positive attitude toward drugs. The ubiquitous public address system makes a plea for audience complicity with its several references to stolen amphetamines or the fact of marijuana being declared an illegal substance. Drugs are agents of the good guys, tools for the surgeons in their nonmedical schemes. Hawkeye and Trapper use drugs to induce sleep in a dentist (in an elaborate scheme to persuade him that he is not impotent—or gay; the two seem interchangeably undesirable). They use drugs to knock the opposition out of a crucial football game. And they use drugs to try to keep their Korean houseboy from being drafted.

If the film's irreverent and antiestablishment attitude made it a success with contemporary audiences, it does not retain its hold on the popular imagination today (to judge by a survey of rentals in video stores). By contrast the television show not only did well during its original decade but has kept its mystique in reruns, which consistently outdraw counterprogramming (Waters, 50). Variety regularly wrote articles tracing *M*A*S*H* as a unique phenomenon that in rerun could "attract and hold an audience at any time of the day" (e.g., Knight, 83).

How much of Altman's *M*A*S*H* was retained for television? The basic premise remains the need to act crazy in order to preserve one's sanity. The film's three cool surgeons are reduced to just Hawkeye and Trapper John. Duke, the third, who is exposed as a Southern bigot in the film, is eliminated. His bigotry is instead ascribed to the two-dimensional Major Frank Burns, who now is not only a pompous zealot, as in the film, but takes on every possible negative (read square) characteristic.

Of the cast, only Gary Burghoff, as Radar O'Reilly, the clairvoyant company clerk, was retained among the principals. (Two minor players had also been retained but were eliminated during the first season: G. Wood, as General Hammond and Timothy Brown as Spearchucker Jones, who was cut when it was learned that there had been no black surgeons in Korea.) However, the personality of the film's Radar had barely been developed. The television character is a cuddly, naive, kind-hearted kid who sleeps with a teddy bear and is hardly allowed to grow up during his seven years' tenure.

One production decision both preserved some of the free-flowing character of the film and allowed for more aesthetic expressiveness than had been seen before in a situation comedy: the decision to shoot not on tape with three simultaneous cameras but rather on film, using the one-camera system. A previously unheard-of rehearsal day was also scheduled before each shoot, a measure that added to the ensemble of the acting.

The film's gore in the operating room and irreverence toward authority are kept but toned down for living room reception. The caustic outlook is mellowed considerably. Perhaps typical of the softening is the treatment of the opening theme song, "Suicide Is Painless," which is retained but without the lyrics, which might offend delicate American sensibilities.

The two stills of eating scenes that accompany this article are meant to illustrate this shift in emphasis. The first is from the film's "Last Supper" scene, in which a dentist prepares to commit suicide as several bystanders serenade him with the "Suicide Is Painless" ballad. (See figure 39.) By contrast, the television still depicts what could be called Radar's First Supper after a tonsillectomy. In one of the last episodes before Radar leaves the

Figure 39. The "Last Supper" scene in Robert Altman's *M*A*S*H* mixes parody and irreverence in a knowing "wink" at the audience (1970).

show ("None Like It Hot," season seven), the doctors go to considerable trouble to get Radar (and themselves) his favorite flavor of ice cream. (See figure 40.) The Last Supper sequence, with its irreverent references to suicide and its religious iconography would have been as improbable on television as the strawberry ice cream episode would have been in the film, which has little appetite for sweetness.

In other words, though the television series adopted the characters, the situation, and the antiwar stance of the film, the values, and the tone shifted dramatically. To be sure, some character virtues remain consistent throughout the film and television versions; in both media the good guys are defined by: 1) their competence as doctors, 2) their tolerance toward the Other (usually a Korean peasant or a black soldier), and 3) their sense of humor. But as for personal style, there is almost a 180-degree reversal. The coolness of the movie surgeon heroes includes an emotional distance— from their own feelings as well as those of others. By contrast, the television episodes valorize those characters who are most sensitive and vulnerable. The change is gradual. It is already discernible in the difference between film and tv pilot. But for reasons I will discuss below, the shift occurs mainly during the latter half of the series.

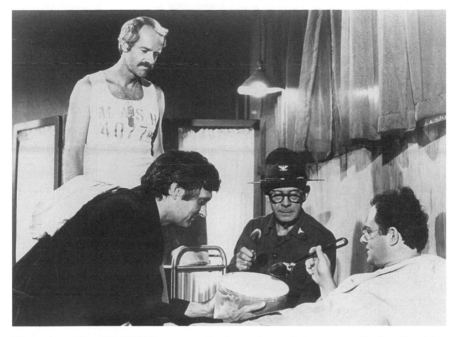

Figure 40. The *M*A*S*H* surgeons feed strawberry ice cream to Radar after his tonsillectomy in the popular television series.

In short, the television producers of *M*A*S*H* were able not only to adapt the original movie to their needs but to reformulate the program over the years so as to emphasize character development. Because of the flexibility of the format the series maintained both its quality and its popularity. When it went off the air in 1983 it was the third-most-watched program—after *60 Minutes* and *Dallas*. What creative, economic, and political factors enabled *M*A*S*H* to adapt and survive?

NETWORK POLICY

M*A*S*H was produced by Fox Television (it was standard practice in a film contract that television rights went to the studio that made a film). Its creators (I shall use the terms "creators" and "producers" interchangeably because nearly all of the principal personnel worked as producers, writers, and directors) brought it to CBS, which had just begun televising the two other most intelligent and revolutionary sitcoms of the seventies, *All in the Family* (1971–79) and *The Mary Tyler Moore Show* (1970–77).

Though more open-minded than the other major networks, CBS still had its rules. In his definitive study of television comedy, *Comic Visions,* David Marc cites a CBS market research study that concluded that the three kinds of characters Americans would not watch on sitcoms were women who were divorced, men who wore mustaches, and anyone from New York City (Marc, 167). In such a climate it is amazing what *M*A*S*H* got away with. One battle that *M*A*S*H*'s creative team did not win involved the laugh track. Despite the *M*A*S*H* producers' vigorous resistance to canned laughter, CBS retained it except in most of the operating room scenes. (However, the laugh track was mixed at a lower level than usual relative to the rest of the sound track.)

CBS clearly felt some ambivalence toward its new product. One measure of a network's support of a new program is its willingness to sustain low ratings to see if the program will catch hold. The network did agree (after sustained lobbying on the part of the show's creators) to continue the show for a second season despite the fact that *M*A*S*H* had finished in the bottom half of the prime-time ratings during its first season. However, CBS may have been responsible for *M*A*S*H*'s slow start in the first place: they had slotted it for viewing at 8:00 P.M. on Sundays, which was a "family hour" slot. But once the network executives did make a commitment to *M*A*S*H* for a second season, they gave it their best slot: 8:30 P.M. Saturday, between *All in the Family* and *Mary Tyler Moore. M*A*S*H* moved up to fourth place and stayed in the top twenty shows for a decade, despite being bounced around to eight different time slots.

Perhaps an indication of industrywide ambivalence toward the program was its results in the competition for Emmy Awards. *M*A*S*H* was nominated for a large number of Emmy Awards (ninety-nine) but won only fourteen, despite its reputation within the industry as one of the best shows on television. *M*A*S*H* producers have said that the relative paucity of these awards (it won many other awards based on audience popularity) reflected the inability of the industry to deal with something uncategorizable. *M*A*S*H* was pigeonholed as a sitcom. However, the producers' favorite episodes were often their most serious in tone, and it was these shows they submitted for nomination (Prelutsky, 19).

GENRE EXPECTATIONS

To some extent, genre expectations will militate against any radical change in a television series. From the start *M*A*S*H* did not fit into the genres of its closest predecessors, the service comedy or the doctor series. It was indeed a situation comedy, but as I have just suggested, eventually *M*A*S*H* remade itself into a genre unique on television. In an industry that banks on reliability and predictability, *M*A*S*H* confounded expectations. Although the series never entirely dropped its dependence on silly sitcom plot devices (e.g., convincing Frank that there is gold to be found in the local hills—"Major Fred C. Dobbs," season one), *M*A*S*H* was what its creators called a "dramedy" (in a documentary called "Making *M*A*S*H*"). Its creators had insisted that the war not serve just as a background for high jinks (as a Nazi POW camp had for *Hogan's Heroes*). During the first season they battled with CBS over one episode in particular ("Sometimes You Hear the Bullet") in which a sympathetic character, an old friend of Hawkeye, dies on the operating table. When the episode aired it became clear that the audience would accept a mixture of reality and comedy previously unheard of on a television sitcom. As recently as 1967 *Bonnie and Clyde* had caused a critical uproar with its mixture of comedy and violence. Its popularity with movie-theater audiences may have helped pave the way for American audiences to accept a mixed genre on television.

POPULARITY

Thus the contract with the audience that usually obtains with sitcoms and other genres was allowed to be modified. It was Alda's belief that once the program gained its viewers' trust and affection, the show could then deviate from rigid expectations: "The audience made a pact with us. We could be as imaginative and exploratory as we wanted . . . because they knew we would never be wanton with them" (Corliss, 65). As the program became a hit, this popularity gained for its producers unprecedented freedom from the network as well as the audience (which was light-years ahead of the network executives). According to Larry Gelbart, "As our ratings climbed, corporate resistance fell. . . . I am convinced that we achieved a creative freedom unheard of in the medium before or since" (Gelbart, 25). The program was equally popular with young and old, men and women (Dougherty, 8). Besides being well written, well acted, and funny, it evidently had something for everyone in the audience, including farce and feeling, buffoonery and literary allusions. The character of Radar, for example, was designed for his appeal to children and older women.

Thus, the audience's loyal acceptance of whatever *M*A*S*H* dished out allowed changes of tone; it became possible to drop completely any pretense of being a comedy for all or part of some episodes. The show's creators also experimented with formal innovations. As often as not, the structure abandoned the classical sitcom formula in which the "situation" is disturbed but the order is resolved within twenty-four minutes. Indeed, there are any number of episodes that have no plot at all. One frequent substitute format is the "letter home" (written by any of the principals, or even a visiting shrink) in which a voice-over provides some narrative structure.

Another episode ("Hawkeye," season four) consists solely of a monologue, in which Pierce, who has sustained a head wound, keeps talking to a family of noncomprehending Koreans so as not to lose consciousness. (This episode is one of the few that were allowed to be aired without a laugh track.) The elegance of this episode is that it takes to an extreme one of Hawkeye's best-known tendencies: volubility. His character has a wisecrack for every occasion, a love of wordplay and alliteration, and a tendency to deliver orations on any occasion (hence the ode to the thumb in "Hawkeye" or the ode to the "tushie" in "Dear Ma" [season four]).

Perhaps the most acclaimed episode is "The Interview," an episode shot in black and white in which the characters are interviewed as if for a stateside newsreel. Although the writers made a number of suggestions, much of this episode was improvised by the actors, who by this time (season four) had become greatly involved with the development of their characters.

Another deviation from convention was the "Dreams" episode (season eight), which ventures into surrealistic representations of the characters' anxieties as they take cat-naps during an operating marathon.

If the above experiments delve into the feelings of the medics, several other experiments emphasize the ordeals of the patients. "Point of View" (year seven) is filmed entirely from the literal perspective of a wounded soldier who cannot talk. "Life Time" (season eight) superimposes a clock on bottom right of the image as we go through the twenty-four minute rescue with a wounded soldier who risks paralysis if surgery isn't undergone within twenty minutes.

WRITERS AND CREATIVE PERSONNEL

All told, the series had seventeen regular writers in addition to any number of freelancers. But one can reasonably divide the series roughly into two eras that match the sensibilities of the two men who perhaps exerted the greatest creative influence: Larry Gelbart, who wrote ninety-seven episodes (and produced and directed many others), and Alan Alda, who wrote and directed over forty episodes.

Larry Gelbart, who was brought in to write the pilot and who stayed for four seasons, was considered the most brilliant writer in the industry (Knight, 83). He has written for television (including *Your Show of Shows*), Broadway (including *A Funny Thing Happened on the Way to the Forum* and the recent *City of Angels*), and film (including *Tootsie*). Judging from the episodes on which he is given writing credit, his imprint on *M*A*S*H* includes: 1) hilarity (he was by consensus the funniest writer the show ever had

[Swerdlow, 6]), 2) a love of formal experimentation, 3) a political edge, and 4) a tendency to prefer sketch formats to dramatic unity.

The departure of Gelbart after four seasons was one of the catalysts for changing the show's sensibility. According to producer (and, often, writer) Gene Reynolds, "The tone of the comedy had to change when Larry left, because we just couldn't equal his comic genius. We were forced to explore other areas, areas that he had not had to bother with, because he was so gifted, so skillful in straight comedy" (Reiss, 116).

Gelbart always said that the character who represented his values and mind-set was Hawkeye. By the time Gelbart left the show, Hawkeye was universally considered the heart of the series. By this time the distinction between the personas of Hawkeye and Alan Alda was getting blurred. Alda was as much a galvanizing force behind the scenes as his Hawkeye was on screen (Waters, 48). Not surprisingly Alda's writing contributions as well as his conscious and unconscious identification with the character he played tended to make Hawkeye both more sensitive and more complex.

Over the years Hawkeye becomes less of a drinker and womanizer and more actively compassionate. His greater sensitivity (as well as the increased introspection of the other characters) was generally attributed to Alda's own self-image. Indeed, as David Marc suggests, "Psychological introspection established itself as M*A*S*H's primary text during the late seventies" (199).

Although it would be impossible to prove the direct links between Alda the person and Alda the writer, one can infer a certain amount from interviews and credits. In 1974 he told the *New York Times*, "All we're attempting is to deal with reality with a sense of humor, to find the fun of behavior and character. I think that's where the best of TV is moving—humor with feeling. . . . To me, only the things that really count are funny, not those old earthshaking questions like should sonny boy tell dad he bent a fender on the family car" (Berkvist, 19). Episodes that appear to reflect Alda's sensibility tend toward: 1) introspection, 2) valuing vulnerability as a character trait, 3) sanctimoniousness, and 4) formal experimentation. Alda's activism as a feminist and his love of pranks also seem to have permeated the show.

Despite individual sensibilities, producers, writers, and performers were apparently pretty much in sync; they were united against a common enemy. Their frustration at having to fight the networks was transposed via the scripts into annoyance with army intransigence. Gelbart once wrote that "[a]lthough turning out a mini-movie on a three-day shooting schedule . . . , battling compromise and complacency all the way, is not of course, in any sense as dangerous or serious as risking one's life in combat, the pressures of making the series gave those of us responsible for it something of the sense of madness, the feelings of frustration and fatigue shared by the surgeons and nurses of the 4077th" (Gelbart, 26). So, for example, when the network censors made the writers remove the word "virgin" from the dialogue, they mischievously introduced a soldier in the next episode from the Virgin Islands (Kalter, 29). This petty kind of reprisal is typical of the rebellion against authority that takes place within the plot.

SUBJECT MATERIAL

In 1974 Gelbart and Reynolds had gone to Korea, visited the MASH unit that inspired Hornberger's book, and interviewed about 150 doctors who had served in frontline hospitals (Darrach, 102). They claimed to have interviewed there and later at home nearly every doctor who was in Korea. Reynolds estimated that these stories formed the basis of some 60 percent of the episodes dealing with military or medical incidents (Corliss, 65). Eventually this source of inspiration had to dry up.

Thus, the combat-hospital situation per se had been exhausted as a source of humor. Gelbart said he left the show at the point when he could no longer come up with new story lines. Considering how long the show had been running, and how few chances there were to expand the characters' experiences (given their restricted lives on the military base), the easiest way to expand the material was to deepen the characters.

And so *M*A*S*H* became increasingly a comedy of character. Linked to this shift of emphasis from situation to character comedy was the emphasis on probing psyches. Conveniently, the two actors (Larry Linville and McLean Stevenson) who played types least capable of changing left the show. These two-dimensional doctors were replaced by characters who were not as silly but were more complex. Most of the remaining principal characters were allowed to evolve. For instance, Corporal Klinger eventually gives up trying to get out of the army on a "Section Eight" by wearing women's clothes.

The greatest change is on the part of the head nurse, Margaret "Hot Lips" Houlihan. Her gradual transition from sex object-martinet to sympathetic woman can be traced through a series of critical episodes. Her first treatment as a human being occurs in season two ("Hot Lips and Empty Arms"), which was written by Linda Bloodworth and Mary Kay Place. Her loneliness and vulnerability are explored in "The Nurses" (season five—also written by Bloodworth). Seasons five and six see Major Houlihan through big changes. She gives up Frank and gets engaged, married, and divorced by season seven and is allowed to grow from her pain. "Hot Lips" is by now called "Margaret" and is treated with respect.

The most striking episode in this regard is "Comrades in Arms" (written by Alda, season six), where Houlihan and Hawkeye, trapped and terrified by gunfire, make love. Although they do not continue the affair after that night, they are no longer antagonists. Indeed, toward the end of the series' run, the only way to introduce antagonists into the script was to import personnel (like the paranoid Colonel Flagg) from off base.

INFLUENCE OF THE ACTORS

On a long-running series there is inevitably a push from serious actors to get meaty parts—to expand their characters' emotional range. On the M*A*S*H set, push did not come to shove. Script development was a matter of ongoing collaboration between writers and players. In addition, most of the principals wrote and directed some episodes.

A second way in which actors influenced the show was unwitting: the writers often wrote the actors' pastimes or behavioral tics into their parts. Hence, David Ogden Stiers's love of classical music is a defining characteristic of Major Winchester. After Loretta Swit took up yoga, Margaret can be found practicing it on-screen. Hunnicut uses his real daughter's real name in referring to B. J.'s baby. Alda wrote and directed an episode "Inga" (season seven) in which he admittedly explored his feelings of being threatened by smart women.

After battles with the military were played down as plot devices and human relationships were emphasized, the group dynamics of the cast was sometimes introduced into the scripts. Thus, when the writers noticed that Gary Burghoff and Loretta Swit were treating veteran actor Harry Morgan as a father figure, they wrote that relationship explicitly into the script for the same actors (Darrach, 103). Of course, there was not always a correspondence between life and art. Gary Burghoff, however cuddly as Radar on-screen, did not fit into the congenial atmosphere of the set (Prelutsky, 21).

Yet another parallel between life and the show was the use of elaborate practical jokes to relieve the arduousness of fourteen-hour days on cramped or cold sets (Kalter, 179). And episodes depicting the departure of characters like the original commander, Henry Blake, were evidently full of genuine tears as the actors played their farewell scenes.

But probably the most extreme case of personal dynamics influencing the direction of the series was the fact that the writers became personally much closer to Alan Alda than to Wayne Rogers. Originally Trapper John and Hawkeye were supposed to have had equally developed parts. But as the writers drew closer to Alda, they developed his role more fully. Wayne Rogers finally got so frustrated at playing second fiddle that he sued the company and left (Swerdlow, 6).

REPLACEMENT OF CAST MEMBERS

Until *M*A*S*H,* industry wisdom had had it that you could not successfully replace more than one principal on a sitcom. Yet *M*A*S*H* replaced three principal cast members. In each case the replacements portrayed more rounded characters. Two transitions occurred at the end of the third season with the departures of Wayne Rogers and McLean Stevenson.

The trade-in of Wayne Rogers's Trapper John for Mike Farrell's B. J. Hunnicut was a shift from a more caustic character to a sweeter guy—one could say from Wayne Rogers to Mister Rogers (B. J.'s overriding attribute is his longing for his family). For the most part, Trapper is a boyish prankster, a drinker, and a womanizer, in short, the character most resembling the doctors in Altman's film. However, as early as the second season, Trapper John is allowed to serve as the center of an episode ("Kim"), when he becomes fond of an abandoned Korean boy who has been found by the MASH outfit. Shortly after he gets his wife's permission to adopt the boy, the child is discovered standing in the middle of an American minefield. The show suddenly shifts from tenderness to tension as Trapper risks his life (metaphorically, love is a minefield!) to rescue the boy. It is useful to compare this episode with "B. J. Papa San" (season seven), in which B. J. becomes a surrogate father to a local Korean family. Whereas the earlier story is played mostly for suspense, the latter story emphasizes the psychology behind B. J.'s behavior.

Oddly enough, the Trapper character got to evolve offscreen. In 1979 a new Trapper, played by Pernell Roberts, reappeared as an older and wiser figure starring in his own spin-off (*Trapper John, M.D.*) This avuncular incarnation of Trapper was chief of staff at a San Francisco hospital, where his wisdom was counterpointed by an idealistic but impatient younger surgeon.

The end of *M*A*S*H*'s third season also saw the departure of McLean Stevenson, who portrayed Henry Blake, a commander whose heart is in the right place but whose mind and body are always several steps behind. He remains a shallow figure whose goofiness in all respects except medicine is visualized by an ever-present cap bestrewn with fishing lures. Henry Blake is not really treated as a serious character until his offscreen death. "Abyssinia, Henry" ends with the announcement that on his way home his plane has been shot down.

Stevenson was replaced by Harry Morgan, who plays Colonel Potter, a career army (former cavalry) colonel whose quaintness is defined by the number of ways in which he can refer to horse dung. Potter's arrival marks a pronounced shift in tone, as he is the first regular army character who is also a regular guy.

Finally, at the beginning of the sixth season there was a change in the chief antagonist. Frank Burns (Larry Linville) had been a cartoon figure with no redeeming qualities. Stories involving Burns come the closest to traditional witless sitcom. The typical *M*A*S*H* episode interwove three plots, with the Frank Burns plot nearly always providing broad comic relief and visual slapstick even if the other two plots were more serious. As an inhuman and inhumane character Burns was an easy target. He was replaced by a character inspired by William F. Buckley (Kalter, 117), the pompous Charles Emerson Winchester III, played by David Ogden Stiers. Winchester has the usual obsessiveness of a comic figure (his snobbishness) but is allowed to be a good doctor and a worthy opponent to the prank-loving Hawkeye. Winchester is also allowed to have occasional moments of generosity and compassion. While there is no doubt that the shift from Frank to Charles resulted in fewer laughs, I happen to greatly prefer the latter. It is a shift from slapstick to wit as a means of battle.

Thus virtually all the replacements of characters in *M*A*S*H* also precipitated a change in type of comedy. The switch from Burns to Winchester was from slapstick to wit; from Colonel Blake to Colonel Potter was from laughing at the former's incompetence to sharing the latter's sardonic sense of humor. And the replacement of Trapper by Hunnicut brought a transition from malicious to gentle humor.

CHANGES IN THE POLITICAL CLIMATE

M*A*S*H's producers met more resistance from the network to its handling issues like adultery and homosexuality than to its antiwar stance. One can make the case, as the producers did, that *M*A*S*H* was neither about Korea nor Vietnam but about the absurdities of the military mentality and all war—especially in regard to the futility of sewing up wounded soldiers so that they could be sent back to the front. Nevertheless, many of the points about the war take particular advantage of the parallels between the situations in Korea and Vietnam. For instance, "Yessir, That's Our Baby" (season eight) raises the problems of Amerasian babies fathered by Western soldiers and left with their Korean mothers, who find their children are outcasts.

The series never lets the viewer forget for long that the war is being fought on the homes and farms of innocent peasant families. Koreans are portrayed most often as orphans, wives, or dispossessed farmers. In addition, some of the episodes deal with issues of cultural difference as Frank regularly misinterprets local customs. Indeed, characters can be measured by their sensitivity to local people. Radar is the only principal who speaks Korean. In the final episode, Corporal Klinger marries a Korean woman.

It is hard to gauge to what extent the series anticipated or reflected the public's growing disenchantment with the fighting in Vietnam. Undoubtedly, the references to pointless slaughter in the Far East lost some of their edge after season five, when Vietnam was no longer a front-page story.

As the nation's interests turned inward, so did the show. The tendency toward introspection of the main characters paralleled the increased self-examination and narcissism of the early eighties. As *Newsweek* put it, "With a canny eye on a new generation of viewers, the series stepped off its leftist, issue-oriented, anti-establishment platform and took on the introspective tone of the Me Decade" (Waters, 50).

One certain parallel between the series and the national psyche was the heightened sensitivity to women's issues. Early episodes regularly exploit the nurses as convenient sex objects. In "Radar's Report" (season two), Hawkeye falls for and proposes to a nurse who then rejects him because she just isn't interested in marriage. However, this is still a story about Hawkeye's feelings, and the nurse's point of view is not examined.

Eventually, homebodies B. J. and Colonel Potter replace womanizers Trapper John and Henry Blake, and Hawkeye stops his inveterate skirt chasing. Perhaps the most direct lecture on feminist pride comes when Nurse Kelly, played by Kellye Nakahara, a regular irregular on the series, is finally foregrounded long enough to proclaim with conviction that she is adorable despite her unglamorous appearance.

ICONIZATION OF THE CHARACTERS

Because *M*A*S*H* revealed so many facets of its principals' personalities, it followed that the audience would feel more attached to them than to most television characters. It also followed that this attachment would adhere to the actors playing them as well. In 1980, a *Ladies Home Journal* survey found that Alan Alda was tied with Sally Field (who was playing a flying nun) as the most trusted personality on television (White, 27). In 1983, the last year of the series, Alda had the highest male TVQ (popularity rating) in the country (Romano, 12-I). Clearly this is a case of viewers confusing characters with the actors who play them. The audience's affection extended to the cast as a whole. In the late 1980s, IBM capitalized on nostalgia for the cast when it reassembled most of the *M*A*S*H* stars in a series of computer commercials. The status of the *M*A*S*H* compound as a national treasure was acknowledged when the Smithsonian placed parts of its sets on exhibition.

Sentimentality for the series was paralleled by sentimentality within the scripts. As *M*A*S*H* shifted from satire to character exploration, its tone shifted from hard-edged liberalism to sentimental liberalism. The final, two-and-a-half-hour episode was an unabashed tear bath. To some extent the series may well have been responding to the political climate in the country as a whole. That is, the growing sentimentality of *M*A*S*H* may mirror the change in the national psyche from post-Watergate cynicism to Reagan-era soft-headedness.

But I suggest that the sentimentalization would have happened in any era. Alda-Hawkeye had become a national treasure. And when a serialized cultural icon becomes a national treasure it goes soft.

To wit: Mickey Mouse, originally a bit of a dirty old mouse (see "Plane Crazy," 1928), became as clean as a cub scout as his popularity rose. Thereupon the Disney company created Donald Duck to play antagonist in the thirties (see "The Band Concert," 1935). Soon Donald mellowed and acquired three cute nephews plus a new antagonist, his Uncle Scrooge. On television Archie Bunker remained a bigot in later years, but he too mellowed considerably by the time *All in the Family* became *Archie's Place*. At the end of *Murphy Brown*'s 1991–92 season, that feisty, female curmudgeon became a single mother. Dan Quayle turned her into an instant icon for the poverty of family values. But what we actually saw in the final episode was a touching endorsement of motherhood—Murphy croons "You make me feel like a natural woman" as a lullaby to her newborn son.

With Murphy as a mother, the show has vacillated between political cynicism and domestic sentimentality. Murphy has indeed become a character very much in the mold of Alda's Hawkeye Pierce. Perhaps the reason both characters (and therefore their shows) have touched something in the American psyche is that they each created a persona that many viewers like to think is their self-image: the tough but tender American, who just happens to have better writers than we do.

Thanks to Lucy Fischer, Krin Gabbard, and Andy Horton for reading the manuscript for this essay and making helpful suggestions.

WORKS CITED

Berkvist, Robert. "*M*A*S*H* Is His Passion." *New York Times*, May 19, 1974, sec. 2, p. 19.

Cooke, Alistair. *M*A*S*H* Was One of a Kind." *TV Guide*, February 12, 1983, 14–21.

Corliss, Richard. "*M*A*S*H*, You Were a SM*A*S*H." *Time*, February 28, 1983, 64–66.

Darrach, Brad, with Suzanne Adelson. "*M*A*S*H*." *People*, March 7, 1983, 100–103.

Dougherty, Philip H. "Advertising: Hot-Selling *M*A*S*H* Air Spots," *New York Times*, February 28, 1983, p. D8.

Gelbart, Larry. "Its Creator Says Hail and Farewell to *M*A*S*H*," *New York Times*, February 27, 1983, pp. B25–26.

Henry, William A. III. "*M*A*S*H*." *Horizon*, September 1978, 84–87.

Kalter, Suzy. *The Complete Book of M*A*S*H*. New York: Harry Abrams, 1984.

Karp, Alan. *The Films of Robert Altman*. Metuchen, N.J.: Scarecrow Press, 1981.

Knight, Bob. "Something Clearly Out of the Ordinary." *Variety,* February 23, 1983, 82, 88.

McFadden, Robert. "*M*A*S*H* Farewells Mix Fun and Nostalgia." *New York Times,* March 1, 1983, pp. B1, 4.

Marc, David. *Comic Visions: Television Comedy and American Culture.* Boston: Unwin Hyman, 1989.

Prelutsky, Burt. "The Troops Scatter—but the Memories Linger." *TV Guide,* February 12, 1983, 18–21.

Reiss, David. *M*A*S*H.* New York: Macmillan, 1983.

Romano, Carlin. "Mustering Out with *M*A*S*H.*" *Philadelphia Inquirer,* February 27, 1983, p. 12-I.

Swerdlow, Joel. "The Staggering Success Story of those Zany Cut-Ups from the 4077." *Washington Post,* April 27, 1980, p. M6.

Waters, Harry F., with George Hackett. "Farewell to the *M*A*S*H* Gang." *Newsweek,* February 28, 1983, 44–50.

White, Diane. "*M*A*S*H* Is More Than a Laugh Track." *Dial,* January 1981, 26–27.

Afterword: Rethinking Remakes

Leo Braudy

"Remake" is a term imported to academia from movie journalism and the movie business. It carries with it the atmospheric shorthand of deal meetings and script conferences. But is "remake" a useful interpretive or theoretical category? Does it tell us anything more than what it says on its face? If it is useful, what would be the most interesting ways to apply it?

More obviously than other forms of art, the remake—like its close kin, the adaptation and the sequel—is a species of interpretation. In pursuit of its nature, virtually all of the essays in this volume therefore emphasize questions of interpretive power and authority, legitimate (if you think it works) and illegitimate (if you think it doesn't). Depending on the different perspectives of these critics, the remake can exist anywhere on an intertextual continuum from allusions in specific lines, individual scenes, and camera style to the explicit patterning of an entire film on a previous exemplar.[1]

The remake summons up both the internal and the external history of film in its relation to past films and past audiences: a film was made and now it is to be remade, revised, or even extended. Along with this invocation of history, there is also often an implicit claim that the intertextual processes of film are aesthetically unique. Both film remakes and successive productions of a play are certainly marked by the era of their making. But different productions of a play, even across the centuries, rarely question the formal processes of theater history. The remade play is often referred to as a revival. Whatever changes in presentation have occurred—if the setting of *Measure for Measure* is shifted from Renaissance Vienna to Freud's Vienna—the purpose is still to revive. While the play thus remains defined almost entirely by its original text, the remade film is less frequently an homage or revival than an effort to supplant its predecessor entirely, as

John Huston's *The Maltese Falcon* supplants the previous two versions and, to a certain extent, the original novel.

Mentioning a novel brings up the other aspect of the remake—the external—in which the kinship with adaptation is stronger. If the invocation of remake is to imply something more than a tracing of local intertextual detail, it must make some claim to relevance not just within cinema but across the relation between cinema and the other narrative arts. An individual remake, like *The Maltese Falcon,* may situate itself historically in relation to previous films as well as to previous literature. The critical category of the remake should be relevant to both.

Although remakes thus derive from and are validated by history, the most apparent reason to remake is economic—the remake as "presold" property. But to conclude that remakes happen primarily for financial reasons obscures the way in which the remaker must also believe that this particular story still inspires what Ira Konigsberg here calls "another attempt to get it right." Beyond the specific circumstances of imitation and recreation, there must therefore also be a basic intuition that the audience will continue to buy this story in its new incarnation because the underlying fable is still compelling.

Such an assumption closely connects remakes to the processes of myth, of which the various avatars of Robin Hood, Dracula, Sherlock Holmes are only a few of the most obvious examples. At the 1992 Modern Language Association session on remakes, David Newman, the co-scriptwriter of *Superman* and *Superman II* and *III,* forcefully insisted that in those films he and his wife, Leslie, were only partially influenced by the history of the comic strip character, his friends, and his adversaries. Instead, they used the original as the keynote to a virtually Jungian narrative medley and allowed its theme to invoke a variety of myths and stories (even seemingly contradictory ones) to which the original version could resonate.

The importance of historical and cultural context was upheld at that session by both Robert Eberwein and Krin Gabbard, who have contributed essays to this volume. But they argued not so much against Newman's mythic reading as they did against a purely formal one, in the same way that Gabbard's essay favors Barbara Herrnstein Smith's view over Seymour Chatman's on the relative importance of intertextual versus contextual readings.

Yet Eberwein and Gabbard diverged, as their essays do here, on the issue of originality. Eberwein's argument for the determinative importance of historical context coincides with his effort to undermine the idea that there is any original—or at least an original with a fixed meaning—to which a remake refers and in terms of which it must be judged. Although just as committed to a primarily contextual reading, Gabbard is much more intent on finding an originatory text against which later examples should be measured. Extending Michael Rogin's analysis of blackface in American drama, he focuses on *The Jazz Singer* as a prime, even unique, source for biopics in which the main character embodies a conflict between his show business aspirations and his ethnic roots. All of these, he argues, should be called remakes—not just those obviously descended from the original *Jazz Singer* but also others (like *The Benny Goodman Story* and *La Bamba*) that share similar narrative elements.

The question of history is therefore also a question of continuity and similarity. Whether the general emphasis is on formal, historical, or mythic elements, several of the essays here—including those by Eberwein, Gabbard, Harvey Greenberg, Andrew Horton, and others—stress the mediating perspective of the psychoanalytic, specifically the male generational patterns of Freudianism. Greenberg and Gabbard both sketch remake genealogies whose oedipal patterns are potentially analogous to cinematic (and to a certain extent social) history. But once again originality is at issue. The oedipal format, whether invoked literally or metaphorically, can hardly remain neutral. The central issue seems to be whether it implies either the superiority of the original—or its necessary supersession. Greenberg for one, as perhaps befits a practicing analyst, explicitly says that remakes are invariably inferior to their originals.[2]

Eberwein's kind of historicism emphasizes instead a deoedipalizing urge that has been called characteristic of postmodernist critical strategy. He denies that any text has priority merely becomes it comes first, and emphasizes instead the many ways the audience and history remake or reconstrue that text. As David Wills remarks about Jim McBride's remake of Godard's *Breathless,* "There can never be a faithful remake . . . because there can never have been a simple original." Some writers connect this opportunistic revisionism and appropriation to the processes of postmodernism, although it was the arch-modernist poet T. S. Eliot, rather than the ur-postmodernist filmmaker Jean-Luc Godard, who first laid down the credo: "Immature poets imitate; mature poets steal."

Once history or even sequence enters the field, originality or the original becomes a central question. "Original" of course has the double meaning of both unprecedented and basic. In 1759 Edward Young, initiating the modern preoccupation with aesthetic originality with *Conjectures on Original Composition,* asked the question, "Born originals, how comes it to pass that we die copies?" To be in history is in a sense to be remade, to be copied. Jorge Luis Borges's "Pierre Menard, Author of the Quixote" is frequently invoked in these essays as a classic of meta-remaking. But it should be remembered that the heart of Pierre's remaking is to recopy Don Quixote word for word. The language, the chapter divisions, the punctuation, everything is the same. Only the historical moment has changed, and that, according to Borges, makes the text completely different.

To frame the tension between originality and history, varying theories and metaphors are possible. Luca Somigli's essay on comics intriguingly formulates the question in terms of the problematic status of the original in translation theory. Chris Holmlund suggests the analogy between celluloid and plastic surgery (which might make *Frankenstein* more an ur-text of remaking than *Dracula*). Peter Lehman finds inspiration in Nelson Goodman's distinction between the "autographic" arts (like painting), in which the original has a special value, and the "allographic" (like music), in which there is no significant distinction between the original and a copy.

But just as the text exists in history, so does the audience. David Newman can detail the many stories he and Leslie Newman drew upon to create their scripts. But we need to distinguish between stories that the audience truly savors and stories that are merely opportunities for those whose greatest pleasure is to catch allusions and write articles about their discoveries. Similarly, reading Gabbard's intriguing foray into the oedipal structuring of generational narrative, I wonder why he stops with *The Jazz Singer* as the progenitor text? Why not trace the line back in intellectual and psychological history to John Locke's argument for a paternal and parental authority to replace the patriarchal power of the monarch? It is, after all, the generative political theory for the founding of the United States, and a pattern that makes its way into many American stories long before that of Jakie Rabinowitz. Why, in other words, pick on *The Jazz Singer*, or *Invasion of the Body Snatchers*, or *Superman*, when these metaphors are embedded in the history and culture of this self-made and self-remade country?

If the intertextual-mythic approach has the problem of knowing where to stop in its search for forebears, the contextual-social construction approach threatens to dissolve the individual work in the same cultural soup that seeps into everything else. Just as every narrative invokes other stories and every new work is a rereading of the past, every audience brings its own context to what it sees—coming upon each film through a web of significant metaphors, images, semiotic fields, and preexisting tales.

What, then, makes the situation of the remake different from that of any other film—or any other cultural production? What is distinctive about the remake as a film form, and how might it be distinguished from genre and adaptation? All these essays have acute things to say about the particular remakes they consider and often about remakes in general. But I miss a theory of significant meaning that would allow us to say which comparisons are central and which are clever but finally local insights.

Ira Konigsberg's essay on *Dracula* suggests the affinity of the remake with genre at large. He complicates the distinction between the intertextual and the contextual views of change by suggesting that similar stories are not so much retold for a new period, but that the new period allows another step in what is otherwise an internal evolution of the story. In this spirit, Krin Gabbard asks us to consider a television version of *The Jazz Singer* to be a remake of the original, while the essays by Elisabeth Weis on the evolution of *M*A*S*H* from film to television, by Peter Lehman on *Stagecoach* from film to radio, and Luca Somigli on comics afford a similarly healthy undermining of cinematic exceptionalism.

Their discussions indicate the way the concept of remake can become independent of medium, without even the underlying story necessary to the mythic-intertextual assumption. Is it more interesting, in other words, to consider Fritz Lang's *The Human Beast* a remake of Jean Renoir's *La Bête Humaine* than to consider both as remakes of Zola's novel? Are James Whale's *Frankenstein* and Tod Browning's *Dracula* originatory texts for the many versions that follow, or are they themselves remakes of the preceding plays, which are in turn remakes of the original novels of Mary Shelley and Bram Stoker? And what are we to conclude when W. R. Burnett's novel *The Asphalt Jungle* is first made "straight" into a crime film and then remade as a western (*Badlanders*, 1958), a caper film (*Cairo*, 1963), and a blaxploitation film (*Cool Breeze*, 1972)?

Such examples impel me to wonder if remake might with more clarity and cogency be distinguished from adaptation and then treated as a subcategory of genre, perhaps as Umberto Eco has sought to distinguish seriality from repetition. Later *Frankenstein*s and *Dracula*s are conceivably remakes, for example, but all share elements of plot, character, mood, theme, motif that we usually refer to as horror.

The tentative formulation these essays inspire is that the remake resides at the intersection of the genetic and the generic codes. In even the most debased version, it is a meditation on the continuing historical relevance (economic, cultural, psychological) of a particular narrative. A remake is thus always concerned with what its makers and (they hope) its audiences consider to be unfinished cultural business, unrefinable and perhaps finally unassimilable material that remains part of the cultural dialogue—not until it is finally given definitive form, but until it is no longer compelling or interesting.

The remake is intriguing because it intensifies basic critical conflicts between the intertextuality of film meaning and its contextuality, between the uses of taxonomy in grouping films and the renewed look at the individual text, between artistic intention as a gesture of originality and artistic intention as a gesture of mediation. It is suggestive that the various versions of *Dracula*, say, including the recent one directed by Francis Coppola, flirt with the question of fidelity to the original text, while the remaking of *Dr. Jekyll and Mr. Hyde* is less significant than its revision into so many different formats: the sharing of identities between a white man and a black man, an older woman and a younger woman, a human and an alien, to mention only a few. Even *Superman* might be seen as a version of the basic *Jekyll and Hyde* format, while the remakes of *Dracula* seem doomed to remain stuck in the repetitive urge to assert their "purer" origin.

The implications of gender for the remaking process also need to be addressed more directly, as Lucy Fischer and Chris Holmlund have done in their essays, in order to question the male bias explicit in the oedipal metaphors used to analyze the remake generations. Krin Gabbard does make the interesting suggestion that *A Star Is Born* takes on the *Jazz Singer* format with a female hero rather than a male. Yet there are few if any genealogies of female remakes to compare with the male versions. Our cultural sense of individual combat is large enough to include male/male, female/female, and male/female pairs. But when we imagine a combat of generations that reflects the tides of history, it seems invariably male/male, in a kind of masculine cultural parthenogenesis. No wonder then that so many remakes are concerned with generational (often father/son) contests of meaning, and conflicts over the proper uses of authority and power—a tendency particularly present in family narratives such as the various *Jazz Singer*s and *Godfather*s. In her intriguing effort to establish an alternative genealogy, Lucy Fischer considers the relation of Almodovar's *High Heels* to Sirk's *Imitation of Life*. But the subject also cries out for an exploration of the connection of remake and melodrama, particularly through the cycle of female generations focused on in fiction, films, and plays such as *East Lynne, Stella Dallas, Mildred Pierce, Back Street,* and *Madame X.*

Our time is particularly heavy in remakes, perhaps the most so since the studio system was cannibalizing novels, plays, and its own past for new material. It is a time of dissatisfaction with the single story and yet a growing uneasiness with heartless and endless referentiality. It is also a time of hyperconsciousness of film history, fed by the availability of old films on cable channels and in video stores. How then does a filmmaker accomplish something personal that will attract an audience and assert the continuity of his or her own career? The two main ways seem to be the much-less-traveled road of originality and the crowded highway of genre and remaking, where the filmmaker's individual moral and aesthetic sensibility is defined by its meditation on the works of the past.

To remake is to want to reread—to believe in an explicit (and thematized) way that the past reading was wrong or outdated and that a new one must be done. One aspect of rereading often present in films but only tangentially considered in these essays is the figuring of generational change and the passage of authority through casting—as Martin Scorsese remakes *The Hustler* as *The Color of Money,* rotating Paul Newman from the younger to the older role, or as he remakes *Cape Fear,* rotating both Robert Mitchum and Gregory Peck from the previous version. Is this a species of quotation that is characteristic of the remake, or is it the stylistic device of a particular filmmaker and, perhaps, his generation?

There is also some distinction to be made between remaking under a studio system, with its high premium on a "product" simultaneously familiar and yet distinguishable by its house style, and remaking in a poststudio film world, where the relation between the time-honored and the innovative takes very different forms. Robert Kolker argues persuasively that Scorsese's *Cape Fear* is also in some important way a remake of Hitchcock's *Stage Fright, I Confess,* and *Strangers on a Train.* His conclusion suggests the central role of remakes in an ongoing personal or general history of aesthetic self-consciousness that experiences periods of both expression and repression. Stuart McDougal traces the same process within Hitchcock's own career as expressed in the two versions of *The Man Who Knew Too Much.* Similar analyses could be made of such self-remakers as Frank Capra and John Ford, Ernest Hemingway and William Faulkner, or those many filmmakers who, like Jean Renoir, have said that their entire careers consist in making and remaking the same film. Scorsese as remaker thus focuses some intriguing aspects of the remaking process—principally the way it highlights a narrative tradition in the act of interpreting itself.[3]

Finally, remaking partakes of the cultural nostalgia so marked now as the century ends and we have passed the one hundredth anniversary of the Lumière brothers' first shows. Like genre itself, remakes emphasize the clash between principles of continuity and principles of innovation in film history—the constant interplay between the desires of artists and the desires of audiences. We're all well schooled in thinking retrospectively and nostalgically, but few if any can translate that into predicting what is to come. Unlike Harvey Greenberg, I think that remakes can easily be better than their originals. And unlike Krin Gabbard, I don't think it's much of a paradox that the "unreproduceable" *Jazz Singer* became godfather to so many other films. It is the audience, or the audiences, that decide what is variable and what is unchanging in art, what vanishes and what lasts, what can be revived and what remains dead. Only one member of that audience is the remaker, and only one is the critic.

NOTES

1. For some acute remarks distinguishing remake from sequel, see Thomas M. Leitch, "Twice-Told Tales: The Rhetoric of the Remake," *Literature-Film Quarterly* 18, no. 3 (1990): 138–49.

2. This is one side of a familiar point of view in the discussion of adaptations, in which the film version can never aspire to the heights of the literary version, unless of course the original work is "bad," i.e., a genre work. See, for example, George Bluestone, *Novels into Film* (Berkeley and Los Angeles: University of Califor-

nia, 1961). The general approach is summed up in a line whose source I wish I knew: "The only good copies are those that make us see the ridiculousness of worthless originals."

3. Harold Bloom's *The Anxiety of Influence* (New York: Oxford, 1973) may be useful here for its proposal of a theory of rereading that stresses that "strong" artists need to actively *mis*read, while "weak" artists are content to be imitative and derivative. But Bloom's judgments, if not his categories, may need adjustment to be applied to film.

NOTES ON CONTRIBUTORS

Patricia Aufderheide teaches film at American University and is a frequent contributor to *In These Times* and other publications, including the *Washington Post.*

John Biguenet is a professor of English at Loyola University in New Orleans. His books include *The Craft of Translation* and *Theories of Translation,* both published by the University of Chicago Press, and *Foreign Fictions* (Random House).

Michael Brashinsky teaches at Brooklyn College, The New School, and the School of Visual Arts in New York. He is coauthor, with Andrew Horton, of *The Zero Hour: Glasnost and Soviet Cinema in Transition* (Princeton University Press, 1992).

Leo Braudy is Bing Professor of English at the University of Southern California. The author of three books and editor of four anthologies dealing with film, his most recent is *Native Informant: Essays on Film, Fiction, and Popular Culture* (Oxford University Press, 1990). He is also a member of the editorial board of *Film Quarterly* and is coeditor of the forthcoming fifth edition of *Film Theory and Criticism.*

Jerome Delamater is a professor of Communications at Hofstra University, the author of *Dance in the Hollywood Musical* (UMI Press, 1981), and a contributor to *The International Encyclopedia of Dance* (Oxford University Press).

Robert Eberwein is a professor of English at Oakland University, where he teaches film theory, history, and appreciation. Among his publications are *Film and the Dream Screen* (1984) and essays in *Wide Angle* and *Journal of Popular Film and Television.* He is currently writing a book on the uses to which film and video have been put for sex education.

Lucy Fischer heads up the Film Studies Program at the University of Pittsburgh and is the author of numerous books, including *Shot/Countershot: Film Tradition and Women's Cinema* (Princeton University Press, 1989).

Krin Gabbard is a professor of Comparative Literature at the State University of New York at Stony Brook. His most recent book is *Jammin' at the Margins: Jazz and the American Cinema* (University of Chicago Press, 1996).

Dan Georgakas is a longtime editor at *Cineaste,* teaches film classes at New York University, and is an author or editor of several books and many articles on various subjects, including not only film but Greek American culture and health-longevity.

Harvey R. Greenberg, M.D., is a psychoanalyst in private practice and a clinical professor of psychiatry at the Albert Einstein College of Medicine in New York, where he teaches adolescent psychiatry and medical humanities. Dr. Greenberg has published widely on cinema and media. His most recent book is *Screen Memories: Hollywood on the Psychiatric Couch* (Columbia University Press, 1993).

Chris Holmlund is an associate professor at the University of Tennessee, Knoxville, where she teaches film, women's studies, French literature, and critical theory. She coedited *Between the Sheets in the Streets: Queer, Lesbian, Gay Documentary* (University of Minnesota Press).

Andrew Horton is a professor of film and literature and an award-winning screenwriter teaching at Loyola University in New Orleans. He is the author and/or editor of ten books; his latest is *The Films of Theo Angelopoulos: A Cinema of Contemplation* (Princeton University Press).

Robert P. Kolker is a professor of English at the University of Maryland, College Park. He is the author of *A Cinema of Loneliness: Penn, Kubrick, Scorsese, Spielberg, and Altman, The Altered Eye: Contemporary European Cinema, Bernard Bertolucci,* and, with Peter Beicken, *The Films of Wim Wenders.*

Ira Konigsberg is a professor of English and film and video at the University of Michigan. He is the author of *The Complete Film Dictionary* and coeditor of a forthcoming volume entitled *The Movies: Texts, Receptions, Exposures.*

Peter Lehman is the director of media arts at the University of Arizona and the author of numerous books, including *Running Scared: Masculinity and the Representation of the Male Body* (Temple University Press, 1992).

Stuart Y. McDougal directs the Program in Comparative Literature at the University of Michigan, where he is also a professor of English, comparative literature, and film and video. He is the author of *Made into Movies: From*

Literature to Film, as well as a number of other publications in the fields of modern literature and film.

Lloyd Michaels is Frederick F. Seely Professor of English at Allegheny College. For the past twenty years he has edited *Film Criticism,* the third oldest film journal in continuous publication in America. He is the author of *Elia Kazan: A Guide to References and Resources* (G. K. Hall) and *The Phantom of Cinema: Character in the Modern Film* (State University of New York Press). His articles have appeared in a variety of journals, including *Film Quarterly, Post-Script,* and *Cinema Nuovo.*

Luca Somigli holds a Ph.D. in comparative literature from the State University of New York at Stony Brook. He has published numerous articles on comics, modernism, and the avant-garde and is the author of *Per una Satira Modernista: La Narrative di Wyndham Lewis.*

Elisabeth Weis is a professor of film at Brooklyn College and the Graduate Center of City University of New York. Her books include *Film Sound: Theory and Practice* (Columbia University Press) and *Film Comedy* (Viking).

David Wills is chairman of French at Louisiana State University and the author of a number of books, including, with Peter Brunette, *Screen/Play: Derrida and Film Theory* (Princeton University Press, 1989).

CREDITS

Quotations from the following works are reprinted with permission from the publishers:

Epigraph to chapter 10: Jacques Derrida, *Positions,* trans. Alan Bass (Chicago: University of Chicago Press, 1981).

Epigraph to chapter 11: Reprinted from *Disturbing Pleasures: Learning Popular Culture,* by Henry A. Giroux (1994) by permission of the publisher, Routledge: New York and London.

Epigraphs in chapter 13: Jean Baudrillard, *Seduction,* trans. Brian Singer (New York: St. Martin's, 1990); James Collins, "Postmodernism and Cultural Practice," *Screen* 28, no. 2 (1987): 11–26; and reprinted from *The Politics of Postmodernism,* by Linda Hutcheon, by permission of the publisher, Routledge: New York and London; and from *Feminism without Women: Culture in a Postfeminist Age,* by Tania Modleski (1992) by permission of the publisher, Routledge: New York and London.

The photographs reproduced in this book appear courtesy of Associated Film Distribution; Columbia Pictures Industries, Inc.; Su Friedrich; Loew's, Inc.; Miramax Films; The Museum of Modern Art, Film Stills Archive; Twentieth Century-Fox Film Corporation; Universal City Studios, Inc., and Amblin Entertainment, Inc.; Warner Bros., Inc.; and Warner Bros. Distributing Corporation.

INDEX

Compositor: J. Jarrett Engineering, Inc.
Text: 10/12 Baskerville
Display: Baskerville
Printer and binder: Thomson-Shore, Inc.